Fighting Stock

John S. "Rip" Ford of Texas

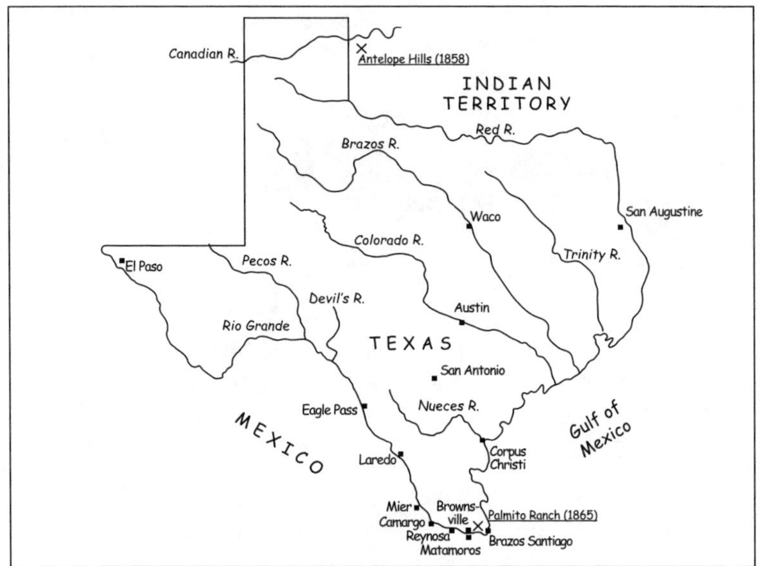

Map courtesy of Robert Citino.

FIGHTING STOCK

JOHN S. "RIP" FORD OF TEXAS

by Richard B. McCaslin

The Texas Biography Series ★ Number 3

A Joint Project of The Center for Texas Studies at TCU
and TCU Press ★ Fort Worth, Texas

Library of Congress Cataloging-in-Publication Data

McCaslin, Richard B.
Fighting stock : John S. "Rip" Ford of Texas / Richard B. McCaslin.
p. cm. — (Texas biography series ; no. 3)
"Joint project of the Center for Texas Studies at TCU and TCU Press."
Includes bibliographical references and index.
ISBN 978-0-87565-421-8 (cloth : alk. paper)
1. Ford, John Salmon. 2. Legislators—Texas—Biography. 3. Texas Rangers—Biography. 4. Frontier and pioneer life—Texas. 5. Texas—History—1846–1950. 6. Texas. Legislature. Senate—Biography. I. Title.
F391.F68M33 2011
328.092—dc22
[B]

2010024241

TCU Press
P. O. Box 298300
Fort Worth, Texas 76129
817.257.7822
http://www.prs.tcu.edu

To order books: 800.826.8911

Designed by Margie Adkins Graphic Design

CONTENTS

EDITOR'S FOREWORD

Through its rich and colorful history, Texas has been home to countless fascinating figures. Some of the state's great works of historical literature, such as Eugene C. Barker's biography of Stephen F. Austin and Marquis James' study of Sam Houston, have chronicled the lives of Texas' larger-than-life leaders. Yet there remain many important personalities who have not yet found their biographer, and many more whose stories are in need of fresh examination in a scholarly biography. The Texas Biography Series, published by the TCU Press and the Center for Texas Studies at TCU, offers a venue for telling their stories. Another major goal of the series is to broaden the body of biographical literature in Texas historiography beyond its traditionally heavy emphasis on the "great men" (which has often meant "great white men on horseback"). While the series certainly includes biographies of nineteenth-century political and military leaders, it also strives to encourage biographers to examine the full range of historical actors who have shaped the destiny of the Lone Star State, including women, members of racial and ethnic minorities, as well as figures from the worlds of business, the arts, science, religion, and even sports. In doing so, the series will contribute to keeping the field of Texas history vital and relevant as it moves into the twenty-first century.

As the third volume in the series, Richard B. McCaslin's biography of John Salmon "Rip" Ford fulfills one of the series' principal aims, which is to place well-known Texas personalities in modern historiographical context utilizing recent scholarly knowledge. With thorough and painstaking research into all phases of Ford's long and varied life, Professor McCaslin cuts through the many layers of myth and misconception surrounding his subject. The Rip Ford who emerges in these pages is a much more complex, and in many ways more compelling, figure than the rough-and-ready Texas Ranger whose famous nickname allegedly derived from the many times he wrote "rest in peace" beside the names of his soldiers in casualty reports during the Mexican War. Moreover, McCaslin devotes long-overdue attention to the many phases of Ford's life apart from his years as a Ranger and Army officer, including his careers as a newspaper editor, political leader, and historian. From the time he came to Texas in 1836 until his death in 1897, Ford was seemingly present at every crucial juncture of Texas' public affairs, often playing a leading role in them. As a consequence of McCaslin's nuanced study, the reader of this book will come away not only with a new and fascinating look at a legendary figure but also with a deeper understanding of sixty years of tumultuous Texas history.

This book and its predecessors in the Texas Biography Series owe their existence to three important institutions. The TCU Press and its staff have furnished the editorial and production expertise to create books equal to those of the leading national publishing houses. The Center for Texas Studies at TCU is a critical partner in launching, funding, and publicizing the series. And finally, Houston Endowment has provided a generous grant underwriting much of the cost of *Fighting Stock* and the next several titles in the series. As series editor, I am grateful to all of these partners who continue to make the series a success.

Gregg Cantrell
Erma and Ralph Lowe Chair in Texas History
Texas Christian University

ACKNOWLEDGMENTS

I would like to thank everyone who assisted me with this project. Gregg Cantrell of Texas Christian University had the foresight to ask me to write a book, and the good taste to allow that book to be on Rip Ford. Archives around the state have shared their materials on Ford, most especially the Texas State Library and Archives and the Dolph Briscoe Center for American History in Austin. I have spent many hours in both places for this and other endeavors, and I greatly appreciate what they have provided to me. My students have brought me materials and new insights from their own research. The Texas State Historical Association gave me their Lawrence T. Jones III Research Fellowship, and the University of North Texas provided several small travel grants. I also must thank my wife Jana, who is especially pleased that I managed to find a place for us in Texas, at the University of North Texas. It has been a journey of many years, but we are finally home.

Richard B. McCaslin
University of North Texas

INTRODUCTION

John Salmon Ford represents Texas as many people want it to be, yet he was never a typical Texan. Renowned as "Rip" Ford, he is remembered as a quintessential Texas Ranger who battled to defend Anglo farmers and ranchers from Indians and Mexicans, and to preserve slavery. But he never owned any farm land or slaves, nor did he grow crops or herd cattle. At the same time, many of those who fought under his command were Indians and Mexicans, and he twice served as an officer under Mexican revolutionary José María de Jesús Carvajal. Renowned as a fighter, he kept the peace during the confrontation that accompanied the potentially violent transition from Republican to Democratic control of Texas in 1874. He spent more time as a newspaper editor than he did in any military assignment, and the only public building in Texas today that bears his name honors his service as an educator. Perhaps most ironic, he won the last battle of the Civil War for the Confederacy, but he lost his Confederate commission more than two years before that victory.

Ford's fame rests on the fact that he excelled in aggressive roles treasured by Texans as part of their evolving mythology. Many young men came to Texas during the first half of the nineteenth century to make a name for themselves, but few did as well as Ford. He seized every opportunity, never earning a lot of money but developing a reputation as a leader in several arenas. Ford later secured his legacy by writing a voluminous memoir. He intended it to be a full record of his life, but Texans were not equally interested in all aspects of Ford's career. During his lifetime, the memoir was never published in its entirety, and only excerpts on his accomplishments as a Texas Ranger and a soldier appeared in various publications. Others used these same fragments in their work even after he died, and an edited version of his memoirs published in

1961 also focused on his accomplishments as a Texas Ranger and soldier. As a result, Ford became a one-dimensional archetype of the nineteenth-century Texan. Having been immortalized as a Ranger and soldier in the published portions of his own writing, Ford became a fixture in a violent frontier culture celebrated by nostalgic Texans as their state modernized during the first decades of the twentieth century.

Every generation has people who seem driven to make a difference. Ford certainly appears to be such a person, if solely because he produced a memoir chronicling the achievements of Texians, and the roles that he played within that cohort. However, it remains difficult to define the motivation that drove Ford to excel and thus to become a prominent part of Texans' history of themselves. He does not provide many clues in his memoirs. Twice he repeats what he wrote in 1844 to Orison Underwood, a Massachusetts militia commander who opposed the annexation of Texas: that his "motto" was "ready, aye, ready."[1] Because this is the motto of the British, and later the Canadian, Navy, it provides little unique insight into Ford. More can be gleaned from his definition of Texians, as the settlers of Texas prior to statehood are known. Ford wrote admiringly of them that "energy, bravery, a practical view of all matters, self-reliance, moderation, and a disposition to act in concert with their fellow citizens were the characteristics of the early settlers." He added, "Danger . . . moulded [*sic*] them into soldiers" who had "correct ideas of what was necessary to preserve order and give adequate protection to person and property."[2] The events of his life indicate that he shared these traits with his fellow Texians, maybe to an extreme degree. Ford always insisted that he was not an original Texian, but by the time of his death, he represented that generation for many in Texas and countless others who admired its early settlers.

A desire to establish a meaningful legacy would certainly explain much of Ford's motive, but what determined the means he adopted to achieve that end? Those who excel in every generation seem more attuned to stories of ancestors, heroes, or other models of behavior. Ford rejected the model of his father, a farmer who eventually followed his son to Texas, and he rarely wrote about any heroes other than Texians, most of whom he met only after moving to Texas as an adult. The answer lies in the attention he devotes in his detailed memoir to the service of his grandfathers, John Ford and George Salmon, in the American Revolution and afterward. After recounting what he knew of their lives, he concludes, "When one comes of fighting stock, he has a right to be proud of it." Living in the shadow of the Revolution, many American men struggled to find roles that seemed as worthy as those played by their fathers and grandfathers, who fought to establish a nation. Historian George B. Forgie, in considering their dilemma, declared that "we can detect among many ambitious men in the post-heroic period a gradual shift from a concern over how posterity would judge them to a concern that posterity might not take the trouble to judge them at all."[3] Faced with this, Ford embraced the aggressive roles defined by his grandfathers in military and political offices. Even as a newspaper editor, he remained assertive and easily crossed the line into the more active role of a public leader.

Of course, in Ford's effort to emulate his grandfathers, it can easily be said that he far exceeded them. They never became well-known historical characters who defined a state's popular, though not always accurate, image. Ford first appeared in literature in the 1870s with the publication of five dime novels about his battles with Mexican border raider Juan N. Cortina and the Comanches. These books, written by Samuel Stone Hall, a Massachusetts native who served briefly with the Texas Rangers before the Civil War, luridly and inaccurately recounted events that Hall, who used the pseudonym "Buckskin Sam," never saw. A generation later, R. H. Williams described Ford, whom he called "Colonel Franks," as "the most inveterate gambler and the hardest swearer I ever met." A popular commander of "deserters and loafers of all sorts," Ford was "free with his money, and equally free with his six-shooter."[4] Williams claimed to have served under Ford in early 1864, but he left before the Texans marched to recapture Brownsville. Such tales supported popular conceptions of life on the wild frontier among many Americans, and even some Texans seemed to relish them.

Ford, who forbade gambling and was noted for his strict discipline, fared better with twentieth-century scholars, who wanted to provide a more accurate perspective on the people who had settled Texas.

But Ford remained a prisoner of his own publicity, unable to escape the labels of Ranger and soldier. Walter Prescott Webb in his landmark study of the Texas Rangers confirmed Ford's stature as one of the four great antebellum captains. More than sixty years later, Thomas W. Knowles included images of the four—Samuel H. Walker, John C. Hayes, Benjamin McCulloch, and Ford—in another thick volume on the Rangers. Not long afterward, Robert M. Utley in yet another popular study of the Rangers actually ranked Ford as the best captain of the decade prior to the Civil War, a period in which Ford spent more time as a newspaper editor and politician than he did as a Ranger. Mike Cox and Michael L. Collins agreed with Utley in the two most recent books on nineteenth-century Texas Rangers. In keeping with this pattern, when Stephen B. Oates edited Ford's memoirs for an overdue appearance in print in 1963, he left out portions that did not focus on Ford as a Ranger or soldier. William J. Hughes in his 1964 biography of Ford followed suit, focusing primarily on Ford's military service for the state, federal, and Confederate governments.[5]

Ford thus was not forgotten by Texans as their state became more modern, but the importance of his career and how it actually shaped Texas, both on the battlefield and off, became lost. While T. R. Fehrenbach in his popular history of Texas published in 1968 admitted Ford was "the only man in Texas history who was involved in a major way in every action or controversy of his time," he dismissed him as "star-following, pragmatic, restless, and apparently without an ideology of any kind." Ford had become a "colorful" man with "prejudices but no philosophy." Nearly twenty years later, Fehrenbach, having had time to think more about Ford, leveled another literary blast at him: "Rip Ford, who was present at the creation but never got the hang of it, wasted years on horseback and being mayor and ended up embittered, having to peddle his memoirs for a living." A popular textbook completed the marginalization of Ford by referring to him as "one of the more ubiquitous and colorful characters in [his] era of Texas history." The damage was only partly undone by the praise offered by Gary C. Anderson in his book on the "ethnic cleansing" of Texas. Anderson referred to Ford as "an aggressive yet responsible ranger." The dual archetype of Ranger and soldier was further restored by the McAllen family, who called Ford a "renowned Texas military hero" in their 2003 history of the Rio Grande Valley.[6] But again, Ford in recent history is at best only a Ranger and soldier, two roles that affirm the frontier image of Texas and leave him a marginal character.

If nothing else, this book seeks to recover the complexity of Ford's career, and in so doing provide a useful perspective on Texas as not solely a frontier state, but also a Southern state. Ford was born in South Carolina and raised in Tennessee, the state that provided the greatest number of antebellum emigrants to Texas. He strongly supported slavery, although unlike his grandfathers and father he did not participate directly in it. Like many antebellum Southerners he became involved in filibusters, or invasions of neighboring countries, to expand the peculiar institution. He served on vigilante committees to confront the threat of slave unrest, supported the Democratic Party as it shifted to become the party of the South and slavery, and became a leader in the secession movement. He continued to fight against the Union even after the Confederacy had collapsed in the East, and he became involved in Reconstruction conflicts and served as a delegate to the 1875 Texas Constitutional Convention that dismantled most of the state's Republican reforms. These efforts do not diminish Ford's great contributions as a Ranger and soldier, nor his involvement in border conflicts along the Rio Grande, but they do make it quite clear that he followed in his grandfathers' footsteps not just as a military and political leader, but as a Southerner. In the end, perhaps he was more like his father, a slave-holding farmer, than he revealed in his memoir. And his aggressive efforts, and those of others like him, made Texas a very Southern state in the nineteenth century.

One final note on an enduring part of the Ford mythology: when did he become Rip? Ford liked the nickname but offered no explanation of it in his memoirs. Lucille T. Cowen, his granddaughter, insisted that it originated during the Mexican War, and her son, Raphael Cowen, told Webb that his grandfather earned the label during the Mexican War by writing "R.I.P.", for "Rest in Peace," after the names of dead Texan soldiers in his reports. Webb included this story in his work, and it entered the public memory. But Lucille Cowen also admitted that Ford had nicknames for many men who served under him after the Mexican War, and Charles L. Martin, who joined Ford's command in 1862, remembered that they called him Rip "in retaliation." Whether Martin and his colleagues did so because Ford never seemed to sleep or because of his aggressive personality was not clear, but the name may also have emerged in the early 1850s when the chronically ill Ford did fall asleep on duty. At least two of the contemporary explanations for the name thus focus on Rip Van Winkle and Ford's unusual sleeping habits, which seems plausible because it would appeal to the rough humor of bored Texas Rangers but would not be the type of story Ford would tell an admiring granddaughter. Ford's original biographers had no such concerns, and they explained the name as an honorary title bestowed upon him as an effective but impetuous frontier commander. H. S. Canfield in an obituary for Ford provided the best example of this, portraying "Rip" as a great but reckless warrior whose "band left behind it a thirty-foot wide trail of blood." Neither he nor Andrew J. Sowell, whose book on the Texas frontier appeared in 1900, three years after Ford's death, mentioned any Mexican War tale. Instead, they focused on Ford's "vim and quick actions." More than five decades later, Tom Lea may have stated this best in his epic history of the King Ranch when he disregarded Webb and wrote about Ford, "He was no mere fighting man, though they did call him Rip for the way he went at it."[7]

CHAPTER 1 TEXIAN

The Republic of Texas provided the stage on which John Salmon Ford developed the roles that he played throughout his adult life. Having declared its independence from Mexico in 1836, Texas struggled to define itself, battling against enemies and insolvency as a nation while also trying to become one of the United States. Ford was among the thousands of penniless young men who came to Texas during this period, but unlike most of them he emerged as a community leader. Driven by a desire to emulate the deeds of his grandfathers who fought in the American Revolution, Ford during his first decade in Texas served in almost every role that later defined his legacy. Opportunities to build a lasting reputation abounded, as well as chances to forge ties with influential leaders, and he took advantage of them. In 1845 Ford, as a first-term congressman of the Republic, introduced the bill to accept annexation by the United States. During the ensuing military and political clashes, Ford expanded further upon his aggressive reputation as a "Texian," but he was just getting started.

Like most Texans before the Civil War, Ford came to Texas from somewhere else. He was born on May 26, 1815, in the Greenville District of South Carolina, to William and Harriet Salmon Ford, who were thirty and twenty-four years of age respectively. Although his mother was still quite young, Ford proved to be her last child to thrive; only he and an older sister, Elizabeth, survived to adulthood. Interestingly, both John and Elizabeth bore the names of grandparents who had memorable experiences in the American Revolution. In fact, John bore the names of both of his grandfathers, George Salmon and John Ford, whose stories made such an impression on Ford that he recounted them in detail when he wrote his memoirs more than seventy years after his birth.[1]

Elizabeth was named for their maternal grandmother, Elizabeth Young Salmon, who married George Salmon at Greenville in 1785. Salmon served as a South Carolina legislator before and after his grandchildren were born, as well as in other offices at Greenville, and he lived until 1837, or long enough for them to know him. He had a colorful record as a South Carolina militia officer that included being captured by the British, though the tale Ford later wrote of his escape during the Battle of King's Mountain is probably no more than a family story told to impress young children. Ford also retold the story of how Salmon was shot through the body while leading militia against Indians, which included the grisly but perhaps more truthful detail of how the wound was cleaned by pulling a silk handkerchief through it. Ford not only recounted Salmon's exploits in his memoir; he also repeated family stories about Elizabeth, Salmon's future bride. A single lady just twenty-two years of age when British Maj. Patrick Ferguson visited her home, she noted his boast of how he avoided being injured in battle by wearing a simple jacket and carrying his sword in his left hand, not in his right as an officer customarily did. She conveyed this information to local patriot militia, and Ferguson was killed when the Americans overwhelmed the British at King's Mountain a few weeks later. Ford's grandmother must have shared this story and others about American Revolution military leaders Francis Marion and George Washington, whom she claimed to have met several times, with her grandson before they both moved west, he to Texas and she to Missouri after the death of her husband.[2]

Ford revered his father, whom he described as "an honest man, always candid in his expressions of opinion, and fearless of consequences," but he devoted more attention in his memoirs to his paternal grandfather, whom he never met. The elder John Ford immigrated to South Carolina from England, but he served as a major in the patriot forces during the Revolution. His grandson enjoyed recounting more than a century later how Major Ford had more than twenty bullet holes in his clothes at the siege of Savannah in October 1779, and later escaped unscathed from the rout of the American forces at Camden in August 1780. With apparent relish, the younger Ford also recounted how his grandfather reacted when Tories, led by a neighbor, raided his home.

Ford got a furlough and confronted the Tory in his house while the latter was eating supper with his gun in his lap. Ford declared why he had come: to avenge the outrages perpetrated on his home. Before the Tory could defend himself, Ford struck him over the head with his sword. He did not kill the man, however, and desisted when the Tory's wife begged for her husband's life. The younger Ford does not make it clear if this happened before or after his grandfather's mother was murdered by Tories and Indians raiding near Greenville in 1781. Like Salmon, the elder Ford remained in Greenville after the Revolution, serving as a state senator and justice of the peace before he died in 1795 at the age of forty-five from a lung disease allegedly contracted during the war.[3]

The greatest number of antebellum immigrants to Texas came from Tennessee, and John S. Ford was among this host. He with his father, mother, and sister moved to Lincoln County, Tennessee, in 1817, when Ford was just two years of age. Ford never explained why his father relocated, but a historian notes that he apparently prospered, adding a little more than two hundred acres to his original purchase by 1832. Another describes the property as a "small plantation," and the census records that William Ford, like his father and father-in-law, owned slaves. He taught his son to ride and shoot, as well as farm, and enrolled him in a one-room school, while Ford's mother insisted that he include the Bible among his textbooks. Ford recalled his childhood fondly, writing in his memoir that he learned to fight and play pranks with boys, and to fall in love with girls. He added, "The old ladies of his neighborhood looked upon him as a sort of a prodigy, and predicted he would be killed for his general 'cussedness' before reaching the age of maturity, or hanged for some infernal mischief he might commit."[4]

As he approached adulthood, Ford made some interesting choices concerning his future. He rejected the farming lifestyle of his father and instead prepared to be a doctor. After five years of school as a teenager, during which he allegedly read every book the teacher had and borrowed others, Ford moved to Shelbyville, in Bedford County, to study medicine under Dr. James G. Barksdale. Ford won attention, and got his name in local newspapers, for his bravery in attending Wilkins Blanton, a friend who was stricken with smallpox. While a slave who assisted Ford with

Blanton died, the patient recovered and lived for another fifty years. Ford was not nearly so fortunate in finding a wife to share his career: he married Mary Davis in Shelbyville, and they had twin children, a son and a daughter, but their marriage ended in 1836 with a divorce.[5] Ford included almost nothing about this relationship in his memoirs, which he wrote while married to his third wife. Perhaps this failure embarrassed him. After all, neither his grandfathers nor his father ever divorced, and while his first daughter stayed with his parents and later accompanied his father to Texas, Ford never again mentioned his first son.

The linkage between Ford's divorce and his interest in Texas is not clear, but in the early spring of 1836, Ford decided to join the Texans in their fight for independence from Mexico. To him, the Texas conflict "appeared to involve all the principles for which our forefathers fought in the Revolution of 1776." He published a flyer to attract recruits for a company, and he persevered even when news of the Alamo and the execution of Texans captured at Goliad cooled the ardor of some potential volunteers. Ford planned to serve as captain of the company, and had about forty members enlisted, when a report of the Texan victory at San Jacinto arrived. Thinking that Texas would have no need for his company, Ford abandoned his recruiting efforts, but he did not give up on the idea of going west. Leaving his daughter Fannie with his parents, Ford traveled west alone. After a steamboat trip down the Mississippi River and up the Red River, he acquired a wagon, affixed a sign advertising his services as a doctor, and rolled into San Augustine, Texas, in the summer of 1836.[6]

Ford found many fellow Tennesseans in San Augustine, and they seemed eager to have a doctor join their community. He practiced medicine there for eight years, earning a reputation as a hard worker who would come when other doctors would not and whose prices were fair. He proved to be quite skillful as well, at one time removing a bone fragment from a child's brain. His rapid rise to prominence became apparent only a month after his arrival when he was invited to attend a reception on July 4, 1836, for Sam Houston, who was visiting San Augustine. Ford was entranced by Houston, later referring to him as the "Washington of Texas" and recalling him as a "splendid specimen of manhood" with a regal "form" and "features," as well as a "mighty mind" and a "gifted tongue." Ford also remembered some of the other Texas revolutionaries present. Jonas Harrison delivered the welcoming speech, but also there were James W. Bullock, who forced the Mexican garrison from Nacogdoches in 1832, Alexander Horton, who served under Bullock at Nacogdoches and Houston in the Texan victory at San Jacinto, Philip A. Sublett, who led troops during the 1835 siege of San Antonio, and Stephen W. Blount, who signed the Texas Declaration of Independence. All in all, it was lofty company for a twenty-one-year-old doctor who had just arrived in Texas.[7]

Ford did not have to wait long for an opportunity to become a soldier like the men he admired. He had been mistaken about Texas not needing more troops—ironically the company he left in Tennessee arrived in San Augustine by the late summer of 1836. It was mustered into Texas service after a United States Army officer exposed the efforts of Mexican agent Manuel Flores to incite Indians in East Texas to attack the Republic. Ford joined another company led by William Kimbrough, a former resident of Bedford County, Tennessee, who had fought at San Jacinto, and they joined the small host gathered in East Texas at Nacogdoches under the command of Houston. Indian leaders soon signed agreements with Houston, defusing the situation for the moment, and Ford returned to San Augustine.[8]

The growing Republic lured new settlers by the thousands with a generous land grant policy, which provided another economic opportunity for ambitious young men like Ford. In February 1838 he became a deputy surveyor, like his maternal grandfather, for Shelby County, in the region that later became Harrison County. He set to work at once even though the weather was wet and cold, and he quickly completed surveys for many large tracts, including that where the town of Marshall would be established. This laudable zeal, however, did not mask his "sheer greenness." A settler on Eight Mile Creek provided shelter for Ford's weary survey crew, so when he asked Ford to locate a league, for which he had a certificate, upon the site of Big Spring Village, despite the fact that Caddo Indians lived there, Ford did so. This not only endangered the delicate truce existing between Indians and settlers in East Texas, it also put Ford and his men in danger of being attacked by Indians, to which he was equally oblivious. He posted no guards, built "large fires," and generally "acted like other inexperienced simpletons would." Fortunately for Ford and his survey crew, "all went merry as a marriage ball." Unfortunately for Ford, while he was making it possible for others to acquire land, he did not take any for himself. He did receive a land grant of 1,280 acres, as did all heads of households arriving in 1836, but he sold this certificate in 1850 without filing a survey. Reflecting on this later in his memoirs, Ford could only write that his failure was due to "improvidence, and the want of a proper appreciation of the value of land acquired by toil."[9] Apparently he had no interest in following in his father's footsteps as a farmer, unlike most of his neighbors.

While he may have been naive, Ford did not let ambition make him a total fool. He met Robert Potter, the volatile former United States congressman and secretary of the navy for Texas, while surveying on Caddo Lake in 1838. Potter, who was determined to remove all Indians from East Texas, wanted local settlers to attack Caddo leaders as they returned from a meeting at Shreveport, Louisiana, with United States officials. He succeeded in having a meeting at which a company organized, with Ford as its lieutenant. Ford at first did not fully understand what was afoot, but when the recruits actually gathered a few days later, their purpose became clear. He then argued against the planned expedition, pointing out that they did not know how many Caddos there were and, if the whites lost, there might be a bloody campaign of retaliation. The men agreed and went home. Ford recalled that Potter was not present for the muster and remarked, "The writer was then quite young, but he had an idea that fire-eating orators are not often found in the front of battle."[10]

Ford would not be led astray by "fire-eating orators," but he remained ready to throw down his surveying tools and take up arms if a valid threat appeared. In August 1838 it was discovered that another Mexican agent, Vicente Córdova, had gathered hundreds of disgruntled Hispanics and Indians on an island in the Angelina River. President Houston ordered Thomas J. Rusk as major general of the militia to respond, and Rusk called on the East Texas volunteers to muster. Ford joined a company of mounted volunteers led by Henry W. Augustine, who had fought at Nacogdoches in 1832 and served two terms as a senator for the Texas Republic. Augustine's company was one of fourteen enrolled in the Third Militia Brigade, commanded by Brig. Gen. Kelsey H. Douglass. Augustine followed Córdova's forces as they marched north between the Angelina and Neches rivers, but not much happened in a campaign noted more for humor than danger in Ford's recollections. Desperate fighting occurred elsewhere before Córdova fled to safety in Mexico, but Ford saw no action before Houston again disbanded the East Texas militia.[11]

Rusk refused to quit his campaign against the Indians in East Texas, especially the Cherokees, which led to another bloodless expedition for Ford. Many whites supported Rusk, either from fear or a desire for land, and the replacement of Houston with the more ruthless Mirabeau B. Lamar as president of the Republic provided Rusk with the official support he needed for a showdown. The discovery of incriminating documents on the body of the hapless Manuel Flores, who had been killed when he returned once more to Texas to convey weapons from Mexico to the Indians, inflamed the Texans, and Lamar ordered the Cherokees to leave or be exterminated. Under the command of Douglass, the First Regiment of the Texas Army led by Edward Burleson marched east in the summer of 1839 to join Rusk's East Texas militia and enforce Lamar's order. Ford enlisted in a new militia company commanded by Kimbrough, but again missed the battles in July when the Cherokees were defeated and their leader, Bowl, was killed. After marching first to disarm the Shawnees, Kimbrough's company had arrived on the battlefield after the fighting ended. Ford saw Bowl's body and recalled that he was dressed "rather in the American style," including a "red silk velvet vest, said to have been a present from General Houston." Any disturbing reflections on the connection between Bowl and Houston were quelled when Ford found a Bible in a nearby deserted home; he claimed in his memoirs that its register of births for a white family "spoke of bloodshed and robbery" by Indians.[12]

Life in San Augustine was not all work and war for Ford. Obedient to his mother's instructions, he allegedly read a chapter of the Bible each day, and he taught Sunday school, though it was not until the 1870s that he was baptized as a Presbyterian. Like many prominent Texans, Ford joined the Masons, enrolling in Red Land Lodge Number 3. He also organized a "Thespian Corp," whose members included a fellow physician, Lycurgus E. Griffith, editor W. W. Parker of the San Augustine *Red-Lander,* merchant John P. Border (who ironically commanded Camp Ford, named for his fellow thespian, during the Civil War), future Confederate general William R. Scurry, and two future Confederate congressmen, William B. Ochiltree and Franklin B. Sexton. Being with such people reinforced Ford's status and provided him with valuable contacts for his future career, but he also enjoyed their company. Scurry he remembered as "versatile, ready to play 'heroes'" as well as "ladies in sorrowful moods." Sexton, "a mere boy," always played the "heroine in a play of any sort—tragic or comic—and never failed." Ford wrote two well-received comedies, and he gleefully recalled how he fancied himself "a genius of sublime proportions." One of the pair, for which Scurry wrote and recited a "prologue," relied on Ford's experiences as it focused on the misadventures of a sharpie who came to Texas with "wild cat" notes to buy land and was hoodwinked by Texans eager to sell spurious land grant certificates. When writing about these activities in his memoirs, Ford concluded, "Young simpletons often enjoy their juvenile follies more than old fools do their worn crotchets, and fancied achievements."[13]

Four years after arriving in San Augustine, Ford tried politics when he reached the constitutionally mandated minimum age of twenty-five in 1840. He had voted for Houston in the August 1836 presidential election, but the lure of winning a public office convinced him to run against Houston and Henry W. Augustine for a congressional seat. Ford's sense of humor got the best of him, and he openly repeated a rumor that Houston would not attend the election because he was on a binge in Nashville. Outraged Houston supporters closed ranks and sent their man and Augustine to the Texas House of Representatives, leaving Ford to grumble that he had been beaten by "grog-shop bullies, cross-road politicians, and self-inflated shysters" who "aped their respective favorites." Digging deeper into his theatrical references, Ford added in his memoirs that the "Jerry Sneaks" and "Ramsey Sniffles" had "a glorious time in blustering and making faces at each other," linking his opponents to characters in Samuel Foote's farcical 1763 play about a mock election in Britain. Ford must not have kept his sharp opinions to himself; when he ran again for the Texas House in 1841, he polled the fewest votes of the five candidates. It must have been quite a bittersweet honor for Ford to serve that fall on a committee to welcome Houston, who won his second presidential race that year, to San Augustine.[14]

Defeated twice in elections, Ford focused on making a living. He had returned to surveying in the winter of 1840–1841, working along the upper Trinity River. Forced by a storm to take shelter at King's Fort, Ford and his crew were joined by a nearly frozen John H. Reagan, who had left his own survey party to get supplies and had been caught by the weather. Perhaps Reagan's close call made Ford begin to reconsider the dangers of surveying. He studied law and passed a bar examination, but he put little effort into a practice. Instead, he formed a partnership with an older physician, Thomas H. Lister, and moved to an office closer to the center of San Augustine. Within a year the arrangement with Lister ended, but Ford continued to work with local doctors such as Lewis V. Greer and Oscar Fitzallen. As he explained in a card posted in the San Augustine *Red-Lander,* "Dr. John S. Ford, having determined to devote his entire attention to the practice of his profession, will attend promptly to every call he may receive." Among his patients were Kenneth L. Anderson, who later served as vice-president of the Republic, his law partner J. Pinckney Henderson, future governor of the state of Texas, and Richardson A. Scurry, when he was speaker of the House of Representatives for the Texas Congress.[15]

Ford's medical work gave him the connections he needed to reenter the political arena. He not only treated Scurry, he also wrote a public statement for him on political matters. When Scurry decided he was too sick to run for another term, Ford ran in his place, focusing on the issues of frontier defense and annexation by the United States. Ford was among the vast majority of Texans who endorsed annexation in the 1836 election, and he bristled at the denunciation of Texas by Orison Underwood, a popular political leader and militia commander, at a meeting in

Milford, Massachusetts. Ford was particularly incensed at Underwood's claim that Texans stole their land from Mexico. He penned a long reply that sternly recounted the settlement of Texas by non-Mexicans and their fight for independence, concluding with "Allow me, sir, to ask if the United States can show a better title to her territory? Royal grants, papal bulls, and Indian treaties, to the contrary notwithstanding?" Ford could not resist adding a pointed inquiry as to when Indians invited the ancestors of the contemporary residents of Massachusetts to settle there. When Ford's missive appeared in the San Augustine *Red-Lander* on June 29, 1844, it must have drawn much attention. He placed first in the polling for two seats in the Texas House, joining his fellow Mason Benjamin R. Wallace in victory and vanquishing Henry W. Sublett.[16]

Having finally arrived in the Texas House, Ford was not content to sit quietly. In the Ninth Congress of the Republic, which met at Washington-on-the-Brazos, he chaired the Committee on Retrenchment and served on the Committees for Indian Affairs and Education. He also introduced a resolution calling for an investigation of the embattled commissioner of the General Land Office, Thomas W. Ward, and he became involved in the ongoing conflict over the site of a capital for the Republic. Initially Ford supported presidents Houston and Anson Jones, agreeing that Austin was too exposed to Indian attacks. When a bill requiring Jones to return the government to Austin narrowly passed the House and became law, Ford was one of nine Representatives who signed a protest against the measure. Jones vetoed the bill, sparking an angry backlash that ended with an override vote by the Texas Congress in late January 1845. That time, Ford voted with the majority to return to Austin. He thus embraced practicality, recognizing that a scattered government did not function well and that public sentiment made it impossible to agree on any other site. After all, the location of a capital was not as vital a matter as frontier defense or annexation, the two issues on which he had campaigned.[17]

Ford wrote almost daily to the *Red-Lander* about his congressional activities, apparently eager to make certain that his achievements were not overlooked. When he delivered a lengthy speech on frontier defense in January 1845, all those who voted for him could read it:

"I care not if a man were placed upon the banks of the Rio Grande, and the sands were crumbling from beneath his feet, if he claimed to be a citizen of Texas, and demeaned himself as such, I would go for protecting him." Ford later recalled that he was "proud of having said this, and still prouder of having acted upon it through a rather long life." He linked the subject of annexation to protection, arguing that an effective defense of the border would secure Texas' boundary claims and make annexation more likely, while at the same time the best frontier protection would only come with annexation to the United States.[18]

Rumors that Britain wanted to buy part of Texas as a homeland for emancipated slaves alarmed Ford, pushing him to redouble his efforts on behalf of annexation by the United States. He owned no slaves, but his father and grandfathers had, and he was every inch a product of the Southern culture in which he was raised. He would not allow the British to make Texas "an instrument to accomplish one of their cherished projects, the abolition of negro slavery," as he wrote to an associate in January 1845. Understanding that Texas was in fact a subject of interest to France as well as Britain and the United States, Ford visited with French chargé d'affaires Alphonse Dubois de Saligny, British chargé Charles Elliot, and American chargé Andrew Jackson Donelson after the Texas Congress had adjourned. He corresponded as well with Kenneth L. Anderson, his former patient who had become the vice president of the Republic.[19]

Donelson had come to Texas to push for the acceptance of an annexation offer approved by the United States Congress in February 1845, and he found a kindred soul in Ford. While Saligny and Elliot hurried to Mexico City to try to secure a treaty that might convince Texans not to accept annexation, Donelson met with President Jones to discuss the entry of Texas into the American Union. Jones called his Congress into a special session in June 1845 at Washington-on-the Brazos, and there Ford introduced a joint resolution for annexation into the Texas House on June 17. He served on a committee to reconcile his joint resolution with several other versions that had been introduced while the Senate considered and finally rejected a treaty from Mexico that recognized Texas independence. Then on June 23 the House and

Senate unanimously approved joining the United States. In Ford's eyes, Texas leaders thus decided to cast their lot with the United States against the two European monarchies, and in favor of slavery, despite the risk of war with Mexico. This proved that they "were true to the principles they had been taught to revere, and to the people with whom they were allied by blood."[20]

Before Texas could become a state, there was one final step: writing a proper constitution. Ford was not a delegate to the constitutional convention that met at Austin in July 1845, but he was there as a correspondent for the *Texas National Register,* a pro-Houston newspaper begun in late 1844. Ford produced a stream of opinionated articles, some of which he later regretted, but he seemed to enjoy himself. One funny highlight came one Sunday afternoon when a black man, mounted on a mule and carrying, rather than wearing, his clothes raced into Austin, shouting that Indians were near. A "motley crowd" led by former president Lamar quickly gathered to confront the enemy. Ford remembered, "We meant business, diabolical, bloodthirsty business." But all they found were some men fishing on the Colorado River, who explained how the man heard their voices while bathing and had "mistaken" them for Indians. Lamar's would-be warriors were of course quite crestfallen.[21]

As Texas prepared to become a state, Ford also began building a new life for himself. After the convention adjourned, he hustled from Austin to Washington-on-the-Brazos, where he married Louisa Swisher Lewis, four years his junior, on September 26, 1845. Later that fall, Ford's father and daughter Fannie joined him and Louisa in Austin, where they had settled. It was a poignant reunion for the Fords; Harriet Salmon Ford had died in Tennessee before her husband and granddaughter left to join her son. Ford had to feed his clan, and so he partnered with Michael Cronican, a veteran of the Texan victory at San Jacinto and a survivor of the disastrous Mier Expedition, to purchase the *Texas National Register* and relocate it to Austin. Because it was a pro-Houston paper that had questioned the need for annexation, Ford's new venture was not initially very popular in the community that remembered Houston's efforts to move the capital. Ford's amiable approach and a quick name change to

Texas Democrat, coupled with the fact that he had voted for a return to Austin, quieted many of his opponents and ended their angry threats to beat him and Cronican, as well as ransack their office at the corner of Congress and Pecan streets.[22]

Ford attended the annexation ceremony at the Capitol in Austin on February 19, 1846, as the editor of the *Texas Democrat.* He stood in the large crowd and watched as the last president of the Republic, Anson Jones, transferred control of the government to the first governor of the state of Texas, J. Pinckney Henderson, who had been a patient of Ford's in San Augustine. Ford recalled how strong, and mixed, his emotions were that day. He was sad to see the banner of the Republic come down, but happy to think of the prospects for a safe and prosperous future. Too, while the "beloved flag of Texas" was furled, seemingly forever, in a ceremony that marked "the funeral of a nation," within a few moments the "glorious banner of our fathers ascended in its stead." The future must indeed have seemed bright for him.[23]

The initial months of statehood brought even more success for Ford. The first Texas legislature chose him and Cronican as state printers in April 1846, which gave the partners a steady income for their newspaper business. When Democrats assembled in Austin on the night of April 27, 1846, to create a state organization, Ford was present, and he was chosen with other prominent politicos as a central committee to direct the organizing. He in fact had made himself a leader in the movement to establish a formal structure for the Democrats in Texas, publishing a call for organization in his *Texas Democrat* on April 15, 1846. Ford and his colleagues made plans for a state convention in the fall of 1846, but the war between the United States and Mexico, which many had expected, interrupted their preparations. When the Democrats actually held their first state convention in February 1848, Ford did not attend because he was serving with the Army in Mexico.[24]

Ford worked hard as an editor but longed to be a soldier again, and tragedy gave him an opportunity. The *Texas Democrat* continued to support Houston but also pushed for effective frontier protection, better schools, and more churches, doctors, and lawyers. Ford was an ardent promoter of the Texans fighting in Mexico, reporting every operation

John C. Hays. William Emerson Strong Photograph Album, Rare Book, Manuscript, and Special Collections Library, Duke University.

they undertook as well as every other bit of news on the war as it developed. He became especially enamored of Ranger leaders such as John C. Hays and Samuel H. Walker, who served under the command of Maj. Gen. Zachary Taylor in northern Mexico, and it was evident that he envied them. His editorial work suddenly ended in mid-July when his beloved Louisa became seriously ill with tuberculosis, and he reverted to being a doctor once more. He tried everything he knew, and when she died on August 21, 1846, at the age of twenty-seven, he was devastated. He published a formal, but tender and sad, obituary in the *Texas Democrat,* and he rarely practiced medicine again.[25] Just as in Tennessee, the end of a relationship, even if it was in no way his fault, gave rise to a fundamental change in Ford's lifestyle.

The chance to fight in Mexico shook Ford from his misery after Louisa died. In the late summer of 1846, he visited the San Antonio camp of Texans who had served in Hays' First Regiment, Texas Mounted Volunteers (Six Months). Hays had enhanced his reputation as a fighter with these men in Mexico, and they took great pride in the title of Ranger as they shared their tales with Ford. His adulatory articles on Rangers resumed in early September 1846, beginning with one that asserted, "There is probably no set of men on earth readier for a fight, a chase, a fandango, or any thing else which may come up, than the Texas Rangers." Noted for his "devil may care, confident, contented look," a Ranger could "ride like a Mexican, trail like an Indian, shoot like a Tennessean, and fight like a very devil." Ford bestowed his own motto, borrowed from the British Navy, upon the Ranger: "his motto seems to be 'ready, aye ready.'" Confessing that he had spent many hours in "a Texas camp," Ford added, "we never let slip an opportunity to spend a pleasant hour with any of the hardy fellows who have helped to add another star to the bright galaxy of the Union."[26]

General Taylor had already discharged Hays' regiment, whose violent excesses in Mexico vexed him, by the time Ford met some of the veterans, but persistent attacks by Mexican guerrillas created a new demand for mobile troops. Hays mustered a second regiment of mounted volunteers with a dual purpose: he was appointed to command the state forces of Texas assigned to frontier defense, while Taylor accepted his companies into Army service to protect his supply lines. This forced Hays to change his troopers' enlistment terms from six months to one year, and to divide his men. He sent a battalion of five companies to the western frontier under the command of Lt. Col. Peter H. Bell, while he led six companies into Mexico. Ford wanted to remain with Hays. He enlisted as a private in Capt. Samuel Highsmith's company of the First Regiment, Texas Mounted Volunteers (Twelve Months), as a private during June 1847, but when the regiment was reorganized in July, Ford became the regimental adjutant. When Highsmith rode west with Bell, Ford stayed with Hays.[27]

Hays' six companies of Texans never joined Taylor. They left San Antonio on August 12, 1847, reached the Rio Grande at Laredo, then crossed and swung east along the far side of the river to Mier. There Hays received orders to join the United States forces gathering to march on Mexico City under the command of Maj. Gen. Winfield Scott. Riding east, Hays had his Rangers board transports at Matamoros for the voyage to Vera Cruz, which Scott had secured as his base of operations. Ford hurried ahead of the main body with a detachment assigned to the task of arriving at Vera Cruz first to secure a campsite. They boarded a steamship at Brazos Santiago, and soon Ford had his first miserable bout of seasickness, which plagued him throughout the voyage. Ford also quarreled with an Irish seaman who tried to appropriate his cabin, but his horse, "Ball Higgins," gained a measure of revenge when he bit the sailor's ear off. With some pride, Ford recalled that his vile-tempered mount had not only won races in East Texas and carried a Texan during Taylor's 1846 Monterrey campaign, but he also "was noted for his extraordinary powers of endurance, his sagacity, and his rascality."[28]

Ford and the advance detachment settled on a sandy, windy campsite north of Vera Cruz on the road to Jalapa, which served as a base for their first operations. Hays arrived with the rest of his Texans on October 17, 1847. More recruits trickled in, until there were about 580 men, and Hays distributed Colt revolvers, which Ford insisted were more accurate than the Model 1841 rifled muskets provided to some of the elite infantry. Ford got his first opportunity to use a Colt when he was ordered to lead a reconnaissance to the ranch of a reputed partisan leader. Ford led a column of hand-picked men out of camp at four in the morning, without a guide as he failed to appear on time. When they spotted suspected partisans, Ford drew his revolver and charged, but Higgins stepped in a hole and flipped, flinging Ford into mud. His fellow Rangers thought he had been shot accidentally by the man following him, but Ford stumbled to his feet and remounted, thus providing a reprieve for the accused. Several Mexicans were shot in the chase, but Ford discovered as he closed on an opponent that his percussion caps were wet and would not fire. The Mexican dismounted and raced into a hut, and Ford pursued with sword in hand but found only a woman. Ford must have smiled as he wrote years later, "The excited ranger ran around the house a time or two, and discovered no man into whose vitals he could plunge his sword." Bitterly disappointed, he returned to Higgins, looking "very much like a fellow who had peeped through a crack and saw his rival playing yum-yum with the gal of his heart."[29]

Ford's tone became more somber when he wrote about what happened when he and his men reached the ranch that was their target. After killing several more Mexicans in a sharp firefight, they searched the buildings, finding "American corn sacks" and other items that they concluded had been stolen. Most disturbing was the discovery of several "American made shirts with ball-holes in them, and blood upon them." For that reason, they burned the main residence and other structures. Ford later remarked that "it was an unpleasant scene, one a man may hope never to witness again." But he took great pride in recording that the Texans made their way back to camp by sundown, having ridden sixty miles in a single day and emerged the victors in several engagements. In Ford's first expedition as a Ranger officer, he believed he had done well.[30]

Ford got another chance at action when Hays ordered the organization of a spy company of fifty troopers chosen from his six companies. They were to serve as scouts when the regiment marched, and to search for Mexican partisans. They elected Ford as their captain. Ford suffered from an unidentified recurring illness, perhaps malaria, in Mexico, and at least once it almost caused him to be killed when he fell asleep during a military operation. The regiment went to Antigua, on the river of the same name northwest of Vera Cruz, and Ford with his spy company led the way. When Ford discovered Mexican pickets near the mouth of the river, Hays decided to send a skiff with Ford and sixteen Rangers across the river, hoping to strike the enemy camp from the rear. Sending his men to search the area, Ford fell fast asleep on the far side of the river and awoke to find himself alone except for a Spanish-speaking black man whom he had convinced his men not to harm. This man repaid Ford by summoning a fellow Mexican to row the Ranger officer back across the river to the safety of his regiment.[31]

Scott captured Mexico City in September 1847, but he found it difficult to patrol the capital and suppress guerrillas without more mounted troops. In response to his call for reinforcements, Hays' Texans joined a column marching inland from Vera Cruz in November. Ford resumed his duties as adjutant after Hays disbanded the spy company, and he kept the records as his fellow Rangers battled efficiently, and ruthlessly, against suspected partisans and regulars who refused to accept a truce. Mexico was still at war, and unwary American stragglers lost their lives. In turn, Ford learned that there was often a discrepancy between the number of Mexicans killed in an engagement and that admitted in official reports. The latter frequently fell short of the actual death toll exacted by Rangers who had lost relatives to Mexican raids, or who had been captured during the Santa Fe or Mier expeditions just a few years earlier and watched as their fellow Texans were executed by their Mexican captors or died of neglect while in captivity. Perhaps shaken, Ford carefully insisted that the Texans with whom he served killed only "armed men," not non-combatants, and did not do anything to sully the reputation of Texas.[32]

Hays arrived in Mexico City with his troopers on December 7, 1847, after more than a month on the trail. The Rangers who entered the capital, including a still-ailing Ford, were a scruffy lot. They wore fragments of garments with which they had arrived in Vera Cruz augmented with a bewildering array of clothing acquired during their march. Many wore fur caps with tails attached, allegedly of everything from bears and raccoons to dogs and cats. They enhanced the impact of their outrageous appearance on the civilians who had gathered to watch their entrance by deliberately putting on a show, in keeping with their growing reputation as fearsome hellions. They rode their horses and mules standing up, sideways, or even backwards. Just as they intended, they made quite an impression.[33]

In Mexico City, the Rangers clashed violently with the rougher elements in the capital's populace, as well as with some innocent bystanders. Several of both were shot by Rangers, some accidentally, some not. Rock-throwing residents and pickpockets alike lost their lives, but also the bodies of three to five Americans would often be found in the streets each morning. The climax came when a Texan was mortally wounded by knife-wielding assailants. After he died, his comrades killed more than eighty Mexicans in retaliation. Ford was visiting with Hays and another officer the night that the Ranger died. About ten they heard pistol shots, but Hays said they were mistaken. When the shots intensified, Hays insisted that it was Army troops training. About midnight the other officer asked why Scott's orderly was approaching the building. There was no one coming, but Hays, not knowing that and also not wishing to be questioned again by the commanding general, retreated into a rear room, asking Ford to tell anyone who asked that he was absent. After an hour, Ford and the other officer smilingly retired as well without investigating the noise outside. This and a few more clashes ended the killing of Americans, but Scott moved the Texans to a camp outside the capital when it became apparent that Hays would not do anything to curb his men.[34]

After a month in Mexico City, the Rangers resumed operations against suspected partisans. Hays led sixty-five men into the field on January 11, 1848. After two days of chasing and not catching Mexicans, he let his troopers rest inside a complex of stone buildings in San Juan Tenochtitlán, near the capital. They quickly fell asleep only to be awakened by an attack led by Celedonio Domeco de Jarauta, a Spanish priest who had taken up the sword against the invaders from the United States. The Texans repulsed at least three mounted assaults and wounded Jarauta. Ford, still suffering from his malady, played a prominent role, shooting and mortally wounding at least one Mexican officer. The Rangers did not lose anyone, while Ford estimated the Mexican dead and wounded at fifteen to twenty, of a total force of approximately four

Fight at San Juan Tenochtitlán. Remington, *Crooked Trails.*

hundred. Angry at residents for taking part in the attack, and believing the town was the site where a captured Texas officer, Ewen Cameron, had been executed in 1843 after the Mier Expedition, Ford hotly advocated sacking San Juan Tenochtitlán. He told a reporter many years later, "I felt like reminding those people that the Texans had come to celebrate the funeral obsequies of their distinguished comrade." Fortunately, he was ignored. Low on ammunition, Hays decided to return to Mexico City; a Mexican cavalry force shadowed him for part of the journey but declined to fight again. The 107-mile ride and skirmish exhausted Ford, and a doctor sent him to bed. He could not even join his comrades when they departed five days later in a futile attempt to catch Gen. Antonio López de Santa Anna, who remained in the field after losing Mexico City to the Americans.[35]

The Treaty of Guadalupe Hidalgo, which provided for an end to the war, was signed on February 2, 1848, but the fighting in Mexico continued as the two governments discussed ratification. Two weeks later, Brig Gen. Joseph Lane rode into the mountains northeast of Mexico

Santa Anna. Prints and Photographs Division, Library of Congress.

City with Hays and 250 Rangers, Maj. William H. Polk (brother of Pres. James K. Polk) with 130 men of the Third Dragoons, and Col. Manuel Dominguez's Mexican lancers. Their quarry was former president Mariano Paredes, who had returned from exile, repudiated the treaty, and joined Jarauta. After a long night of hard riding, Lane entered Tulancingo. Ford with Lt. William B. Bate of the Dragoons persuaded a Mexican to show them where Paredes was hiding, but Polk called to them to join him because he had the ex-president. In fact, Polk had Paredes' brother, who was somewhat amused at the confusion, which allowed his more famous sibling to escape after hastily dressing. Ford himself was intrigued to think that a president's brother had captured a president's brother.[36]

Frustrated at losing Paredes, Lane led his command, minus Dominguez's lancers, to the village of Zacualtipan, where informers said Jarauta had settled. The Americans arrived on February 25, discovered Mexican regulars and partisans, and decided to attack. While Hays and Lane directed the main assault force, Ford with Maj. Alfred M. Truitt of Hays' regiment led a detachment in an attack on some Mexicans barricaded inside a stone house. Ford noticed that many of his enemies were slipping away over a stockade wall. He and Pvt. Jacob M. Horn made their way closer using a wood fence for cover, and with revolver fire prevented the Mexicans from using that escape route. Horn was shot in the chest, but other Rangers joined Ford, and the Mexicans, seeing their pathway to safety was blocked, surrendered. Ford and Truitt gathered twenty prisoners, half of whom were wounded, including their commander, who had been mortally wounded by Ford. Eleven Mexicans had been killed, three of them by Ford. Truitt, who had worked closely with Ford since they left Texas with the advance detachment, gave him much of the credit for their victory: "He was in the thickest of the fight—mounted the wall, exposed himself to the fire of the enemy, and encouraged the men by word and deed." Horn unfortunately proved to be their single fatality when he died later in the hospital—Ford could not resist remarking that he probably would have lived if the doctors had been bold enough to pull the bullet from his wound.[37]

While Ford and Truitt fought at the stone house, Hays and Lane crushed the main Mexican force at Zacualtipan in a house-to-house fight that allegedly claimed the lives of as many as 150 Mexicans and three Americans assumed to be deserters who joined the partisans. Jarauta escaped, but among the dead was his second-in-command. Like Ford and Truitt, Hays and Lane suffered relatively light casualties, losing only three men wounded, bringing the total for the encounter to six Texans wounded, including the dying Horn. Both Hays and Lane joined with Truitt in praising Ford in their official reports of the fight. In fact, Ford's quick thinking prevented the Texans' losses from becoming much worse. He did not have much time to rest before he noticed that the building where his vile-tempered horse, Higgins, and other officers' mounts had been quartered was on fire. Ford was exhausted, but still saddled and led a half dozen horses to safety, including Higgins, before help arrived.[38]

Patrols and fighting continued into March 1848. Ford was sick again as Hays led his Rangers toward Vera Cruz that month, and occasional clashes with Mexican partisans did not improve his mood. Nor was he pleased when he was sent on a patrol to search for partisans, and local officials refused to provide him with rations and quarters. A prefect of police tried to make amends by serving a lavish supper to Ford, but the Texan and his companions, an interpreter and a guide, kept their weapons in their laps during the meal. Conversely, when Santa Anna, who had been given a promise of safe passage to leave Mexico, passed by the Ranger camp at Jalapa in March 1848, Ford and Truitt intervened to convince their comrades not to kill the former dictator. The Texans lined both sides of the road and stared in stony silence as Santa Anna with his wife and daughter in an open carriage, escorted by American and Mexican soldiers, sped past their camp as his worried driver frantically whipped his mules.[39]

The Rangers mustered out of federal service at Vera Cruz by early May, and Ford and Hays and others climbed aboard a ship bound for Texas. Ford wanted to remain in Ranger service with the state of Texas, but when he learned that Hays intended to resign, he decided to do so as well. Ford idolized Hays for his fighting skills, leadership ability, and endurance, and he was apparently reluctant to serve on the frontier without him. The enthusiastic greeting of a large, happy crowd at Port Lavaca and the "elegant" dance they provided for the Texans, as well as other celebrations as Ford and others traveled inland, did not persuade him otherwise. It was nice to be a hero, but Ford mustered out of state service with his company on May 14 and went home to Austin on Higgins. There he might have expected a hero's welcome as well; after all, he had written constantly to Cronican while he was in Mexico with the assumption that his partner would publish his letters in their *Texas Democrat.* Instead, he discovered that Cronican had decided the communications were too lengthy and had thrown them away. Copies kept by Ford had been lost on the journey home when he left his papers on the ship and never saw them again. Regarding his reaction when Cronican confessed what he had done, Ford wrote, "Truth requires the admission that this information caused an uncommon emission of profanity."[40]

Ford returned to publishing the *Texas Democrat* with Cronican, despite his great transgression, and the partners also got contracts for publishing the laws adopted by the current legislature as well as the tax assessment lists. When the legislature did not renew their contracts, however, and it proved as difficult as always to sell subscriptions, Ford decided to quit. In January 1849 he and Cronican sold their newspaper to William H. Cushney, who had originally printed the *Texas Democrat* at Washington-on-the-Brazos under the title of *Texas National Register* before he sold it to Ford and Cronican. What Ford wanted to do was to be a Ranger, a desire probably magnified when he served on a "Committee of Invitation" for a formal ball hosted for United States Army officers at the Texas Capitol in December 1848. When Indians threatened Austin, Ford led volunteers into the field in October 1848 and again in early 1849. He failed to locate Indians, and when the legislature refused to accept his volunteers into state service, he found himself unemployed. As he did when he returned from Mexico, he wrote articles on Rangers and Indians for the *Texas Democrat,* which Cushney regularly published, but it was a poor substitute for being a Ranger.[41]

The Gold Rush, which ironically began just after Mexico ceded California to the United States in the Treaty of Guadalupe Hidalgo, generated much demand for a practical wagon road from central Texas to the Pacific coast. Thousands of people were traveling west; if they came through Texas, and later maintained business ties, that would benefit the new Lone Star State. Too, American traders regularly traveled from Independence, Missouri, to Santa Fe, New Mexico, and some pushed on to Chihuahua, inside Mexico itself. Their trade was lucrative, and Texans wanted their own pathway into it. During the era of the Republic of Texas, this desire had led to the disastrous attempt to annex the Santa Fe area, and as debate began in the United States Congress on boundaries, Texans again wanted to establish a claim to the region. San Antonio citizens in 1848 hired Hays to lead an exploration west from their community to the Rio Grande, hoping to establish a wagon road from San Antonio to Chihuahua by way of El Paso. This expedition became hopelessly lost and ultimately only reached Presidio del Norte on the Rio Grande, whence a wagon road wended its way to Chihuahua. Hays found an easier route for their return journey to San Antonio, where they arrived 107 long days after their departure.[42]

When Maj. Gen. William J. Worth was ordered to Texas in December 1848, among his instructions was the charge to explore other options for a wagon road from the interior of Texas to the west. During the next year, he authorized seven new expeditions. Robert S. Neighbors, Indian Agent for Texas, led one of these. Neighbors spoke with the general about a route from San Antonio to El Paso, but changed his itinerary when he stopped in Austin, on his way north to secure Indian guides, and talked with Ford at his home. Austin businessmen had asked Ford to help establish a wagon road from their town to El Paso. At a meeting on February 20, 1849, they appointed a committee to produce a report showing the most practical route. Ford and Stephen D. Mullowny actually wrote the document, which relied heavily on that written by Hays after he tried to blaze a trail from San Antonio to El Paso. Neighbors accepted the change in his plans, and Ford as a partner, perhaps in part because Austin businessmen agreed to underwrite much of the cost of his expedition. The two men made an unlikely team: both of them were thirty-four years of age and had tall, muscular physiques, but Ford was loud and outgoing while Neighbors was quiet and reserved. But they apparently had a common ground in their ambition and love of jokes, and they forged a friendship that lasted until Neighbors' death at the hands of an assassin just ten years later.[43]

Ford agreed with Neighbors that Hays had failed because he did not have "an able and efficient guide." Indians knew the country better than anyone else and were effective interpreters, so Neighbors traveled north to Barnard's Trading Post near modern Waco, where he recruited Delawares Jim Shaw and John Harry, Shawnees Joe Ellis and Tom Coshattee, and Patrick Goin, a Choctaw. To complete his small band, Neighbors hired Buffalo Hump, a Penateka Comanche who had battled with Texas settlers before signing a treaty in 1846. Ford rode Higgins to the rendezvous point at Barnard's Trading Post, but sent him home with his friend Thomas M. Woolridge because Neighbors wanted his entire party mounted on mules. Buffalo Hump was late, so Ford visited with Shapley P. Ross, who had commanded a company under Bell while Ford campaigned with Hays in Mexico. When Shaw insisted that the group needed to be larger, two Anglos from Ross' company were added: Daniel C. "Doc" Sullivan and Alpheus D. Neill. Sullivan, who had survived the Mier Expedition, was a small albino prankster with white hair and pink eyes. The latter stayed "in constant motion, as if under the influence of a current of galvanism." Ford was fascinated with and instantly liked Sullivan, whom he praised as "a terror to pretenders and windbags." Sullivan's "constant companion," Neill, was not nearly as impetuous or mischievous, nor as entertaining, but Ford liked him, and Neill served several times under his command.[44]

Buffalo Hump finally arrived, and the expedition departed on March 23, 1849, for El Paso. Ford rode Tantrybogus, a lazy mule who fell down with annoying regularity. The Indians proved to be skillful hunters, especially Harry, and kept the party fed on the march. Ford, in good health and high spirits, entertained the Comanches by jumping on rattlesnakes, secure in the protection of his knee-high boots, but when confronted by an especially large specimen, he reconsidered the idea and never did it again. Sullivan, on the other hand, performed silly songs and imitations of animals, which initially led the Comanches to conclude that he was crazy but harmless. But when he persisted in sticking pins in the Comanche warriors and flirting with Comanche women, much to the irritation of Buffalo Hump and his men, the latter's patience wore thin. The breaking point came when Neighbors' group arrived in the Colorado River camp of Sanaco, a Penateka leader whose father had been killed by the Texans at the Council House Fight in 1841. Buffalo Hump quit the expedition despite having been given goods by Neighbors for his services to El Paso. Ford recalled that this decision was not just based on Sullivan's bad behavior, but also arose because some of Buffalo Hump's associates reminded him that men in El Paso had pledged to kill him if he went there again. Too, it cannot be discounted that Buffalo Hump had become aware that the proposed road would bring more settlers west, which he had opposed in a treaty with President Houston in 1844.[45]

Ford's experiences in Sanaco's camp brought into focus his own ideas about Indians and their conflicts with whites. He spotted a captive red-haired white woman whose "face seemed the personification of despair." He was deeply moved not just by her sad expression, but also by the long cuts evident on her cheeks. She was apparently miserable with the Comanches, whom Ford assumed treated her brutally and kept her from a previous happy life to which she could not return now that she was the consort of an Indian, however unwilling. He considered trying to rescue her but was dissuaded by Shaw, who explained to Ford that such an effort would be foolhardy and fatal. Years later, Ford declared in his memoir, "The writer has since that period done some rather rough Indian fighting. When leading a charge against the red men, the woman with auburn hair, slashed cheeks, and countenance of extreme sorrow, has appeared to lead him. She was before his mind's eye, and he struck for her and for vengeance." This grim encounter as much as any other convinced him that "if savagery is right, civilization is wrong. There can be no middle ground."[46]

Neighbors persuaded Guadalupe, also known as Tall Tree, to serve in Buffalo Hump's place, and the new recruit, with his family group, stayed with the expedition throughout their journey despite Sullivan's continuing harassment. The trip became an ordeal. Neill got lost while hunting and had to make his way back east with the assistance of other Comanches. Water became increasingly scarce as the remaining members of the party made their way across the prairies. Their mules stampeded one morning, leaving them afoot until the Indians retrieved their wayward mounts. Ford's Tantrybogus was accused of leading the stampede, despite his laziness and the fact that he was hobbled. Remounted, Ford had a tense encounter with a Comanche warrior that ended peacefully when Guadalupe recognized the stranger and intervened. Told that the party was short on food, the stranger even killed one of his mules and prepared it for all to feast upon. The hungry Texans crossed the Pecos River at Horsehead Crossing, where they ate the last of the meat they brought with them. They later devoured an abandoned horse they found on Toyah Creek and also supplemented their meager supply of corn meal with half-roasted mescal and maguey. Ford was miserable: he hated the taste of horsemeat, eating mescal and maguey made him dangerously sick, and he was plagued by mosquitoes. To cap it all, an ice storm hit the party in mid-April, dumping sleet and snow on the travelers while they struggled for hours to find anything to make a fire.[47]

Ford and Sullivan finally rebelled against Guadalupe, who insisted upon leading the group over a series of steep ridges, and struck south to the Rio Grande. Ford recalled that he and Sullivan rode for several miles along the Rio Grande before Sullivan told him that it was a river; Ford had mistaken it for a pond. A deer was killed that night, raising the Texans' spirits even further. The expedition stumbled up the Rio Grande, through an amazing number of rattlesnakes, into El Paso by late April 1849. Ford there encountered the subject of an article that had appeared in his *Texas Democrat* in September 1846: the "Great Western," a woman who operated a hotel that offered "a variety of refreshments." Her name was Sarah Knight, and she had followed her husband, a soldier with Zachary Taylor, to Fort Brown. When Mexican troops attacked the post, she grabbed a musket, and a grateful Taylor gave her a battlefield commission as a colonel. By marrying twice more she was able to stay with the Army as it marched into Mexico, but her luck ran out and she settled in El Paso. An infatuated Ford described her as "a huge, powerful woman who . . . could whip any man, fair fight or foul, could shoot a pistol better than anyone in the region, and at black jack could out play (or out cheat) the slickest professional gambler."[48]

Neighbors was not happy with the route chosen by Guadalupe, who was clearly lost by the time they approached El Paso, and so he decided to find another way home. This trail, along which they were led by a Mexican guide, proved to be easier and better-supplied with water. The superiority of this route was indicated by the fact that Ford and his colleagues encountered several groups traveling west. Neighbors assigned members of his party to guide them. Most of the Indians left on a more direct route back to their starting point, while Ford and others accompanied Neighbors to San Antonio. There the residents were fascinated with the sulking Guadalupe, who had only reluctantly left El Paso with its prospects for profitable raiding, and with Ford, who apparently wore only fragments of the garments in which he began his trek in late March 1849. Ford himself described his clothing as "a pair of old drawers and a breech clout, no coat, and a shirt chock-full of the free-soil element."[49]

With Ford's assistance, Neighbors produced an official report on his expedition in June 1849 for Col. William S. Harney, who had replaced Worth when the latter died of cholera the previous month. It had taken the Texans only fifty-five days to complete the 1,160-mile trip from central Texas to El Paso and back to San Antonio, and they reported that their return march was along a level, all-weather route. Nonetheless, Army officials decided to build their posts along a more southerly pathway explored by Lt. William H. C. Whiting, whose journey from San Antonio to El Paso and back at about the same time had taken longer than that of Ford and Neighbors. Ford could take some consolation from the high praise accorded him by Neighbors in his report: "In Dr. John S. Ford, I found an energetic and able assistant, the services rendered by him were important to the successful termination of the expedition. I cheerfully recommend him to your favorable notice." Furthermore, when Robert Creuzbaur published a popular guide for travelers in 1849, he included a detailed map of the route from Austin to El Paso drawn from Ford's notes, not from an Army report or any other source. Finally, on August 3, 1849, Sullivan arrived in Austin from El Paso, having made the trip in twenty-three days with a wagon along Ford's and Neighbor's route. He found hundreds of wagons being prepared for the journey west, indicating that many people were already making their way along the route explored by Ford and Neighbors.[50]

Ford was not about to let the people, and businessmen, of Austin forget what he had done. He produced several articles on his trip for the *Texas Democrat,* beginning with a long, detailed report on June 23, 1849. In it, he outlined the best route for a wagon road, extolled the virtues of West Texas, and proposed building a rail line along the same route. Just as Neighbors had done for him, Ford graciously praised his traveling partner. Nonetheless, Ford did not follow Neighbors when he was appointed by the legislature to organize the western lands claimed by Texas into counties to establish a clear hold on the disputed region. Neighbors traveled west, completed the organization of El Paso County by March 1850, and continued to Santa Fe, earning a denunciation from Zachary Taylor as president of the United States. Both federal and state officials declared they would fight over the matter, but cooler heads prevailed, and Gov. Peter H. Bell, Hays' former lieutenant colonel, accepted the terms of the Compromise of 1850, which ceded much of the western lands to the territory of New Mexico in return for a substantial cash payment to Texas.[51]

Rather than play a greater role in the final settlement of the claims of the Republic of Texas, Ford briefly returned to practicing medicine in 1849, buying an office on Pecan Street. He also became active in the Sons of Temperance, joining the Austin chapter and traveling to other towns to speak. He of course excelled at it, and when a committee of ladies presented a banner to the Sons in Austin on July 4, 1849, Ford accepted the gift on their behalf with a long, gracious speech in which he compared the "war on drunkenness" to the independence fight of 1836 and the recently concluded war with Mexico. He had continued to read his Bible every day as he promised his mother, even in the field, and he resumed teaching Sunday School classes for young men, using crude humor to keep them amused and make his points.[52] Along with writing occasional columns for the *Texas Democrat,* it made for a full, if not very profitable, life, and he apparently enjoyed the peacetime roles he had defined for himself.

Ford by 1850, when he was just thirty-five years old, had been a doctor, surveyor, lawyer, congressman, editor, soldier, and explorer. The many roles he played reflected the opportunities for an ambitious young man in the Republic of Texas, which expanded rapidly despite attacks from Mexicans and Indians and the constraints of an impoverished government. It was not an easy lifestyle for many who lived in the Republic, and Ford also endured the deaths of his mother and his second wife. But Texas triumphed in the war with Mexico and prospered as one of the United States, and Ford advanced with it, continuing to take advantage of the chances a new frontier state offered to a man determined to meet or pass the mark that he believed had been set by his Revolutionary grandfathers. Most important for the next decade of Ford's life was the fact that he had clearly proven to be of the same "fighting stock" as they. Texas would need aggressive leaders during the decade prior to the Civil War, and Ford would build upon his previous roles to become not just a popular journalist and political leader, but also one of the best-known Ranger commanders on the eve of that conflict.

CHAPTER 2 RIP

When historians who study the Texas Rangers discuss the great captains of the era prior to the Civil War, John S. Ford is always included on the list. Some argue that he should be the top name on that roster. Ford secured this reputation during the period from 1849 to 1860, when he campaigned aggressively as a Ranger captain against both Indians and Mexicans. He did not devote all of his time to being a Ranger; in truth, before 1858 he played many other roles, including editor, Mexican revolutionary, Texas state senator, and mayor of Austin. But it was as a Ranger captain that he became known as "Rip" Ford, and that role provided him with the opportunity to make the lasting contributions to antebellum Texas, and his own legacy, that he longed to make. As a Texas Ranger and in other roles, Ford continued to follow the examples of his Revolutionary grandfathers and focused on public service; at the same time, he never forgot that he was of "fighting stock." He also remained committed to the Southern political and economic system based upon slavery that his father and grandfathers had embraced, never doubting that it was the correct path for the development of Texas as it had been for the other Southern states.

The Treaty of Guadalupe Hidalgo, which had ended the Mexican War, committed the United States and Mexico to control the Indians who had raided Tejanos and Anglos on both sides of the Rio Grande for several decades, but neither government proved capable of suppressing the violence along the border. Texans expected much of the United States Army, but peacetime reductions left that organization unable to prevent Indians, especially foraging Comanches, from riding east through a line of forts constructed along the frontier after the war with Mexico. The Comanches could not support themselves by only hunting buffalo, and they refused to quit their raids. Col. George M. Brooke of the

John S. "Rip" Ford. Collection of John N. McWilliams.

United States Army, who succeeded Col. William S. Harney in command of Texas in July 1849, initially declared that he did not need Rangers to assist in patrolling on the Rio Grande, but within a month he changed his mind and asked Gov. George T. Wood for three companies of state troops, to operate from Goliad to the Rio Grande. Texas Adjutant General John D. Pitts selected Ford, John J. Grumbles, and Henry Smock to organize the units. Each Ranger company numbered seventy-eight men, all of whom received a rifle and pistol from the state but had to provide their own horse and tack. Ford's volunteers, sworn into federal service at Austin on August 23, were eager to fight Indian, Mexican, or white outlaws, and they elected Ford as their captain, the first time that he held that rank. Governor Wood had apparently promised Ford's command to another man, but when he asked Brooke to dismiss Ford, the colonel responded "upon the legal advice of Volney E. Howard," United States Representative from Texas, that a removal would be impossible unless Ford was court-martialed or his commission expired. Mounted on Higgins, and with his friend Thomas M. Woolridge as a lieutenant, Ford led his new command south.[1]

Ford's Rangers arrived in Corpus Christi on September 5, 1849. They got their weapons at a depot there, and Ford hired Andrew J. Walker, a veteran Ranger, as a guide. Then he set up camp at Henry L. Kinney's ranch south of Corpus Christi, though he later relocated to Santa Gertrudis Creek, on the site of the future King Ranch. Indian and bandit raids had made it almost impossible to raise crops or herd livestock in this region, and Ford issued a declaration to his command that an "aggressive policy" was the only way to deal with Indians effectively. He explained: "Cost what it may the pioneer settlers must be protected. It is the imperative duty of the State to do so. It matters not what motive carried them to the frontier. They had a right to go, and they are entitled to the fostering care of the Government." Ford's Rangers patrolled constantly, and at least once as far as Laredo in a rainstorm, but they found no Indians or bandits. The greatest excitement for Ford came when he was wrongfully accused of stealing goods from the customs house at Mier. Ford and Walker had been at a party in the town that night. When the Mexican consul at Mier complained to the Department of State

Comanches. Brown, *Indian Wars and Pioneers of Texas.*

that Ford had been involved in the theft, Secretary of War George W. Crawford ordered Ford's arrest. Brooke once more defended Ford, and the matter was dropped.[2]

Ford's original six-month enlistments expired in February 1850, but the muster was renewed. While new recruits replaced those who left, Philip N. Luckett remained as the company doctor and Walker became first lieutenant. Among the seventy Rangers in the ranks were the irrepressible Daniel C. "Doc" Sullivan, his shadow Alpheus D. Neill, and Edward Burleson Jr., who arrived in camp carrying orders from Brooke to Ford and a letter from his father asking Ford, who had served under him as a volunteer during the Republic era, to "treat him as he would his own son." Another was John L. Wilbarger, whose father survived for eleven years after being scalped by Indians in 1833. The unit's new guide was Roque Maugricio, a renowned tracker who was half-Indian and half-Mexican. Ford also had a personal servant, Francisco de la Garza Falcón, who boasted that he was a hero of the battle of Monterrey but apparently spent most of that engagement trying to flee the field. Falcón proved adept at avoiding combat with Ford as well, but he finally declared he was on strike until he got the full wages of a Ranger, $23.50 per month, and not the $10 per month paid to a servant.[3]

This lively crew may be the source of Ford's enduring nickname. Every one of these men had a nickname bestowed by Ford, who apparently had trouble remembering names. For example, there was "Doc" Sullivan, or even more memorable was the title of "Don Monkey," as Ford referred to Falcón because of his lively and erratic mannerisms. In turn, these men began referring to Ford as "Rip." It may have been that they were impressed with his inclination to attack any foe he met, or "rip into them." Or it may have been that he suffered recurring bouts of the malady, perhaps malaria, that had first wracked him in Mexico; he thus found it difficult to stay awake at times, like Rip Van Winkle. At least one Ford biographer speculated that Doc Sullivan pinned the label on Ford, which would certainly fit their relationship. Ford recalled all of these men fondly in his memoirs, declaring, "They did right because it was right." They generally behaved themselves; those that survived became good citizens and husbands, and in sum they made excellent subordinates for a man like Ford who was determined to be known as a fine Ranger captain.[4]

After reorganizing with his new recruits, Ford moved closer to the Rio Grande, settling at San Antonio Viejo, a ruined hacienda forty-five miles north of Rio Grande City. There his men lived in tents, with a "rude building" for storing their supplies, but they had potable water. Ford, unlike most Ranger officers, insisted that his company drill regularly, becoming proficient in the manual of arms and tactical maneuvers. Those who did not found themselves ordered to guard the camp or perform other onerous duties rather than serve on escorts or ride on patrols. One of the latter led to Ford's first major engagement with Comanche warriors. While patrolling with forty men, Ford discovered a recently killed deer with a Comanche arrowhead in it. He divided his command and sent half to the south with Walker while he rode north with the rest. Ford guessed that the Comanches would bolt from one party and run into the other. Comanches did attack Walker's group, then raced north as the Texans pursued them. Walker's men fell behind and quit, but on May 12, 1850, Ford crossed the trail on the Nueces River and overtook the Comanches who were riding slowly, confident they had outrun all pursuers. Seventeen Rangers, led by Ford, attacked the same number of Comanche warriors. Only Ford and another Ranger had Colt revolvers; the remainder had muzzle-loading rifles, while the Comanches used bows and lances. The latter withdrew slowly, hoping to lure the Texans into firing and then attack before they reloaded. Ford had his men fire alternately, so some had loaded rifles at all times. When the Comanche leader was hit, Ford ordered a charge of his own while his foes were in disarray. The Comanches bolted, but several fell to Ranger bullets, including a warrior who tumbled from his horse and was shot by Ford before he could loose an arrow.[5]

Ford had won his first victory as a Ranger captain, demonstrating the combination of thoughtful planning, disciplined execution, and personal bravery that characterized all of his victories. He had carefully anticipated his opponents' tactics, had his men fight as a unit and not as individuals, and stayed in the forefront of the fighting as it developed. It was a particularly vicious engagement in that it involved Comanches with whom Ford and others had camped on their expedition to El Paso in 1849 with Robert S. Neighbors. When one Comanche asked during the fight whether the Texans would kill their friends, Sullivan shot him through the body. In all, four Comanches were killed and seven wounded, while Ford's Rangers had only two slight wounds. Ford was one of the two wounded Texans. He had a scratch from an arrow on the back of his right hand, and did not pay much attention to it. But it proved to be very painful, and he later sought the attention of another doctor, suspecting the arrow had been tipped with poison, probably rattlesnake venom. No one could treat the wound effectively, and he suffered a temporary paralysis of his right arm several years later. Too, a "skin eruption" appeared annually on the hand for the next twenty-five years. Ford also lost his mount; hit by another poisoned arrow, it died three days later.[6]

The Comanches did not give up easily. That night they nabbed two horses that strayed from Ford's camp, partial compensation for twelve mounts they lost in the fight, and eluded Ford's pursuit the next day. On the night of May 13, joined by many other warriors, they surrounded Ford's command, waiting for an opportunity to strike. This standoff continued for three days and nights as Ford slowly made his way south while keeping his men in a tight defensive formation. His objective was Fort Merrill, a new post on the Nueces River, but the Texans' rations ran low as no one could be allowed to venture out for a hunt. Boiled mesquite with lots of sugar substituted for coffee by the time Ford got close enough to Fort Merrill for the Comanches to abandon their siege, but the Indians hovered close and continued to watch for a chance to harm or rob the Texans. When some bold Comanches did attack Ford's camp near Fort Merrill before daylight on May 26, they were repulsed and at least one Indian was killed.[7]

A handful of Rangers arrived from Corpus Christi with one hundred single-shot dragoon pistols for Ford's men, greatly enhancing their firepower. Among the five was William Gillespie, astride Higgins, and he tragically became the first to die under Ford's command. Ford left Fort Merrill for San Antonio Viejo on May 27, 1850. When the Rangers encountered Comanches and gave chase, Ford warned Gillespie that

Higgins could not be trusted. Sure enough, when the young man was aiming at a dismounted warrior, Higgins shied, ruining his shot and allowing the Indian to loose an arrow that penetrated Gillespie's left lung. His comrades quickly rallied around him as Ford rode to the scene. Spotting Comanches nearby, Ford ordered a charge and rode forward, then fumed when his men did not follow. He assumed they balked from cowardice, but one interrupted his tirade and explained the situation. Ford had Gillespie taken to cover, and then organized a two-front attack on the Comanches. At first the Indians maintained good order, with mounted warriors shielding those on foot, but a Ranger charge scattered them and the chase resumed as the Comanches rushed for nearby timber. Ford spied a Comanche leader, Otto Cuero, and fired a revolver shot that hit the Indian in the left arm at a distance, he claimed, of 125 yards. When Cuero turned to ride away, Ford ordered Ranger David Steele to dismount and take a shot with his rifle, which he did, hitting the Indian in the head and killing him. The other Comanches fled, having lost four killed and seven wounded. Ford had two men wounded, and Gillespie soon died.[8]

After the Rangers reached San Antonio Viejo, Ford submitted a report that won praise from Brooke, and Steele sent Cuero's accoutrements to Gov. Peter H. Bell. Ford's men had another prize as well: a wounded young warrior who said his name was Carne Muerto. Ford later speculated that he was in fact a son of Santa Anna, a feared Penateka Comanche leader who died of cholera in 1849, but what he knew for certain in June 1850 was that he was a troublesome trophy. In just a few weeks the Texans took him to Fort McIntosh near Laredo when Ford led forty Rangers to that post in response to reports of a Comanche attack on twenty of his men under Walker's command. Sent to Laredo after a series of Comanche raids, Walker's Texans had killed seven Comanches during a confused fight, while only one Ranger was wounded—future Bexar County sheriff Ed Stevens, who was shot in the head with an arrow that lodged under the skin. Among the dead was Bad Finger, a cousin of Carne Muerto who before he died told Rangers that the Comanches planned another raid. In fact, discovering that Ford was at Laredo, the Comanches attacked San Antonio Viejo, defended by only twenty-six Rangers. Ford returned by a forced march of seventy-five miles, but Army troops arrived first and the attackers were gone when Ford approached. Both sides suffered few casualties, but Comanches grabbed Higgins. Ford pursued his horse's captors but failed to catch them through his own fault: he was capping a shotgun when his thumb slipped and discharged the weapon. Startled Indians left their cover on the far side of the Rio Grande and rode away as he watched, knowing he did not have the authority to cross into Mexico.[9]

Higgins was not Ford's greatest loss in the summer of 1850. At Fort Merrill in May he had given furloughs to Doc Sullivan, Alpheus Neill, and John Wilbarger. The latter wanted to visit his family, while the first two had been summoned to testify in legal suits. The three Rangers met at San Antonio for the return trip to San Antonio Viejo. Having overstayed their leave, they were in a hurry and ignored Ford's warning about traveling with large parties. Sixty-five miles south of San Patricio, they were attacked by thirty Comanches. Instead of running, they decided to fight. Sullivan was shot through the body at long range and died when a second shot slammed into his head. Neill had dismounted to help Sullivan to the ground; when he remounted, his horse bolted under the rope securing Sullivan's mount and sent Neill flying. On foot, without the weapons secured to his saddle, Neill became an easy target for Comanches, some of whom caught his horse and armed themselves with his guns. Seriously wounded, Neill fainted and was shot with five or six arrows as he lay on the ground, then was stripped of his clothing. He awoke as the Comanches were leaving, but feigned death. Several days later, sunburned and with the broken shafts of arrows protruding from his infected wounds, he staggered naked into San Patricio, where amazed residents nursed him back to health. The bodies of Sullivan and Wilbarger, who killed several Comanches in a running battle before being killed, were soon located; Sullivan's had been mutilated and dragged across the prairie.[10]

Ford was discovering that being a Ranger captain was not all exciting adventures. His men faced a hard choice after the fight that claimed the life of Bad Finger. Walker's Texans had actually killed six Comanches, and took a seventh warrior alive but mortally wounded.

They carried him to the ranch of Basilio Benavides, where an examination revealed that their captive had both hips shattered and other grievous wounds. The end seemed apparent, the "chance of recovery was deemed hopeless," and it was decided to end his suffering. No Ranger would shoot him, but a Mexican teamster "performed the sanguinary part of an executioner," according to Ford, who later described the affair as an "act of mercy." Whether it was or not, such words provided scant comfort to Ford when Carne Muerto's mother, together with the mother of the Comanche warrior killed when his wounds appeared too serious for recovery, visited Ford's camp at Los Ojuelos in the summer of 1850 to plead for their sons. Ford through an interpreter told Carne Muerto's mother that he was safe at Fort McIntosh and would remain so. Ford did not record what he told the other Comanche woman; after all, there was not much he could say that would appease her.[11]

Ford had shifted his camp to Los Ojuelos because it lay much closer to Laredo and Fort McIntosh. His company mustered into federal service there for a third term of six months on September 24, 1850, but Ford and his Rangers probably did not remember that enlistment very fondly. Being close to a federal post forced the Texans to be more diplomatic in their response to Comanches. Ford encountered a group while on a night march from San Antonio to Laredo, and he was dissuaded from attacking only when an Army officer identified himself and explained that he was leading the Comanches to Fort McIntosh. One of them, Saddle Blanket, later formally declared that he and Ford were brothers, and apparently he kept his pledge not to fight when Ford took the field against the Comanches in 1858 and 1859. The Comanches left without incident, but they did so at night and quite suddenly, increasing the uneasiness of the Rangers. At the same time, the advanced location of the post forced Ford and his Rangers to travel long distances for supplies. A trip to San Antonio in the fall of 1850 became an ordeal when wagons had to be manhandled across a flooded Rio Frio, whose cold water gave ample evidence of how the river earned its name. Ford became ill and was bedridden for much of the next winter, while his reorganized company patrolled under the command of lieutenants Walker and Burleson.[12]

Carne Muerto was ordered to be moved from Fort McIntosh to San Antonio in January 1851, together with his mother and sister, who had joined him after the interview with Ford in his camp. Ford warned Burleson, who commanded the Comanche's escort, to expect trouble. Walker scouted north and east of Laredo with a detachment and found a Comanche campsite on Gato Creek. He laid an ambush and sprang his trap on January 25, killing four Comanches returning from a raid and wounding six. The only Ranger seriously injured was David M. Level, whose hand was pinned to his saddle by an arrow. Walker recovered a captive Mexican boy as well as two hundred horses and mules, but he did not prevent an attack on Burleson. Two days later, Burleson was returning from San Antonio when his Rangers spied three Comanches. Burleson gave chase with only eight Rangers, sending the remainder to Laredo. When eleven Comanches on foot joined their quarry, the Rangers dismounted to fight them, misunderstanding an order from Burleson. The engagement became a confused melee; of the nine Rangers, Baker Barton was killed and William Lackey was mortally wounded, while five, including Burleson, had serious but not fatal wounds. Of the fourteen Comanches, four died and eight were wounded.[13]

Ford had dragged himself from his sickbed to chase Comanches who had killed a Mexican, and he was recovering in Laredo when news came of Walker's and Burleson's engagements. Hamilton P. Bee reported from Laredo that Ford left immediately for Los Ojuelos, adding "I have no doubt that, although entirely unfit for duty, he is now in the saddle in pursuit." When he arrived in his camp, Ford heard more alarming details about Burleson's casualties from an excited courier. Hurrying up the San Antonio road with reinforcements, Ford had to be lifted from his saddle when he got to Burleson's camp, where Walker had also arrived. Burleson and others were being treated by a surgeon, and Ford must have been relieved to discover the injuries were not as grave as the messenger had indicated. Nonetheless, he was clearly displeased, as a hapless civilian discovered. About one month after Walker's fight, a lawyer appeared in Ford's camp to complain that his client had recovered only twenty-eight of the thirty-five mules stolen from him by the Comanches. When Ford explained that all of the captured mules had been given to the Army quartermaster at Fort McIntosh, the visitor declared that a suit would be filed for the missing animals. Ford blandly told him that if he were Walker, and if he were sued, he would cut the lawyer's ears off. As Ford recalled, "The suit was not brought."[14]

Ford's company mustered again for its fourth and last time on March 23, 1851. It proved to be a peaceful enlistment, with many patrols but no combat as the Comanches stayed to the west. A few Seminoles came north across the Rio Grande, but they did not seek battle. In September 1851, at his own request, Ford mustered his men out of federal service at Laredo. He praised his Rangers in a farewell address and admonished them to focus on a peaceful "transition" from their "wild life" to the "bounds of civil life." He also asked his men to support the Union and the Constitution, perhaps reflecting on the sectional conflict that had attended the Compromise of 1850, which provided a temporary solution to several of the key arguments concerning slavery. A few protests against the disbanding of the Rangers appeared in some Texas newspapers, together with appeals to Governor Bell to retain the companies at state expense, but Ford did not publicly support these demands.[15]

Ford left state service because he saw a greater opportunity to advance the causes of both democracy and slavery. José María de Jesús Carvajal, a native of San Antonio who had been educated in Virginia before becoming involved in the Texas Revolution, issued the Plan de la Loba at Camargo in 1851. In it, he called for the establishment of an independent republic carved from northern Mexico along the Rio Grande. He had earlier been defeated in efforts to achieve the same goal, but this time he had the support of Texas volunteers, led by Ford, and prominent Texas merchants such as Charles Stillman, Richard King, and Mifflin Kenedy, the trio who had united to dominate trade along the lower Rio Grande. Kenedy and King had already begun expanding into ranching, and they anticipated that a victory by Carvajal would enhance their prospects. Ford had more grandiose ideas, declaring that he and other "Texians" would join Carvajal not only to "assist a people" who were "resisting tyranny, and battling for the exercise of their privileges as free men," but also with "the hope of strengthening the institution of

José María Jesús de Carvajal. Prints and Photographs Division, Library of Congress.

slavery in Texas and in the South." Ford and others believed there were thousands of runaway slaves in northern Mexico. In addition to promising open trade on the Rio Grande to Texas businessmen frustrated by Mexican taxes and laws, Carvajal agreed to assist in returning runaways to Texas masters and, if his revolution succeeded, to make it illegal for slaves to flee to northern Mexico. Some Texans funneled money to Carvajal, while others enlisted to fight for him. They assembled at Rio

Grande City, then crossed the river with Carvajal and took Camargo in September 1851.[16]

From Camargo, Carvajal appealed for reinforcements. Ford, as they previously had agreed, joined him with twenty-nine former Rangers, including Walker. Carvajal soon appointed Ford as a colonel to command all of the Americans while Walker took charge of the Rangers, whom Ford had allegedly equipped at his own expense. The revolutionaries marched on Matamoros, where they seized Fort Paredes on the outskirts of the city. This prompted Edward R. Hord to lead as many as four hundred Americans from Brownsville to join Ford, under whom Hord took command of a company. Ford's large force included many prominent Southerners. C. Roberdeau Wheat of Louisiana directed the artillery as a major, the same rank that he would hold when he fell mortally wounded as a Confederate officer at Gaines' Mill in June 1862. Joseph D. Howell, the brother-in-law of future Confederate president Jefferson Davis, led a company from New Orleans. Not just future Confederates served with Carvajal—among the Texans was John L. Haynes of Brownsville, who would become the colonel of the Second Texas Cavalry (USA) during the Civil War. Furthermore, not everyone was American; Ford had to cope with a zealous Hungarian who spoke no English and refused to step down from his post in charge of guarding the artillery one night. The situation was resolved only when Ford found another soldier who could speak Magyar.[17]

Ford led an assault in Matamoros on October 22, leading his Americans in house-to-house fighting. When artillery blocked his advance at the main plaza, Ford asked for reinforcements and was told by Carvajal to withdraw. He ignored these instructions until Carvajal issued them a third time, after which Ford convinced his revolutionaries to retire to Fort Paredes. There they slept in a downpour outside the main works, glumly trying to keep their powder dry. Ford had lost one killed and two wounded, but he believed he had inflicted heavy losses and could win if he made another effort. He attacked again on October 23, pushing to the edge of the main plaza before heavy small arms and artillery fire pinned his forces. Ford himself had his scalp creased by a musket ball that gave him a serious concussion and left him unable to think clearly. Carried across the Rio Grande to Brownsville, Ford had his wound dressed by a United States Army surgeon. There he remained until Carvajal withdrew from Matamoros a week later, having heard that enemy reinforcements under Gen. Antonio Canales were finally approaching.[18]

The Texans had fought on without Ford, who in his delirious state penned grand addresses to his troops "*à la Napoleon*," which "Hord had the 'cussedness' to preserve." Still not healed, Ford rushed to join Carvajal as he fell back. Arriving by steamboat at Reynosa, Ford found the revolutionaries there, but he also learned that many Americans and Mexicans had deserted, having not been paid, and Carvajal had suspended operations while he searched for more recruits. Another problem was that the Mexicans had begun to suspect the operation was nothing more than an effort by the Americans to seize more land. Too, the Texans were a rough-looking group, and reports surfaced that they had deliberately set fire to parts of Matamoros. Ford also perhaps began to understand the complexities of the political situation when Carvajal explained to him that he retreated rather than fight Canales because the general was a friend who was expected to join the revolutionaries. In fact, Canales had a son, Servando Canales, who was serving as an officer with Carvajal, and the general had delayed his advance on Matamoros to avoid a confrontation while hoping that Carvajal could complete his occupation of the city. Ford wryly recalled that the two Canales men did eventually reunite as fellow officers under Carvajal's banner.[19]

While at least one Texas leader associated with Carvajal carried a permit from Governor Bell for the recovery of runaway slaves, indicating state support for the operation, the United States government was not at all pleased with the escapades of Ford and his men. The involvement of Americans with Carvajal derailed negotiations to amend the Treaty of Guadalupe Hidalgo and settle Mexican claims because it inflamed public opinion in Mexico. President Millard Fillmore on October 22, 1851, issued a proclamation warning all United States citizens who became involved in the conflict in Mexico that they faced severe penalties from both governments if caught, and that his administration would not intervene to protect them. At the same time, the president ordered military authorities in the southwest to block any efforts to organize for the fighting in Mexico. The Army proved ineffective in enforcing this directive, but the message from Washington was clear.[20]

Ford's confidence in Carvajal's military abilities eroded quickly, but not his support for his cause. Carvajal told Ford at Reynosa that Kenedy offered him ordnance and supplies to declare himself leader of a provisional government and leave military affairs to someone else, but Carvajal declined because he wanted to "be the Washington of my country." It was just one of many public allusions to the American Revolution by Carvajal that may have endeared him to Ford, who privately believed that his commander probably should not lead an army. Ford became a brigadier general for his service at Matamoros and was assigned to recruit Texans. He returned to Austin with a three-man escort and a little money, and he warily tried to enlist men without openly violating the federal laws for neutrality. He had limited success because he had no funds to equip his recruits. When Edward Burleson Sr. suddenly died on December 26, 1851, Ford won his seat in the Texas Senate in a special election on January 12, 1852, in which he lost in Gillespie and Hays counties to Clement R. Johns, future comptroller of Texas, but triumphed with a strong majority in Travis, his county of residence. He served in the Senate for a month, beginning in January, while continuing to hold a commission in Carvajal's revolutionary army, a fact that apparently sparked no public protest.[21]

Ford worked hard as a state senator, introducing and securing the passage of a bill that defined the city limits of Austin, authorized the city to collect taxes, and imposed an extra fee on businesses that sold liquor. He also delivered a speech on the sorry state of frontier defense in Texas and, as chair of the Senate Committee on Indian Affairs, worked closely with his counterpart in the House, Robert S. Neighbors. The two successfully introduced a joint resolution authorizing the state to negotiate for the establishment of a federal Indian reservation in North Texas, which was not actually done until 1854. Ford paid particular attention to measures intended to pay debts of the Republic, especially the money owed to Frederick Dawson, a Baltimore shipbuilder who had constructed six ships for the Texas Navy. Ford gallantly supported

Henry L. Kinney. Prints and Photographs Division, Library of Congress.

paying all such obligations. Almost all of the Texas senators in the 1850s served one term, and Ford did likewise. When the Senate adjourned in February 1852, he made no apparent plans to retain his seat.[22]

Ford intended to rejoin Carvajal, but his commander had fallen on hard times. Defeated twice at Cerralvo and Camargo, Carvajal had retreated into Texas, where he was arrested near Rio Grande City for violating neutrality laws. He was not convicted, but Ford informed him there that no recruits could be had, primarily because there was no money to equip volunteers. A fundraiser during May 1852 at Corpus Christi, hosted by Henry L. Kinney and attended by Carvajal and such "distinguished

Texians" as Ashbel Smith (who served as manager for the event), Hugh McLeod, Benjamin F. Terry, H. Clay Davis, and Ford, did not generate much money. Carvajal spoke to a crowd on May 13 after being introduced by Smith. He was warmly applauded, but McLeod addressed the same people and said what many thought: he warmly endorsed Carvajal but politely refused to become directly involved. Unable to recruit Mexicans, who distrusted him as an Americanized Tejano who welcomed too many Anglos into his army, Carvajal had to accept that he had failed. Many Texas merchants who once supported him had already abandoned his cause after Mexican authorities lowered tariffs along the Rio Grande in late 1851. Carvajal would try again and be arrested in 1853, but once more he would be released. Ford had not seen the last of Carvajal, but in 1852 he walked away from him, which may explain why he was not among the Texans indicted, but not convicted, with Carvajal.[23]

Forced into unemployment by the collapse of Carvajal's revolution, Ford retreated into another familiar role: newspaper editor. He purchased the *South-Western American* in October 1852. His office stood on Congress Avenue, directly across from that of the *Texas State Gazette,* which in fact was his previous publication under the title bestowed upon it by William H. Cushney in 1849. The owner by 1852 was Joseph Wade Hampton, and he greeted Ford with an editorial that hailed him as an "old Texian" who happened to be a "good writer and a courteous gentleman." Ford intended to join with Joseph Lancaster, whose press in Washington-on-the-Brazos had burned, and resume printing his newspaper, the *Texas Ranger,* in Austin, but Lancaster decided not to move. So Ford changed the name of his paper to *Texas State Times* in 1853 and worked with a series of partners. The first was Joseph Walker, a former Ranger and founder of the San Antonio *Ledger,* followed by Wilson T. Davidson. Ford failed to win the state printing contract as he planned, but with Walker's and Davidson's help he claimed to enjoy the second largest readership of any Texas weekly (behind the Galveston *News*). Walker left in November 1855, about the time Ford moved his office to Pecan Street, and Davidson departed in February 1856. Ford then acquired another partner, William E. Jones, and Walker returned to keep the operation going under the abbreviated title of *State Times.*

By the fall of 1856 Jones and Walker were gone, replaced by Ed Finnin, and the paper was again known as the *Texas State Times.* Fenton M. Gibson bought Finnin's share in March 1857, while at the same time Xavier B. DeBray became a silent partner. Ford three months later sold his press to DeBray, who changed the title of the publication to *Texas Sentinel.*[24] Ford thus had six partners in just five years, which indicates the great difficulties of producing and supporting a newspaper in antebellum Texas.

As an editor, Ford expounded on topics that had become of great interest to him. He called for more effective frontier defense, focusing upon a permanent Ranger force, while denouncing both the state and federal government for their efforts. He promoted the use of land grants to fund railroad development, but he did not endorse the idea of creating a state-owned rail line. He was particularly vituperative in his comments on Gov. Elisha M. Pease's refusal to accept the stock offered as security for the Mississippi and Pacific Railroad, part of a transcontinental scheme in 1854. About other editors who defended Pease's action, Ford wrote, "It is probable so much was seldom written about railroads by men who knew so little about them." Austin residents apparently admired Ford's position on rail operations, and they sent him as one of their representatives to a meeting on the subject at La Grange in 1855. In other editorials, he supported funding the Republic debt in full, regardless of currency fluctuations. On morality, he advocated the total prohibition of alcoholic beverages and condemned bullfighting and prizefighting. Public education also received support from Ford, who later wrote about Texans: "Educate him at home, with those who are to be his companions for life, and he will acquire no foreign habits, no aristocratic airs, and stoop to ape no brainless fop because he is a nobleman."[25]

Ford had become a revolutionary to sustain slavery, and he remained convinced both of that institution's righteousness and the threat to it posed by Texas' proximity to northern Mexico, where he believed many runaway slaves found a refuge. He made his position clear on slavery, if there had ever been any doubt, in a February 1857 editorial that asserted "Slavery . . . is an institution founded by God." He declared that the Bible sanctioned slavery, so "if slavery is wrong the

Bible is wrong. They must stand or fall together. There can be no middle ground." In other articles Ford noted that Jesus never spoke against slavery. Ford also embraced a secular justification for slavery, later writing that it "came to the Southern man authorized by the Supreme Law of the Land. It came to him authorized by time, custom, and law." When Thomas Jefferson wrote in the Declaration of Independence that all men were created equal, Ford believed he did not intend to include blacks. He opposed congressional intervention on the issue of slavery, applauded the Dred Scott decision, and opposed popular sovereignty because it vested territorial legislatures with power equal to that of state legislatures on important matters such as slavery. When Mexicans encouraged runaways, helped them, and gave them sanctuary in northern Mexico, as Ford and many Texans believed that they did, they defied God and the law. He endorsed the demands of Texas leaders for extradition treaties to recover the thousands of runaways he thought were hiding across the Rio Grande, and he lamented the failure of the United States government to secure any such agreements.[26]

Ford of course commented freely on politics, which led to conflicts with his rivals at the *Texas State Gazette.* While it is true that "two newspaper firms seldom preserve harmonious relations when divided by a street only, and it is hard for either of the editors to do anything the other does not find out," Ford and Hampton did have some substantial disagreements. Hampton sharply criticized Carvajal while Ford continued to defend him. In fact, Ford in November 1852 published Carvajal's agreement to return runaway slaves. Hampton in the meantime printed accounts of Carvajal's defeats, including the names of Texans executed for joining his army. Later each man allied with a different faction of the Democrats. When John Marshall bought Hampton's share of the *Texas State Gazette* in 1854, Ford gained a foe even more worthy of his editorial steel. Ford rarely missed a chance to poke fun or even ridicule Marshall, who responded in kind. For example, Ford sharply criticized Marshall for his work as the state printer in 1857, but Marshall in turn chided the "old coon," as he called Ford, for complaining about a monopoly when he had the contract ten years earlier. It was a respectful, if amusing, rivalry. When Ford left the *Texas State Times* in 1857, allegedly disgusted because Sam Houston did not properly support "Southern Institutions," he served for several months as an editor for the *Texas State Gazette* while Marshall was absent. This arrangement benefited from the fact that Ford's old partner, Walker, had become part owner of the *Gazette*.[27]

Ford could not resist returning to the political fray in person. Rejecting an offer in 1853 to edit another newspaper in Washington-on-the-Brazos, he stayed in Austin, secured an appointment to the Democratic Central Committee, and endorsed Middleton T. Johnson for governor. The campaign became quite ugly. When Ford planned a trip to the Rio Grande, Hampton, who in 1853 supported Pease against Johnson, reported that his rival was going to spread leaflets to persuade the Tejanos to vote for Johnson. Ford retorted that in fact he was going to get affidavits so that he could collect unpaid salary for his Ranger service, but that he might indeed distribute leaflets advertising "a worthy candidate." Hampton in turn declared that it mattered little what Ford took with him, because he was mentally incompetent as a result of the head wound suffered at Matamoros, which had allowed Ford's "not overly plentiful supply of brains to leak out." Hampton in his next issue admitted he had gone too far, and Ford agreed. In the fall of 1853, Texans elected Pease to his first term as governor, but Austin residents again endorsed Ford by overwhelmingly electing him as their mayor, which doubled subscriptions to his newspaper.[28]

Ford's single term as mayor of Austin was marked by temperance and economy. He endorsed a new law that forbade the sale of liquor on Sundays, while he also reduced public salaries and even eliminated positions. This provided the context for one of the most popular stories concerning Ford as Austin's mayor. He insisted upon serving as the town marshal after firing the incumbent for being drunk on duty, and calmly confronted a drunken pistol-toting ruffian in a local bar. Told by Ford that he had one hour to leave Austin, the garishly attired stranger profanely replied that he had no intention of leaving, whereupon Ford quietly informed him to do as he wished but to tell the barkeeper where to send his horse and personal effects. After Ford left, the intruder asked the barkeeper for the name of the marshal who had confronted him and was told that it was Ford, the famous Ranger captain. The stranger finished his drink and left Austin.[29]

As mayor, Ford was called upon to serve as a not-so-reluctant member of a vigilance committee. Whites in early Austin were always worried about lax enforcement of laws intended to restrict the activities of blacks, and this intensified in the fall of 1854 with the arrival of a group of Mexican laborers. The *Gazette* led the way in denouncing Mexicans in general and the newcomers in particular, accusing them of associating with blacks and providing them with contraband, including weapons. Ford's *Times* by early October joined its counterpart in urging that immediate action be taken. After Seguin and San Antonio hosted public meetings about Mexican migrants, Austin did likewise on September 27. Mayor Ford chaired that assembly, as well as another on October 7. The first meeting organized an investigation of the situation, and when it was reported there was indeed a problem, the second gathering declared that "transient Mexicans" had ten days to leave Austin or be expelled, and that a vigilance committee should enforce the existing restrictions on black conduct. Those in attendance were careful to make it clear that not all Mexicans were suspect, only those "associating and interfering with negroes." Ford did not chair a final meeting on October 14, but he joined the "steering committee" along with Marshall. When some again expressed concern at expelling every Mexican, amended resolutions, supported by Ford and Marshall, allowed those who had the support of an Anglo to stay. Vigilantes and supporters then marched to the Mexican camp, where the resolutions were read aloud. Within a few weeks, the Mexican migrants departed, much to the apparent delight of writers for the *Times* and the *Gazette*.[30]

Ford's persistent concern with the Mexican threat to slavery, as he perceived it, led him to become involved in new filibustering schemes by late 1854. Texans, with the support of leaders such as Governor Bell and Sam Houston, participated in the Narciso López expeditions to Cuba in 1850 and 1851, and in 1854 preparations were again made for a Cuban filibuster. Ford met at New Orleans with former Mississippi governor John A. Quitman and others involved in the "Order of the Lone Star," a secretive organization created to continue efforts to establish a

John A. Quitman. William Emerson Strong Photograph Album, Rare Book, Manuscript, and Special Collections Library, Duke University.

pro-slavery republic in Cuba after the execution of López in 1851. Upon his return to Austin, Ford organized his own chapter, known as the "Order of the Lone Star of the West." Ford and other prominent Texans worked hard to raise money and recruit men, but Quitman had to postpone his plans to invade Cuba in December 1854. Official support for filibusters declined in the wake of public protests against the Ostend Manifesto, which proposed that the United States buy Cuba, or use force to take it if Spain declined to sell. Quitman found it prudent to abandon his Cuban scheme, and Ford and most Texans did likewise. Ford was proud of his organization, writing later that its initiation rite was "impressive and intensely unique," and that "its cabalistic pass-words were indelibly impressed on the mind." However, he also admitted about his decision to abandon the project that "the risk of landing in Cuba, of being left without the means of withdrawing, and of being garroted might have had an influence."[31]

Ford and others might have turned their backs on Cuba, but not on filibustering. Governor Pease in the summer of 1855, in response to reports of Indian raids, asked for mounted federal troops to patrol the frontier west of San Antonio. When the national authorities did not act quickly enough, Pease authorized James H. Callahan to raise a company, among whom was Ford's former lieutenant, Edward Burleson Jr. While Callahan was patrolling the western frontier, William R. Henry, an Army veteran and filibusterer who was a grandson of Patrick Henry, called for volunteers to join a rebellion in Mexico against Santa Anna. The former general had been appointed as emperor of Mexico, and Henry accused him of supporting Indian raids against Texas. Henry and perhaps twenty men did cross the Rio Grande and had their services refused before Santa Anna resigned as emperor and left Mexico in August 1855. Undaunted, Henry asked Pease to appoint him to command a company, as he had one year earlier. The governor did so after visiting San Antonio but assigned Henry's volunteers and another company to a battalion led by Callahan. The group rode to the Rio Grande ostensibly to look for Indians, but most understood the true objective was to recover slaves, and they followed Callahan and Henry into Mexico. A fight ensued, and the Texans retreated to Piedras Negras, which they burned before crossing the Rio Grande into Texas during the first week of October 1855.[33]

Reflecting on the turmoil in Mexico in the summer and fall of 1855, Ford wrote in the *Texas State Times* that a march by thousands of members of the Order of the Lone Star of the West into that country might solve many of its problems. Months earlier, after delegates from Austin attended a meeting on runaway slaves at Gonzales, the *Times* opined, "The affair is of some importance; and the government may redress the grievance or look for trouble on the Rio Grande frontier." Seeking support for an occupation of Mexico, Ford wrote to Quitman, pointing out that a Mexican port might make a fine base of operations against Cuba. Ford in September 1855 represented Austin in another meeting at Bastrop to discuss methods to prevent runaways and reclaim fugitive slaves from Mexico. The Texans decided to send Ford and Bennett Riddells to talk with Santiago Vidaurri, whose troops controlled much of northern Mexico. Riddells owned a hotel in Chihuahua, where he also served as United States consul and had already met with Vidaurri's secretary about the slave issue. Callahan's disastrous raid into Mexico during the fall of 1855 disrupted their trip. Ford decided it was unsafe to cross into Mexico and stopped at San Antonio, while Riddells continued to the Rio Grande before he abandoned the quest, having learned that Vidaurri was more concerned about political machinations in Mexico than the travails of Texas slave owners.[32]

Many Texans apparently assumed that Ford rode with the filibusterers. One of Callahan's volunteers, resting on the Texas side of the Rio Grande near Piedras Negras, wrote to Burleson that "Old Rip is here and will go without fail" if the Texans attempted to ride into Mexico again. But Ford denied this in his memoirs. Instead he, with Henry E. McCulloch, was still in San Antonio trying to raise support for Callahan, including a company of one hundred men, when a wounded man arrived with the disappointing news that the fragments of Callahan's expedition had returned to Texas. As it had been with Cuba, Ford's decision not to fight was again based on practicality, not principle. His *Texas State Times* was among the newspapers that defended Callahan and Henry, and many years later he wrote that "Callahan was actuated by pure and patriotic

Henry E. McCulloch. Brown, *Indian Wars and Pioneers of Texas.*

motives in attempting to give peace and security to the suffering frontier of Texas." While federal authorities viewed Callahan and Henry and their followers as thugs, Ford blamed the national government for initiating the affair by not properly securing the frontier.[34]

Callahan's failure did not dissuade Ford from contemplating an occupation of at least a portion of Mexico, despite heated denunciations from his rivals at the *Texas State Gazette.* Ford wrote to Burleson, his former lieutenant, in February 1856 that Houston and Burleson's father "and a host of other chivalrous spirits redeemed and annexed Texas—Why may not others of less note secure another slice from the grasp of anarchy and place it under American control?" He explained, "I look upon the movement as a political necessity—a duty we owe to Texas and the South. It has occupied my thoughts for years." Ford did not want to lead the operation himself "because I have said and written so much on the subject I begin to think people don't believe me." Instead, "If you, or McCulloch or Callahan, would go upon the Brazos you could get money." For those who doubted the need for invading Mexico, Ford had a ready answer: "There is no government in Mexico—everything is in confusion. The people are oppressed, ground down by taxation, debased by ignorance and paralyzed by the influence of the priests. She is a dangerous and harmful neighbor." Furthermore, because Mexicans supported raids on Texas and Texans, "we have the right by the laws of nations, by the right of self-preservation and self-defense which we acquired from God himself—to demand 'indemnity for the past and security for the future.' This can only be obtained by placing the country between the Rio Grande and the Sierra Madre under the control of Americans and by giving protection to slave property in Texas and the South." Ford concluded, "I conscientiously believe we would be right and that Heaven would bless the enterprize [*sic*] with success."[35]

Failing to goad his associates into yet another filibuster into Mexico, Ford turned his attention, like many Texans, to the efforts of the ill-fated William Walker to establish a pro-slavery government in Nicaragua. During February 1857 Ford chaired at least two meetings in Austin to raise money and volunteers for Walker's forces, which were then in Nicaragua. Ford also chaired the committee actually organized to solicit recruits and the funds to equip them, which proved to be a mixed success. Nine men volunteered at the meeting on February 11 at the courthouse in Austin, but ten days later Ford reported in his *Texas State Times* that only six young men had left the capital with the intention of joining Walker. Although the filibusterer surrendered to the United States Navy in May 1857 and left Nicaragua, Texans continued to support him, and the idea persisted that Ford would eventually join him. When Ford quit the *Times* in June, the *Eastern Texian* declared that

"Col. John S. Ford has withdrawn from the editorial management of this spirited paper [*Texas State Times*]. His reasons are not given, though the junior hints that ere many months have elapsed, he may be again leading troops to victory in a foreign land."[36]

Ford's concerns with foreign intrigues may have been the primary factor that led him briefly into the Know-Nothing fold. After serving for two years, 1853 and 1854, on the Democratic Central Committee in Texas, Ford in January 1855 endorsed John T. Cleveland, a member of the American or "Know-Nothing" Party, in a successful bid to become the mayor of Austin. After also electing a mayor in Galveston, the Know-Nothings held a state convention at Washington-on-the-Brazos in June 1855. They chose candidates for governor, lieutenant governor, and Congress, which so alarmed Democrats that they quickly organized their own meeting in Austin to nominate a list of candidates. The unexpectedly large turnout for the Democrats dismayed Know-Nothings, and many of them abandoned their new cause. While nineteen Know-Nothings were elected to the legislature, and Know-Nothing candidates dominated the polls in Travis County, the 1855 elections were disappointing for the party. Undaunted, Know-Nothing diehards in 1856 hosted a ball for their second candidate, Edward R. Peck, to be elected as mayor of Austin and held another convention in the Capitol. Ford, together with his partner William E. Jones and Edward Burleson Jr. helped organize the event for Peck, and Ford joined the committee on resolutions. The latter called for only native-born citizens to serve in office, preservation of the Union, strict interpretation of the Constitution, rejection of congressional power to regulate slavery, and frontier protection. Ford's fellow Texas Know-Nothings again endorsed a full slate of candidates, including Millard Fillmore for president, only to be soundly defeated at all levels in the fall.[37]

In his memoir, Ford dismissed his immersion in Know-Nothing politics with the flippant statement that it was just "one of those inconsiderate things men do sometimes," but for more than a year he was passionately devoted to the cause. He strongly denied allegations that the Know-Nothings wanted to ban Catholics from public office, insisting instead that they simply wanted to extend the constitutional requirement that presidents be native born to include all offices. He was certainly not above publishing scurrilous material in the *Texas State Times,* including anti-Catholic articles, but it is not clear how much of it he wrote and, perhaps more importantly, how much of it he believed at the time and later learned was not true. Nonetheless, Ford's defense of the Know-Nothings became quite strident in 1855, and only the intervention of friends prevented him from fighting a duel with a man who criticized the organization's secret ritual. Ford actually did get in a fistfight with Carl D. A. Douai, a tiny but fiery German who as the editor of the San Antonio *Zeitung* opposed both slavery and the Know-Nothings. Douai declared in an editorial that Ford lied when he wrote in his own newspaper that Douai was paid by Northern abolitionists. Ford came to Douai's office to demand a retraction, and when the German refused they began punching. Douai proudly wrote that he got the best of Ford: "I quietly beat him up until he bled," adding that "as soon as he had enough punishment," Ford "begged me for water and a towel to clean himself up." Ford apparently was not completely vanquished because he again asked Douai to "expunge the word 'lie,'" and the German editor concluded that "I was good natured enough to do it."[38]

Beyond Ford's concerns about immigrants and their alleged dangerous influences, many of the reasons for his brief allegiance to the Know-Nothings probably emerged from the political conflict that attended the adoption of the Kansas-Nebraska Act in 1854. Ford always believed that the ballot was a sacred right that should only be used intelligently and in an informed fashion, and that a person, foreign-born or not, who could not speak and read English should not vote. He also supported a delay of twenty-one years for any foreigner to be naturalized, reasoning that men born in the United States had to wait for the same number of years until they could vote. But in the Kansas-Nebraska Act he saw a threat to the Union, which he revered, because it promoted popular sovereignty, which he hotly opposed for giving territorial legislatures the same stature as state legislatures in deciding about slavery. At the same time, he denounced efforts by Congress to mediate the slavery issue, declaring they had no power to do so. Both, he thought, undermined the Union by reducing the power of the states, with whose consent the Constitution had been adopted, and threats of disunion from Democrats did not reassure him. When he heard that Houston, whom he admired, had voted against the Kansas-Nebraska Act and joined the Know-Nothings, Ford followed suit, as did Jones and Fenton M. Gibson, his partners in the *Texas State Times.* Ford always seemed uneasy about the anti-Catholic sentiments of Know-Nothings, and he later declared that any such articles in his newspaper were written by assistant editor James A. Beveridge. The arrival of Ed Finnin, a Catholic, to be Ford's partner in the fall of 1856, may mark a final decision on the topic by Ford.[39]

The Know-Nothings in Texas began to fall apart in 1856, with many returning to the Democrats. Ford posted a card advertising the Know-Nothing candidates, including Fillmore, but there were no fiery editorials as in 1855. Houston reaffirmed his ties to the Democrats, and Ford did likewise. In April 1857 he declared himself a Democrat, and in May he attended the state convention as a news correspondent. On a motion by John P. Border, his fellow actor in San Augustine, Ford was invited to take a seat as a delegate. He later made a good-natured speech about his political apostasy and thanked his fellow Democrats for letting him return. On May 23, 1857, Ford published a fuller *mea culpa* in the *Times.* While admitting that he "still has great respect for Know-Nothings," Ford wrote that he had to become a Democrat again "to perpetuate the Union and to preserve inviolate the 'peculiar institution' of the South." His decision to return was based upon his sense of "duty to the country, and particularly to the South." He offered no apology because his change in political alliances "suits him, and he does not care a 'continental dime' whether it suits other people or not." Marshall, who had never joined the Know-Nothings, welcomed Ford back with a gracious column, and in turn Ford set to work, serving on committees to welcome Robert Toombs of Georgia to Austin, to recruit new Democrats, and to raise money. As conflict deepened among Texas Democrats over the two goals that had brought Ford back into their party, perpetuation of the Union and preservation of slavery, Ford joined the majority in choosing slavery over the Union, parting with Houston and others who refused to accept this choice. The latter group included

Ford's partners Gibson and DeBray, which contributed to his decision to sell his interest in the *Texas State Times* and temporarily replace Marshall at the *Gazette,* where he battled in print with George W. Paschal, pro-Houston editor of the Austin *Southern Intelligencer.*[40]

Ford by 1857 had become a familiar figure to Texans who operated in public circles, such as state politics and newspapers, and even among some Rangers. He had not become famous, however, and he yearned to return to the field of battle where glory could be won. In 1852, when the Travis Guards organized at Austin under the state militia law, they elected Ford as their captain, but they never campaigned under his command. Two years later Governor Pease asked him to assist with Texas Rangers at Goliad, but Ford's assignment was only to inspect and muster the volunteers enrolled by Henry, who would lead another company under Callahan at Piedras Negras the following year. Ford thought Henry's company and others would make excellent recruits for a filibustering expedition in early 1855, but that did not happen, perhaps in part because Henry's volunteers sacked the small Texas town of D'Hanis. The closest Ford came to actual combat during the years since he had been with Carvajal was in the fall of 1856, when he joined another vigilance committee and served as a patroller at Austin during an insurrection scare.[41]

Ford's chance to return to the field came when the Indian situation worsened in Texas in 1857. The number of settlers had increased rapidly during the decade, almost tripling the population in just ten years. The line of settlement moved west, marked by an increase in the number of counties from 36 at the time of annexation in 1846 to 119 by 1860. Indian raids increased, especially by the hard-pressed Comanches in North Texas, but the number of federal troops was cut. Many people resented rather than approved the creation of two reservations as a solution to the dilemma of how to control Indians. Hardin R. Runnels defeated Houston for governor in part by declaring he would provide more security on the frontier. Brig. Gen. David E. Twiggs, commanding the Department of Texas, suggested to Secretary of War John B. Floyd that Congress should fund the organization of a regiment of mounted volunteers in Texas. Congress moved slowly, and Runnels, with Twiggs' support, decided to goad them into a decision. In his first message as governor, he urged Texas legislators to provide him with more Rangers, and they responded by creating another new company to supplement several already in the field, in a bill that Runnels signed on January 27, 1858.[42]

Many people urged the appointment of Ford as captain of the new company while the legislature debated, and Ford visited Runnels to discuss the matter. The terms of the measure as passed must have whetted Ford's appetite: the appointee would not only lead a company of one hundred men, enlisted for six months service, but also serve as "senior captain" in charge of all other state units. Since the bill also provided an ample budget of $70,000, there was much potential to strike a telling blow against the Indians to show the federal government what could be done. After a "lively talk" with Runnels, Ford became "senior captain of all state troops" on January 28, 1858. The decision met with warm approval among those who knew Ford, including his rival, Marshall. It also made Ford the most likely candidate to command the new regiment of mounted volunteers, if Congress ever created it.[43]

Governor Runnels' instructions to Ford were very broad, and Ford prepared for a campaign against the Comanches, who most often raided settlers in Texas. He kept two companies already in the field, under the command of lieutenants James H. Tankersley and Allison Nelson, disbanded another, and ordered the muster of a new company led by McCulloch. In his own company, Ford unanimously won election as captain and welcomed the election of Edward Burleson Jr. as his senior lieutenant. William A. Pitts served as second lieutenant, and Robert Cotter was the orderly sergeant. Ford expected support from peaceful Indians in Texas, many of whom hated the Comanches as much as whites and Tejanos did, and he was not disappointed. Neighbors, as the Indian agent for Texas, had asked for an expedition into the Indian Territory in January 1858 and pledged the cooperation of a company of Indians; learning of Ford's appointment, he issued orders for a muster in early February. Twiggs, in response to an inquiry from Runnels, declined to accept Ford's Rangers into federal service, which kept them from buying weapons with federal money, but each of Ford's volunteers brought at least one Colt revolver and a muzzle-loading rifle. The *Texas State Gazette* declared that Ford and his men could fire 1,500 rounds without reloading, which was an incredible show of firepower for that era.[44]

Ford's company left Austin for the northern frontier of Texas in February 1858. He understood that he had a difficult task, and that many eyes were upon him. Runnels had tried to warn him about the difficulties of balancing the demands and expectations of civilians, military authorities, and Indian leaders, concluding that "your position, in this respect, will be one of some delicacy; but I hope your sense of duty, your desire to be useful to the state, and your judgment will be sufficient to steer you safely through any difficulty." At forty-three years of age, Rip Ford looked like a man who could become a great Ranger captain. His right arm was still weak from the wound inflicted by a Comanche during his prior Ranger campaign, but Ford was lean and athletic, with clear blue eyes. Stern and quick-tempered, he had the respect of the men he commanded, in part because he was a good shot with a revolver.[45] All of these traits would serve him well during the next phase of his life, when he again showed that he was of "fighting stock" in combat on the Texas frontier and his legacy began to overshadow that of his grandfathers.

CHAPTER 3 RANGER

A handful of events defined Ford's stature among Texans, and two occurred in the last few years just prior to the Civil War. While the nation discussed Kansas and John Brown in the wake of the Dred Scott decision by the Supreme Court, Ford inflicted a stinging defeat on the Comanches, and then joined with Army troops on the Rio Grande to crush an uprising led by Juan N. Cortina. His triumphs were not greatly appreciated by many federal officials, who had to be concerned with political matters beyond the boundaries of Texas, but his victories established him as one of the great antebellum Ranger captains. The young man who had traveled west in 1836 to join a revolution finally found the role that made him a legend among his fellow Texans, who long remembered the Canadian River expedition of 1858 and the Cortina War of 1859–1860. Having come to Texas in search of opportunities to emulate his grandfathers' roles in the American Revolution and the early development of the United States, Ford surpassed them in establishing his own legacy within the context of these two events.

Ford in March 1858 established Camp Runnels on the Clear Fork of the Brazos River, twelve miles from present-day Breckenridge. Here he was near enough to observe the two Indian reservations in North Texas, one intended for the Comanches and another for Indians who were considered to be more peaceful. He was also close enough to Fort Belknap to obtain supplies and support if he needed them. Lieutenants James H. Tankersley and Allison Nelson joined him with their companies in March. When word came that Henry E. McCulloch had failed to raise a company, Ford authorized the muster of two smaller units led by William G. Preston and William N. P. Marlin. All of Ford's volunteers endured long days of drill, marksmanship practice, and fruitless patrols

Hardin R. Runnels. Institute of Texan Cultures, UTSA, #078-0056 *02.02.

in which they did not encounter any Comanches. To make matters worse, Ford forbade gambling, a common pastime for the Texans.[1]

An irritable Gov. Hardin R. Runnels sent Ford a stream of advice based more on political than military concerns. He pushed Ford to strike the Comanche raiders hard, but not to gather more men or spend more money than absolutely necessary. The governor grumbled about those who criticized him, reminding Ford that "to justify the keeping of a force on the frontier, the people will want to hear of some thing being done, to hear of Indians and of their being whipped." At the same time, he admonished his senior captain, "the howlings of corrupt and designing or mad men, will not be permitted to have any influence on your action I hope, as I am determined they shall have none on mine." By way of explanation, Runnels continued, "Do whatever you are going to do quietly and let the thing be put a stop to as soon as possible, as I have said to you upon your reputation and mine the good and welfare of the country depend on something being done to justify the belief of an existing emergency." Finally he concluded, "If something is not done the people who have the bill to foot will regard the whole affair as a humbug gotten up for the benefit of a few croakers whose wish it is to live from the public crib and those of us who have lent a willing ear to reports as miserable dupes only."[2]

Ford assured Runnels that he had a plan to augment his force without cost to the state. Shapley P. Ross, a former Ranger officer who had served as the federal agent to the non-Comanche reservation until earlier in 1858, had agreed to lead a company of one hundred reservation Indians into the field as part of Ford's expedition. Ford insisted that these Indians under the tutelage of Ross and current agent Robert S. Neighbors had made great progress in "becoming civilized," dressing like whites and planting crops of wheat and corn. Ford added, "There is no disorder, no discontent, and no disposition to give trouble to the Agent or the Government." Joining with Neighbors in opposing those who wanted the reservations closed, Ford declared that such would be a "serious misfortune." After all, making Indians "civilized" was cheaper in lives and money than fighting them. Conversely, Ford had little good to say about John R. Baylor, who during his term as agent for the Comanche

Shapley Ross. Brown, *Indian Wars and Pioneers of Texas.*

reservation, which lay near the one praised by Ford, had proven to be a "cipher, and worth as little on the right, as the left." Ford attributed much of the unrest on the Texas frontier to Baylor's "inefficiency." It did not improve their relationship that, in response to rumors that Congress was considering accepting a Ranger regiment into federal service, Baylor had told settlers in North Texas not to enroll in Ford's command. Instead, Baylor urged them to wait and join him when the time came to muster a company from the region for the proposed regiment.[3]

The Indians that Ford accepted as allies were primarily Caddos and Tonkawas. He and several of his Rangers attended a dance at their reservation in April 1858 that served as a recruiting event. About the dancers' efforts to appear ferocious, Ford later remarked in his memoirs: "The sight of one was enough to stampede a regiment of dudes, and a battalion of school-marms." But he needed their services, and they hated Comanches and were willing to fight. More than a hundred, with Ross as their captain, joined Ford as he rode north to the Canadian River in search of hostile Comanches during late April. A ceremonial rattlesnake feast hosted by the Tonkawas fortunately only intrigued, rather than disgusted, their new commander, though he apparently did not join them in their repast.[4]

Ford's command included some familiar faces. Lt. Edward Burleson Jr. had to leave for home just before the expedition departed, and Martin had to be left behind with his Rangers to provide protection for the reservations, but 102 heavily armed men rode with Ford. Once again Francisco de la Garza Falcón, or Don Monkey, accompanied Ford as his

Fight on Canadian River. Remington, *Crooked Trails.*

servant. Also among the retinue was his father, William Ford, who at the age of seventy-three arrived in Camp Runnels with an ambulance and declared his intention to accompany the march. His son quietly added the ambulance to his pack train and wagons. Ross joined Ford on April 26, after four days on the trail, with 113 Indians.[5]

Ford crossed the Red River on April 29, 1858, and made his way to the Wichita Mountains. There his men spent two days on Otter Creek, hunting and eating buffalo, to the delight of Ford, who savored both the excitement of the hunt and the taste of buffalo meat. Ford knew he was far outside of Texas, in the Indian Territory, and had no legal jurisdiction, but there is no evidence that this concerned him. When his scouts captured a runaway slave, Ford sent him back to his owner. He crossed from the North Fork of the Red River to the upper Washita River and there found a clear Comanche trail. Within days he closed on his quarry, who were traveling in a large group near the road from Fort Smith to Santa Fe. Leaving his father in charge of a small group of Rangers and drivers with the wagons, Ford pressed forward to find the enemy camp. By nightfall they had located the Comanches' encampment, and under the cover of darkness Ford moved his Rangers and Indians into position for an assault.[6]

Ford attacked just after sunrise on May 12, 1858, across the Canadian River. He had Ross and his command, who wore "white cloth badges" to distinguish them from the Comanches, approach the enemy camp first, which gave the Comanches the impression that they faced only Indian foes. Ford had learned that Comanches might avoid a fight with Rangers, but they had a great disdain for other Indians. Iron Jacket, a Kotchateka Comanche leader, confronted Ross' Indians before they reached his lodges. Leading a few warriors, he rode forward wearing a mail shirt, puffing hard to blow aside the enemy arrows as he had always been told he could. His opponents paused momentarily, amazed perhaps at the sight, but they were galvanized into action by a yell from Lt. William A. Pitts: "Kill the son-of-a-bitch!" Two volleys from Ross' Indians shattered the illusion of Iron Jacket's magic. The first toppled his horse; the second felled him. The ensuing chaos among the Comanches gave Ford an opportunity to order his Rangers to charge, and the enemy scattered. Ford had organized his command in two parts, wanting to lead his right wing into the Comanche camp while his left wing cut off their retreat. Instead, the battle soon dissolved into a series of fights between single combatants as Comanches fled and both Rangers and Indians chased them.[7]

The arrival of Naconi Comanches from a neighboring, larger camp after noon forced Ford to reassemble his men. At his request, Ross again led his Indians forward to challenge the newcomers, which lured them down from the hills onto the flat land in front of Ford. The plan failed, however, when an ambushing force of Rangers and Tonkawas attacked too soon on the left flank, alerting the Comanches to the danger and allowing them to slip away. Ford prudently decided not to confront an even larger group led by Buffalo Hump and retired to his wagons, camping twelve miles south of the Canadian River on the night of May 12, 1858. From there, Ford decided to return to Camp Runnels because supplies were low and his Indian allies had decided to go home. The Texans' wagons broke down and were abandoned in a hasty march south, but they reached Texas in a week. Ross and his Indians turned toward home at Cottonwood Springs, and Ford accompanied them to their reservation. His weary Rangers continued without him and reached Camp Runnels on May 21, almost exactly one month after they departed.[8]

Ford praised Rangers and Indians alike in his report to Runnels on the Canadian River fight. His losses were one Ranger killed during the main fight on May 12, and one Indian killed with a lance in the second fight, in which two other Indians and a Ranger were wounded. Ford reported that his command had killed seventy-six Comanche warriors and captured eighteen women and children, but he insisted more men must have died after escaping from the battlefield. Also 300 horses were taken, most of which went to Ross' Indians. About his own company, he declared, "I think that they have fully vindicated their right to be recognized as Texas rangers of the old stamp." Concerning his Indian allies Ford added graciously, "They deserve well of Texas and are entitled to the gratitude of the frontier people." He gave full credit for the killing of Iron Jacket to Jim Pockmark, a Tonkawa leader with Ross, though pieces

Robert Cotter. Lawrence T. Jones III Collection, Southern Methodist University.

of Iron Jacket's coat of chain mail were given to several people including Ford's sergeant major, Robert Cotter, who apparently sent the largest portion to Runnels. Ford brought a more interesting memento home for himself: a Comanche boy about four or five years of age, supposed to be the son of Iron Jacket. The "novelty" of having the child, Little Owl, soon "wore off," and the widowed Ford, whose own daughter Fannie was an adult, sent him to live with a family in Harrison County.[9]

When the *Texas State Gazette* published Ford's report, they included a letter from Cotter that gave all credit to Ford for planning the march and battle. Other less positive allegations soon surfaced, but they had little impact on Ford's growing reputation among Texas settlers. Ford actually took sixty prisoners, but he reported only eighteen. In his later memoirs, he explained that many of them were given to the reservation Indians, and that "many of them married and seemed content." When reports surfaced that Comanche women had been killed in the fighting, Ford attributed that to the confusion of combat and the fact that Comanche men and women dressed much alike. Charles E. Barnard, who operated a trading post near the North Texas reservations, wrote to his brother that Ford and his men brought back seventy-six scalps from the Canadian River expedition, but there was no further mention of that grisly assertion. The Tonkawas shocked Ford and his Rangers by cutting the hands and feet from some dead Comanche warriors, which they boiled for a "victory feast," but no one held Ford responsible for this ritual cannibalism. Federal officials charged with negotiating a treaty with the Comanches were unhappy with Ford, as his attacks derailed their efforts. But the Army did not complain, and in fact it mounted its own expeditions against Comanche raiders later that same year.[10]

Ford hoped to capitalize on his Canadian River triumph to secure an even more prominent appointment, but in this he was disappointed. Runnels firmly believed that Congress would accept a volunteer regiment into federal service in Texas to defend the frontier, and that Ford was the best candidate to command it. Sam Houston spoke at length in the Senate on the necessity for a Ranger regiment, and John A. Quitman guided the bill successfully through both chambers of Congress. During his march north in late April, Ford reminded Runnels that he had a fine company ready to join. One day after he submitted his official report, Ford penned a private letter to the governor in which he asked if his request to muster his men into the proposed regiment was being ignored. He declared that he would be a better colonel than Henry E. McCulloch, adding sharply, "[I]f the game is not too far advanced I should like to shuffle and have a hand dealt to me. I think there is a combination to beat me, and under the circumstances it is equivalent to defeating you." Runnels congratulated Ford and his Rangers and conveyed the news of their operation to the Texas delegation in Congress, but the Senate quashed a measure to fund the proposed expansion of the military.[11]

Ford did not abandon his quest to command a regiment without one last salvo. When Runnels asked him to report on frontier conditions, Ford used his pen to assail at length, and floridly, the federal government's failure to provide proper frontier defense. While men had been murdered, women had been ravished, and children had been taken captive, federal officials had responded with "a sneer of cold, derisive incredulity" to pleas for help from Texas. Infantry had been sent to confront "the best horsemen in the world," Indians "fond of war, of plunder, and of deeds of violence." The solution was to raise a state regiment to "carry the war into Africa" and attack the Comanches and their allies, including those who traded with them. Protect the settlers in this manner, Ford wrote, and the federal government "cannot avoid footing the bill." After all, "Protection and allegiance go hand in hand." In a reversal of his earlier support for the Union as a Know-Nothing, prodigal Democrat Ford added, "There is no principle better established than that when a Government fails or refuses to protect its citizens the ties of allegiance are dissolved, and they have a perfect right to take care of themselves. In my opinion Texas has already had ample cause to sever her connection with the Union on this very head." In a second letter written one day later, Ford snarled at Runnels as well, asking for more pay for his services while pointing out that if he had failed, it would have been a "severe, if not fatal blow" to the governor's administration as well as "an argument against the use of Rangers for all time to come."[12]

Ford's frustration at not securing command of a regiment charged with defending the Texas frontier reflects not only his wounded pride, but also an important shift among many Texans concerning the federal government's responsibilities. After the annexation of Texas, expectations were high among Texans that the United States Army would be able to defend its new borders. Victory over Mexico, and the apparent success of joint operations involving Texas and federal units during the first few years of statehood, led people to believe that the frontier would soon be secure. Ford, who commanded Rangers in this period, was among those who warmly praised the Army personnel with whom he worked. As it became obvious that a reduced Army would not be able to protect all on the frontier, many Texans became bitter. The *Texas Democrat* in August 1852, noting that Pres. Millard Fillmore had sent three warships to protect American fishermen in the Gulf of St. Lawrence that year but no additional troops to Texas, angrily declared that "blood is daily spilt by the marauding Indians and Mexican, hundreds of valuable lives have already been lost on our frontier, yet these are treated far more lightly than some squabble about a fishing smack in the northern waters." The editor added, "The fact is, that the life of a Texian is held at Washington at such a discount, that it cannot enter into competition with a kit of codfish." Six years later, John H. Reagan lavishly praised Ford in the Dallas *Herald* for accomplishing more in a single campaign than the thousands of soldiers stationed in Texas, and he repeated this praise in Congress in early 1859. Ford came to share this disdain for the Army, except for the elite Second United States Cavalry, and he resented the lack of protection afforded by the federal government on the Texas frontier.[13]

Runnels tried to mollify Ford by authorizing him to enlist more volunteers, but the money soon played out. Despite Ford's insistence that a large standing force was needed to defend the frontier, the governor ordered the disbanding of Ford's command when its enlistments expired. In mid-August 1858 the Rangers left Camp Runnels. Nelson took his company to Stephenville, where it mustered out and enjoyed a barbecue, while Ford led the remainder to Lampasas, where they also mustered out and indulged in an even more lavish barbecue. Runnels warmly praised Ford, perhaps in part because he had spent only half of the $70,000 appropriated for his expedition and the public greeted the Rangers as heroes, but the disbandment still disappointed Ford.[14]

An idle Ford found himself drawn into the controversy surrounding Neighbors and the North Texas reservations, which many people still believed were sanctuaries for hostile Indians. When Ford had arrived at Camp Runnels, he heard that some Comanches from the reserve did attack settlers and declared, "If I fix it upon them I shall give them hell and trust to the people to sustain me." He asked his officers to look for evidence that reserve Comanches were guilty, but only Nelson reported that he found anything. Ford sent Nelson's report to Runnels, then exploded when Nelson mentioned in a meeting that such information could, and should, be fabricated. Nelson reluctantly joined his fellow officers in reporting that there were no signs of cooperation between the Comanches on the reserve and those away from it, convincing Ford that "unreasonable" settlers reported "many imaginary and dreadful evils they persuade themselves are near." Ford in turn became a proponent of the reservations. Reserve Indians, he wrote to a friend, helped to keep the peace on the frontier—"place them on the opposite side, throw into the scale some four hundred of the best warriors in the United States, imbued with a belief that we have been unfaithful to our pledges, and thirsting for revenge, then tell me where you think the line of frontier settlement will be within five years and when the war will end." About those who wanted to take the law into their own hands, he sharply added, "Once let an infuriated mass of men attack the Reserves, break them up, interfere with the United States Government in the consummation of a settled Indian policy, and we may apprehend danger, trouble and bloodshed from Red River to the Rio Grande." On the other hand, if the national government did not honor its treaties, "we should then have worse than a Florida war saddled upon us."[15]

After returning from the Canadian River fight, Ford asked Lt. William G. Preston to tell anyone with accusations against the reserve Comanches to submit their complaints in writing to Ford. Not a single person did so. As a consequence, more of Ford's men changed their minds about Comanches who lived on the reservation, but not Nelson. He did not directly challenge Ford, but he launched a covert attack on Neighbors. He allied with Baylor, who schemed to replace Neighbors with Nelson. The matter became even more sordid when Nelson wrote to Pres. James Buchanan, portraying himself as a good man caught between an incompetent Neighbors and a scheming Baylor. Among other documents that arrived in Washington was a petition asking for Nelson's appointment in place of Neighbors and a report from Ford to Runnels that had been given to Nelson for delivery to the governor. Having his confidential communications to the governor sent by Nelson to Washington led Ford to conclude that the young officer was ambitious; when Nelson began insisting to Ford that Neighbors was not really his friend, Ford decided that Nelson was not just ambitious, but bad. Sadly for Ford, who submitted an affidavit supporting Neighbors, federal authorities conducted investigations that resulted in the removal of the Texas reservations to locations north of the Red River in 1859. Neighbors, who led the Indians north, was assassinated when he returned to settle his affairs, while both Baylor and Nelson enjoyed political success and became high-ranking Confederates.[16]

Hungry Comanches resumed their raids in North Texas during the late summer of 1858. A joint expedition of federal troopers and reserve Indians, led by Maj. Earl Van Dorn and Lawrence S. Ross respectively, provided only partial relief. They won, but both Van Dorn and Ross, the son of Shapley P. Ross, were severely wounded, and the raiding continued. James G. Bourland mustered a company of Rangers in North Texas, but Ford in late November met with Runnels to press for more. The governor, as always, worried about the cost of a muster, but Ford had spent only half of the money allotted to him earlier, and so Runnels agreed to let him have another six-month company. Before the month ended, Ford led new recruits out of Austin. Edward Burleson Jr. remained behind this time, but he got the corn contract for Ford's command. His cousin, Aaron Burleson, who had served under James H. Callahan at Piedras Negras, took his place as Ford's lieutenant. The Rangers settled into Camp Leon, on the South Leon River in northern Comanche County, where Ford drilled them, as he always did.[17]

If Ford had any grandiose plans, they were curtailed by Runnels' order not to venture "into the Indian country." The governor pointedly explained that "there is much dissatisfaction in many portions of the country at what has already been done." That winter Ford settled little in a series of minor engagements with Comanches, even with the aid of reserve Indians as scouts. At least once an Indian leader refused to lead Ford near a large group of Comanches, rightly believing Ford would attack in spite of the odds against him. In late February, Ford was at Camp Cooper to muster out another Ranger company when he received a request for help from Shapley P. Ross. Hostile Indians had attacked his charges and taken some horses. Ford and his Rangers joined Ross and his Indians in a pursuit, but Ford also decided to enlist the support of a detachment of the Second United States Cavalry, posted at Camp Radziminski under the command of Van Dorn. That officer decided that cold and snow made a joint operation unwise, but Ford settled nearby with his Rangers and Indians to wait for warmer weather. After a week, they rode west for an extended patrol during which they found no enemies. Tired and discouraged, Ford led his command into Camp Cooper on March 30, 1859, and from there returned to Camp Leon, having trekked a total of 700 miles for nothing. That Van Dorn would take the field again and fight a battle in May 1859 did not improve Ford's disposition.[18]

Ford's second campaign in North Texas was also marred by the Peter Garland affair. After four years of conflict between settlers and reserve Indians, Garland, a local settler with a reputation for fighting Indians, led an attack in Palo Pinto County on seventeen Caddos, mostly women and children, who had left their reservation with Ross' permission. Seven Indians were killed while they slept on the morning of December 27, 1858, and several other women and children were badly wounded. Ford reported the next day to Runnels: "What this may portend I cannot say. There appears a determination in certain quarters on the frontier to make war indiscriminately on the reserve Indians. This may be the beginning." He assured the governor, as well as Neighbors, that he would assist with any legal actions, but when Judge Nicholas W. Battle confronted Ford at Camp Leon, deputized him, and ordered him to arrest Garland and seventeen others, the Ranger balked, insisting only Runnels could tell him what to do. The governor had indeed admonished Ford during his first muster in 1858 to defer to civilian authority and "not to intermeddle with the affairs of others in matters outside your line of duty," but in February 1859 he ordered Ford to work with civil officials in arresting Garland and his followers. Ford still stalled, writing to Runnels that what he really wanted to do was avoid a conflict between his Rangers and settlers. When Judge Battle, Neighbors, and Edward J. Gurley (counsel for the Indians) united against Ford, the latter repeated that civil war would erupt if he arrested Garland, with supporters on both sides.[19]

Fortunately for Ford's reputation, events called him into the field in March, when Runnels ordered him to go on the offensive against raiding Indians while telling him one more time to assist in the arrest of Garland and others. Neighbors saw a chance to protect the reservations by arresting men such as Nelson and Baylor, who were implicated in the Garland attack. His angry letter to Ford, however, went unanswered. He, with Battle and Gurley, continued a campaign for justice in the press and in letters to the governor, but to no avail. No one was arrested; the grand jury for Palo Pinto County ignored the matter when it next met; and Neighbors, attacked repeatedly by Baylor and his followers, agreed to remove the reservations from Texas. As for Ford, he staunchly defended his inaction then and later. On February 16, 1859, he wrote to Runnels, "I feel conscious of having acted right, and if any thing in the shape of a sacrifice of position should be demanded I shall make it most willingly." He would assist a civil officer in his job, if one would lead the way, but he would not do his job for him, especially if that would lead to bloodshed and would result in no positive good, such as a conviction. Fifty years later, after a long and unhappy recounting of the affair, Ford concluded, "I thank God, that my hands are not red with the blood of my fellow citizens, shed under the orders of Judge Battle, and at the instigation and advice of the ciceronian E. J. Gurley." His appropriation at long last completely spent, and with rumors circulating that the North Texas reservations would soon close, Ford mustered out his Rangers at Austin on May 10, 1859, and went home in a foul mood.[20]

A petition circulated at Austin in May 1859 calling on Ford to run for governor, but he declined to do so. Instead he watched as Sam Houston defeated Runnels, who had twice given Ford commissions as a Ranger. Ford attributed Runnels' loss to his failure to provide an effective solution to the problem of frontier defense. He wrote to Edward Burleson Jr. that "you may rest assured if Gen. Houston does not accord a very liberal degree of protection to the frontier he will [catch] h-ll from that quarter and very soon too." He added, "Gov. Runnels ran his boat against that rock and went overboard—Gen. Houston should profit by the example." The greatest border challenge for Houston came not in North Texas but on the Rio Grande, when Juan N. Cortina, a rancher and accused cattle rustler who was a folk hero to some local Tejanos, shot the Brownsville marshal and fled into Mexico. Cortina returned to occupy Brownsville with a small force in September 1859, intending to murder those who had secured an indictment against him. He and his followers did kill several people before José María de Jesús Carvajal, the commander of the garrison in Matamoros, convinced his cousin Cortina to stop. Cortina retired to Rancho del Carmen, his mother's ranch upriver, where he gathered more men by declaring that he would fight for the rights of Mexican Texans. The federal units at Brownsville and other posts along the lower Rio Grande had been removed due to the relative peace that had fallen over the region, as well as a general decline in the town after the creation of a free trade zone in northern Mexico, so Brownsville militia had to battle with Cortina's men. Cortina could not take Brownsville, but he controlled much of the surrounding countryside, and his ability to cross the Rio Grande repeatedly showed he had little to fear from either Texas militia or Mexican troops.[21]

To cope with Cortina, Maj. Samuel P. Heintzelman was sent with a small federal force. Runnels, who did not relinquish the governor's office to Houston until December 1859, in turn commissioned William G. Tobin, a merchant from San Antonio, to recruit a Ranger company and go to Heintzelman's assistance. When it became apparent that Cortina had only a few hundred men, plans to send even more Army personnel were cut, which forced Heintzelman to rely more heavily on the Rangers. Unfortunately for him, when he arrived at Brownsville on

Juan N. Cortina. Lawrence T. Jones III Collection, Southern Methodist University.

Samuel P. Heintzelman. Prints and Photographs Division, Library of Congress.

December 5, he discovered that Tobin had not done well. One day after Tobin's Rangers rode into Brownsville, some of them participated in lynching one of Cortina's lieutenants who had been captured by militia from the town. Fighting escalated with violent retributions on both sides, and casualties mounted. Cortina repulsed an attack by militia and took two cannons from them, killed four of Tobin's Rangers in an ambush, and then repelled an attack by Tobin two days later.[22]

Federal authorities might not have taken Cortina seriously, but Texas leaders did. When a rumor surfaced that he had burned Corpus Christi, Texas Senator Forbes Britton of that port stopped Ford on an Austin street and demanded that he do something. Ford thought he had convinced Britton that the rumor was untrue when Runnels, the lame duck governor, happened upon them. Convinced by Britton that the danger was real, Runnels ordered Ford to rescue Corpus Christi. Whether Britton believed the rumor, or was just concerned about an impending election, always puzzled Ford, but he knew many Texans had expected him to be appointed to command. With a six-month commission and eight men, Ford rode to Goliad, where in November he received instructions from Runnels to lead a company of Rangers to the Rio Grande, not Corpus Christi, and take command of all state troops there. Ford lobbied for more support by explaining to the governor that Cortina was a much more dangerous enemy than the Comanches. Ford believed that Cortina's support came from his convincing Mexicans that slave-owning Texans stood alone, abandoned by the federal government, and that Americans who did not own slaves would help against Texas. Warming to his subject, Ford wrote that there was "no doubt that an insolent foe has unfurled his banner within our limits and invites us to the combat. Shall we accept the challenge of the nation whose sons committed the massacres of the Alamo and of Goliad, who fled before us at San Antonio, San Jacinto, and many other fields? Can we allow foreign hordes to invade us, to murder and hang our citizens, and to escape unharmed, without tarnishing the honor of a good name gained by deeds of daring, by fortitude in adversity and in the endurance of privation? It seems to me there can be but one course for Texas. Expel the invaders let it cost what it may in blood and treasure."[23]

Ford assembled fifty-three men at Banquete, a day's ride west of Corpus Christi. Volunteers from that community had joined Tobin but returned home after his defeats. Now some responded to a new challenge from Ford: "Have you any desire to wipe off the reproach that has been cast upon Texas by her allowing a foreign flag to wave upon her soil with impunity? Come if you wish to fight!" They rode south with Ford, arriving in Brownsville on December 14 as cannon boomed in the distance. Mifflin Kenedy, who had mustered his militia to confront the newcomers only to discover it was his friend Ford, reported that Heintzelman had taken his soldiers and Tobin's Rangers upriver that morning, December 14, to engage Cortina. Ford and his riders rushed to the battlefield, thirteen miles from town, but arrived too late to participate in the main fight. Cortina had ambushed Heintzelman and in turn had been forced to retreat. After a rest, Ford and his Rangers joined in pursuing Cortina and his men, most of whom escaped when rain dampened the powder of the pursuers that night and made further effort useless. Ford, after taking command of all of the Rangers, returned with Heintzelman to Brownsville the next day.[24]

Heintzelman was not impressed with the Texans' first fight under his command. In fact, he angrily wrote in his journal, "We would undoubtedly have done better without the Rangers." Initially he did not know quite what to do with Ford, referring to him as doctor, captain, and even colonel in his journal as their first meeting approached. Having met him on the battlefield, he accepted the title of major, but even that was problematic. Runnels in his first orders to Ford appointed him as a major, but just one week later he instructed Ford to have his men and those in Tobin's company "immediately" choose who would serve as major in charge of both commands. Instead, Ford simply assumed the rank of major upon arriving in Brownsville and then delayed the election, apparently worried that he might lose to Tobin. Heintzelman dryly noted that "Capt. Tobin & Major Ford do not get along well together." His solution was to send them on separate patrols, with a third column composed of the only federal troopers he had: a company of the Second United States Cavalry under the command of Capt. George M. Stoneman. They found nothing, and thus when Heintzelman marched upriver again on December 21, 1859, with about 150 federals and almost 200 Rangers, he still had little confidence in the latter. Meanwhile, Ford had purchased Sharps carbines for some of his men, enhancing their firepower in anticipation of another fight.[25]

Cortina had settled near Rio Grande City, and Ford found his camp. He had been assigned to guard Heintzelman's flanks as he marched, and on December 26 his Texans located their quarry. Ford was told to slip around Cortina's left flank with three Ranger companies and occupy a position on the road from Rio Grande City to Roma by daylight on December 27. The main attacking force would advance into Rio Grande City at dawn. Unfortunately, Ford discovered that the brush was too thick for his march, that Cortina's pickets were posted to prevent a flanking movement, and that Cortina's force was much larger than anticipated. Ford stopped near Ringgold Barracks to wait for Heintzelman; when he arrived, Ford asked to lead an attack upon Cortina's left flank. Heintzelman agreed and assigned the remaining Rangers to Ford. Before sunrise on December 27, Ford drove in Cortina's pickets, repulsed a reconnaissance party, and then swung around Rio Grande City to attack Cortina's command post. There he found Mexicans arrayed in a defensive line. He assigned Tobin to attack their left, at a cemetery, while Ford led an assault on their right, across the road from Roma to Rio Grande City near the river itself. He left the center to Heintzelman's federal troops, who had artillery.[26]

Ford ran into trouble when he came under fire from two Mexican cannons as he crossed the road to Roma. He sent a detachment to silence the guns, which they did with small arms fire from the protection of a fence. Ford joined this group, intending to seize the guns, which were those Cortina had taken in November. While Ford's men drove the gunners from their pieces, a charge by some of Cortina's mounted men prevented a capture. The gunners returned, fired a blast of grapeshot that slightly wounded Ford and more than a dozen of his men, then withdrew with their guns. Tobin, repulsed at the cemetery, joined Ford just after the Mexican riders retired. Heintzelman, who could not tell exactly what was occurring because of a heavy fog, arrived and gave Ford permission to pursue the Mexicans, who had begun a slow retreat. Stoneman cleared the river bank of Cortina's stragglers, and when Cortina himself rallied some men about five miles down the road to Roma, Ford shattered his lines and finally captured a cannon. William R. Henry, the erstwhile filibusterer, fired the piece at the Mexicans as they resumed their retreat.

Cortina and some of his followers avoided capture by crossing the Rio Grande, but others simply fled into the brush, abandoning the other gun to Ford. That night Stoneman with his company garrisoned Roma while the Rangers retraced their steps to Ringgold Barracks. There Ford's guests included Samuel J. Stewart, a justice of the peace and former sheriff in Rio Grande City whose execution by Cortina had been prevented by the arrival of the Texans and federals.[27]

The clash near Rio Grande City on December 27, 1859, also known as the Davis Ranch fight, reportedly cost Cortina at least sixty men dead and forced him to flee across the Rio Grande. It also convinced Heintzelman to support Ford over Tobin in the dispute about who would command the Rangers as major. He wrote in his ever-present journal: "I hope [by] all means that Ford will be elected the Major. He is by all odds the better man. He controls his men & Tobin is controlled by his. I would rather have Ford with 50 than Tobin with all his men." Despite this, when Ford decided to hold the elections for major on New Year's Day in 1860, Tobin won. Heintzelman was told that many of the Rangers voted against Ford because he wanted to stop the rough behavior that Tobin tolerated. A significant number of Texans, led by Ford, subsequently decided not to serve under Tobin. Ford's former newspaper partner, Joseph Walker, who had been elected to lead Ford's company in the Davis Ranch fight, refused to stay, as did most of Ford's original recruits. Tobin ordered the malcontents to Brownsville to be mustered out, while he asked Houston, the newly inaugurated governor, to allow him to enlist replacements.[28]

Ford led Walker and many others to Brownsville, where to their delight they were hailed as heroes. They also found a pair of commissioners, Ángel Navarro and Robert H. Taylor, sent by Houston to investigate matters along the Rio Grande. The two men had endured a hostile reception from local leaders, who assumed the outsiders might actually sympathize with Cortina, but the atmosphere changed when it soon became apparent that Navarro and Taylor disliked Cortina and supported Ford over Tobin. The two had little choice about the latter decision—people in Brownsville told them that Tobin's men were undisciplined and dangerous, perhaps even more of a menace than Cortina in looting local settlers, and that Tobin had been repeatedly defeated by Cortina. Conversely, Ford required discipline, and he won. Within days of their arrival on the Rio Grande, Navarro and Taylor ordered Tobin to Brownsville to be discharged. At Heintzelman's request, the Rangers were reduced in number and reorganized as two companies with Ford as senior captain. He could not be a major because there was not a battalion of five companies to command, but he took charge of all of the Rangers, in cooperation with Heintzelman. To the great pleasure of many local leaders, Navarro and Taylor declared that Cortina was in fact a "thief, assassin, and a murderer" who had been allowed to do as he wanted for too many years because the Mexican majority followed him and the Anglo minority needed his influence. The result had been chaos, with Mexican officials supporting Cortina, and Ford and Heintzelman were to work together to restore order by eliminating him.[29]

Ford later claimed that his announced decision to resign was just a ruse to get out from under Tobin's control and move to Brownsville, where he expected Cortina would strike next, and he knew his company would follow him there. If so, his maneuver had worked brilliantly. Tobin and his troublesome recruits were vanquished, and friendlier faces now served with Ford. Matthew Nolan, who had been a bugler for the Army in the Mexican War and for Ford in both 1850 and 1858, now became his first lieutenant. John J. Dix Jr., who would be a lifelong friend, was one of Ford's second lieutenants. Walker and others went home, but Ford's second company was commanded by John Littleton, a Karnes County sheriff who had been wounded in fighting against Cortina in November. He decided to stay, and like Nolan would lead a company again under Ford during the Civil War. Ford christened his new command as the "Rio Grande Squadron." There were many veterans in the ranks and, with Ford as senior captain, much was expected of them when Cortina showed signs of staging an unexpected resurgence.[30]

In the aftermath of his victory at Davis Ranch in December 1859, Heintzelman had confidently declared that "Cortina's forces" were "entirely dispersed," and he told his subordinates "to keep out small parties to pick up any stragglers who may be disposed to be troublesome." Ford never harbored any such misconceptions about his opponent, and he warned Houston that Cortina was not finished as he could draw support from those in rebellion against President Benito Juárez in Mexico. When Houston sent a proclamation to Ford for Cortina and his men, promising amnesty if they would lay down their arms and return home, Ford delivered the missive but expected no positive result. He also did not trust the reassurances of Gen. Guadalupe García, who commanded the garrison at Matamoros (and had done so during the infamous James H. Callahan incursion in 1855). Perhaps Ford understood better than other Anglos the larger context for the unrest along the Rio Grande because he was again being offered a command by the ever-hopeful José María de Jesús Carvajal, who saw in the travails of Juárez a chance for personal glory. Ford declined to join Carvajal. Instead, he and Littleton, along with many others, met repeatedly with Heintzelman to urge an attack on Cortina, even if they had to cross the Rio Grande into Mexico to reach him. By early February Heintzelman reluctantly agreed, and he ordered Ford into the field in tandem with two companies of Army troopers.[31]

On February 1, 1860, Ford rode out of Brownsville with his Rangers alongside United States cavalry under the command of Stoneman and Lt. Manning M. Kimmel, whom Ford had first met at Camp Radziminski during his unsuccessful try to secure Van Dorn's cooperation against the Comanche in 1859. The combined force moved slowly up the Rio Grande, searching for raiders. On the second day Ford arrived at the ranch of Cortina's mother, María E. G. Cavazos de Cortina, to whom he was formally introduced by Savas Cavazos, Cortina's half brother by their mother's earlier marriage. Ford was impressed and deeply affected by her gentle manner, as well as her earnest plea to not harm her son, and he promised to protect her. The Americans scattered along the Texas side of the river to prevent any crossings, which led to the first engagement for the Rio Grande Squadron. Ford on February 4 sent a small party of Rangers to establish a camp at a bend in the river opposite Bolsa Ranch. They encountered about thirty of Cortina's men, and a fight ensued that quickly escalated. Tobin with his command, riding to muster out at Brownsville, joined the melee, while the steamboat *Ranchero,* laden with specie and cargo worth $300,000, chugged into range as well. Army gunners on the deck of the *Ranchero* opened fire with the guns captured by Ford at Davis Ranch. A courier raced to get Ford, who arrived with additional Rangers several hours into the fight.[32]

Believing Cortina had several hundred men across the Rio Grande, Ford decided to attack. Tobin swam the river with ten mounted men to secure the far bank while the *Ranchero* ferried Ford and three dozen Rangers, including Littleton and Dix, across the border. Ford in his haste forgot to grab his guns from his saddle, but he led dismounted Rangers in a flank attack on Cortina's men firing from behind a fence. The Mexicans broke and ran, seeking shelter in the brush while Cortina himself served as a solitary rearguard. Only one Texan, Fountain B. Woodruff, was killed, and none were seriously wounded, while Cortina's losses were reported as twenty-nine killed and forty wounded. Bolsa Ranch was set ablaze, though not by Ford's order, and Tobin resumed his march for Brownsville shortly before midnight, when Stoneman and Kimmel arrived with their troopers.[33]

Ford and Stoneman, as the ranking captains on the field, consulted that night and decided to escort the *Ranchero* downriver. To do this effectively, Ford would ride down the Mexican side with Rangers, while Stoneman would parallel him on the Texas side, close enough to provide support if necessary. Informed of this, Heintzelman responded with admonitions not to venture too far into Mexico and to maintain strict discipline. Ford's original orders from Runnels in November 1859 had forbade him to cross the Rio Grande without permission from Mexican authorities, and when Heintzelman informed García of Ford's plan and asked for his cooperation in catching Cortina, the Mexican general responded with a demand that Ford leave Mexico and reported that he had already sent troops to intercept the Rangers. Ford met the Matamoros militia at Las Palmas Ranch. A tense negotiation ensued, during which Ford became convinced that some of the Mexican troops he faced were Cortina's men. A clash was averted when the Matamoros authorities decided not to protest Ford's escort, while he, in obedience to an order from Heintzelman, agreed to let the Mexicans guard their side of the river for the remainder of the *Ranchero's* journey. Ford and

Stoneman, with their men, returned peacefully to Brownsville on the Texas side of the Rio Grande.[34]

Ford reported to Houston that Cortina had been badly beaten at Bolsa Ranch, but he expected his opponent to recruit another force. Heintzelman within a week sent Ford to patrol again along the Rio Grande, but this time he told the Texans to stay on their side of the river. Rangers, when not being drilled by Ford, continued to patrol together with cavalry for the next six weeks. Ford also enforced strict discipline, forbidding alcohol in his camp and telling Houston that his men "gambled very little" because "they have had nothing to gamble for." The main casualty during this quiet interlude was Ford, who was badly injured when his horse stepped in a hole at full gallop and fell on him. He had to be carried to his quarters, blood dripping from his nose and mouth.[35]

Ford and his Rangers returned to Mexico in March 1860, when García reported to Heintzelman that Cortina was camped at La Mesa, just a few miles from Ford's base at Agua Negra Ranch. Heintzelman conveyed the news to Ford just to alert him, but an idea grew. Ford secured permission from Carvajal, now appointed as the governor of Tamaulipas, for the Americans to cross the Rio Grande, and Heintzelman ordered Stoneman with two companies of cavalry to accompany Ford, who for once moved slowly. He claimed that he still suffered from the injuries sustained when his horse fell, but he also worried that Cortina might be setting a trap, perhaps with the assistance of García. A reconnaissance indicated an ambush had indeed been set, and Stoneman agreed to an indirect march that brought the Americans close to the Mexican camp before they were detected. Ford's Rangers formed the right wing and Stoneman's cavalry became the left for a charge that enveloped a hastily formed defensive line. After the fight, it was discovered that the Americans had overwhelmed a Mexican militia unit, killing four or five men and even mortally wounding a woman. Ford and Stoneman quickly released all prisoners and restored captured property to its owners, or at least most of it.[36]

Later that morning a larger Mexican force approached. A Mexican officer asked for Ford, whom he addressed as colonel, to meet with his commander, who actually was a colonel and refused to speak with Stoneman, a captain. The Mexican colonel berated Ford and demanded an explanation for entering Mexico and firing on Mexican militia. Ford in turn asked why an ambush had been prepared on the main road, forcing the Americans to take another route to avoid being attacked themselves. The colonel, rather than answer, boasted that if the Americans had attacked him earlier that morning, they would have been defeated. When Ford angrily asked whether he would like to try his luck, the Mexican colonel declined. Further discussion revealed that mounted men driven from the field by Stoneman's troopers at La Mesa were indeed Cortina's, working with the militia. Irritated at this clear evidence that Mexican officials supported Cortina, the Americans, rather than obey the colonel's order to wait for further instructions from Matamoros, returned to their camp on the north side of the Rio Grande.[37]

Ford again led his Rangers in tandem with Stoneman's cavalry down the Mexican side of the Rio Grande in late March and found some of Cortina's men at Bolsa Ranch. One, Faustino, was an "old Mexican Indian" notorious for leading raids and killing at least six Americans. When he was captured by the Rangers, Ford simply declared that he did not wish to see him. He later wrote in his memoirs, "A shot was heard—the scene closed." Because this incident became the source for stories of many alleged killings by Ford's men, a few months after Ford's death in 1897 a former Ranger, Will Lambert, claimed responsibility for the execution. An Austin newspaperman in 1859, Lambert had been with Ford only a short time when he caught Faustino. Told by Ford that he did not wish to talk with the captive, Lambert marched Faustino into the brush and shot him, then told Ford that he had escaped. Ford responded quietly, "You'll do." Whether or not Ford condoned this act, he reported every atrocity committed by both sides to Heintzelman and was never called to task for excesses, though his report of Faustino's death omitted much of the detail provided years later by Lambert.[38]

While resting his horses at Bolsa Ranch, Ford was approached by a courier who delivered an order from Heintzelman to return to Texas. Ford and Stoneman grumbled; they had been hoping for orders to ride into Matamoros. Instead, acting on a tip from an informant, Ford led his

Will Lambert. Daniell, *Personnel of the Texas State Government, 1887.*

Rangers and the cavalry to Cortina's ranch south of Matamoros. Hearing gunshots as they approached, the Americans assumed their advance had been attacked and raced into the settlement, only to find they had interrupted a Saint Joseph's Day celebration, during which it was customary to fire blanks. One Mexican was killed when he fled into the brush, loaded live rounds, and angrily began firing at the Rangers. That night another spy told Ford that Cortina had fled toward Monterrey, and the Rangers took up the pursuit. They missed their quarry again at a ranch forty miles away, and so Ford and Stoneman decided to return to his camp at Agua Negra Ranch in Texas, which they reached on the night of March 21, 1860.[39]

Ford could not resist one last strike, against Reynosa, whose residents sheltered some of Cortina's veterans and boasted they would not fall as easily as La Mesa. Ford and Stoneman laid plans by which the Rangers would cross the Rio Grande and occupy Reynosa. When firing began, as they expected it would, Stoneman would hurry across the river to support the endangered Texans. Ford smoothly occupied the smaller village of Reynosa Vieja at midnight on April 3–4, 1860, but Cortina's veterans escaped. Ford's Rangers consoled themselves by organizing a fandango, but at daylight Ford continued to Reynosa, where the alarm had been raised and several hundred defenders had gathered, thinking they were being attacked by bandits. The Rangers divided into three columns, led by Ford, Littleton, and Nolan, and entered the town, but despite their best efforts they could not goad the Mexicans into firing a first shot. Instead, once the defenders realized they were not being attacked by bandits, Ford was invited to meet with the town council at the courthouse. A tense meeting ended with Ford agreeing to return to Texas and send demands in writing for the surrender of Cortina's followers. The disappointed Texans were escorted to the ferry, and settled for the night near Edinburg, where Stoneman had waited anxiously for shots to be fired.[40]

Ford sent his written demand for Cortina's veterans to the Reynosa council, and they politely replied that they had no such men. Ford fumed and the council prepared to meet his attack, which they fully expected. Tension mounted as bullets from the Texas side of the

Rio Grande wounded several Mexicans, and bullets from the Mexican side fell in the Ranger camp. The situation did not improve when Littleton and other Rangers, with Ford's approval, built a realistic-looking gun emplacement with bricks and placed a log on an oxcart inside of it, which looked to Reynosa residents like a cannon aimed at them. To complete their jest, the Texans filled a cow horn with gunpowder and grease, and then launched it with a boom toward the town by exploding powder in a small hole underneath it. The flaming missile convinced Mexicans they had been fired upon, and many of them stayed on guard through the night for the attack that would surely follow. In turn, Kimmel raced his troopers to the river crossing when he heard gunfire, which again proved to be a religious procession celebrating a saint's day.[41]

Lt. Col. Robert E. Lee arrived with more federal troops on April 7, 1860, less than twenty-four hours after the horn was launched. After talking with Ford, who had joined his column as it approached the river, Lee sent a note to assure Reynosa officials that he did not want a war, but he also admonished them not to support Cortina. They responded that they also did not wish to fight, that no Cortina followers were in their town, and that Ford should not have entered their town. Lee agreed on all counts. This brought an end to Ford's campaign, which was not unexpected. While Ford operated on the Rio Grande, Duff Green came to Austin on a fact-finding mission and reported to the James Buchanan administration that Texans were as guilty as Mexicans in creating havoc along the border. Heintzelman also decided that the Rangers were impediments to peace; after all, Ford had ignored his orders on several occasions. With Cortina apparently deep in Mexico, Army leaders did not need Ford. Finally, Houston, like Ford, had considered attacking Mexico to seize territory or to distract his fellow Americans from the impending sectional crisis, but he dropped this notion by late January 1860, when he appointed an agent to muster Ford's command out of service. Navarro urged Houston to establish a protectorate over northern Mexico, and Houston discussed the matter with Lee, but when the latter refused to take part in such a scheme, Houston ordered Ford to Goliad. Houston's agent, George McKnight, asked Lee if Ford could enter federal service, but Lee declined, and Ford led his command away from the

Robert E. Lee. Shorter Mansion Photograph Album, Alabama Department of Archives and History.

Rio Grande without further protest. After all, he could not satisfactorily answer the governor's queries about atrocities committed by Tobin's men, and he had actually asked for a leave of absence in early March.[42]

Ford left the Rio Grande as a conquering hero among the Texans, and with warm praise from Army leaders as well. Before riding north, he and his Rio Grande Squadron enjoyed a banquet and dance in Brownsville that was attended by Lee and other officers, who perhaps appreciated a speech by Ford assuring everyone of his love for the Union. Lee certainly defended Ford when García tried to complain about the Reynosa intrusion. Heintzelman had already heaped accolades upon Ford in his official report submitted in March; after all, Cortina had lost more than 150 men killed while American losses were only fifteen. Perhaps another eighty Mexicans also died during the conflict, but Cortina's surviving followers abandoned him and he had fled far south, away from the Rio Grande. In a letter to Houston formally declining to accept the Rangers into federal service, Lee repeated the praises of Heintzelman for Ford and Littleton. The attention lavished by the people of Brownsville on the Texans did not suit Heintzelman, however, and he left town without Lee and Ford on May 7, 1860. The two joined him on the road on May 10, and they rode together for three days until Ford left to rejoin his command at Goliad. There McKnight mustered out the Rangers and thought he had collected all of their state-issued weapons, but Ford was amused to encounter some of his men along the road to Austin still carrying their arms and laughing at how they had hoodwinked Houston's agent. Like his Rangers, Ford had not yet been paid, and he did not indicate later that he did anything to correct their theft.[43]

After settling his accounts in Austin, Ford returned to Brownsville. Rumors flew that he would lead a filibuster into Mexico by the Knights of the Golden Circle. That pro-slavery organization had begun in Kentucky, but no southern state had more chapters than Texas. The Knights in Texas wanted Mexico to become part of an expanded slavery empire that embraced the entire Caribbean region. This seemed to fit what people knew about Ford, especially since many believed Mexican leaders such as Carvajal would cooperate in this effort. Hundreds of Knights had descended on Brownsville in the early spring of 1860, prompting Houston's condemnation of filibustering. When money ran out and leaders began to bicker, the would-be invaders drifted home. A convention at Raleigh, North Carolina, in May 1860 reunited and revived the Knights, who issued a plan for an operation by an army of thousands recruited in the United States and Mexico. Once more Knights rode into Brownsville, but again there was little money and no effective leaders, and so the effort collapsed for good. Ford had not stepped forward to publicly declare his support for the movement, and there is no evidence that even privately he still entertained the notion of invading Mexico again. Knights continued to agitate and establish chapters in Texas, and some of Ford's associates such as Littleton joined, but not Ford.[44]

What brought Ford back to Brownsville in 1860 was not war but love. Soon after defeating the Comanches on the Canadian River in 1858, Ford had responded to a gibe in a letter to Governor Runnels, declaring that he "always could have married" if he "could have found the right woman." He added, "I was only hunting after her." He met Adeline Norton Smith when he arrived on the Rio Grande to chase Cortina. "Addie" was twenty-one and never married; he was forty-four and a widower as well as a divorcé, but they courted throughout the late summer and early fall of 1860. Addie was unlike either of Ford's previous wives. Born in Connecticut, her father was Elihu D. Smith, a prosperous merchant who moved to the Brownsville area about 1831. His brother, Daniel W. Smith, served as the United States consul at Matamoros. Ford later explained in his memoirs that while Addie "was of Yankee descent," her "relatives were, nearly all, democrats," and she became a "consistent friend of the Confederacy." They married in March 1861 and had three children during and just after the Civil War. One of their granddaughters wrote that her grandmother Addie was "handsome" and "gracious," and that her grandfather fondly referred to her as the "red headed institution."[45]

By the late summer of 1860, a smitten Ford could reflect on a busy two years in which he had become one of the most, if not the most, prominent Ranger captains in Texas. It was a role that he relished, even if it led at least one congressman, Abram B. Olin of New York, to denounce him as a "coward and an enemy to the Red man." Ford in June 1860 confessed to Edward Burleson Jr., his erstwhile subordinate, that he missed "Bob Potter and Monkey S----," his former sergeant major and attendant respectively, "though Billy Stinkfinger and a bob-tailed, pot-metal dog compensate a little for their absence."[46] If the nation had remained at peace and whole, Ford would probably have taken the field again with them as a Ranger in pursuit of either Indian or Mexican raiders, and he would have further cemented his role among Texans. But the country did not remain united, and when the Texas government asked him once more to take charge of troops on the Rio Grande, he campaigned against the Union his grandfathers had fought to establish in the American Revolution, and which he had repeatedly claimed to love during the decade prior to the Civil War.

CHAPTER 4 SECESSIONIST

John S. Ford in 1861 finally got his chance to help create a new nation as his grandfathers had done, but the first year of the Civil War proved to be disappointing for him. Other Texas leaders left the state and won glory on distant battlefields, but Ford remained on the Rio Grande, far from the primary theaters of national conflict. He became in part a victim of his own fame. While he had established a reputation as an aggressive defender of slavery and the South as a politician and editor, he had also won fame as a Ranger captain defending the frontier. So although he used his political skills to promote secession, as Texas left the Union he was assigned once more to play the role of frontier defender. There his stubborn pride, and allegiance to friends, undermined any chance he had to become a national leader for the Confederate States of America. Ironically, as the war entered its second year, Ford found himself exiled from the field, despite his leadership in the secession movement and his initial military success along the Rio Grande. It was a bitter fate for one who boasted of being from "fighting stock."

Texans in 1860 faced a monumental question in the presidential race. Stephen A. Douglas secured the nomination of the Democratic Party and embraced a platform that endorsed popular sovereignty for settling the issue of slavery in the territories, whereupon many of the Southern Democrats withdrew from their national convention and nominated John C. Breckinridge, whose support for slavery was unequivocal. Republican nominee Abraham Lincoln made his opposition to slavery very evident, try as he might to appear conciliatory, while John Bell of the Constitutional Union Party avoided addressing the subject directly. The Texas Troubles in the summer of 1860, when several North Texas towns burst into flames, convinced Texans that they confronted a violent challenge from abolitionists. They reacted violently and became more determined to support pro-slavery leaders such as Breckinridge.[1]

Ford was initially unsure whom to support in the 1860 race, but he was clear on the issue of slavery and the related topic of whether secession might be justified as a way to protect that peculiar institution from an abolitionist challenge. About the election, he wrote to Ed Burleson Jr., "I am at a loss who to vote for and, like Micawber, I am waiting for something to turn up to determine the matter." But about slavery, Ford had no doubts that it was politically, economically, and morally correct. Furthermore, for him there was a direct link between abolitionist threats and the necessity for secession. His resentment at the failure of the federal government to provide adequate protection for the frontier, a sentiment shared by many Texans, enhanced his growing conviction that secession might be necessary. He had written to Hardin R. Runnels in 1858 "that when a Government fails or refuses to protect its citizens the ties of allegiance are dissolved." As to whether the Constitution allowed a state to leave the Union, Ford like many Southerners looked beyond that document to the Declaration of Independence, in which his revolutionary ancestors had asserted their right to revolt against a government that did not protect their lives and interests. In the end, such beliefs led him in August 1860 to declare in favor of Breckinridge at a rally in Brownsville.[2]

After the presidential election of 1860, Ford hurried to Austin. He believed that Lincoln, once in office, would take some action against slavery, and Ford did not want to surrender the initiative to a man he considered an enemy of the South. Secession had become necessary, in Ford's mind, and this meant war. He had served with Northern officers and soldiers on the frontier, and he understood that they would fight to preserve the Union. For these reasons, Ford joined Texas Attorney General George M. Flournoy and others to discuss what to do. Justice Oran M. Roberts of the Texas Supreme Court, who like Ford had resided in San Augustine in the 1840s, suggested three courses of action: demand that Gov. Sam Houston call a special session of the Texas legislature to authorize a convention, organize a campaign to win enough seats in the legislature that it would later call a convention, or immediately

Sam Houston. Prints and Photographs Division, Library of Congress.

Oran M. Roberts. Lawrence T. Jones III Collection, Southern Methodist University.

begin a grassroots push for a convention. William P. Rogers reported that Houston had already declined to call a special session, and no one recommended waiting while prominent newspapers such as the *Texas State Gazette* were calling for action. The group chose the third option, and Ford assisted Roberts in writing a call for a convention. Ironically, the two had co-authored resolutions calling for the annexation of Texas that had been adopted by a caucus at San Augustine in 1845; now they worked together to undo what they had done fifteen years earlier. Copies of their call for a convention were sent to communities throughout Texas in December 1860. The delegates were to be elected on January 8 and convene in Austin on January 28, 1861. While ostensibly the convention would discuss the merits of secession, the intention was to take Texas out of the Union quickly, before Lincoln was inaugurated.[3]

Ford and his allies were not content to let matters take their course without some guidance. Several hundred secession supporters attended a meeting in the Travis County courthouse at Austin, where they heard speeches by John R. Baylor and Thomas Harrison of Waco, both of whom would become prominent Texas Confederates. A Union meeting at a local hotel days later resulted instead in a voice vote in favor of defending Southern rights. Ford joined with his fellow secessionists in breaking up other Union meetings in Austin and denouncing all who opposed secession, although some observers noted that he proposed reestablishing the Republic of Texas, not joining a Southern confederacy. He persisted in his campaign even as his efforts threatened to alienate old friends. In 1854, Aaron B. Burleson had written to his nephew, Edward Burleson Jr., asking him to secure Ford's support for him in the forthcoming election. Six years later, the elder Burleson angrily reported to his nephew that "me and Old Rip had like to have got to fighting the other night and dam him I will whip him if he does attempt to stope me from speaking my sintiments [*sic*] at any place or time in these United states." Undaunted, Ford served as marshal of a pro-secession parade in Austin on January 5, 1861. He rode a white horse at the head of the procession with Thomas E. Sneed, a former mayor of Austin who wed the sister of Edward Burleson Jr. just three weeks later. Among the horde of participants was Ford's daughter Fannie, who carried a banner with the Georgia coat of arms while other ladies carried the flags of other Southern states. Bands, riders, carriages filled with women waving Lone Star flags, and yelling walkers comprised the rest of the boisterous procession. They paraded down Congress Avenue, turned on Eighth Street, and gathered at a tall flagpole on the corner of Colorado Street, where Ford presided over the raising of a Lone Star flag.[4]

Secessionists dominated the elections for delegates in most Texas counties, and Ford won in Cameron over Edmund J. Davis, even though Davis lived in Brownsville and Ford did not. The other two delegates from Cameron County were Edward R. Hord, who had joined Ford's command under José María de Jesús Carvajal in 1851, and Francis W. Latham, a New England Yankee like Ford's father-in-law who served as collector of customs at Brownsville. Among the other delegates were two of Ford's former Ranger subordinates, John Littleton and Allison Nelson. Ford had much in common with them and other delegates—most were middle-aged, middle-class lawyers and farmers born in states where slavery was legal. But there were differences as well: most of them owned slaves, which Ford did not, and he was the only delegate who had no occupation listed in the convention journal. Nonetheless, he shared their support for secession.[5]

Governor Houston called for a special session of the legislature to meet in January 1861, hoping they would condemn the impending convention, but they overwhelmingly endorsed the idea, quashing any plans he might have had to veto their approval and avoid an override. When the Secession Convention met on January 28, Ford helped to get Roberts elected as its president and spoke in favor of secession, though he did warn that war would be the likely result of leaving the Union. Ford also endorsed the legislature's requirement that a secession ordinance be submitted to a popular vote before ratification. Anticipating a majority vote in favor of secession, and mindful of Ford's reputation as a Ranger, Roberts appointed him to the Committee on Public Safety, which was charged with securing federal property in Texas and providing for frontier defense. Roberts also allowed Ford to guide the appointment of other committee members, which included Latham and Phillip N. Luckett, who had served as the surgeon of Ford's Ranger company in

1850 and 1851. The committee members in turn apparently shared Roberts' opinion that Ford was "unquestionably the very best military man" in Texas, and so they followed his lead in planning how to remove federal troops and replace them with state units. The posts on the Rio Grande, from Brownsville to Laredo, were assigned to Ford, who helped to write his own orders. With 600 volunteers, he was to secure all federal property in the Military Division of the Rio Grande, supervise the evacuation of ten companies of Army regulars, and defend against "hostile invasions" while maintaining friendly relations with Mexico.[6]

With a commission as a colonel of state troops in his pocket, Ford issued muster orders to fellow convention delegates Littleton and John Donelson as captains of two of his companies, as well as to Matthew Nolan, who like Littleton had previously served under Ford's command as a Ranger. Ford left these three to their tasks and traveled by stagecoach to Hempstead, where he mustered another company and boarded a train for Houston. There Ford enlisted other recruits, but he also talked with Ebenezar B. Nichols, who had been appointed by the Secession Convention as its receiving agent for all federal property. The convention expected Nichols to provide Ford with the money, supplies, and transportation he would need to take possession of the Rio Grande line. By the third week of February 1861, Nichols had obtained arms and large donations of money from New Orleans, and he leased two steamers, the *General Rusk* and (ironically) the *Union,* and a schooner, the *Shark,* to carry Ford and his volunteers to Brazos Santiago. Located near the mouth of the Rio Grande, Brazos Santiago served as the supply depot for Fort Brown and posts further upriver. With a total of 500 officers

Fort Brown, 1861. *Harper's Weekly,* March 21, 1861.

and men, Ford formally organized his first regiment at Galveston with former Texas adjutant general and longtime associate Hugh McLeod as his lieutenant colonel and Benjamin F. Terry, a wealthy planter and fellow convention delegate, as major.[7]

Ford, with Nichols and McLeod, sailed from Galveston for Brazos Santiago on the night of February 19, 1861. After two days at sea, Ford landed peacefully at Brazos after convincing an Army lieutenant and his gunners not to fire the heavy guns they had trained on the water approach to the island. Ford and his troops stood at attention in a ceremony that included the firing of thirty-three guns for the United States flag as it was lowered and twenty-one guns for the Lone Star as it was raised. Ford officially reported that all was done with great civility, but he confessed privately many years later that it was a difficult moment for him. As he explained, "This was the first time the writer ever saw the flag of the United States lowered to an opposing force. His ancestors had fought to create and sustain it, and he had marched beneath its victorious folds. Now to see it lowered, even to men who were born beneath it, was a trial of no ordinary character." Some solace could be taken in the fact that he captured twenty-one pieces of artillery that had been sent by Capt. Bennett H. Hill, the commander of Fort Brown, from Brownsville to Brazos Santiago to be shipped out of Texas, which sorely needed such ordnance as the war approached.[8]

Ford and his troops escorted Nichols on February 22 to Brownsville, where Nichols met with Hill the following morning to discuss a surrender of Fort Brown. Nichols told Hill that Texas was "virtually out of the Union" as the election on secession was being held that day, and he asked Hill to evacuate his troops peacefully from the again "sovereign and independent republic" of Texas. This of course was somewhat premature; while the convention had approved an ordinance of secession, the popular referendum had not yet concluded. Whether or not Hill knew this, he declined to hand over the post, saying that he had no authority to do so. Nichols later described Hill as "taunting, threatening, and insulting" during their meeting, and Hill apparently did declare that he had ordered the arrest of Nichols, Ford, and other state officers but had been persuaded not to do so by his subordinates, who were divided in their views on secession. He also told Nichols that he had ordered the destruction of all stores at Brazos Santiago, but his order had not arrived before the Texans occupied the place. He would carry out such an order at Fort Brown if forced to surrender. Nichols and others decided to give Hill until March 2, the actual effective date for the secession ordinance, to surrender and "acknowledge the Texans own Texas." If he did not, Nichols later reported, "we intended to whale him into a knowledge of that fact certain." Nichols returned with McLeod and some of Ford's men to Brazos, whence he left for Galveston to get reinforcements. There he learned that Texas voters had indeed approved secession, and that Brig. Gen. David E. Twiggs had met with Benjamin McCulloch, Luckett, and others at San Antonio and agreed to withdraw all federal troops from the Department of Texas.[9]

Musing over whether Hill would leave quietly or try to fight, McLeod wrote to Ford on March 1, 1861: "It [is] useless . . . to speculate upon the motives or designs of such an ass." He added that his defenses at Brazos Santiago, and his men, were ready for a fight if it came. Nichols returned from Galveston with another 325 troops under the command of Terry on board the *General Rusk,* while Littleton, Nolan, and Donelson arrived overland, bringing Ford's total strength to more than 1,000 men. But Hill had four companies of Army veterans and artillery with trained gunners, so Ford knew he could make it difficult for the Texans to win, if not impossible. One figure emerged to provide some encouragement for Ford: his old comrade Capt. George M. Stoneman, with whom he had campaigned against Juan N. Cortina, served as an intermediary with Hill. Stoneman was among the officers who had counseled Hill not to arrest Ford, and he also worked with the Texan to keep him from doing anything rash. Stoneman and Ford were not always cordial while waiting at Brownsville—the former once boasted that he could march all over Texas with his companies, to which the latter responded with "derision." But when Hill, informed of the terms signed by Twiggs, finally agreed to an evacuation on March 2, Stoneman accompanied Ford to Brazos to meet Maj. Fitz John Porter, who arrived with a steamer to transport the

George M. Stoneman. Prints and Photographs Division, Library of Congress.

federal troops. Porter traveled to Brownsville with a relieved Ford and Stoneman to make final preparations and also urged Hill once more to abide by the agreement endorsed by Twiggs. [10]

Stoneman intervened one last time to ensure a peaceful evacuation. McLeod sent a note to Ford on March 4, 1861, declaring that his troops at Brazos Santiago could hear artillery being fired at Fort Brown and assumed that it was in honor of the inauguration of Lincoln. McLeod's Texans, who had voted unanimously for secession, regarded this as a "menace" and an "insult," and McLeod begged Ford to reply "that the firing of today is not of an insulting or hostile character to the State, or your Regiment will be in full march on tomorrow to settle the question with the US Troops in the field." Stoneman responded quickly and satisfactorily to an inquiry from Ford, who in turn assured McLeod that any gunfire was part of a daily drill and not a salute to Lincoln. Furthermore, the evacuation was proceeding smoothly. When the last Federals left Brownsville on March 21, 1861, Ford watched them go with mixed feelings. He was pleased, but also sad to think that he might have to fight friends some day. At the same time, he was proud of having avoided a fight. On March 7 he boasted to John C. Robertson, chair of the Committee on Public Safety, that Texas might secede without a war, adding, "If it is revolution, it is thus far a bloodless one, and challenges the world for a parallel." Ignoring Stoneman's key role in events, as well as Nichols and even McLeod, Ford declared, "I have used every effort to avert civil war, and shall feel to have done the country a service if in the slightest degree I have been instrumental in preserving peace." Of course, a peaceful evacuation persuaded those Federals who wanted to join the Texas cause to do so, and Ford briefly put Nolan in charge of a camp for them.[11]

Despite Ford's requests for a continuation of enlistments, his force at Brownsville was quickly reduced, and the men who remained were often troublesome. Both Terry and McLeod resigned by mid-March, leaving to seek more prominent assignments far from Texas. Nichols, ill, left for Galveston on March 13, 1861, taking with him a third of Ford's force to be discharged, along with most of the small arms taken at Brazos Santiago and Brownsville. Many of Ford's recruits, especially those enlisted at Helena and Seguin by Littleton, had been members of the Knights of the Golden Circle, and they apparently wanted a battle to replace the one that Ford had avoided. On the other hand, the Davis Guards of Houston, who were principally of Irish descent, refused to board the *Union* for the trip from Galveston to Brazos Santiago, declaring it to be unsafe, and once there they balked at leaving their quarters, arguing that their new billets were inferior. McLeod in a fury declared the mutinous company disbanded before he departed, but Ford rescinded the order, and the Davis Guards remained in service for the duration of the war, although not with Ford.[12]

Ford lost his temper with at least one of his captains. He wrote to his adjutant, Joseph E. Love, in mid-March about William Edwards, who claimed not to have enough rations for his men. Ford exploded, "With wagons for transportation, pen and ink, and the capacity to write his name, or his command[,] it will be something peculiar if Capt. E. cannot keep his company supplied for the few days it is expected to remain near the Brazos." Warming to his subject, Ford added, "It is not possible, at present, to procure a supply of feather beds and night glasses for delicate and hysterical gentlemen who cannot 'keep up' with rough camp fare. If they can manage to live a while longer, perhaps the convention may, in mercy, restore tranquility to their disordered nerves by sending down a few hotels with a full supply of the articles required to give peace to their troubled minds, rest to their wearied bodies, and in that may preserve them from horrible deaths." He concluded his letter with a quote from Alexander Pope's *Essay on Man:* "Meantime beg them not to 'die of a rose in aromatic pain.'" Edwards continued to provoke Ford, demanding a leave of absence and accusing his commander of being rude when he did not answer. Ford responded sarcastically: "The receipt of your two communications burdened with jeremiads is acknowledged. Some people have real sorrows, others invent their own griefs and simulated misfortunes. Your official correspondence is a tissue of complaints and personal matters which do not affect the public interests. Through my instrumentality you were made a captain and my appointment made you a major, yet you are not satisfied. Your vaunting ambition accuses me of not having placed you high enough. Would general of division suit you?"[13]

Despite the annoyances, Ford remained with his troops at Brownsville. He made Fort Brown his headquarters and posted the remaining members of his command as five companies along the Rio Grande. The convention on March 18 created the Second Texas Mounted Rifles and appointed Ford as its colonel, with John R. Baylor as his lieutenant colonel. The legislature provided funds and authorized the discharge of Ford's original troops, expecting that many of them would simply join the new regiment. In turn, the state, which had joined the Confederacy, offered Ford's regiment for Confederate service. This transfer was accepted by late May, and so Ford believed himself to be a Confederate colonel. When Brig. Gen. Earl Van Dorn, who had the responsibility for interpreting the tangled assignments of units as commander of the District of Texas, addressed the issue of what to do with Ford, he ordered the Texan to move his troopers to the Rio Grande line beyond Laredo, leaving Brownsville to be defended by infantry under Ford's distant command. Rather than comply, Ford left the direction of his companies in the far west to Baylor, who had ambitions for an invasion of New Mexico, and stayed at Fort Brown. The infantry never arrived, and Van Dorn was called east before he could insist on Ford's relocation. Thus the Second Texas Cavalry, as Ford's regiment was known in Confederate nomenclature, effectively divided into two parts under Ford and Baylor.[14]

Ford never fully explained why he refused to leave Brownsville in 1861. He wrote cryptically in his memoirs: "Circumstances compelled Colonel Ford to remain on the lower Rio Grande . . . This state of affairs requires no comment. It speaks for itself." In truth, on March 31, 1861, ten days after the Federals departed, Ford married Adeline N. Smith, his third wife, in the Presbyterian church at Brownsville. At the age of forty-six (she was twenty-three), Ford started a new family. The couple had a daughter in August 1862, and a second daughter in July 1864. "Addie," as everyone apparently called Ford's third and last wife, had strong ties to Brownsville, where both of her parents still resided as well as her older brother, William, and younger sister, Mary Louise. William suffered from a lung disease that would claim his life in January 1864. Ford also had to be concerned about family matters in the Austin area, where his elderly father lived and his daughter from his first marriage, Fannie, married William G. Thomas, a quartermaster officer, in 1863. Obviously the "circumstances" keeping Ford from riding west included concerns for family, both his and Addie's.[15]

There were of course military matters that concerned Ford at Brownsville. After the Federals left, many people feared that Indians would increase their raids in the region. Stoneman gave all of his company's weapons to Ford upon the latter's "touching appeal" for "the means of keeping the scalping-knife from the heads of the people at and near Brownsville." Nichols concluded a report to Ford from Galveston with the admonition, "Do look after the rascally Indians." After receiving a plea for protection from residents in Corpus Christi, Ford dispatched Littleton and Nolan in pursuit of Indian raiders who killed more than two dozen people along the Nueces and Frio rivers in late March 1861. Littleton led his troops west and found many abandoned ranches. He talked with settlers who repeated rumors of impending attacks but encountered no Indians.[16]

While his subordinates chased Indians, Ford turned his attention to Fort Brown. He believed that a Union fleet would soon attempt to land on the Texas coast, perhaps at the Rio Grande, and that Juan N. Cortina would resume his destructive raids as well. He wrote to Edward Clark, who replaced Houston as governor after secession, that to remove troops from Brownsville "would be a blunder of the worst imaginable character." Ford's concern increased after news arrived of Fort Sumter's surrender, which swept away any illusions that secession could be accomplished peacefully. He conferred with some of his officers and local leaders, and they decided that Brazos Santiago could not be defended. It was too exposed to fire from Federal warships, had no guns large enough to defend against an invading fleet, had no good sources of fresh water, and was too difficult to supply. Ford reported his decision to Nolan: "We shall repair Old Fort Brown and hold this point or leave many a bone to attest the pertinacity and desperation of our defence [*sic*]." He penned a more dramatic letter to Clark two days later, declaring that if the Federals landed at Brazos, "Their march [to Brownsville] shall be no holiday parade. I shall hold Fort Brown as long as I can offer resistance. Do not think however, that we have the most distant idea of not being able to beat back the Black Republican hordes, who would come sword in hand to force a President upon us elected in violation of the spirit of the Constitution, and as an enemy to the constitutional rights of the South."[17]

Fort Brown required a lot of hard work to prepare for a defense. Ford's troops, encouraged by liberal rations of whiskey left behind by the Federals, rebuilt and repaired the eroded earthworks. Extensive renovations to other structures included the creation of a bombproof magazine. Israel B. Bigelow—a New England Yankee who had arrived in Texas as a soldier during the Mexican War and stayed to served in the Texas Senate (with Ford) and as a county judge and first mayor of Brownsville—hired Mexican laborers and directed them in clearing the brush from the walls to create an open field of fire. Cannon were hauled from Brazos Santiago, increasing the fort's complement to twenty. A flag was sewn by a group of women led by Bigelow's wife, Mary, and Bigelow presented the banner to Ford, who raised it over the fort. By late April Ford learned that the secession of Virginia had changed the focus of Federal operations, removing Texas from the list of immediate targets, but he continued the work on Fort Brown, completing the project during the first weeks of May 1861.[18]

While watching for Federals, Ford also tried to cultivate good relations with Mexicans. He issued a proclamation on March 6 to explain his perspectives on national events to residents on both sides of the river. The United States government, he wrote, was just an "agent of the sovereign States which are a party to the Constitution." That agent "failed to . . . exercise properly the powers thus delegated," while a president was elected "in accordance with the forms of the Constitution" but "upon principles violative of its plain intent and spirit." Because this president intended to trample upon the rights of people in the slave states, Texas had resumed the portion of its sovereignty it granted to the United States and once more became a "free, sovereign, and independent power." Ford predicted that Texas would soon join the Confederacy, but he assured his readers that Texas intended to avoid civil war and protect the rights of everyone. For Mexicans, who were just emerging from their own revolution with the entry of Benito Juárez into Mexico City in January 1861 and his election as president in March, much of this rhetoric must have sounded familiar. Rumors flew that Ford intended to invade Mexico, but he followed his proclamation with orders to his troops not to cross the Rio Grande and not to molest civilians. Not all of them obeyed. Some of troublesome Major Edwards' men crossed the river to Camargo, were arrested, and were rescued in a manner that brought a reprimand from Ford. He wrote to Edwards: "We are at peace with the government of Mexico. It is the policy of the Confederate States to remain so. Every act endangering our amicable relations with that government is in disobedience to the known wishes of our rulers, and prejudicial to our interests." Edwards was told to treat Mexican officials with respect, and to keep his men from crossing into Camargo again.[19]

Ford's efforts to maintain peace on the Rio Grande were suddenly interrupted by Antonio Ochoa in Zapata County. Ochoa, a rancher and supporter of Cortina, called for a revolt against allegedly corrupt local officials on April 12, 1861. He gathered more than fifty Tejano and Mexican followers, then delivered a proclamation denouncing Anglos and the Confederacy to County Judge Isidro Vela, one of the political leaders who had delivered a unanimous vote for secession in Zapata County. Vela persuaded most of the rebels, including Ochoa, to return home, but some clashed with Major Edwards' troopers, prompting Henry Redmond, another pro-secession leader, to write to Ford for help. Ford, who had visited Redmond's ranch as a Ranger officer ten years earlier, believed Cortina was behind the entire affair, and he told two of his captains, Nolan and Santos Benavides, to provide any aid requested by the authorities of Zapata County. He was particularly explicit to Nolan, who had campaigned under him previously: "If the parties resist the execution of a civil process, or have embodied with the intention to defy the law, they are public enemies, and should be treated accordingly." Ford further explained his legalistic perspective on Ochoa's challenge to Redmond: "The authority of the Convention is the paramount authority in the State—It represents the people in their sovereign capacity and all power is inherent in them. Resistance to the Convention is treason to the State of Texas, and if these persons have arms in their hands, they must be treated as public enemies, or if they purpose resisting the present State Government it is sufficient to justify ulterior measures to prevent them from consummating their design."[20]

Ford need not have bothered with his long-winded justification to Redmond. By the time his orders reached Zapata County, matters had already come to a bloody climax. Nolan had been informed on April 13 by John D. Mussett, deputy collector of customs at Carrizo and an ally of Vela and Redmond, that fifty-two men had organized to prevent officials from taking the Confederate oath of allegiance and possibly to take funds and property belonging to those who supported the Confederacy. Nolan led twenty troopers to Carrizo, where he met with Mussett, Redmond, and Vela, who issued an arrest warrant for the fifty-two alleged conspirators. Nolan escorted Vela and Sheriff Pedro Díaz to a ranch where twenty of the rebels had gathered. Arriving about daylight on April 15, the sheriff ordered the Mexicans to surrender, which a "few of them" did. But one allegedly fired at Nolan's men, "and then—all tried to make their escape." In the ensuing melee, nine of the Mexicans were killed and two wounded. Doubt later surfaced as to whether the Mexicans, who may have gathered at the ranch to surrender themselves, fired first, but Ford warmly praised Nolan in his official report of the affair to Governor Clark. To the former Ranger himself Ford wrote, "Your conduct in quelling the Zapata rebellion is highly praise-worthy. You acted with prudence, activity, and propriety; and I think you did good service."[21]

Nolan reported to Ford that his attack settled matters in Zapata County, but he warned that Ochoa had escaped to Mexico and might return. He proved correct in his latter concern when Ochoa allied with Cortina in early May and crossed the Rio Grande with forty men. Vela fled with his family to Redmond's ranch, whence they sent another call for help. Nolan had left Laredo, traveling east with his troops, and was in Rio Grande City when the alarm was raised. The responsibility thus fell on Benavides at Laredo to confront the raiders. Cortina with reinforcements surrounded Benavides at Redmond's ranch and, under a flag of truce, asked Benavides to withdraw and leave Redmond and his allies to fend for themselves. This of course Benavides refused to do. His courier reached Laredo, and reinforcements hurried upriver under the command of Basilio and José del Refugio Benavides, the uncle and older brother, respectively, of the besieged Confederate. The Laredo contingent encountered Cortina's outposts on the morning of May 22, 1861. Both Cortina and Santos Benavides joined the fight with more men; the result was a rout of the raiders, nine of whom were killed. Cortina and Ochoa escaped to Mexico while Benavides executed eleven more of their men whom he had captured.[22]

Ford again praised his subordinate for the harsh measures taken in Zapata County, rather than reprimanding him for executing prisoners. While complimenting Benavides for his "judgment, ability, and gallantry" in the affair, Ford added that "you and the people of Webb county have furnished indisputable evidence to the world of your devotion to the cause of true, constitutional liberty." He repeated his praise in a report to Governor Clark, who did not respond with any chastisement himself. Perhaps the reason lay in Ford's assertion in early May, as unrest resurfaced once more in Zapata County, that "bold measures" were often the most effective, and that "Mexico can be awed easier than persuaded." Ford promised he would not cross the Rio Grande to get Cortina, as it would be a "great harm" to the South to "cause a needless war," but he pledged to beat him if he came to the Texas side of the river. When Clark apparently approved and even praised the actions taken in Zapata County, Ford took the opportunity to insist that Cortina was not yet finished, and that he probably was supported by Unionists and Federal agents. Cortina's men in fact continued to take potshots at Americans, and Donelson captured several men accused of being Cortina's followers at Las Cuevas and hanged one for his involvement in the killing of two Americans. Others who claimed to be under Cortina's command raided along the Rio Grande, killing and stealing cattle and horses. By the late summer, Cortina had worn out his welcome with authorities on both sides of the river, and so he disappeared into central Mexico again.[23]

Ford's battles with Cortina fortunately did not seem to endanger his relationship with a much more important figure: Gen. Guadalupe García, who commanded Mexico's defensive forces on the lower Rio

Grande from his headquarters at Matamoros. Ford met with García as early as February 25, 1861, to assure him that no threat was intended by the Texans. García responded in a friendly manner, and he later cooperated in efforts to recover stolen livestock. Van Dorn in late May complimented Ford on his success in securing such influential friends south of the border. After Cortina's raid into Zapata County, García offered to aid Benavides in "breaking up the lawless bands which have invaded" Texas from the area around Guerrero. Ford allowed Benavides to cross the Rio Grande to work with García, but he warned his subordinate to be careful because what was afoot might be "revenge for the beating you gave Cortina." Ford added, "If they should I shall take bloody vengeance for the deed, but that would not bring you and your gallant men back. We need you and them. Don't let them get the advantage of you." Perhaps Ford was recalling March 1860, when Cortina's men fought alongside Mexican militia after preparing an ambush that failed to catch Ford. García's subsequent efforts to confront Cortina and Ochoa convinced Ford that his new ally was sincere this time, if not entirely effective in suppressing the raiders. García ultimately met with Cortina and was influential in convincing him to leave the border.[24]

García actually had good reason to mistrust Ford, though the latter would not have seen it that way. Ford in a letter to Governor Clark in mid-July 1861 graciously praised García and other Mexican authorities for their assistance in what Ford referred to as the "Second Cortina War." But the Texan felt compelled to add that "I shall always believe the logic of the guns at Fort Brown, and the rifles that sounded the note of welcome to the traitors and invaders, convinced them of the necessity of this step." Because he did not trust Mexican officials to behave properly without the presence of a military threat, he once more repeated that it would be unwise for him to leave Brownsville. Having made it clear that he did not entirely trust Mexican leaders, he revealed why they should not have complete faith in him. He had maintained good relations with Mexican authorities because a "policy of peace and justice will do more towards bringing Mexican states into the Confederacy than many heavy Battalions." Even as he worked for the security of the Confederacy, Ford still had the mindset of a Texas filibusterer.[25] He was certainly not the only Southerner considering the annexation of northern Mexico, but ironically his ideas would lead to actions that undercut his support among the Confederate leadership.

By the late summer of 1861, Ford and his troops spent their time chasing Mexican raiders and escaped prisoners, and still trying to improve Fort Brown. Rumors flew of hostile Mexicans and disloyal Tejanos alike conspiring to cooperate in a Federal invasion of the Rio Grande area. This situation did nothing to improve Ford's mood, and he began to complain about the lack of support being given to his command. He had already been sharply criticized for ordering the Cameron County tax collector in June 1861 to give him all of the funds in his possession, claiming there was no other way to support his troops. Ford became convinced that there was a "plot to slander and disguise me," as he wrote to his old comrade Oran M. Roberts in late September 1861. He admitted that his reports to Van Dorn and Clark had never brought criticism from either man, but he worried about their associates, especially the governor's. As Ford explained curtly to Roberts, "The small fry officials of San Antonio were exceedingly active in circulating falsehoods and condemning me upon orders originating only from their prolific imaginations." Clark's silence only served to convince Ford that he was right. Brig. Gen. Hamilton P. Bee, then in charge of the militia on the Texas coast, did arrange for an English steamer to sell its cargo, which included food, to Ford's Confederates, and then to carry hides to Havana to be swapped for guns, but a storm sank the ship near the mouth of the Rio Grande as Ford fumed.[26]

Ford was right to fret about Clark's allies, especially Charles G. T. Lovenskiold. Van Dorn before leaving Texas had demanded that the transfer of Ford's regiment from state to Confederate service be completed, and Lovenskiold arrived in September 1861 as the agent of the state to muster out Ford's men. He declined any help from Ford, and in fact was dangerously candid and even critical of him in his reports to the governor. In one of his letters, Lovenskiold said Ford's troops were hungry and had been "reduced almost to nakedness," while Ford spent much of his time in bed sick with a fever. He admitted that Ford's command was as good as any in "military discipline and behaviour [*sic*]," and

Hamilton P. Bee. Lawrence T. Jones III Collection, Southern Methodist University.

he agreed with Bee that more reinforcements and supplies should be sent to Brownsville, but he also asked Clark to send a "competent and reliable officer" to assess the situation, implying that those were two qualities Ford lacked. Lovenskiold quickly completed his mustering out at Fort Brown, but he stayed in Brownsville for months as the process took longer for units scattered at other posts. By November, he was writing to a new governor as Francis R. Lubbock succeeded Clark in Austin. The last company to be transferred was that commanded by Santos Benavides at Laredo in January 1861, by which time serious questions had been raised about the condition of Ford's command.[27]

Ford always suspected that Henry E. McCulloch was part of his problem with getting support, for good reason, but Ford also became a target for another ambitious officer, Bee. When Ford had been given command of the Rio Grande line in February 1861 by the convention, McCulloch had taken charge of the northern frontier of Texas. Ford later became the colonel of the Second Texas Mounted Rifles, while McCulloch took command of the First Texas Mounted Rifles, and both men became Confederate colonels when their regiments became the Second and First Texas Cavalry, respectively. When Van Dorn departed, McCulloch briefly served as the acting commander of the Department of Texas. As such he angrily reported that "considerable confusion" existed in Ford's regiment because of the divided manner in which it was led, with Ford at Brownsville and Baylor in the west. Frustrated at the lazy manner in which many reports had been submitted while demands for support seemed to multiply rapidly, McCulloch vented his frustration on Ford, declaring that he had no reliable information on the location of his companies. Bee was somewhat more generous in his comments on what Ford had done at Brownsville, where Bee found Fort Brown in good shape with twenty-five pieces of artillery and a garrison of four companies, but he declared that the fort's location made it of little use in defending the city or its vital trade with the outside world. Ford certainly noticed that by the spring both McCulloch and Bee had become Confederate brigadier generals, while his own military career appeared to be in jeopardy.[28]

Ford finally did get reinforcements in the late fall of 1861, when two companies from the Third Texas Infantry, commanded by his old comrade Philip N. Luckett, arrived along with a light battery. Luckett's arrival allowed Ford to take an overdue furlough, after which Ford returned to duty with an assignment from McCulloch as the commander of the Western Sub-District of Texas. Ford once more commanded all troops on the Rio Grande line, as he had a year earlier under the instructions of the convention. This time, in accordance with the wishes of McCulloch, and perhaps in response to more negative reports from those who had commanded at Brownsville during his furlough, Ford proved more dutiful in reporting his strength and unit locations. He had 33 officers and 369 men present for duty in early 1862 at Fort Brown, with another 102 soldiers sick or otherwise not eligible for duty and 62 absent. At his other posts he had a total of 15 officers and 296 men present, with 19 more not on duty and 72 absent. Luckett's complement had grown to six companies and there were four artillery companies, though like Ford's units most of them were not at full strength.[29]

During March 1862 Ford received instructions from McCulloch to do something to counteract the Federal blockade of the Rio Grande. When Ford occupied Brownsville in 1861, he had welcomed all trade through the river port. The Confederate Congress, at Pres. Jefferson Davis' request, embargoed the shipment of cotton from southern ports but specifically exempted the export of cotton to Mexico. As a result, the Rio Grande became the focus of much commerce. But on the first day of February 1862, a Federal blockader, the USS *Portsmouth,* settled at the mouth of the river, interrupting the flow of ships under Confederate registry. Mifflin Kenedy, Richard King, and Charles Stillman—Ford's former sponsors during the brief rebellion led by José María de Jesús Carvajal in 1851—owned the principal steamboat line on the Rio Grande. They experimented briefly with operating under the British flag, but in March 1862 Ford approached them with an idea. Through an arrangement with Santiago Vidaurri, strongman ruler of the northern Mexico states of Nuevo León and Tamaulipas, they could register their ships as Mexican, which would exempt them from the blockade under

Mifflin Kenedy. Daniell, *Personnel of the Texas State Government, 1892.*

the terms of the Treaty of Guadalupe Hidalgo. In other words, while British and French support for the Confederacy remained uncertain, the partners could take advantage of Ford's good relations with Mexico. Some such as Stillman grumbled about having to sail under a flag emblazoned with a "turkey buzzard," but the scheme worked. Trade blossomed at Brownsville, as well as Matamoros on the other side of the Rio Grande and Bagdad, a town that developed at the mouth of the river. Matam-

Richard King. Daniell, *Personnel of the Texas State Government, 1892.*

Santiago Vidaurri. Prints and Photographs Division, Library of Congress.

oros became in effect an extension of Brownsville, through which the Confederacy traded with Mexico, the Caribbean world, Europe, and even the northern United States, swapping cotton for much-needed supplies.[30]

Ford's trade scheme did not proceed without some protest from Federal officers and even a few Confederates. Lt. Charles Hunter, whose USS *Montgomery* took the place of the *Portsmouth* at the mouth of the Rio Grande, sent a note ashore on April 29, 1862, demanding the surrender of Confederate forces along the river and threatening to bombard their positions if they did not capitulate. In response, on April 30 from Fort Brown Ford sent a defiant note expressing his regret that he could not fight the Federals "on the sea" and inviting them all to come ashore, where they would be "met as brave men ever meet the invaders of their soil, who come to execute the edicts of a despotic government." Ford prudently withdrew his outposts from Brazos Santiago in preparation for the Federals' response, but neither a bombardment nor a landing ensued. The next protest came when Luckett, who took charge of Fort Brown after Ford's removal in May 1862, complained that the registry scheme did not allow Confederate officials to control the ships. Asked to comment, Ford pointed out that the steamships actually belonged to civilians and thus should not be under the control of Confederate officers, that Mexican registration protected them from the Federals, and that these ships often carried cargo intended for the Confederacy. He heard no more about the matter.[31]

Ford's efforts to maintain peace along the Rio Grande and promote trade along the river brought mostly praise from his superiors, but his inability to avoid becoming personally involved in border diplomacy led to his removal from command. This was particularly ironic because Ford himself in July 1861, after deposed Mexican president Ignacio Comonfort had passed through Brownsville and Laredo on his way back into Mexico, had "cautioned Capt. Benavides and other officers to have nothing to do with Mexican revolutions." The Confederates tried to establish relations with Benito Juárez and sent John T. Pickett to Mexico City, but Juárez believed the Southerners were too expansionistic and made clear his support for the United States. Frustrated authorities in Richmond decided to rely more on local leaders, and Vidaurri was the most dominant in northern Mexico. Vidaurri had done little in response to Confederate protests about the Cortina raid during May 1861, but a few months later José A. Quintero, a Cuban-born resident of Texas, arrived on the Rio Grande as the Confederacy's "commissioner" to Vidaurri, whom he had known for several years as a friend. Initially matters went well—Vidaurri promised his support and even proposed joining the Confederacy with the states that he controlled, a Texan filibuster dream that Richmond authorities politely declined. More important to Ford, Quintero reported to Secretary of State Robert M. T. Hunter that Ford, who like Quintero had supported filibusters in Cuba less than a decade earlier, was doing a splendid job and should retain command on the border.[32]

Ford's troubles began when the Juárez regime once more came under attack from within. Jesús de la Serna won an election as governor of Tamaulipas in the fall of 1861, but his opponent Cipriano Guerrero refused to accept these results and called for a revolt. When General García declared for Guerrero, Serna attacked him at Matamoros and was repulsed, whereupon Ford allowed Serna and his men to take refuge on the Texas side of the Rio Grande. Reports surfaced that Cortina might be among Serna's supporters, but Serna turned to José María de Jesús Carvajal—Ford's former commander and a friend of King, Kenedy, and Stillman—for military support. Serna prepared for another attack on García, who asked Ford to speak to Carvajal. Ford did so, but when his friend refused to negotiate, Ford at his request reviewed Carvajal's forces and advised him to attack García at once, before desertion and disease reduced his army as it had in 1851. Carvajal instead besieged Matamoros until he was driven away by Vidaurri, who had been appointed by Juárez as the military commander of Tamaulipas in addition to his duties as governor of Nuevo León. Once again Ford allowed the defeated Mexicans to take refuge in Texas while Vidaurri consolidated his hold south of the Rio Grande.[33]

The turbulence on the far side of the river disrupted the flow of trade and supplies through Brownsville, which concerned Confederate authorities. Ford assumed the defeat of Carvajal at Matamoros would settle matters, and to pacify Mexican leaders he ordered all of his former commander's troops to surrender their arms to Luckett. Both Serna and Vidaurri demanded that Luckett give the weapons to them, but Carvajal intervened when Ford returned from leave. Describing his forces as men "who peaceably sought refuge in your state from the persecution of a lawless and savage foe," Carvajal reminded Ford that the surrender of his small arms and two pieces of artillery was just a "temporary deposit." Ford apparently gave the weapons to him. Within a week Col. Julian Quiroga, who had earlier asked permission, as commander of the Mexican forces south of the Rio Grande, to cross the river and attack Carvajal as the Texans had once pursued Cortina into Mexico, complained that his forces were fired upon by "una partida de los bandidos que obedezen al traidor Carvajal." Ford sent detachments to investigate, one commanded by the trusted veteran Littleton, and they all reported that while shooting had occurred, the bullets flew both ways, and there was no evidence that the men in question were anyone but bandits with no clear allegiance, unless it was to Cortina.[34]

Reinforced and re-supplied, Carvajal raided several Mexican towns in April 1862, apparently using the arms returned to him by Ford as well as others provided by King, Kenedy, and Stillman. Vidaurri, incensed, asked for permission to pursue Carvajal into Texas, which Ford did not grant. In retaliation, Vidaurri doubled the tax on cotton and other goods being transported across the border, claiming he needed the money to bolster his defenses against Carvajal. Confederate authorities contacted McCulloch, who told Ford to give Vidaurri any arms taken from Carvajal, to stop anyone from providing aid to Carvajal, and to arrest any person who gave assistance to Carvajal for violating the laws against neutrality. Meanwhile, Vidaurri wrote to Governor Lubbock demanding that Carvajal be arrested and delivered to him. Understanding that meant certain execution, Ford warned his old friend, who escaped into central Mexico. He later joined the Juárez forces fighting the French, who invaded Mexico to establish a protectorate as part of the expansionistic schemes of Napoleon III.[35]

Vidaurri reduced his taxes in response to Confederate protests, but Ford was in trouble. Quintero, the Confederacy's representative with Vidaurri, reported to Governor Lubbock that he had spoken several times with Ford about maintaining friendly relations with the proper authorities in Mexico, especially Vidaurri, but his advice seemed to have little effect. Instead, Ford sent "threatening communications" to Mexican commanders engaged in fighting Carvajal's incursions, and he continued to allow Kenedy and others to supply Carvajal with weapons and other goods. Quintero explained Ford's previous relationship with Carvajal to Lubbock, and that Ford was the primary threat to "friendly relations" with important figures such as Vidaurri, who as a friend of the Confederacy would sustain its trade with Mexico. McCulloch agreed with Quintero that Carvajal had to be quashed, as did Bee, who took command of the Sub-District of the Rio Grande on April 24, 1862. Three days later Benavides, in response to orders from Bee, attacked and dispersed the main part of Carvajal's forces.[36]

Ford always thought that the decision to remove him came from Bee, but in fact the instructions came from much higher up the chain of command. It is correct that Bee ordered Ford in early May 1862 to San Antonio, where he was soon placed in charge of enforcing conscription in Texas while Luckett took command of the units at Brownsville. But it was President Davis who decided that Ford must be removed. Judah P. Benjamin, as the new secretary of state for the Confederacy, wrote to Quintero on the last day of April 1862, chastising him and Vidaurri for their "entire misunderstanding of facts." He informed Quintero that Ford had submitted reports and documents that indicated he had "given the most prompt and stringent order for the suppression of any acts on the part of Carvajal and his followers." Furthermore, Ford had sent several officers to check on the allegations of misconduct by Carvajal and his followers, and none seemed to be true. Nevertheless, to mollify Vidaurri and maintain good relations with him and all Mexico, Davis had "directed" that a higher ranking officer than Ford be assigned to the border. Benjamin did not mention it, but pressure for Ford's removal had also come from Texas leaders such as Congressman William P. Ochiltree, who was concerned that a war might erupt along the Rio Grande. Ford's loyal support for his revolutionary friend Carvajal had proven to be his undoing.[37]

Ford greatly resented losing his Rio Grande command, and that he had to leave a pregnant Addie in Brownsville when he went to San Antonio. Just a few months earlier, in January 1862, he had received a joint resolution of thanks from the Texas legislature for his services, and now he was an exile from the field.[38] Called once more to play the role of frontier defender, he had supervised a peaceful exodus of Federal forces from the Rio Grande and had crushed a challenge from his old foe, Cortina. He had also done his best, as he understood it, to cope with the ever-changing political factions in northern Mexico. Many Texans might agree with him, but not all, and his military future was in the hands of men whose political views did not entirely coincide with his perspectives. Having helped Texas leave the Union, Ford might have reflected upon the irony that he had been put aside by the new Confederacy that his beloved state had joined. For a man determined to emulate his revolutionary grandfathers, it must have been painful to recall that neither of them had ever been removed from command.

CHAPTER 5 PHOENIX

Removed from command on the Rio Grande, Ford appeared to be doomed to obscurity, especially after he lost his commission as a Confederate colonel. But his great popularity among Texans, and his frontier experience, led to a new opportunity from Maj. Gen. John B. Magruder, who took command in Texas after being exiled from the Army of Northern Virginia for his less-than-stellar performance in the Seven Days battles. Just as Magruder redeemed his reputation in Texas by recapturing Galveston, Ford triumphantly returned to Brownsville on the heels of a retreating Federal army. Once more called to the public stage, Ford won an improbable victory and restored his stature as a defender of Texas. He also proved conclusively that he was of the same "fighting stock" as his grandfathers who had fought and won the American Revolution.

Hard-pressed on many fronts, the Confederacy in the spring of 1862 enacted a draft, which was expanded in September to include white males from eighteen to forty-five years of age. Ford's popularity among Texans made him a good choice to be given the often controversial assignment of enforcing conscription in Texas. This became more imperative when Maj. Gen. Paul O. Hébert declared martial law in Texas, primarily with the intent of enforcing the draft. Hébert appointed Ford as superintendent of conscripts for Texas on June 2, 1862. Ford was also to command a conscript camp at Houston, but instead he established his headquarters in Austin, near where his father, William Ford, and daughter Fannie lived. His staff in the capital city included Capt. William C. Walsh, who had ridden alongside Ford in the secession parade at Austin in January 1861, before he was crippled at Gaines' Mill while leading a company in the Fourth Texas Infantry. Ford appointed enrolling officers for more than a hundred counties, while his former

John S. "Rip" Ford. Lawrence T. Jones III Collection, Southern Methodist University.

John B. Magruder. William Emerson Strong Photograph Album, Rare Book, Manuscript, and Special Collections Library, Duke University.

Paul O. Hébert. Prints and Photographs Division, Library of Congress.

surgeon for the Second Texas Cavalry, William J. C. Rogers, served as his medical superintendent and selected physicians to inspect draftees in seventy counties. Other officers under Ford's authority staffed two training camps, one at Tyler and another near Austin. The latter was known as Camp Lockridge, while the former was named in Ford's honor.[1]

Ford recalled that many of his records were destroyed after the Civil War due to concern that Confederates involved in conscription might be prosecuted, so recounting his activities as superintendent of conscripts can be difficult. He issued a circular soon after taking office that delineated an aggressive program. Most Texas officials agreed with him, but the strong reaction of at least one state officer clearly revealed the wisdom of appointing a popular figure such as Ford to administer an unpopular program. John Sayles, a brigadier general of state troops in Bonham who had been a noted author and professor of law before the war, complained to Gov. Francis R. Lubbock that Ford's assertion of authority over enrolling officers, especially those appointed by state brigadier generals such as himself, was unlawful. Sayles added, "The authority of the State is Supreme. This question is politically of the last importance. It is the principle for which this war is waged & amid the din of arms, it should not be allowed to become dormant lest it should sleep a sleep that knows no waking—lest the principle for which the war is waged be lost in the contest." But rather than have the governor worry unduly about such matters, his agitated officer concluded, "Practically, I do not suppose that under the administration of Col. Ford, who is a Texan & a man of sound judgment & undoubted integrity, that the law will be oppressively enforced."[2]

Sayles proved correct. Ford sympathized with those who wanted to stay out of the war for good reasons, in part because he also resented the exemptions provided for wealthy slave owners. More important, he understood the need for manpower to defend the frontier and to sustain Texas' role as a source of supplies, especially cotton and beef. He was quick to exempt those whom he could under the draft laws, and even some whom he legally could not. He excused plantation overseers and suppliers of essential goods, and he endorsed a successful request to Lubbock from Mifflin Kenedy and his associates at Brownsville for exemptions based upon their efforts in supporting the garrison there. When Ed Burleson Jr. resigned his commission as a major, Ford secured a contract for his former lieutenant to procure horses for Simeon Hart, the erstwhile quartermaster at El Paso. Going beyond the law, Ford tried never to enroll Unionists into Confederate units for the simple reason that "the man of one party could not honestly serve in the ranks of the other." A Unionist recruit might desert and take information to Federal authorities. Among the prominent Unionists whom Ford protected was John Hancock, an Austin judge and legislator who opposed secession. He put Hancock's name on a list of men assigned to salt production near Austin, and later he allowed Hancock to slip away to safety in Brownsville, which was occupied by Federal troops in the fall of 1863.[3]

Ford's record was far from perfect with Texas Unionists, but he quietly shared their relief at the departure of Hébert and martial law. When Confederate units clashed with Hill Country Germans in August 1862, in what became known as the Nueces River Massacre, Ford had no comment then or later. He later apparently carried out the orders of a Confederate military court that convened at San Antonio to address the persistent problem of desertion in the region. Those orders were to return soldiers to their units, however, not to execute them. Concerning the most spectacular legal travesty in Civil War Texas, the Great Hanging at Gainesville in October 1862, Ford said nothing at the time but was more forthright later. Reflecting on that killing of more than forty men, he declared that "it was difficult to form a correct idea of the real character of the matter," although he admitted that it was a "deplorable affair" and was to be "regretted." He in fact was contacted by local leaders and asked to assign a partisan Ranger battalion to the area to disrupt the communications that they thought existed between Unionists in North Texas and Kansas, but they said nothing about possible arrests, much less executions. When he revised his memoirs, perhaps anticipating publication, he deleted his original words in favor of a brief declaration that he knew nothing about the event but was sorry that it occurred. Ford also remained silent when Confederate President Jefferson Davis annulled martial law in Texas on September 10, 1862, and then removed Hébert soon afterward, but he made his low opinion of his former superior quite clear in his memoirs with the comment: "if there was any place or spot in Texas which Gen. Hébert proposed to defend it was not made evident by his orders."[4]

Ford may have been unclear about events in the late summer and early fall of 1862 because he was distracted by the loss of his commission as a Confederate colonel. While he was serving on the Rio Grande, at least half of his regiment, the Second Texas Mounted Rifles, was involved in the futile effort by Texas Confederates to occupy New Mexico. Renamed the Second Texas Cavalry, the regiment received recruits and new companies until September 1862, when Brig. Gen. Hamilton P. Bee, as commander of the Sub-District of the Rio Grande, decided to complete the task of officially organizing the regiment, which had been assigned to him. This included making a final decision on who would be its commander. Ford publicly insisted that he had been appointed colonel by the Secession Convention and could not be dismissed, but privately he expressed grave concerns about his appointment as early as the late summer of 1861, when Charles G. T. Lovenskiold came to Brownsville to muster Ford's companies out of state service. At that time he survived what he later described as the "quirky accusations of a mustering officer," but Bee, who had issued the orders for his exile from the field in April 1862, was a more formidable foe. Elections were held during the first week of October over Ford's protests, and Lt. Col. Charles L. Pyron, who had commanded the companies in New Mexico, became the new colonel of the Second Texas Cavalry. Many years later, Ford wrote that his argument that his commission from the Convention could not be revoked "was perhaps not well founded." By November, Hébert's impending departure from Texas made it clear that Ford would be replaced as superintendent of conscripts as well.[5]

Ford's removal accelerated the efforts of those who wanted him to be promoted to brigadier general. The Texas delegation in the Confederate Congress wrote to Davis in late September 1862 asking for Ford's promotion. Texas Supreme Court Justice George F. Moore in November 1862 wrote to John H. Reagan, his fellow Texan who served as the Postmaster General of the Confederacy, asking him to intervene on

John H. Reagan. William Emerson Strong Photograph Album, Rare Book, Manuscript, and Special Collections Library, Duke University.

Ford's behalf. Reagan added his own endorsement when he forwarded Moore's letter to Secretary of War James Seddon. Ford's old friends at Brownsville—including Capt. Matt Nolan and Confederate collector of customs Francis W. Latham—wrote to the president before the year ended, asking that Ford be given both a Confederate commission and an assignment to the Rio Grande. More than sixty Texas legislators signed a petition to their delegates in Congress on February 2, 1863, asking them to renew their efforts to secure a brigadier general's star for Ford. At the same time, sixteen East Texas leaders sent a second note to Seddon, asking that Ford be promoted. None of these inquiries resulted in a promotion for Ford; perhaps his transgressions on the Mexican border in early 1862 were too well remembered in the Confederate White House.[6]

Magruder took charge of the District of Texas, New Mexico, and Arizona in late November 1862, and he initially appointed Maj. James P. Flewellen, a West Point graduate who had been appointed to work for Ford in September 1862, as the new commandant of conscripts. Flewellen quit within a few months, and so in March 1863 Magruder contacted Ford. The latter had already decided that he liked the general, who had also fought in the Mexican War and chased Comanches. While Magruder had not done well with the Army of Northern Virginia, he had a reputation as a hard fighter that was borne out by his recapture of Galveston from the Federals on New Year's Day 1863. Magruder appointed Ford as commandant of conscripts on March 21, but there was a problem: Ford had no commission. Magruder sent a series of letters to Lt. Gen. Edmund Kirby Smith, commander of the Department of the Trans-Mississippi, asking that Ford be commissioned as a colonel, and Ford himself visited Smith, but Smith only confirmed Ford's appointment as commandant. Richmond authorities again failed to act on a request to confer a military rank on Ford, although Magruder paid him as a colonel. Rumors circulated that Ford had a commission—Magruder had to reassure Bee in June 1863 that Ford had not been promoted to brigadier general and was not being sent to replace Bee on the Rio Grande. But in fact Ford had lost his Confederate commission, and he would never have another.[7]

Edmund Kirby Smith. Prints and Photographs Division, Library of Congress.

Magruder usually gave his subordinate commanders wide latitude in carrying out their tasks in Texas, but he asked Ford to become more diligent in enforcing conscription as a swelling tide of deserters threatened to undermine Confederate authority. To make matters even more complicated, state officials also divided bitterly over the draft. The Texas Supreme Court endorsed conscription, but Governor Lubbock and his successor, Pendleton Murrah, protested enrollment efforts that reduced the state's ability to defend its own borders. Ford strongly supported the Confederacy, but he agreed that Texas had a responsibility to protect its frontier citizens. As he wrote to a supporter in March 1863, "Cost what it may the pioneer settlers must be protected." Lubbock in September 1863 asked for exemptions for all those willing to serve in frontier defense units. Brig. Gen. Elkanah B. Greer, director of conscription for the Department of the Trans-Mississippi, responded with a denunciation of the practice of enrolling recruits into state units rather than Confederate commands, which he said created "confusion & dissatisfaction." Ford proved more amenable, declaring that the muster of frontier defense companies was "in accordance with the motives inducing me to furlough them until further orders." He added, "the proposed course meets my approbation." As for Greer, Ford remarked that "should the Brig. Genl. in control of the conscripts of this Military District call for these men they would have to respond but I am satisfied they will not be required to enter upon any other duty." This arrangement apparently satisfied Lubbock, who joined Ford and other speakers at a pro-war rally in late September 1863 at San Antonio, where hundreds enjoyed barbecue and a dance.[8]

The organization of camps around Austin by Unionists and others who opposed the Confederacy did alarm Ford, who asked for troops to confront the dissenters. He had futilely requested soldiers to defend the city during the summer of 1862, but Magruder in 1863 was more cooperative. He ordered Col. Edward J. Gurley with five companies of the Thirtieth Texas Cavalry to join Ford, but when that command was called to Arkansas he sent A. H. Davidson with his First Texas Cavalry Battalion. This was certainly more to Ford's liking, because it had been Gurley who argued with Ford over efforts to arrest Peter Garland and others for killing seven Indians in December 1858. Ford at the same time mustered three companies of local men, with the approval of Lubbock. In the late summer and fall of 1863 he sent them to capture or expel "jay-hawkers, deserters, and men of conscript age." The leaders of each detachment, who were usually successful, were authorized to use force, but in fact little blood was shed. Ford led some of the expeditions, with similar results. On one occasion, vigilantes approached one of the Unionist camps, intending to attack in retaliation for a murder committed in Gonzales County. Alerted, Ford led soldiers and citizens to the camp late at night, and somehow someone fired a gun not once but twice to awaken the Unionists, who escaped unscathed. Ford recalled with pride that "the plan formed to disperse the Unionists about Austin was productive of no bloodshed; no laws were violated, and no one was mistreated." He finally convinced Magruder not to press the Unionists, though the General may not have had much choice in the matter considering the attitude of his chief conscription officer in Texas.[9]

Ford's determination to avoid bloody conflicts in Texas led him to organize the Order of the Sons of the South with the assistance of his adjutant, Capt. John J. Dix Jr. Together they wrote a constitution and by-laws that included pledges to keep prices fair, provide aid to the dependents of indigent soldiers, and prevent military authorities from abusing civilians. Ford worried about clashes between soldiers who returned to Texas on furlough, often with the intent of redressing real or imagined wrongs, and prominent men who had avoided service and loudly criticized the military. His bylaws therefore stressed obedience to law, subordination of military to civilian control, and the supremacy of the constitution as an expression of the will of the people. To abandon these principles, Ford warned, was to become like the "Black Republicans" in violating well-established laws.

Unfortunately for Ford, enforcement of the draft continued to generate conflicts. His enrolling officers, who once angered Magruder by arresting three of his couriers, were part of the problem. Ford himself, while trying to muster forces to retake Brownsville, had to intervene twice to prevent them from taking his recruits. Others protested as well. Ford left enforcement of the draft in late 1863 to Walsh, who in a few weeks complained that "they are deviling my life out with Hab[eas] Corp[us] cases. I feel like I was being stung to death with piss-ants." Walsh signed his letter as "Your friend in a 'cussin' humor." Ford certainly understood, as both an enforcer and as a victim of overzealous enforcement.[10]

Ford might have spent the rest of the war on conscription duty if the Federals had not decided to invade Texas. After Union Maj. Gen. Nathaniel P. Banks' feeble seaborne probe was repulsed at Sabine Pass in September 1863, he launched an overland campaign through south Louisiana while sending a substantial force to occupy the Texas coast and the lower Rio Grande. President Abraham Lincoln was concerned about Confederate trade through the region and also wanted to prevent any cooperation between the French and the Confederacy, so he had overridden the objections of some of his primary officers and ordered a landing. Elements of the XIII Corps landed at Brazos Santiago on November 2, 1863. Other units soon disembarked and occupied Fort Brown within four days while Bee retreated from Brownsville. By the end of the month, Union forces held the Rio Grande from its mouth to Rio Grande City, as well as the Texas coast from the Rio Grande north to Matagorda Bay. Bee settled near Richard King's ranch to regroup, while Col. Santos Benavides withdrew west to Laredo. All Confederate goods bound for Matamoros, and from that town to the outside world, had to cross at Laredo or Eagle Pass, increasing the travel distance and cost, while much of the southern coast of Texas lay open to Federal raids.[11]

Supporters of the Confederacy along the Rio Grande called for Ford's return to the field to counter the Federal invasion, and Magruder responded by sending Ford to San Antonio to organize a defense. Capt. James A. Ware of the First Texas Cavalry asked that Ford be given command of an expedition, describing him to Magruder as an "officer with a known ability as a partisan leader with a knowledge of the country, and the people." Members of the legislature addressed a plea to Murrah, requesting that Ford be made a general in state service. At San Antonio, Maj. Andrew G. Dickinson, post commander and former chief of staff for his cousin Magruder in Virginia, urged Ford to organize an

Santos and Augustina Benavides. Collection of Hector Farias Jr.

expedition to the Rio Grande. In turn, Dickinson and Murrah sent letters to Magruder, adding support to the grassroots campaign for Ford. Magruder on December 19 sent instructions to Ford to raise as many companies as he could for a march on Brownsville, but he did not assign Ford to lead these units. Ford, fuming, fired a letter to Magruder on Christmas Day declaring that if he did not get a Confederate appointment, Murrah would certainly give him a state commission to retake Brownsville. Referring to Magruder's greatest victory in Texas, Ford declared, "There is no doubt of success. The results of an expulsion of the Yankees from the Rio Grande would be almost equal to those following the recapture of Galveston." He need not have blustered; on December 27, instructions arrived from Magruder for Ford to take charge of troops and anything else he needed to accomplish his mission. These orders had been written five days earlier.[12]

Ford announced his return to command with great gusto. He issued a ringing call to arms on December 27, asking, "Shall it be said that a mongrel force of Abolitionists, negroes, plundering Mexicans, and perfidious renegades have been allowed to murder and rob us with impunity? Shall the pages of history record the disgraceful fact, that Texians have tamely and basely submitted to these outrages, and suffered the brand of dishonor to be inflicted upon an unresisting people?" He answered with a charge: "For the honor of the State, for the sake of the glorious memories of the past, the hopes of the future, you are called upon to rally to the standard and to wash out the stains of invasion by the blood of your ruthless enemies." Ware had been one of the first to demand Ford's appointment, and Ford placed him in charge at San Patricio with firm orders: "You will explain to the people the great public necessity requiring them to aid their country in the arduous struggle for liberty, that should they withhold assistance and cause the expedition to fail, they will but reserve their wagons and teams, and other property for the heartless invaders, who have come to rob & enslave us, that the man who refuses to lend his services or the use of his property to the South in this perilous crisis can not be a friend to our cause." Ford concluded, "Tell . . . all my old friends to put their shoulders to the wheel—to work with body, mind, and soul for their homes, the protection of their families against insult and outrage, for the consecrated rights of freemen, and for a cause that is holy."[13]

Magruder in appointing Ford to command admonished him to keep his ultimate destination a secret. Ford initially told the general that his plans for taking Brownsville included a feint toward the coast and an announcement in newspapers that Indianola was the real target. But when potential recruits proved uninterested in recapturing Indianola, the truth somehow became public knowledge by early January 1864. Dickinson hurried to Magruder's headquarters to reassure him about Ford, who had also shifted from a plan that would force the Federals to attack him on ground of his own choosing to another that included an assault on Brownsville. Ford himself assured Magruder that "if activity, hard labor, and perseverance can achieve anything the expedition will be successful."[14]

Magruder had a much more important concern about Ford than a loss of secrecy. Ford still had no official commission. Magruder suggested to Murrah in December 1863 that he appoint Ford as a brigadier general in state service, with the intent of transferring him to Confederate rank. As he explained to the governor, "There is a question whether Colonel Ford is an officer at all at this moment, and I am embarrassed in ordering officers to report to him lest they may legally decline doing so." Two days later, Magruder asked Kirby Smith to appoint Ford as a colonel. He repeated this request several times, adding on December 24, "I have recognized him, he having already taken the field at the call of the people, who have confidence in him." Kirby Smith responded only by relieving Ford from his duties as superintendent of conscripts and ordering him to report to Magruder, but Murrah appointed Ford as a brigadier general of state troops on December 28, 1863.

Unfortunately, plans to transfer him to Confederate service fell through, and so in March 1864 Ford was officially assigned to command the state troops in District Number 1 of Texas. That same month Magruder made clear his opinion on Ford's rank in a letter to Col. James Duff of the Thirty-Third Texas Cavalry: "Colonel Ford has received the appointment of brigadier-general of State troops, and though I have not the authority to receive him into the Confederate service as such, his orders as such must be obeyed by all who are not of equal rank in the Confederate service." To confirm this, Magruder on April 27 issued a general order declaring Ford to be a "temporary" brigadier general in charge of the Western Sub-District, Bee's assignment at the time that he abandoned Brownsville.[15]

Magruder's appointment of Ford as a temporary general ended the conflicts over rank that initially plagued Ford as he labored to organize what he called the Rio Grande Expeditionary Force. One of the first to annoy Ford was Benavides, who had been given command of a border regiment to be mustered in Mexico as well as Texas. Ford praised Benavides for his efforts but also conveyed Magruder's instructions that Benavides was to obey Ford. Benavides did not respond at first, but by mid-January he assured Ford that he would follow his directions. Next was Duff, who tried to claim that Ford in fact had to obey him. As with Benavides, an appeal to higher authorities brought a resolution in Ford's favor. The most stubborn challenger was Col. Spruce M. Baird of the Fourth Regiment, Arizona Brigade. In February 1864, in response to orders from Ford, Baird led his men west, then refused to accept more instructions from Ford until the issue of rank was settled. When Ford asked Baird not to use his supplies until a resolution had been reached, Baird responded that he was "highly gratified" at the "prospect" of Ford becoming a brigadier general, but until Ford was "legally assigned to command in the service of the Confederate states over me," Baird would not accept his authority. Waxing eloquent, Baird recalled how he had fled from New Mexico and "sacrificed every thing I had on earth." With great hardship he had traveled "with a family of helpless children to the country and people I loved—as a matter of choice through a desert country of 1200 miles." He had personally recruited his regiment and therefore could "not regard it very generous, in any one who has had so many favorable opportunities, to try to root me out of my little obscure and as I thought undesirable field." Baird like Benavides and Duff lost his challenge, but unlike them he resigned rather than serve under Ford.[16]

Ford intended to strike quickly at Brownsville after taking command, but quarrels over authority proved to be just one of many problems that caused delays. He explained to Magruder in February 1864: "I have had serious obstacles to surmount—exhausted resources—a population almost drained of men subject to military duty—opposition from rivalry—and the relentless disagreeable retardations incident to an undertaking of this character." To assist him, Ford assembled an interesting staff. Maj. Felix A. Blucher, a grandnephew of Field Marshal Gebhard L. von Blücher of the Battle of Waterloo, served as his chief of staff. Blucher could speak five languages and knew the region between the Nueces River and the Rio Grande well because of his work as a surveyor, but he was unfortunately a drunk. Ford had to remove him in September 1864 "on account of his intemperate habits." Ford had better luck with Maj. Albert Walthersdorff, an "awesome giant" with tremendous strength who served as his tactical officer and trained Ford's troops in battlefield maneuvers through the end of the war.[17]

To the surprise of no one except perhaps Governor Murrah, Ford and his staff devoted almost no attention to organizing state troops; in fact, Ford asked that Dickinson be appointed in his place to command the militia in District Number 1. Instead, Ford and his officers scrambled to fill the ranks of the Rio Grande Expeditionary Force. Males who were normally exempt from the draft, especially youths, were welcome. Magruder ordered all unassigned conscripts to join Ford and sent commands from all over South Texas to him. The long list of units included Ware's battalion, Benavides' and Baird's regiments, Walthersdorff's two-company battalion, and companies led by men such as Capt. George H. Giddings, a former stage line operator who had previously worked as a contractor for the Army of Northern Virginia. The number of unattached conscripts was potentially significant as well; Thomas H. O'Callahan, provost marshal at San Patricio, reported to Ford in January 1864 that he had three or four hundred men ready to join if they could be assured that Ford would lead them. Magruder expected Ford to have 700 troopers. Estimates of his strength grew to three times that number by February 1864, but when Ford took the field in March he actually had 1,300 men with him.[18]

Ford respected few boundaries in his quest for recruits. He approached Murrah for companies assigned to the Frontier Regiment months before Magruder declared such men subject to Confederate service. He also contacted deserters in Mexico, promising to "do all in my power to procure a full pardon for past acts." If he failed to secure amnesty for them, he agreed that they would "be allowed to return as they came." He insisted they could be trusted; after all, "They have withstood the temptations of Yankee promises and Yankee gold." In his letter assigning John B. Davis to recruit deserters in Mexico, Ford appealed to more crass motives: "Now is a dark hour of trial with Texas, and they have voluntarily offered their services to aid in driving her cruel and heartless foes from her soil. I know they can have no sympathies, no interests, in common with the Yankees who have come to enslave and degrade the white and to free the negro and place him upon an equality with us. Would any one of them be willing to see his mother, his sister, or his daughter, led to the altar by an African upon whose head rests the degradation, the ignorance, of thousands of years of slavery and heathenism, and who has never shown any evidence of improvement? Would they be willing to see the homes consecrated by every recollection and every tie dear to man, desecrated, plundered, and finally sold to pay the immense debt the Yankees have contracted in order to make the Southerners their slaves? I feel sure they will answer these questions by the argument of the rifle and the bowie knife, as freemen ever respond to the call of their country." Many deserters did respond to this call, and Ford secured an amnesty for all who served with him.[19]

Ford's recruitment of deserters in Mexico encouraged many others to leave their units with the avowed intention of joining him. Most never arrived, but the commanders of other units became convinced that Ford's ranks were filled with their deserters and complained bitterly. Ford actually refused to accept such men. He carefully told each of his officers not to recruit soldiers from other commands, and even issued orders to arrest some deserters, but certainly a few of his subordinates, under pressure to complete their musters, arranged some unofficial transfers. Ford even issued a declaration in February 1864, in response to rumors that he would accept deserters who left other commands to join him, which said in part, "The man who deserts his post in presence of the enemy can expect no support or sympathy from me." He urged all such soldiers to return to their units and try by good service to "wipe from their names, and those of their children, the foul stain of desertion." Perhaps the most bittersweet reports were about men leaving his old regiment, the Second Texas Cavalry, to join his new command, but Ford held firm. The only exceptions were soldiers who secured official transfers, which Ford was willing to consider if there were compelling reasons. If not, their requests often met with a terse refusal. Ford certainly knew that his general stand against recruiting deserters was not always honored, and he even admitted as much to Brig. Gen. James E. Slaughter in July 1864, but he also recalled with pride that most who searched his ranks for deserters "seldom found the men they desired to see."[20]

Ford's amnesty program for deserters did not always work to his advantage. In February 1864, Giddings, who had been promoted to command a battalion, forwarded the resignation of William N. Robinson, one of his captains. Robinson, whose father fought at San Jacinto for Texas independence, had traveled to Texas from California when the war began, but his commitment to the Confederate cause had faded due to the chaos in Ford's command. Soldiers defied their officers or deserted and joined other units, and when challenged they declared that they should not be punished because they had been encouraged to act in such a manner by others. Giddings himself revealed that he was considering quitting as well, especially after five of his men robbed a wagon train and fled with their loot. Ford apparently convinced both officers to stay with him because they fought under his command at Palmito Ranch in May 1865, but it is hard to say how many of the enlisted men about whom they complained were still in the ranks as the war ended. The company of deserters raised by Davis in Mexico also drew angry complaints for their behavior, and their commanding officer had to be arrested in the fall of 1864. Not all were as grateful for a second chance as Ford expected them to be.[21]

Ford generally refused to pay "exorbitant sums" to entice recruits, but he made an exception for Mexican troops. From the beginning of his efforts to create the Rio Grande Expeditionary Force, he pressed Confederate authorities to provide him with specie, or cotton to be sold for specie, to entice Mexicans. He believed they would do well, but he needed to pay them to counter the allure of the money and equipment offered by Federal recruiters. Ford was even willing to consider the recruitment of his old nemesis, Juan N. Cortina, who had returned to Matamoros in the fall of 1863 with a military commission from Benito Juárez. By January 1864 Cortina had seized power and declared himself to be the governor of Tamaulipas. Federal authorities were courting him, and Ford did not want to fight both them and Cortina. He told Magruder through Dickinson that Cortina was "uneasy in Mexico, and anxious to live on this side." While he had been indicted in Texas, he had not been convicted, so no pardons were needed. If "assurances" could be given "that the indictments will be withdrawn," or a final decision would be made not to prosecute, then Cortina "will be with us." Ford added that his enemy's brother, José M. Cortina, "has already made overtures to that effect." While Ford continued to fret about Mexicans in Federal service, he was only able to enlist a small contingent, which never included his former quarry.[22] Part of this failure can be attributed to his lack of cash, but also many Mexicans preferred to join Benavides if they served the Confederacy at all.

Both Magruder and Ford found it difficult to enlist artillerymen. Texans wanted to be cavalrymen and, while they might grudgingly accept the ignominy of infantry life, they abhorred the mundane duties of a gunner. Ford was absolutely convinced that he needed artillery to take Brownsville. He found some cannon, including the famous Twin Sisters of San Jacinto, but the accoutrements and horses proved hard to obtain without a ready supply of cash, and few wanted to join a gun crew. In early February 1864 he asked for volunteers, declaring, "Those unprovided with horses and arms are hereby offered a fine opportunity of doing noble duty in the defense of their State, in what is considered the most agreeable arm of the service." Magruder tried offering furloughs, but Ford could not do that and conduct a campaign. He assigned one company from the Fourth Regiment, Arizona Brigade, to his guns, but when they balked he grumbled that if he actually forced anyone to serve "they will either desert or be inefficient." Magruder had Capt. H. H. Christmas send a two-gun section of his light artillery battery to Ford, but the horses died, the men deserted, and upon Christmas' request Magruder transferred what remained of his small detachment east, much to the distress of Ford.[23]

A lack of money contributed greatly to Ford's troubles in recruiting and equipping his forces, but that proved to be a riddle with no solution, as those along the Rio Grande, such as Benavides, already knew too well. Cotton could be traded easily for supplies in Mexico, but the low prices offered by Army officers seeking to buy or impress bales meant that they could not get sufficient quantities to trade. Ford demanded greater efficiency, arguing that military success must not be "sacrificed to a mis-called economy," but little could be done, in part because state and Confederate officials clashed with each other over jurisdictions. Ford sent copies of orders to Benavides forbidding the transfer of vital foodstuffs over the Rio Grande, but there were simply not enough troops to guard effectively against smugglers.

Ford learned from his associates in Matamoros that there were goods there to be had in exchange for cotton. He convinced John M. Swisher, his former paymaster for the Texas Rangers who had been removed as a state financial agent due to accusations of Unionism, to serve as his representative in Matamoros to acquire or tax cotton crossing into Mexico, and then use the proceeds to buy supplies. Santiago Vidaurri's decision to seize cotton entering Mexico through Eagle Pass in February 1864, in response to a dispute between his son-in-law Patricio Milmo and Confederate officials, made Laredo the principal gateway, and Benavides redoubled his diplomatic efforts to keep that pipeline open.[24]

While Ford struggled to find money to buy supplies, he also had to forge a system to convey goods to his troops. Nolan and others by March 1864 were complaining about lacking everything from guns to soap. Ford appointed Charles H. Merritt to be his chief quartermaster, then battled constantly with him and everyone else engaged in the process. When Lovenskiold, employed as a commissary agent, wrote, "Honestly, it seems to me the machinery is sadly out of gear somewhere," Ford responded that he did not expect "miracles" from him. He added, "I have a right to employ any man under my command in any way I see proper & you have no right to complain." Lovenskiold within a few days learned exactly what Ford meant when he was replaced with Dix as a commissary agent. Assistant Quartermaster Edward P. Alsbury also received a hostile communication from Ford: "I understand you have scruples of conscience concerning the impressment law. If so you ought to resign because the duties of your position require you to enforce the laws. This is no time to indulge in refinements of any kind." Even Merritt, who initially received praise from Ford, was under fire by April 1864. Early in the month, Ford was almost civil with his demands: "I am confident you have neglected nothing, yet we have no supplies—Where are they? For the sake of the cause, do send supplies." Three weeks later, Ford explained curtly, "I am taking steps to supply myself, come what may[,] but I would prefer having your assistance."[25]

Ford could berate or replace subordinates to improve his logistical system, but there was little he could do about another transportation problem: the weather. A severe drought plagued the region between the Rio Grande and the Nueces River in early 1864. Maj. Lieuen M. Rogers reported to Ford from the lower Nueces in February: "You can not immagine [*sic*] how desolate, barren, and desert like this country is; not a spear of grass nor a green shrub, with nothing but mooving [*sic*] clouds of sand to be seen on these once green prairies." Benavides described the upper Nueces as "dry for miles." It was scant consolation to Ford that the drought also prevented the Federals at Brownsville, who greatly outnumbered him, from taking the field. Searching for a solution, Ford tried camels, which had been brought to Texas as an experiment by the Army during the mid-1850s. He sent troops with camels from San Antonio to Guadalupe County, a fairly short distance, to retrieve corn, but two of the animals died on the trip. Apparently they needed grass and could not live on corn, which subordinates were gathering in anticipation of his campaign. Disappointed, Ford sent the camels into retirement and waited for rain.[26]

While the drought kept the Federals in Brownsville, Ford worried about threats from other directions. Rumors of a Union march from El Paso not only concerned him, but also led him to scheme of taking New Mexico. Encouraged by reports of Southern sympathizers in the mining camps of Sonora, Mexico, Ford proposed sending agents to recruit them for a march into New Mexico, in conjunction with a campaign from

North Texas to seize control of the road from Santa Fe to Independence, Missouri. When this failed to gain support, Ford settled for arguing that a defensive line should be established at the Devils River, far to the west of Eagle Pass. By late February 1864 Ford realized that the danger from El Paso was far less than that closer to home. He sent scouts to the Devils River, but he also reinforced Eagle Pass in response to rumors of an impending attack from Mexico. This proved prudent when his pickets there repulsed an attack by "renegades" on February 12. Elsewhere, state troops under Ford's command nervously watched for Indians, bandits, and deserters. While their most serious casualty occurred when Walthersdorff was severely bitten by an "unchained mastiff," Ford asked Magruder to declare martial law in the counties along the Rio Grande and send an "energetic, fearless, Provost Martial [*sic*]." Ford had learned that "the disloyal and the timid are leaving us," and he wanted "to check this tide of immigration before it becomes formidable." An efficient officer with the proper authority could protect the loyal and intimidate the disaffected, and thus remove another worry from Ford's long list.[27]

Ford's command embraced the coastal counties as well, where the Federal Navy supported more effective and deadly operations. Union raids on Corpus Christi during early 1864 forced him to dispatch the Fourth Regiment, Arizona Brigade, and several independent mounted companies to that area. Nolan, whose house was among those ransacked by the Federals, remained in the area after the alarm passed and watched in frustration as another Union force larger than his single company again landed in Corpus Christi in late March. He had more luck when he captured the son of Cecilio Balerio, a Mexican who led Unionist attacks on Confederate cotton, horses, and cattle around Corpus Christi, where he also lived. The son, Juan Balerio, led Nolan's Confederates to his father's campsite before daylight on March 13, but the young man managed to warn his comrades before Nolan could attack. In the ensuing firefight two of Nolan's men were killed, but the Balerios lost five before they escaped to Mexico, where they stayed for the duration of the war. Ford, who arrived in the area a few weeks later, congratulated Nolan, but it worried him that "appearances indicate that we shall have to fight the Mexicans as well as Yankees."[28]

Ford's primary concern remained Brownsville. During the first week of January, Union Maj. Gen. Napoleon J. T. Dana, commander of the XIII Corps, bragged that his defenses could withstand an assault by 5,000 men. His successor, Maj. Gen. Francis J. Herron, reported the next month that he had 3,015 infantry, cavalrymen, and artillerymen, with two black infantry regiments at Point Isabel with another 632 effectives. This was far more than Herron understood that Ford had, which was about 600 to 700 men, but Herron and others worried that Federal strength might be reduced as Ford recruited. At the same time, Ford received fairly accurate reports of Union dispositions at Brownsville, and so he fully realized his difficult position. To attack a numerically superior enemy settled in earthworks and supported by artillery seemed to be, as Herron boasted in April, a clear "impossibility."[29]

An attack on Brownsville might have appeared impossible, but Ford had been told to try, and Federal decisions gave him an opportunity. In late February and early March 1864 he finally acquired enough troops and supplies to attempt an advance, while at the same time Banks began withdrawing Union troops from Texas in response to orders from a new general-in-chief, Ulysses S. Grant. In truth, Banks did not protest much, because he could use the relocated units to support his Red River campaign in Louisiana. As he left San Antonio for Corpus Christi, Ford explained to Lt. Col. Daniel Showalter, who had succeeded Baird as commander of the Fourth Regiment, Arizona Brigade, that "the Yankees are of opinion the Expedition is a failure, and a quick move to the front will surprise them." Ford had been urging the high probability of success by a "sudden dash" for weeks; now he would get his chance. The drought had not yet ended, and some of his men still lacked proper arms, but Ford hoped the boldness of his move in tandem with Federal force reductions might yield him a victory.[30]

Benavides proved to be the first hero in Ford's drive on Brownsville. While Ford was camped near Corpus Christi, he received reports that several hundred Union cavalry had attacked Laredo on March 19, 1864. Although Benavides was quite ill, and his local force had been reduced by disease to seventy-two effectives, the attackers could not force their way into the town before nightfall, when the defenders reinforced

Francis J. Herron. Prints and Photographs Division, Library of Congress.

and barricaded the streets under the cover of darkness. Alarmed by the sounds of Confederates celebrating the arrival of more troops, the Union force fell back to Rio Grande City, where the rest of their comrades waited. Benavides believed the combined Federal strength totaled about 500 troopers, but he asked only for more reinforcements and ammunition, which Ford sent before starting himself for Laredo, where he arrived in mid-April. By then, matters were improving rapidly. While his units were still scattered, the ones he had assigned to march with him to Brownsville were converging on his camp at Los Ojuelos, where he had camped with his Rangers in 1850. Morale was high among Ford's troops, and rain began falling, raising their spirits even higher. And Benavides, who had been effusively praised by Ford for his defense of Laredo, reported the Federals "were in full retreat." Ford from Los Ojuelos, forty miles outside of Laredo on the road to Corpus Christi, could hit the Federals at Rio Grande City and follow the river down to Brownsville, avoiding the arid region to the north of that town.[31]

Ford's return to the Rio Grande thrust him into the role of border diplomat again. Napoleon III of France had invaded Mexico in early 1862 along with Spain and Great Britain. The latter nations soon abandoned the venture, but the French persevered and during May 1864 would install Ferdinand Maximilian as emperor of Mexico. Vidaurri allied with the French against Benito Juárez, refugee president of Mexico, but his bid for power did not succeed. Juárez drove Vidaurri north, and Ford found his nemesis from 1862 in Laredo when he arrived. This placed Ford in a ticklish situation. Confederate officials wanted French support, but Ford sympathized with Juárez as the legally elected president of Mexico. To complicate matters, Vidaurri had fifteen million percussion caps he was allegedly willing to sell, while reports indicated that Juárez might allow Union units to cross Mexican soil and attack the Confederates in Laredo. Ford understood that if this happened, "it would almost be tantamount to a declaration of war on the part of the Juárez government against the Confederate States." He wrote grimly to Magruder: "If President Juárez sees proper to transfer the theater of operations from Texas to Mexico he should be gratified." This would make Ford and his Confederates allies of Vidaurri and the French, but "I have never viewed the fact that we might be placed side by side with the French in Mexico as portending evil to our cause." Magruder pressed Ford to remain friendly with Juárez, but he agreed that if Federals attacked across the Rio Grande, Ford should "cross over and whip them, as it would be a declaration of war." Ford's decision was made for him when Vidaurri refused to sell the caps and Juárez did not allow Union troops into Mexico, but he would face similar dilemmas later at Brownsville.[32]

Excited by the Confederate success in driving Banks' Federals back on the Red River in April 1864, Magruder urged Ford onward, declaring, "Now is your time." Ford marched from Laredo to Rio Grande City, where he found no Federals, by the first week of May. As his force continued to increase, with only a few skirmishes with Federals and Mexicans to distract them, Ford struggled to keep his men under control. Before leaving Laredo he issued a ringing declaration: "The grasping avarice, the overbearing insolence, and the insatiable desire to plunder, evinced by the Yankees upon all occasions, have disgusted and estranged the Mexicans disposed to aid them." Admonishing his troops to treat Mexicans well, he reminded them that trade from Mexico was vital for their success. Therefore, "it is the interest and the duty of every Southern man whose heart is warmed with the love of country to make friends of all the world but our heartless & inhumane Yankee enemies." Once in Rio Grande City, Ford invited all Mexicans to return to the Texas side of the river, where they could live in peace. When the alcalde of Camargo, J. María García Villarreal, asked Ford about his intentions, the Texan responded warmly: "I desire to respect the rights of all classes and to give no just cause for complaint to our co-terminous sister republic." Appealing to Villarreal's patriotism, Ford explained that his only purpose was "to defend our liberties against the assaults of a despotic government which is endeavoring to centralize all power." By late May Ford could brag that "our relations with the Mexican authorities and people are becoming daily more amicable," and he claimed to be making progress in convincing Mexicans to desert from the Union army. Herron grudgingly concurred in his reports to Federal authorities.[33]

Within weeks Ford established a supply line to Matamoros, where another old nemesis, Juan N. Cortina, continued to rule in the name of

Juárez. Putting aside their differences, the two men agreed to free trade along the Rio Grande, which allowed Ford to bypass Laredo, where Benavides now struggled to sustain a flow of commerce. Ford harbored no illusions about Cortina—he fully understood that the resilient Mexican was also trading with the Federals. As he recalled in his memoirs, Cortina "was known to be friendly to the Union men, yet he was not averse to allowing his friends to earn an honest penny by supplying Confederates." This was made brutally evident when the Federals in Brownsville seized Manuel G. Rejón, Vidaurri's fugitive secretary of state, and delivered him to Cortina, who had him shot. Undeterred, Ford paid an official visit to Matamoros, lured by the possibility that Cortina, rather than lose his prizes to the French, might sell ten cannon donated to him by the Federals. Ford did not get the guns, but Confederate sympathizers in Matamoros did present him with a splendid trophy: one of Herron's own horses, which had somehow been pilfered. Cortina continued to tease Ford by offering to sell him arms, but Ford discovered that Federal deserters were more reliable suppliers than Cortina. Nevertheless, he instructed Benavides that "it is our duty to recognize the government de facto of Mexico," which meant Cortina at Matamoros. Benavides was to tell Vidaurri to abandon his plans for an attack from Texas, and if he did not desist, then Benavides was to treat his troops as "public enemies."[34]

Ford's visit to Matamoros allowed him to thank Cortina in person for a favor: he had extended his protection to Ford's wife, Addie, and her family. When Ford had left Brownsville in 1862, a pregnant Addie had remained there at the residence of her father, Elihu D. Smith. Addie delivered a daughter, named Mary Louise for Addie's younger sister, on August 15, and a few months later the two joined Ford in Austin, escorted by George W. Morris, a family friend from San Augustine who died of yellow fever soon thereafter. Ten days after Ford left San Antonio for the Rio Grande in March 1864, Addie, who was expecting their second child, left for Piedras Negras with Lula, as they called their first daughter, and Manuel Treviño, a prominent Brownsville merchant who was accompanied by his wife and sister-in-law. Ford tried to intercept the party after hearing of the attack at Laredo, but his wife continued. She apparently wanted to be with her family again when she delivered,

Charles B. Combe. Brown, *Indian Wars and Pioneers of Texas.*

and her mood could not have been improved by the fact that her older brother William had died of a respiratory ailment at Matamoros in January. The party, traveling down the Mexican side of the Rio Grande after leaving Piedras Negras for Matamoros, had a horrific scare when an ambulance rolled over on top of Lula, but she was tended at Camargo by Dr. Charles B. Combe, who had served with Ford against Cortina in 1859–1860. The tired and shaken family arrived in Matamoros after a month on the road, only to be told by Addie's sister Mary Louise that she might be arrested if she crossed to Brownsville. Recalling Ford's kindness to his mother in 1860, Cortina had his half-brother Savas Cavazos, who had introduced Ford to their mother, escort him to see Addie. She refused their offer of money, but Cortina spoke with his contacts among the Federals and visits across the Rio Grande were arranged.[35]

Ford must have been relieved to see his family safe, but he had a campaign to lead, and so he left them in Matamoros. Swisher, who had been sent by Ford to purchase supplies in Matamoros, had written to Ford that his daughter had "recovered entirely" and was "lively as a cricket." Combe wrote a month later that Lula had become everyone's "pet" and asked slyly, "who in the H_LL told you I was spoiling the child's disposition?" Rather than wait for Ford's response, Combe continued in his letter: "you have got D—n little to do to believe such statements. Why don't you write me or are you endeavoring to maintain one of your infernal dignified & stubborn fits of genteel silence." The best news came in mid-July when Ford received reports that his wife had safely delivered their second child. Swisher, who was apparently much better at finances than obstetrics, excitedly wrote that the new arrival was a boy, but Robert West, who attended at the delivery, informed Ford that he had another daughter in a letter written the same day. West, a partner in a ranch near Cortina's mother's estate, had somewhat better medical credentials than Swisher: he worked as a dentist in Brownsville. The child was named Addie Julia, for her mother.[36]

While Ford's friends kept him informed about his family, they also told him about Federal activities around Brownsville while he fussed and fumed and prepared to march. He snarled at Giddings that if he insisted upon using his own route to Rio Grande City rather than the one that Ford had chosen, then "I shall anticipate your arrival sometime in September." Or perhaps "you will next conclude to fortify Eagle Pass, and winter there." Pendleton Murrah, the hard-pressed governor of Texas, next received a verbal broadside from Ford, who complained that his communications to and from Austin did not seem to be arriving at their intended destinations. Ford also constantly worried about money as little cash and no cotton seemed to be forthcoming from Confederate or state officials. The frustrated Texan issued orders to his troops about behavior, admonishing them to be civil and barring them from drinking or gambling. This was especially important for his officers; after all, he wrote, "a drunken officer is powerless except for evil."[37]

Ford could not resist a few rhetorical flourishes as he exhorted his men to do their best. His general order on May 10, 1864, concluded with a typical declaration: "The fiendish outrages of our enemies upon our families must nerve our arms to strike for revenge. The spirits of our murdered brethren will hover around in the hour of battle. A just cause, a resolution to do our duty, and a reliance upon the aid of the Almighty will give us victory." His troops had to understand that "if we resolve never to yield we can never be defeated or conquered" by the "enemy who comes to plunder & enslave us."

Appalled by a report from Capt. John Littleton that some recruits on the Nueces River had refused to muster, Ford told his former partner against Cortina not to feed the men until they obeyed. Perhaps consciously invoking the Shakespearian image of Henry IV at Agincourt, Ford added, "It will be a nice thing to be handed down as a family heirloom that when a forward movement was ordered against the invaders of Texas the members of certain companies were on the San Fernando in a state of mutiny, because a mustering officer had been sent to them in pursuance of an order from their Maj. Gen. Cmdg. Every one will be eager to say—'My father was one [of] that glorious number who preferred growling to marching against the enemy.'"[38] Ford's troops might not have understood all of his literary references, but his words had the desired effect as his numbers grew and weeks passed without any serious conflicts within his ranks.

By mid-June 1864 Ford had 1,300 men in his command. He had no artillery, but he did have rain and reports that more Federals had been withdrawn from Brownsville, which had become the last Union outpost in Texas. Ford left 600 troopers at and near Ringgold Barracks while ordering 700 to ride down the Rio Grande on June 16. His orders to the rank and file were simple: "Good order and silence must be observed—no straggling allowed; and the discharge of firearms except at the enemy is prohibited." When Showalter grumbled that he could not find enough pack saddles for the march, Ford told him to "cease complaining," as Showalter had as much equipment as could be

Brownsville. *Frank Leslie's Illustrated Weekly,* December 5, 1863.

provided and also had the shortest route to the main rendezvous point, the Laguna del Como Se Llama, northeast of Brownsville. Ford turned north from the Rio Grande road to join Showalter there, then led his combined forces due south to return to the river road near Las Rucias Ranch, where the westernmost detachment of the Brownsville garrison had settled. Ironically, these Federals, who numbered about one hundred, had been sent to catch Ford after the latter detained Anglo John F. Webber, his black wife, and their mixed race children at their ranch near Hidalgo. One son escaped, but he told Union authorities that Ford had only sixty-two men. Unaware that Ford had many more riders with him, Capt. Philip G. Temple had led two companies of the First Texas Cavalry (USA) west to crush the Confederates. Meanwhile, Ford knew exactly what Temple had, having been told by Mexican prisoners, and he deliberately left the river road and then returned to avoid detection as he approached his target.[39]

Ford checked his ground carefully, then hit Temple hard on June 25, 1864, at Las Rucias. He sent Lt. Col. John J. Fisher to make sure there were no Federals concealed at nearby Carricitos Ranch, then slipped to within a few hundred yards of Temple's camp because the Union commander had not posted pickets. Ford's initial probe of the enemy position, however, met with heavy fire, and he had to feed reinforcements into the fight to sustain his attack in a steady downpour. Federals took cover in wood and brick buildings and behind wooden fences and piles of bricks. The Confederates drove them from their protected positions to the banks of a lagoon, which again concealed the Federals as they continued to fire rapidly. Ford told Capt. José del Refugio Benavides, Santos

Benavides' brother, to attack the Union right flank, but instead the captain was repulsed twice as he charged the enemy's left. A frontal assault by Ford's troopers on foot, led by Refugio Benavides, Showalter, and Capt. Thomas E. Cater, compelled the surviving Federals to surrender or swim the lagoon. Some of those who tried to do the latter were drowned, and Ford later learned the Texas Unionists had been told that if they surrendered, their Confederate counterparts would kill them. Reports later surfaced that Ford had executed prisoners, but the thirty-two that he delivered to authorities in Houston, as he told his subordinates to do in such cases, corresponds with the number reported as captured by Union officials. In fact, the latter arguably were more negligent than Ford: they did not send ambulances until three days after the fight to retrieve four wounded prisoners who could not walk.[40]

Ford boasted that only eight of Temple's Federals returned to Brownsville, while he lost only three men killed and four wounded. He estimated that his troopers had killed twenty Federals and wounded ten or twelve, while thirty-six had been captured and the remainder scattered. Temple himself had been wounded and left the field "early." Ford probably did not inflict as many casualties as he claimed, but Herron preferred not to address the issue directly in his report of the Las Rucias affair. Instead, he focused on the fact that after that fight, Ford's probe of the Union picket lines at Brownsville had been repulsed. Then Herron had lost only two men killed, five wounded, and twenty-three captured, while he was confident his troops had killed five Confederates and wounded twelve. Regardless of the numbers, Ford had crushed a Federal detachment and scared their commander, Herron, into reporting to his superiors that Ford had 1,800 men with him and another five regiments with a battery marching from San Antonio to join his expedition. While one of Herron's associates dispatched a letter to a newspaper in Iowa, Herron's home state, describing the debacle at Las Rucias and the chaos that followed, Herron withdrew into his defenses at Brownsville, and panicked Unionists fled across the Rio Grande to Matamoros.[41]

Herron got a small measure of retribution when Texas Unionists led by Thomas P. McManus briefly occupied Eagle Pass at about the same time as the Las Rucias fight, but Ford paid scant attention to the matter. McManus was an interesting character who had served with the Army in Utah and delivered mail and freight across Texas and Mexico from his home in San Antonio before the war. In 1861 he claimed to have sold his slaves and equipped a militia company, whom he led to Mexico and then to Union-occupied New Orleans. When the Federals took Brownsville in 1863, he returned to Texas and slipped up the Rio Grande to Piedras Negras by early 1864. There he found much cotton stockpiled in that town and across the river in Eagle Pass while Vidaurri and Milmo argued with Confederate authorities over control of the cotton trade. Soon afterward Vidaurri was defeated by Juárez, and much cotton remained unsold in Eagle Pass. McManus was apparently behind the unrest at Eagle Pass in February 1864, and in June he attacked again with about eighty men, burning many bales and capturing some Confederates who had been accused of killing Texas Unionists. Ware managed to retain control of the town, but he begged Ford for reinforcements.[42]

Ford was more concerned with taking Brownsville than protecting Eagle Pass by July 1864, when he received Ware's plea. Plagued with transfers of individuals and units to other commands, expirations of enlistments, and the persistent refusal of some officers to cooperate with him, he complained bitterly to Confederate authorities that his authority was constantly usurped by superiors or ignored by subordinates, that he needed supplies, and that his efforts were not appreciated. In response he got praise and $4,000 in cash, with instructions to make it last as long as he could. He also received support from his superiors in a showdown with Lt. Col. Oliver Steele, who had told Ford's officers not to gather corn in his district earlier in the year, and then diverted a company of men from Ford in the summer. Ford exploded: "I may labor under erroneous impressions, but I am led to believe that had Lieutenant Colonel Steele offered an opposition as persistent and determined to a Federal officer's intentions and plans as he has to mine he would have done the country good service." Magruder was preparing to leave for a new assignment in Arkansas, but his chief of staff, Slaughter, acted in his place. His staff instructed Steele to cooperate, and he again placated Ford with praise and assurances of support, though he may have unwittingly done more harm than good when he revealed that Magruder never expected Ford to take Brownsville, only to disrupt its supply lines.[43]

A great opportunity presented itself to Ford in mid-July when reports surfaced that Herron had been told by Federal officials to abandon Brownsville and leave only a small force at Brazos Santiago. Ford at first refused to believe his luck, but it was true. Swisher wrote to him from Matamoros, urging Ford to move swiftly and give Herron a "parting kick." He explained that "it would be a feather in your cap if you could make it appear that you had forced them to leave." Furthermore, "if they are permitted to leave without a blow struck on the retreat, it will mar the sweep of your operations." Ford hardly needed such advice—he rode out of Ringgold Barracks with 1,500 troopers on July 19. Weeks later, he received a communication from Slaughter that left the decision for an attack in Ford's hands. Summer heat and a lack of rain made grass scarce, and Cortina became increasingly unreliable in allowing trade on the Rio Grande, but Ford continued. On July 22, so ill he had to be helped onto his horse, he led an attack on the Federal picket lines at Brownsville that forced them to retire into the city. Hearing that 3,000 Union troops remained inside the defensive works, Ford stopped his advance to watch and wait.[44]

Ford battled illness and Federals while waiting anxiously for Herron to withdraw more of his troops, if not all of them. Picket fighting raged every day, although Ford's Confederates prudently remained outside the range of Union artillery. Combe, along with Swisher, crossed from Matamoros to tend Ford, who could hardly walk but still insisted upon taking the field on horseback. On July 28 Ford got his wish: the Union garrison abandoned Brownsville. Showalter led a detachment into the city on July 30, finding it to be, according to Ford, "in better condition than we had been led to expect." In fact, when the Federals left Brownsville, Maj. Eber W. Cave, the former secretary of state for Texas who had been a volunteer aide for Magruder, crossed from Matamoros with forty Confederate sympathizers and organized a militia to protect against looters. A grateful Ford arrived on July 31, established his headquarters at Fort Brown, sent for his family, and collapsed into bed, leaving Showalter and Fisher in charge of the city for which he had fought so hard. Ford trusted Showalter to send patrols to harass the retiring Federals, which he did. Ironically, the malady that had first plagued Ford in Mexico and later as a Ranger resurfaced to mar his triumphant return to Brownsville.[45]

Ford may not have immediately enjoyed his triumph, but many pro-Confederate Texans certainly did. The editor of the Houston *Telegraph,* Edward H. Cushing, wrote for them when he declared, "Everybody has believed all the time that he would do it, and everybody is glad now that he has." Five days later, Cushing was more effusive, writing, "Good for the Old Rip. Long may he wave. He is the pride of his country." In September Cushing printed a letter from an anonymous correspondent who crowed, "Ford certainly has displayed remarkable versatile talents in the important part he has had to perform; and all this without extraneous aide [*sic*] from those who are in command of the Trans-Mississippi Department that includes the Rio Grande frontier." Referring to Ford by his state rank, he concluded, "That Gen. Ford will hold Brownsville free from the polluting tread of our bitter foes I am satisfied." Ford certainly had groused about not getting proper support, but he might not have agreed entirely with the claim of no "extraneous aide." Magruder, in his farewell message to Texans on August 16, 1864, congratulated Nolan and Benavides for their victories, as well as the "gallant Ford" for his win at Las Rucias. He did not mention Bee, who had sent Ford away from Brownsville more than two years earlier only to abandon the city to the Federals in 1863.[46] Ford had regained his rightful place in the eyes of many Texans, and he had once more secured the right to consider himself the equal of his grandfathers, who won their revolution. No one could anticipate that within a year he would expand his legacy by winning the final battle of the Civil War, though ironically the fight to establish the Confederacy would already be lost.

CHAPTER 6 LEGACY

Maj. Gen. Lew Wallace in March 1865 reported to the general-in-chief of the United States Army, Maj. Gen. Ulysses S. Grant, that he had met with the "most influential Confederate soldier in Texas," John S. "Rip" Ford, to discuss a scheme for ending the Civil War in the Trans-Mississippi west.[1] While Ford might claim to be influential among Texans, he in fact did not have a Confederate commission at the time he spoke with Wallace, and he was second-in-command to Brig. Gen. James E. Slaughter, who also met with Wallace. Slaughter's attempts to dominate Ford in fact complicated the latter's efforts to maintain control of the lower Rio Grande in a four-way power struggle between Confederates, Federals, the French who had installed Ferdinand Maximilian of Austria as emperor of Mexico, and Benito Juárez, the refugee president of that country. Ford kept a watchful eye on Matamoros, where Gen. Tomás Mejía commanded an Imperialist occupation force of French and Mexican troops. To the west, Juan N. Cortina still campaigned, vacillating in his loyalty to Maximilian or Juárez as their respective fortunes waxed and waned. All of these matters worried Ford in his role as the defender of the Rio Grande border, across which an invaluable stream of trade flowed. He had no idea that just a few months after meeting Wallace he would gain immortality by winning the last battle of the Civil War. By once again proving that he was of the same "fighting stock" as his grandfathers who fought in the American Revolution, Ford became a Southern legacy, celebrated by those who looked back fondly on the Lost Cause of the Confederacy.

Ford arose from his sickbed at Brownsville on August 1, 1864, to face a variety of challenges. He assigned Lt. Col. Daniel Showalter to direct a select group of mounted Texans in harassing the Federals, while Lt. Col. John J. Fisher took charge of the garrison troops. Ford's command expanded to include a naval element when Showalter's men captured a small steamer, the *Ark,* which had run aground. The captain of the vessel hid his United States flag and hoisted a Mexican one in its place, but then confessed what he had done while drinking with his captors. Ford arrived and told his men the steamboat would have to be released because it was Mexican, but they replied that the captain had concealed his true colors. Ford promised to free the prisoners if they would show him where the banner was hidden; when they did so three days later, he held them anyway, apparently for having made him wait. Sent to Brownsville, the hapless crew enjoyed a brief parole, then went to Houston, whence they were released in December 1864. Ford ordered Lt. Henry de Wolf of Showalter's Fourth Regiment, Arizona Brigade, to skipper the *Ark,* and the steamer ferried supplies to Confederate posts along the Rio Grande. Plans were discussed to reconfigure the steamboat so it could ply even shallower waters beyond Brownsville, but Ford acceded to the demands of his superiors, who were not interested in an expensive refitting. He had to allow the vessel to be sold at auction to Thomas Gilgan of Matamoros, who used the steamer to trade along the river. Selling the *Ark* also rid Ford of the troublesome de Wolf, who was arrested for selling shares in his own vessel.[2]

Having returned to the Rio Grande, Ford resumed the role of border diplomat. Juan N. Cortina was absent from Matamoros fighting the French near Tampico when Ford occupied Brownsville, but the Texan immediately contacted Col. José M. Cortina, the general's older brother who was in charge of the Mexican troops loyal to Juárez on the lower Rio Grande. Ford, who appreciated Colonel Cortina's efforts to combat outlaws in the region, thanked him for his "many acts of kindnesses to our citizens." General Cortina, worried about the French landing at Bagdad at the mouth of the Rio Grande on August 22, hurried back to Matamoros, adding complexity to the diplomatic situation Ford faced. Ford had been told by Confederate authorities to work with the French in the hope of gaining their support, and yet he preferred to see Juárez triumph in Mexico. Now confronting him across the Rio Grande, as Juárista commander of Matamoros, was General Cortina, his old enemy, and he wanted to fight the French. So Ford assigned

Francis W. Latham to serve as an unofficial consul in Matamoros with Cortina, while he sent Fisher to meet the French. With Fisher went Maj. Waldemar Hyllested, a Swiss-born veteran of the United States Army in the war with Mexico who had commanded a Zouave battalion from Louisiana earlier in the Civil War and later became a provost marshal. A. Veron, commander of the French forces, received the two envoys graciously and penned a message to Ford assuring him that if the French occupied Matamoros, "all persons and property covered by the flag of your nation" will be "duly respected." Ford gleefully reported the tacit recognition of the Confederacy as a nation and assured Veron that he looked forward to a warm friendship.[3]

Despite Ford's contact with the French, he recalled that "Gen[eral] Cortina felt compelled to be more or less friendly." While Cortina imposed a forced loan after his arrival in Matamoros, and arrested consuls and people from other nations for not paying, he did not harass Confederates. Ford even planned to buy arms from him and chastised Showalter when his men fired at Cortina's troops while they were skirmishing with the French. Ford soon realized that Cortina was not a potential ally, however, when the two men began to quarrel over the right to cross the Rio Grande, and Ford had to ask Cortina to investigate sniping by his units on Confederate positions. Reports soon surfaced that Leonard Pierce, United States consul at Matamoros, had told Cortina that if he assisted in pushing the Confederates out of Brownsville, the Union Army would help him drive the French from Bagdad. Ford also understood that Cortina had been offered an appointment as a Federal brigadier general. It was easy for Ford to believe that Cortina would attack him. As he reported at that time, Cortina "hates Americans, particularly Texians. He has an old and deep seated grudge against Brownsville . . . If he could force his way through our lines, plunder our people, and get within the Yankee lines, it would be a finale he would delight in." Ford prepared for a showdown by warning Showalter and Veron to be watchful, and he assured his superiors that "if Cortina crosses I shall beat him."[4]

After meeting with Pierce to make plans for an attack in conjunction with a Union advance, Cortina blockaded the Rio Grande on

September 3 and emplaced artillery facing Brownsville. Dr. Charles B. Combe, who had tended Ford's oldest daughter when she was injured during his family's journey to Matamoros in the spring of 1864, raced to warn the Texans of the impending danger. Ford ordered Showalter to be ready, told de Wolf to burn the *Ark* if necessary to avoid being captured, and posted Lt. Col. George H. Giddings' cavalry battalion to support Showalter. Cortina on September 5 made a weak feint toward the French at Bagdad while his cavalry crossed the Rio Grande and camped with the Federals. The remainder of his forces, led by Col. Servando Canales and others, shifted to face the Confederates but would not ford the river, in part because Pierce had refused to guarantee that officers would retain their ranks if their units joined the Federal forces. Col. José M. Cortina also did not cross above Brownsville with his troops as his brother had ordered. Nevertheless, Showalter nervously reported to Ford on September 5 that Cortina had about 600 troops with artillery across the Rio Grande near his position at Palmito Ranch, and that the Mexican general himself was present and clearly planning an attack. Furthermore, the Federals at Brazos Santiago had been greatly reinforced by the arrival of black infantry.[5]

Cortina's guns fired on Showalter's camp from across the river on the morning of September 6, while Col. Henry M. Day approached the Confederates with 900 Union and Mexican troops. Showalter in turn advanced skirmishers to harass Cortina's gunners and probe Day's forces. Capt. José del Refugio Benavides, who had fought valiantly under Ford at Las Rucias, captured some Federal wagons but had to abandon them when he saw Showalter retreating with many of his men. As Day wrote, "the last seen of [Showalter] he was flying in confusion back to Brownsville." Giddings arrived and, despite being peppered with Mexican shells, stabilized a defensive line by nightfall, when rain and mud prevented any further Union advances. While his troops battled at Palmito Ranch, Ford in Brownsville sent his wife and two daughters to a convent for safety and shuttled his troops to create the illusion of having a larger force to dissuade Cortina from using the artillery trained on the town or attempting to cross the Rio Grande and attack. Cortina in fact was elsewhere, being repulsed in another assault on the French and then fording

Servando Canales. Prints and Photographs Division, Library of Congress.

the river downstream to join Day. Many of Cortina's troops at Matamoros were under the command of Canales, who marched his men there rather than follow Cortina. Canales had served alongside Ford under José María de Jesús Carvajal in 1851, and he did not want to fight the Confederates. Unusually high water in the river provided him with an excuse to do nothing. Ford's main concern became his wife Addie, who refused to stay in the convent and rejoined her husband as he waited tensely for the next development.[6]

Ford expected an attack on Brownsville on September 7. It never came, so he joined Giddings at Palmito Ranch. There to his great relief he found the Federals were retiring toward the coast, though they took with them cattle gathered by the Confederates to sell to the French. Ford, with Giddings and Hyllested, followed them but avoided any contact. Having already reported Cortina's attack to his superiors, Ford spent the next day demanding explanations from both Cortina and the French. To the former, he wrote that there was no just cause for an attack; if Cortina was concerned about Confederates meeting with the French, as he claimed, he should realize that they could do so as freely as he met with the Federals. Colonel Cortina answered for his brother, assuring Ford that efforts were being made to eliminate conflict and avoid war. Ford took comfort in this evidence of a division of opinion among the Mexicans, but he was much less happy with the response from Veron. While Ford had been told "by a Mexican officer in the French Service" that Veron would help against Cortina on September 6, and he asked for support from Veron, the Frenchman declared that his "position of perfect neutrality" precluded helping the Confederates. Ford fumed and later wrote in his memoirs that "Com. Veron only squirmed, and did not do his duty." Veron actually did protest the involvement of Cortina with the Federals, but Day initially ignored him.[7]

Ford planned his next step carefully. Heeding the advice of Brig. Gen. Thomas F. Drayton, his immediate superior, Ford refrained from attacking the Mexicans across the Rio Grande. Instead, he decided that defeating the Union Army, alongside which Cortina had fought, should make it obvious to the French that the Federals were not good friends, and that the Confederates could be better allies. He later explained

Thomas F. Drayton. William Emerson Strong Photograph Album, Rare Book, Manuscript, and Special Collections Library, Duke University.

to one of Drayton's staff officers: "I thought this course preferable to attacking Matamoros, concentrating the Mexicans, endangering the safety of millions of dollars worth of Confederate property, and thus staking everything upon the hazard of a single battle." Although suffering from a recurrence of his chronic illness, Ford shuttled companies in and out of Brownsville to maintain the illusion of having a large force, and waited for an opportunity to strike. He trusted that persistent heavy rains would make it difficult for his opponent to use his superior numbers of artillery and infantry effectively.[8]

Capt. W. H. D. Carrington of Giddings' battalion gave Ford the news he wanted to hear on the morning of September 9. During the night 250 Federals and Mexicans had advanced to the San Martin Ranch, near the Confederate position at Palmito Ranch east of Brownsville, and Carrington insisted that a quick movement might capture the entire lot. Carrington skirmished with the enemy until mid-afternoon when, told that Giddings was coming with reinforcements, he had his riders fall back. He then sent a few men forward with orders to fire and run, hoping to draw his foe into a foolish attack. Unfortunately about 150 Federals reacted so quickly that Carrington had to lead a force forward to shield his skirmishers as they recovered their horses and hid in the brush. Urged by Ford to make a "sudden dash," Giddings led his troops, with Carrington in the center, in a headlong rush at the Federals, who were driven back at least five or six miles. When Union resistance stiffened, and a Confederate flank attack failed because of heavy brush, Refugio Benavides joined Carrington in a rush on the Federal center while others struck the Union right, crumpling it and initiating another retreat. Day had disarmed many of Cortina's men; in the face of Giddings' attacks, he frantically returned their weapons. Most of the rearmed Mexicans fled across the Rio Grande during three days of pursuit by the Confederates, and Cortina joined them when it became apparent that he was not welcome in the Federal camp. Day's artillery prevented the Confederates from coming too close to Brazos Island and threatening Cortina's sanctuary there, but renewed French protests convinced Day, in the wake of his defeat on September 9, to rid himself of his erstwhile Mexican ally, enhancing Ford's victory.[9]

Ford was pleased with the fighting done by his men in September 1864, with one obvious exception. He and others claimed that they had inflicted hundreds of casualties on the Federals while suffering very few of their own. In truth, Ford lost three men killed while Day had eighty-six killed, wounded, and missing. Most of the latter were Mexicans. Ford made polite inquiries about a dozen Mexicans he had captured, all of whom were Cortina's men, and then declared that they were prisoners of war, to be held by him until properly exchanged. Agapito Longoria, the alcalde of Matamoros, demanded their release, but to no avail. The primary focus for Ford's legalistic wrath was Showalter, whom he arrested and sent to San Antonio for a court martial. Not only did Showalter retreat on September 6, but he was also drunk, a sin Ford would not forgive. Ford wrote that when Showalter arrived in Brownsville that night, he had "spread reports upon the streets calculated to demoralize the command." These included a claim that he had been flanked and routed by overwhelming numbers. Showalter was in fact acquitted on every count, but he did not serve again under Ford, who may not have paid much attention to the verdict. Years later he generously wrote that Showalter, "when not under the influence of liquor . . . was as chivalrous a man as ever drew a sword." In September 1864, Ford was more interested in the growing rift between the Federals and the French, especially after Day admitted to Veron that Mexicans had found sanctuary in the Federal camp. Too, Ford noted that the Mexican guns pointing at Brownsville had disappeared.[10]

Drayton, as the commander of the Western Sub-District of Texas, became worried about the reports of fighting and hurried to Brownsville. Ford welcomed his superior, assuring him while he was on the road that the Confederates still held Brownsville and would "until the last brick is knocked from its place." Ford posted accurate reports to Drayton on his activities, which Drayton confirmed during a personal inspection after his arrival. From Palmito Ranch on September 12, Drayton excitedly reported that five French steamers had passed that point on their way up the Rio Grande, and he ordered Ford to support operations against Cortina. Four days later, shells from Mexican guns fell in Brownsville when Cortina confronted the French near Matamoros, but Gen. Tomás

Mejía, in command of both the French forces and their Mexican allies, did not accept the challenge to fight. A relieved Drayton joined Ford in Brownsville, where he delivered a treasured relic: a battle flag sewn by the ladies of the town that had flown over units led by Brig. Gen. Hamilton P. Bee in the Confederate victories over Maj. Gen. Nathaniel P. Banks during the Red River campaign in Louisiana. Ford, while watching Mejía and Cortina sparring with each other at Matamoros, wrote to Bee that the flag "will be upheld by the Expeditionary Forces as long as human endurance can allow a stout arm to wield a keen blade."[11]

Pinned in Matamoros by Mejía's larger force, and knowing he would get no help from Day and his Federals, Cortina resorted to negotiations. Ford desperately wanted artillery, and he had been talking with Cortina since the early summer about obtaining his guns. The Mexican general contacted the Texan, and they met at the Matamoros ferry landing. Ford wore pistols and had riflemen posted on the Texas side of the Rio Grande in case of treachery. But all remained quiet, and afterward Ford carried an agreement for reopening trade along the river to Drayton for his signature. Ford also understood from his negotiation with Cortina that he would be able to buy Cortina's guns before his surrender to Mejía, which appeared imminent. He was apparently unaware that Cortina also had a treaty with the French, which included giving them his artillery in return for being accepted as an ally. When Ford returned to the ferry landing for another meeting about cannon on September 26, he was surprised to see Mejía marching his troops into town. Ford angrily scrambled back to Brownsville, rather than risk a confrontation with Mejía, who might be upset to find the Texan doing business with a new ally the French still did not trust. Ford of course blamed Cortina for the affair, claiming in his memoirs that he later learned the Mexican general had told Mifflin Kenedy that he would never sell a single gun to the Confederates.[12]

Ford soon realized that he was not the only person threatened by Mejía's entry into Matamoros. On the evening of September 26, Texas pickets at the ferry landing on the Rio Grande watched as a Mexican regiment of 300 to 400 men approached the far bank of the river. It was Canales, who dispatched a message to Ford asking for asylum in Texas.

Tomás Mejía. Prints and Photographs Division, Library of Congress.

Ford agreed as long as the Mexicans surrendered their arms, which they did after crossing and being met by two companies of Confederates arranged in a line of battle. Canales and the officers who accompanied him to Texas explained that they still wanted to support Juárez and not become allies of the French. Veron, informed of their actions, assured Ford that he had complied properly with international law in disarming Canales' troops before providing sanctuary. Many of the refugees were expected to join Col. Santos Benavides in Laredo, but instead they lingered and became, like Carvajal's men in 1862, a nuisance for Ford. Drayton, just before he departed in early October, advised Ford to pay Canales for the confiscated weapons as soon as possible, which would allow the worried Mexican colonel to settle accounts with his unpaid soldiers and dismiss them. Carvajal wrote to Ford soon afterward, explaining that Juárez had appointed him as the military commander in Tamaulipas and asking that Canales' guns be given to him so he could fight the French. Ford instead assured Mejía that he still had Canales' weapons, and if the Juárista colonel had found others and was raiding into Mexico, then he would "be treated as a public enemy, and an abuser of our hospitality." Mejía ultimately sent Cortina in pursuit of Canales as well as his own brother, Col. José M. Cortina, who had taken refuge at Camargo rather than ally with the French. Cortina smashed Canales at Guerrero after he defeated his brother.[13]

Ford was pro-Juárez, but practical concerns dictated cordial relations with Mejía and his troops. While Ford discovered that it was much easier to work with Mejía than Cortina, and even respected Mejía, he never mistook their working relationship for true friendship. Ford did what was necessary and as he was instructed by Maj. Gen. John G. Walker, who had taken command of the District of Texas, New Mexico, and Arizona. Walker understood Ford's dilemma; after all, he demanded that Cortina be executed as a criminal in the same communication that told Ford to pursue friendly relations with the French. José A. Quintero, the tenacious Confederate diplomat, remained in Matamoros, and he facilitated communications with Mejía. Perhaps through his offices, Ford and Drayton crossed the Rio Grande to visit Mejía within days of his entry into Matamoros. Escorted by eight troopers under the command of Carrington, the Confederate leaders met Mejía at the governor's palace and accompanied him to a restaurant for a banquet. Mejía returned the compliment on October 3 despite a "Plutonean thunder shower." He was met by a company of Ford's men wearing not only their best uniforms but carrying new Enfields complete with bayonets. Drayton provided a feast, and again compliments flowed in profusion. Mejía toasted Confederate independence, while Drayton toasted Maximilian. Not to be outdone, Mejía the following day invited the Texans once more to Matamoros, where in a "large hall of the Bishop's palace" they enjoyed a dinner that was even more magnificent than what Drayton provided. More drinking, speeches, and toasts ensued, and Drayton and Mejía later exchanged photographs of themselves.[14]

Ford reaped immediate benefits from his diplomacy. Mejía honored the trade agreement between Cortina and Drayton, and commerce boomed along the Rio Grande. When Lew Wallace arrived in March 1865, he found more ships at the mouth of the river than in Baltimore Harbor. He assumed the cargo was for Texas and the Confederacy, but George L. Robertson, a veteran of the Fourth Texas Infantry serving in Giddings' battalion, was more skeptical. He saw the same activity but wrote to his mother, "I wonder if the government derives any benefit from it?" It is true that trade through Matamoros never met Confederate expectations, but while Federal blockaders harassed all who came and went at Galveston, Rio Grande traffic remained lively and enriched local leaders such as Richard King, Mifflin Kenedy, and Charles Stillman. On other matters, Bee had signed an extradition agreement in 1863 with Juárista officials, which of course was nullified with the incursion of the French. Ford, in response to a request from Drayton, asked Latham and Maj. Nestor Maxán, a lawyer fluent in French, to meet with representatives from Mejía to negotiate an arrangement for the extradition of prisoners and the return of stolen property, deserters, and runaway slaves. Talks stalled after two weeks; on their part, the Mexicans refused to return any slaves and declared that chasing deserters might lead to a conflict with the United States, while the Confederates declined to detain people who might be political prisoners. Brig. Gen. Slaughter later proved more successful and signed an extradition agreement with

George L. Robertson. Lawrence T. Jones III Collection, Southern Methodist University.

Mejía in December 1864. In individual cases Ford did better, delivering Mexican deserters from the Federal Army to Mejía, who in turn suppressed Union recruiting in Mexico and dismissed the protests of United States consuls against the extradition arrangement.[15]

One of the greatest challenges to Ford's authority along the Rio Grande came from within the Confederate command structure. Brig. Gen. Paul O. Hébert became the temporary commander of the District of Texas, New Mexico, and Arizona on August 16, 1864, after Maj. Gen. John B. Magruder returned to the field. Just six days later, Hébert issued orders for a reorganization of Ford's forces. New recruits were forbidden to join Ford, "or any other command on western service," while the troops with Ford were to be consolidated, under the direction of Lt. Col. Matt Nolan as acting inspector general, into two regiments commanded by Showalter and Santos Benavides. After filling these regiments, any remaining men were to march to Columbus, Texas, for other assignments. When Walker succeeded Hébert in September, he appointed Slaughter, who had served as chief of staff for Magruder, to command the Western Sub-District in place of Drayton. Neither Walker nor Slaughter made any effort to repeal the order issued by Hébert. In fact, Nolan, who had served several times under Ford before and during the Civil War before he was reassigned in April 1864, arrived on the Rio Grande in October to carry out a consolidation. Showalter had departed, but Nolan was to organize Giddings' and other commands into one brigade to be commanded by Slaughter and another for Benavides, for whom a Confederate appointment as brigadier general was allegedly pending. This would usurp Ford, who remained a state brigadier general.[16]

The proposal for making Benavides a general complicated an already damaged relationship for Ford. Benavides had played a key role in Ford's march on Brownsville, using his contacts among the Mexican and Tejano communities on both sides of the Rio Grande to gather information and hinder Federal efforts to communicate. For example, when Benavides learned that a Union courier hired a Mexican to carry dispatches from Nuevo Laredo to Fort Lancaster, he asked the garrison commander at Piedras Negras, a "personal friend," to arrest the Mexican as a horse thief. The man was arrested and shot, and his dispatches were

Matt Nolan. Brownsville Historical Society.

taken. But Benavides' ambition was fired when he received permission to raise and command a regiment, and by the late summer he was ignoring Ford's requests for help and seizing cotton to be sold to pay his expenses. Ford, rather than welcome the prospect of Benavides becoming a general, instead asked Slaughter to arrest him in October 1864. He was not suspected of disloyalty—although Ford claimed later that he had refused an offer of a Federal brigadier generalship—but he was openly insubordinate. When Nolan arrived, Ford heatedly explained that many of his men had joined his command specifically because they understood they would not be mustered into Confederate service and thus become eligible to serve outside of Texas. Meanwhile, Giddings made his way to Austin, where he asked Gov. Pendleton Murrah to intervene and secured the support of Drayton and two Texans in the Confederate Congress, Sen. Louis T. Wigfall, and Rep. William S. Oldham, for Ford. After talking with many of Ford's troops, Nolan suspended his efforts to reorganize the troops on the Rio Grande, while Benavides also met with Ford and decided not to press the issue.[17]

Slaughter arrived in early November and made arrangements to settle the issue of the Western Sub-District's organization for good. He assigned Ford to command his Southern Division, Benavides got his Western Division, Col. Charles L. Pyron of the Second Texas Cavalry (Ford's original regiment) assumed command of his Northern Division, and Col. Alexander C. Jones took charge of his Eastern Division. Slaughter may have understood the wisdom of heeding Ford's warnings that any effort to muster his men into Confederate service would cause many of them to leave, legally or not. Ford explained to Nolan that "this diminution may be so great as to render the evacuation of the Rio Grande a necessity should the enemy make a forward movement." To Ford, it was quite simple: "the re-occupation of the Rio Grande by the Yankees would be paying very dearly for the filling up of two regiments." Nolan and Ford parted as friends when the former returned to Nueces County, where he had been elected sheriff. Tragically, Nolan was shot to death in December by a pair of assassins who may have been trying to murder a man with whom he was walking. As for Benavides, he and Ford maintained a polite but not friendly relationship for years.

About the Tejano colonel, Ford smugly wrote in his memoirs, "If a bee of the brigadier general species got in Benavides' hat and stung him, and caused insanity, he deserves our sympathy. He has not our condemnation or ill-will."[18]

Having solved the organizational problems that threatened to undermine efforts to defend the Western Sub-District, Slaughter remained in Brownsville, rather than return to San Antonio, and feuded with Ford. He believed that Ford had done a poor job with his command, which he described as "wild bands of men, scattered from San Antonio to this point." Cortina's attacks in September, before his arrival, he attributed to depredations by Ford's troopers, whom Slaughter believed to be unruly and demoralized. Described as an officer who did everything "in an old army style" by the veteran Robertson, Slaughter did his best to chase away anyone accused of having deserted another unit to join Ford and to discipline those who remained. He developed a rough division of labor, staying in town to direct the Western Sub-District while letting Ford oversee, and often join, the men in the field. Robertson noted that the men had "great faith . . . and confidence" in Slaughter, but his conflict with Ford was evident. The Texan obviously did "not like the idea of being superceded [*sic*] by Slaughter and sent to the woods." Robertson reported that one evening Ford joined him and others for a visit, adding that "he seemed to be in a good humor, which is unusual." The men of course supported Ford; as another of them, John H. Jenkins, remembered, "Gen. Slaughter was <u>called</u> commander, but Ford in reality owned and ordered our force of nearly eight hundred Confederates."[19]

Jenkins' remark reveals a vexing problem with Ford's command: it was shrinking. His strength in September 1864 was reported to be 1,630, with reinforcements expected. Two months later, he had 1,300 officers and men, and by January 1865 he mustered only 812, or half what he had just four months earlier. A March 31, 1865, report revealed that he had five of Benavides' ten cavalry companies with him at Brownsville, as well as two battalions of troopers led by Capt. Thomas E. Cater and Giddings, who commanded three and six companies respectively. Maj. Albert Walthersdorff had three independent cavalry companies and Capt. O. G. Jones' artillery battery to garrison Fort Brown. Part of the problem was Slaughter's zealous policing in response to new instructions from Lt. Gen. Edmund Kirby Smith, the commander of the Trans-Mississippi Department, to transfer many of Ford's command, whom he declared had been "illegally organized, and made up of deserters and conscripts." In February 1865, the last of the Fourth Regiment, Arizona Brigade, rode away from the Rio Grande. At the same time, desertion reduced Ford's strength, beginning soon after Slaughter's arrival and increasing through the early months of 1865. Some may have feared or resented Slaughter's discipline, but others simply tired of skimpy rations, ragged clothing, inadequate weapons, and no pay. Anglos and Tejanos alike slipped away, and Ford apparently made little effort to pursue them beyond sending letters asking others to apprehend the most brazen deserters, such as a captain who tried to entice others to leave with him.[20]

Fortunately for Ford, he did not have to worry much about the Federals at Brazos Santiago or attacks from any Mexican forces. Both fronts were relatively quiet, with only some occasional skirmishes. After receiving one section of Captain Jones' light artillery battery in October 1864, Ford did plan an attack on the Union position. Slaughter agreed to lead the operation, but bitter cold forced the two to cancel the advance after some light skirmishing. Perhaps it was for the best; Brig. Gen. William A. Pile, who supplanted Day as the commander at Brazos Santiago in November 1864, had three well-equipped infantry regiments: the Ninety-First Illinois, Sixty-Second Infantry (United States Colored Troops), and Eighty-First Infantry (USCT). By the end of the year, the Ninety-First Illinois had departed, but the Thirty-Fourth Indiana Infantry arrived to take its place. As for Union operations, in spite of rumors that Juárez had asked them to re-occupy the river valley, they did not venture far from Brazos Santiago, further reducing Ford's worries. Beyond the Rio Grande, Cortina devoted his attention to Imperial service, while some of his new colleagues pounded Carvajal and forced him to withdraw into the San Carlos Mountains, where he made plans to depart for the United States with permission from Juárez to seek arms and recruits.[21]

A Federal scheme to bring the Civil War to a swift and successful conclusion in the Trans-Mississippi while the final Union victories were being won in the East led to a strange encounter that involved Ford. The Confederacy since the fall of 1863, after its losses at Gettysburg and Vicksburg, had expended much effort to secure an alliance with France against the United States. West of the Mississippi River, Kirby Smith penned his own inquiries to the French, seeking their support for his isolated command. One serious complication in Kirby Smith's plans was the great antipathy of many Texans toward the French, especially after the exposure of an alleged conspiracy by the French consul at Galveston, Benjamin Theron, to separate the state from the Confederacy. An inquiry from Theron on this subject in 1862 led to an angry denunciation from Gov. Francis R. Lubbock, and Confederate Secretary of State Judah P. Benjamin had Theron expelled. Some suspected Theron's purpose was to leave Texas exposed to annexation by Imperialist Mexico.[22] It was not unreasonable to suppose that a Federal overture to the Texans at this late stage in the Civil War might lead them to abandon the failing Confederacy and cooperate in a joint venture with United States forces against the French in Mexico to insure both the security of Texas and the protection of the South from French intrigues.

The idea of a joint invasion of Mexico became a favorite of such leading Federals as Francis P. Blair, who asked that it be one of the topics of the meeting in February 1865 between Abraham Lincoln and Confederate officials at Hampton Roads. Lincoln did not endorse the proposal before the conference, and when Confederate Vice Pres. Alexander Stephens raised the issue at Hampton Roads, Lincoln rejected it. Apart from the obvious risks of war with France, the president did not like the fact that the Confederacy would not be required to surrender in order to engage in the operation, nor would it be asked to accept emancipation. Thus his two cherished goals, the Union and abolition, would be sacrificed. At least one Federal officer, Wallace, thought he had a better solution. Convinced by an old school chum from Texas, S. S. Brown, that Texans were eager for an honorable exit from the war and would welcome a defensive buffer against the French, Wallace asked another friend, General Grant, for permission to travel to the Rio Grande and contact the Confederate leaders there. He would propose a joint invasion but also require them to surrender and accept emancipation. As a

Lew Wallace. Prints and Photographs Division, Library of Congress.

bonus, he explained to Grant how lucrative the trade through Brownsville had become. He added that success on the Mexican border "would stagger the rebellion next to the giving in of the state of Georgia." With the support of a skeptical Lincoln, Grant dispatched Wallace to make an inspection tour of the Rio Grande region, understanding that he would present his idea. If it did work, a Confederate force would surrender, valuable economic support for the western Confederacy would be interdicted, France would be blocked from directly assisting the Confederacy from Mexico, and national reunification and abolition would be a giant step closer. As Wallace wrote, "It is worth a trial anyhow."[23]

Charles Worthington, who had been appointed by Lincoln as collector of customs for Brownsville in 1864, before Ford's Confederates reoccupied the town, accompanied Wallace to Brazos Santiago. Wallace's plans became more grandiose as he traveled, and he asked Grant in late February to appoint him as commander of the Department of Texas and send reinforcements. With more troops, Wallace assured Grant that he could create a new territory or state. Grant did not encourage these proposals, and Wallace returned to the task at hand: convincing Confederates on the Rio Grande to cooperate in an attack on the French. He invited Slaughter, as the highest ranking Confederate at Brownsville, to meet with him at Point Isabel on March 9, 1865, and Slaughter graciously asked Ford to go with him. On the appointed day Giddings had a detachment watching for the Federals at Point Isabel while others waited to escort Slaughter's party, but bad weather delayed the conference. On March 11, still under a shroud of secrecy and with pickets posted to watch for signs of Federal treachery, Slaughter and Ford joined Wallace and Worthington at Point Isabel.[24]

The meeting lasted for two days, and Wallace reported to Grant that it was a great success. Both Ford and Slaughter, he wrote, declared that they could fight "indefinitely," but they admitted that "the North would ultimately conquer the South as a desert." They discussed the terms of a general surrender for the entire Trans-Mississippi that included abolition, which Ford and Slaughter accepted but asked that it be implemented gradually. Of course, Wallace made it clear that he did not represent the government of the United States, and Slaughter and Ford insisted they could not speak for Confederate authorities. But the latter agreed to convey the proposals to their superiors, Walker, Kirby Smith, and Wallace declared that they "entered heartily into the Mexican project." Peace would be established in Texas, and then a combined army would cross the Rio Grande. Cotton in Texas that belonged to

James E. Slaughter. Richard C. Young Confederate Officer Album,
Courtesy of Alabama Department of Archives and History.

the Confederate government would be sold to fund the operation. Ford worried that Kirby Smith would reject cooperation because newspapers reported that he was negotiating with Maximilian for "Imperial annexation," but he told Wallace "that if such a sale was attempted he would instantly bring about a counter revolution." Slaughter spoke more about his own fate than that of Texas, explaining that he believed the best way for officers in his situation to earn clemency was to assist in conquering two or three Mexican states from the French and arrange for their annexation by the United States. Wallace added that Ford would deliver the proposal to Walker and Kirby Smith "in person, and as he is politically the most influential Confederate soldier in Texas that fact gives me additional confidence." Wallace would follow Ford to Galveston, arriving a few days after the Texan, and meet with Kirby Smith. He asked that Edmund J. Davis of Brownsville, the colonel of the First Texas Cavalry (USA), accompany him as he was a friend of Kirby Smith.[25]

Ford in his later writing on the meeting at Point Isabel did not indicate that either he or Slaughter was as supportive of the scheme as Wallace believed, and his actions at the time tend to support his postwar explanations. He believed the only binding decision had been to establish a truce on the Rio Grande; anything else was simply to be reported to his superiors for their consideration. And if he had ever agreed to deliver the proposal in person to Walker, he prudently changed his mind. On March 17, 1865, Wallace wrote to Slaughter, asking that Ford go with him to see Kirby Smith at Galveston. The Federal officer envisioned Ford and Davis, "each representing his side in this unnatural struggle," talking to Kirby Smith together and convincing him to surrender. Slaughter was away, so Ford replied for him, explaining that his increased duties during Slaughter's absence made it impossible for him to go to Galveston. Nor could he go without Slaughter's permission. Rather than endanger the new truce, Ford added cagily, "You do not mistake when you suppose me willing to make any sacrifice short of honor to restore peace." When Wallace repeated his request on March 24, Ford again declined to accompany him, writing that he had sent a courier to Slaughter, but no reply had come. Instead, Lt. Col. E. Fairfax Gray carried Wallace's proposals to Walker at Galveston. Wallace, joined by Davis, arrived offshore only to receive a hostile note from Walker rejecting any consideration of a capitulation. Walker's concluding line even questioned the propriety of "seeking an obscure corner of the Confederacy to inaugurate negotiations."[26]

Wallace, stung by Walker's rebuke, vainly struggled to salvage his proposal. He angrily responded to Walker, demanding that he send the proposals to Kirby Smith. In an aside that was a backhanded compliment to Ford and Slaughter, he remarked that "it is impossible for me to believe that accident or policy has located all the sane men of your Confederacy in its obscure corners." Apparently ignored, he sent copies of Walker's note and his response to Ford and Slaughter on April 6, referring to Walker as "childish" and declaring, "If Texas should be invaded you and I will not be responsible. Not ours the blood, the ruin, the horrors that will ensue." Worthington, at Wallace's request, made his way to Matamoros and contacted Ford and Slaughter, asking if they would act without Kirby Smith's permission. There is no record of an answer. Wallace in the meantime sailed to New Orleans, where he asked Maj. Gen. Stephen A. Hurlbut, commander of the Department of the Gulf, to contact Kirby Smith, who cordially refused the proposals on May 7. By this time, Kirby Smith's response was irrelevant; newspapers in Texas had already denounced the proposal for a joint operation, while he months earlier had opened negotiations for a position in Maximilian's army. Ford, as well as Slaughter, had proven judicious in not challenging public opinion and the personal arrangements of superiors. In fact, to curry favor with the French, Kirby Smith sent copies of Slaughter's, Ford's, and Wallace's letters to Paris. Slaughter sent copies of Wallace's communications to Mejía, in Matamoros, perhaps as a similar gesture of good faith.[27]

Ford and Slaughter, after speaking with Wallace, did take his overture as a sign that there would be no more fighting on the Rio Grande, and so Ford scattered many of his companies to forage. Magruder resumed command of Texas from Walker on March 31, 1865, and did not press for operations against the Federals. The only concerns Ford had in early April focused on political developments south of the river. He learned that his old commander, Carvajal, had joined Wallace at Brazos

Santiago to discuss Federal support for himself and Juárez. Ford revealed that he had not yet quit the Confederacy by ordering Cater to arrange ambushes between Brazos Santiago and the mouth of the Rio Grande. If his troops could capture Carvajal on his return to Mexico, this would expose the connection between Juárez and the Federals and might push France into supporting the Confederates. Unfortunately for Ford, Wallace sent Carvajal to Washington to speak with Federal officials there. Matters became more complex when Juan N. Cortina declared in favor of Juárez, abandoning the Imperialist cause, and then raided Matamoros to recover the artillery he still had stored there. His brother José M. Cortina, who had made peace with the French, also denounced Maximilian and allegedly began making plans to raid across the Rio Grande. Reports that Federals were involved in recruiting and equipping Mexicans, and rumors that Santos Benavides might join Cortina against the French, convinced Ford that Matamoros could be a target for a full-scale attack, to be followed by towns in Texas. He redoubled his efforts to secure a formal alliance with Mejía, and advised the troops he still had on duty to watch the Federals closely.[28]

Tensions increased on the Rio Grande as April passed into May 1865. Magruder wrote to Smith on April 28 that the situation made the defense of Brownsville imperative because the Federals well knew the importance of stopping all trade between Mexico and Texas. At the same time, loss of the Rio Grande line would prevent effective cooperation between Texans and the French if the United States became involved in a conflict with France. At Ford's request, Magruder asked that reinforcements be sent to Brownsville. Cortina did assault Matamoros on May 1 and was repulsed, but he continued to gather men and money steadily. He also resumed his communications with the Federals, asking them to attack Brownsville and to return guns he had sent over the Rio Grande during the fall of 1864. Ford prepared to cross the river into Matamoros if Confederate citizens had to be protected from Cortina, and he also had his pickets watch for steamboats. Those at Brazos Santiago might be bringing Federal reinforcements, while Cortina had seized one on the river and could use it for an invasion of Texas.[29]

Matamoros. *Frank Leslie's Illustrated Weekly*, December 5, 1863.

Ford remained confident that the men who stayed with him would still fight even as the Confederacy collapsed in the East. To prevent bad news from spreading, Slaughter had ordered on March 10, before he and Ford talked with Wallace, that no United States newspapers could cross the Rio Grande into the interior of Texas. But Houston papers reported the surrender of Gen. Robert E. Lee on April 22, 1865, and the capitulation of Gen. Joseph E. Johnston on May 6. New Orleans newspapers reporting both surrenders arrived at Palmito Ranch, where some of Ford's men camped near Brownsville, by early May. Ford and his men thus knew, like many other Texans, that the two principal armies of the Confederacy had been vanquished. At the same time, however, Gov. Murrah penned a statement admitting Lee had surrendered but exhorting Texans to continue fighting. Kirby Smith and Magruder made it quite clear that they were determined to fight, and reports circulated that Confederate Pres. Jefferson Davis was making his way to Texas, where he would take charge of efforts to sustain a shattered but not yet moribund Confederacy.[30]

Robertson spoke for many of his colleagues in Ford's command when he wrote to his sister Julia in mid-April that the "Expeditionary Force" remained "in good condition and wood [*sic*] rejoice should an order come to go east." Despite their efforts at secrecy, he reported on Ford's and Slaughter's meeting with Wallace, who apparently wanted to "feel the pulse of our commanders on the Rio Grande and learn how they stood on the peace question." Robertson gleefully wrote that "Old Rip" must have "horrified" Wallace when he "told him that he preferred Louis Napoleon, as a ruler, to Lincoln. The old fellow left with a flea in his year [*sic*]." Having not heard the bad news from the far side of the Mississippi River, Robertson admonished his sister: "As long Julia as Robt. E. Lee is at the helm never say our prospect is gloomy. If God will only spare him to us, we cannot but succeed." On May 8, he wrote to Julia that Lee had surrendered but Johnston remained in the field after his terms for capitulation were rejected by Andrew Johnson, who had succeeded Lincoln as president. Robertson declared that "Andy Johnson calls for blood." The South would be completely subjugated and forced to pay reparations through the confiscation and sale of property, while government in the South would be controlled by blacks. Southerners were to become "menials, slaves of our own slaves," and so there was "nothing left to us but to fight." Ford received pleas from his men for everything from food to pants, but most agreed with Robertson. As Sgt. A. J. Murry of Santos Benavides' regiment reported, any claims that Ford's companies were "bursting up is all false."[31]

Despite the bravado of Ford and his men, the Civil War might have ended quietly on the Rio Grande, and Ford would have missed his chance to become a legacy, if not for the great ambition of Col. Theodore H. Barrett of the Sixty-Second Infantry (USCT). He arrived at Brazos Santiago in February 1865, and in late April assumed temporary command of the garrison, which included his regiment as well as the Thirty-Fourth Indiana Infantry, several companies of the Second Texas Cavalry (USA), and a few artillery companies. Ignoring the informal truce that had been followed for more than a month, and apparently in defiance of instructions from his superiors, Barrett decided to advance a detachment of his forces toward Brownsville. He never explained his motives, but speculation ranged from his desire to secure a victory to further a planned career in politics to the more plausible assertion that he had heard the Confederates had deserted Brownsville. Whatever his purpose, on May 11 he sent 250 men from the Sixty-Second Infantry (USCT) and 50 from the Second Texas (USA) into the field under the command of Lt. Col. David Branson of the Sixty-Second regiment.[32]

If Branson expected to find no Confederates, he quickly discovered otherwise. Rain drenched his men as they marched to White's Ranch by nightfall on May 11. The next morning he deployed an infantry company as skirmishers and advanced on Palmito Ranch, where Confederates had camped since the previous summer. The Federals met pickets from Giddings' cavalry battalion, commanded by Capt. William N. Robinson in Giddings' absence, and drove them back. Ford ordered Robinson to hold his position, so he counterattacked and again occupied Palmito Ranch by sundown on May 12, while the Federals retreated to White's Ranch and Branson sent to Barrett for instructions. Barrett responded by marching to reinforce Branson with the Thirty-Fourth Indiana Infantry, joining his subordinate at White's Ranch about daybreak on May 13. Leaving the Indiana troops to rest, Barrett once more advanced toward Palmito Ranch with half of his Sixty-Second Infantry and the Second Texas in a line of battle, preceded by the remainder of the Sixty-Second regiment serving as skirmishers. Robinson's troops fell back, allowing the Federals to retake Palmito Ranch and be reinforced there with the arrival of the Thirty-Fourth Indiana. Barrett, having decided to continue into Brownsville, rearranged his battle line with his regiment on the right and the Indiana troops on the left, with the Texans in the center. This fairly strong force of at least 500 soldiers pushed west until it again encountered Robinson's skirmishers, whose resistance convinced Barrett to abandon his march to Brownsville. Retiring to Palmito Ranch with his troops, he prepared to return to Brazos Santiago.[33]

Ford joined Robinson about two miles from the Federal position at Palmito Ranch at 3:00 in the afternoon on May 13, 1865. Told about Barrett's advance the previous day, Ford had hurriedly assembled a force to confront him. Showalter's regiment had been ordered away months earlier, and Santos Benavides' companies were far upriver. Other commands, in recognition of the informal truce, had scattered to forage, while desertion depleted those that remained. Ford gathered about 250 men and a motley collection of six guns, at least some of which may have been loaned to him by Mejía, before he joined Slaughter at dinner on the night of May 12 to discuss a battle plan. Slaughter revealed his intention to retreat, which caused an angry Ford to insist profanely that he would fight. Chagrined, Slaughter agreed to join Ford, and a defiant general order was issued that declared, "The Brig Ge[nl] Comdg is determined to contest every inch of ground and if possible, drive back the insolent foe who advances to enslave us." The writer added that "men resolved to be free can never be conquered," but who exactly wrote the order was not clear. Both Ford, with his state commission, and Slaughter could claim the rank of brigadier general. It became a moot point on the morning of May 13 when Ford led his command out of Brownsville without Slaughter, who had failed to appear. To his credit, Slaughter did not accompany Ford because he feared a raid by Cortina on Brownsville. He had Quintero ask Mejía to intervene if Cortina attacked, which he agreed to do, while the militia and other units were mustered and defenses were prepared.[34]

Ford with Robinson had a combined force of about 360 troopers, and he decided to attack. O. G. Jones, the artillery captain, tried to say that his Confederate commission outranked Ford's state title, but he quietly agreed to take charge of his battery after Ford had him arrested. Ford placed two guns of Jones' battery in his front and another pair on his left, with the remaining two in reserve, then delivered a stirring speech to his troops. Using hills and brush to mask his artillery while delivering a heavy fire on both Federal flanks, Ford struck hard. Startled, Barrett fell back, abandoning his skirmishers, and the Confederate troopers fought isolated small groups in a pursuit that covered seven miles in three hours. Ford peppered pockets of strong resistance with shells after being reminded that he had to shout commands in French to some of his gunners as they had come across the Rio Grande from Mejía's command. After Ford ended the chase because of darkness and his men's exhaustion, Slaughter arrived with Cater's cavalry battalion under the temporary command of Carrington. Slaughter insisted that Ford resume the fight. When the latter refused, Slaughter led troops to the edge of the narrow channel separating the mainland from the Federals on Brazos Island. After brisk skirmishing, Union gunners responded to the Confederates with shells, prompting a burst of profanity and a last futile rifle shot from a startled young Texan. Slaughter insisted that Ford hold his ground, but again the latter ignored orders, leading his men back toward Brownsville that night rather than risking envelopment in his exposed forward position.[35]

Palmito Ranch became Ford's legacy to the South as part of the treasured myth of the Lost Cause. One last time outnumbered Confederates had defeated more numerous and better equipped Federals. The latter lost 104 men captured, two killed, six wounded, and two missing, while only seven of Ford's men were wounded. Ford believed he had killed more Federals, but it did not matter—he had done enough. The Confederates also captured two flags, the national and the state banners of the Thirty-Fourth Indiana, which had been lost when the soldier carrying them was taken prisoner. Confederates found the flags in the brush on May 14. Ford was puzzled at Barrett's ineptitude, but that did not stop him from enjoying warm praise from Slaughter, who declared that Ford's victory "comes like a bright gleam of hope, to illuminate the dark cloud of disaster which has lowered upon us, and may be the harbinger of future successes and of prosperity and happiness." The luster of Ford's legacy was threatened when accusations surfaced that he executed Texas Unionists and Confederate deserters who had joined the Federals, or that many of these men died in battle rather than be subjected to summary justice. The fact that only two Federals were killed in the fighting belies the second part of those claims, while the first is undermined by the fact that some of the ex-Confederates captured at Palmito Ranch by their former comrades were allowed to escape on the march to Brownsville. Ford then paroled and released all remaining prisoners by May 15 rather than feed them. He even recognized some of the prisoners as Unionists he had chased while serving at Austin as supervisor of conscripts for Texas, and he freed these as well in a practical coda to the legacy of Palmito Ranch. To cap it all, Ford returned the state flag to the Indianans at about the same time that he paroled their colleagues.[36]

After Palmito Ranch, Ford again kept a wary watch on the Federals, telling his pickets near Brazos Santiago to watch for any transports bringing reinforcements. Brig. Gen. Egbert B. Brown arrived from New

Egbert B. Brown. Prints and Photographs Division, Library of Congress.

Orleans to take command of the Brazos garrison with orders to prevent Jefferson Davis and any other Confederates from reaching Mexico. While Davis had been captured on May 10, others remained at large, and Brown's orders included taking Brownsville if necessary to block their escape. To ascertain what Ford and Slaughter had, Brown sent a party of six officers under a flag of truce to Brownsville on May 20, 1865, just a week after the clash at Palmito Ranch. Slaughter had Ford tell the Federals that he was "too unwell to tend to business" and then serve as their host. To impress the visitors, Ford took them to Matamoros to meet Mejía and watch a review of his troops. While Ford clearly wanted to convince the Federals that he had strong allies at Brownsville, he also savored the confused reaction of both Mexicans and French when he walked into a Matamoros restaurant with his blue-clad guests. The visit had the effect Ford desired: Brown reported that Slaughter had 1,000 men and great support from the Imperial forces, and that most Confederate property had been removed to Matamoros, which had been reinforced and fortified. Brown thus asked for reinforcements before he would attempt to approach Brownsville.[37]

Ford also conveyed another message, intentional or not, during his interview with the Federal officers. While Slaughter appeared committed to fighting and supported the Imperialists, Ford and most of his men wanted peace and favored Juárez to the extent that they would join in any Federal effort to expel the French from Mexico. Brown continued his public correspondence with Slaughter, but he began writing privately to Ford. In an unofficial communication on May 26, Ford assured Brown that "we are anxious to do all in our power to secure an honorable peace, but candor compels me to remark, that we are unauthorized to treat. However, much may be done to avoid scenes of bloodshed and violence—by a proper understanding between all concerned, and by mutual forbearance." Ford understood the changing temperament of his troops, which had been made clear at a meeting at the Brownsville courthouse where the men balked at Slaughter's proposal to keep the command together and cross into Mexico if necessary to continue resistance to the United States. While some such as Robertson still argued for war, most were ready to go home. As Carrington wrote to Ford on May 22, "The men are not only radical but in a radically bad humor." An increasing number of them began leaving, knowing their comrades would not use force to detain them.[38]

An open break occurred between Ford and Slaughter when the latter sold the guns from Fort Brown to Mejía for $30,000 in specie, which was deposited with a merchant in Matamoros. Ford had his unpaid soldiers surround Slaughter's quarters on May 25 and force his commander to agree to distribute $20,000 in return for a signed receipt for the entire deposit. Ford had not been paid in eighteen months, so he kept $4,000 while the rest was given to the troops, all of whom allegedly got something. With his receipt in his pocket, as well as proceeds from the sale of cotton and travel permits, Slaughter left soon afterward with some of the men, crossing the Rio Grande far upriver and joining other Confederate refugees in Mexico. Ford made his own preparations to seek sanctuary with Mejía in Matamoros, asking Robinson, who had served so well at Palmito Ranch, to bring his remaining troopers to secure Brownsville in place of the departing garrison. Ford also sent his family across the river. On May 28, commanding in the absence of Slaughter, Ford sent a final communication to Mejía, probably from his new residence in Matamoros, asking for his assistance in posting guards along the Rio Grande to guard against "robbers." Brown led his Federals into Brownsville two days later, effectively relieving Ford of his responsibilities for protecting that town and its people.[39]

The Civil War ironically ended with Ford exiled from Texas, where he had played so many roles for almost four decades. Less than nine months after retaking Brownsville from the Federals, he could only watch from across the Rio Grande as they once more occupied the river port. Having secured his place in history at Palmito Ranch as a legacy for Southerners who revered the Lost Cause, and having proven himself once more to be of the same "fighting stock" as his revolutionary grandfathers, Ford found himself living in Matamoros. There he and his family were dependent on the protection of Imperialist forces that he hoped would soon be defeated. And if that happened, he might finally fall victim to Cortina, his old enemy who waited outside of Matamoros with a growing army of Juárista soldiers, whom Ford, ironically, supported in their efforts to regain control of Mexico for their refugee president. It was a strange turn of affairs, one that provided little encouragement for Ford and the many other Confederate fugitives from Texas and the rest of the Trans-Mississippi region who found refuge in Mexico. At fifty years of age, though, despite chronic health problems, Ford still had a lot of energy left. He had returned from administrative exile to become a legacy, and he would expand that legacy by retaking the public stage in Texas.

CHAPTER 7 STATESMAN

In the two decades that followed the collapse of the Confederacy, Ford again played many of the public roles he had defined for himself in Texas, as well as Mexico. He became, in turn, a soldier, newspaperman, lawman, politician, and finally a teacher, to the surprise of many. Like his grandfathers after the American Revolution, Ford became best known as a politician, albeit a conservative statesman devoted to opposing Republican reforms and restoring a Democratic hegemony. This, coupled with his persistent focus on extending the Texas border further south into Mexico, made him notorious in circles outside Texas, but within the state he was noted for his leadership in a peaceful transfer of power in Austin, for his efforts to secure peace along the Rio Grande border, and for his service as a state senator. Some grumbled that his appointment as superintendent of the Deaf and Dumb Asylum was nothing more than a sinecure, and the experience did end on a sour note when he was removed, but Ford in fact worked hard and accomplished much good, providing a suitable coda to his last years as a public servant for Texas.

Ford in 1865 settled in Matamoros under the protection of Gen. Tomás Mejía, but he watched Brownsville closely. For his host, Ford often secured information from his contacts in Brownsville on the operations of Benito Juárez and his supporters, but more important were the operations of the United States Army along the Rio Grande. Many of the opportunists who flocked to Matamoros during the Civil War disappeared, but Ford was not the only former Confederate to take refuge with Mejía, and this worried Federal officials. Maj. Gen. Philip H. Sheridan assumed command of the Military Division of the Southwest, which included Texas, during late May 1865, and within a few months 52,000 Union troops flooded into the state. Maj. Gen. Frederick Steele

Frederick Steele. Prints and Photographs Division, Library of Congress.

marched a division of the XIII Corps into Brownsville in early June, and Maj. Gen. Godfrey Weitzel sent elements of the XXV Corps up the Rio Grande. By June 19, when Maj. Gen. Gordon Granger debarked at Galveston and declared the Emancipation Proclamation to be in effect for Texas, the migration of ex-Confederates into Mexico had been slowed considerably. When Sheridan himself paid a visit to Brownsville during the last week of June 1865, he was greatly reassured to discover there was little threat from them or their potential allies among the French, for whom Mejía worked. At the same time, Ford retained the United States flag his troops had captured from the Thirty-Fourth Indiana Infantry at Palmito Ranch, just in case Sheridan or any Federal officer decided to reduce their concerns further by ordering his arrest. The precious relic could serve as a valuable item for bartering.[1]

Ford need not have worried about being arrested; he was too useful to the Union occupiers of South Texas, as well as influential Texans in the region. According to the terms for the surrender of the Trans-Mississippi signed on June 2, 1865, six Confederate officers were appointed to supervise the tedious process of issuing paroles to their fellow Confederates at designated sites in Texas. Because Brig. Gen. James E. Slaughter had disappeared upriver to join with die-hard Confederates marching deep into Mexico, Ford became the parole commissioner at Brownsville. Fortunately for him, his wife Addie had a cousin, Lt. Richard P. Strong, on Steele's staff, and he helped Ford establish a friendly relationship with the Federal commander. Ford brought Mifflin Kenedy, Richard King, and Felix A. Blucher with him to his first meeting with Steele, which proved productive. After receiving assurances of their support, Steele allowed Ford to parole them, which permitted Kenedy and King to rebuild their business operations on the Rio Grande while Blucher remained in Matamoros as Mejía's principal engineer. Others followed suit as Ford, who continued to suffer from his recurrent ailments, worked with Col. J. Charles Black, a Mississippi native who had been disabled and received the Medal of Honor as commander of the Thirty-Seventh Illinois Infantry. Among the last to cooperate was Col. Santos Benavides, who tardily submitted muster rolls for assigning paroles in late August 1865, almost two months after Ford and Black contacted him.[2]

Ford served in other roles as well. Col. Theodore H. Barrett had Lt. Col. Robert G. Morrison tried by a court-martial at Brownsville for his actions on May 13, 1865, at Palmito Ranch, which Barrett insisted had led to the capture of many Federals in that engagement. Morrison hired Israel B. Bigelow as his attorney, and Bigelow called his old friend Ford as a defense witness. Ford's testimony proved as damaging to official efforts to prosecute Morrison as any of Bigelow's other countermeasures, and Morrison was declared not guilty on every charge in August 1865. Reports surfaced during the same period that Slaughter had removed the lenses from the Point Isabel lighthouse and destroyed them. In fact they had been removed at the onset of the war and safely stored in Brownsville, and Ford led a Federal officer to the storage place. While stories of Ford's participation in destroying the lighthouse apparatus continued to circulate for many years, it actually was fully operational by February 1866.[3]

Ford, despite being paroled in July 1865, continued to live in Matamoros, but he urged others not to follow his example. He enjoyed a warm relationship with Mejía, but not with the French troops who comprised part of the town's garrison. Mejía had to intervene at least once when a zealous French officer tried to evict the Fords from their rented home, intending to billet French soldiers in their place. Ford later explained that while the Confederacy existed, he and others had been "friendly" to the French and their Mexican allies in the hope of advancing the Southern cause. After the Confederacy fell, "we raised our voices in favor of a government for the people and by the people," and thus supported Juárez. Mejía was willing to tolerate this; apparently the French were not. Ford did more than speak against the French—he discouraged former Confederates from supporting them in more substantial ways. Francis C. Zacharie of New Orleans, formerly the colonel of the Twenty-Fifth Louisiana Infantry, contacted Ford soon after the war, proposing to bring ex-Confederates to Matamoros to join the armies of Ferdinand Maximilian, who continued to serve as the emperor of Mexico with the support of the French. Ford convinced him not to do this, insisting there was "no future" outside the United States and that there was more honor in remaining in the South than in going abroad. Furthermore, "no true republican could take service under [Maximilian] and fight to establish a monarchy in Mexico."[4]

Life in Matamoros quickly became more complicated for Ford. He remained pro-Juárez, but he liked José María de Jesús Carvajal and Servando Canales, and hated Juan N. Cortina. It certainly did not improve matters that Cortina visited frequently with the Federals in Brownsville, which he used as a base for recruiting and launching attacks on Ford's hosts in Matamoros. To add insult to injury, the Federals returned guns they had confiscated from Cortina to him, while the French were pressed into surrendering the ten cannons Slaughter had sold them as the Confederates abandoned Brownsville. Juárez dispatched Gen. Mariano Escobedo in the late summer of 1865 to coordinate efforts to expel Mejía and the French from Matamoros. Escobedo negotiated with both Canales and Cortina to secure their cooperation, while reports circulated that Carvajal would return to Mexico from the United States and join the trio with money, munitions, and even troops. Ford became an informal messenger between Mejía and the Juáristas as the latter approached Matamoros and then besieged the town for more than two weeks. The Federals in Brownsville supported the Juáristas, and many Union veterans served with Escobedo, while some ex-Confederates fought for Mejía. Finally the attackers retreated, having suffered heavy losses. Escobedo's alliance then unraveled, with Cortina, Canales, Carvajal, and Francisco de León all claiming to be the legitimate governor of Tamaulipas by the end of 1865.[5]

Under increasing diplomatic pressure from the United States, the French agreed to leave Mexico, through a staged withdrawal, in January 1866. Within just a few months Carvajal, with strong support from Sheridan, forced Escobedo, Cortina, and Canales to accept him as leader of the Juárista forces threatening Matamoros. Mejía resisted their united attacks until he lost two-thirds of his troops at Santa Gertrudis in mid-June 1866. Eight days later, he left quietly for central Mexico, leaving Matamoros to be occupied by Escobedo's men. With them came Carvajal as the official governor of Tamaulipas under the resurgent Juárez. Carvajal in turn offered Ford, who stayed in the city, a commission as a brigadier general, with the understanding that the Texan would recruit other former Confederates to serve under him. Ford visited with Sheridan at Fort Brown to discuss the offer, and the general declared that the continuing enmity of ex-Confederates concerned him and that such men should not be encouraged to cross the Rio Grande and take up arms again. Ford assured him that the United States was not the target, and Sheridan reluctantly agreed not to interfere. After all, he had supported Carvajal's return to power as an acceptable substitute for Mejía and the French in Matamoros.[6]

Ford's return to service as a brigadier general under Carvajal, a position he had briefly held in 1851 and 1852, led to another short-lived reunion. Lew Wallace arrived in Matamoros with a weapons shipment for Carvajal. Wallace had worked hard to acquire support for Carvajal since the last year of the Civil War, and he allegedly participated in a raid on Bagdad in January 1866, when former Federal soldiers and bandits took the town from its pro-French garrison. Weitzel had sent troops to restore order but gave the place over to Escobedo rather than to its original garrison, again indicating support for any who opposed the French. In the late summer of 1866 Wallace became a brigadier general like Ford, but their alliance did not last long. Within weeks Carvajal, whom many Mexicans thought was too pro-American, further alienated his supporters by demanding loans and confiscating property. Escobedo complained about letting Mejía escape, while Juárez denounced the agreement with Mejía and ordered Carvajal court-martialed. Cortina took the opportunity to declare himself governor of Tamaulipas, but Canales preempted him by declaring a coup against Carvajal, announcing that he would be the military governor of Tamaulipas. When Ford hurried to Carvajal's office to warn Wallace, Carvajal joined them and confirmed the report, then told the Texan to return to his post. Later, Carvajal shot an officer who tried to detain him and fled to Brownsville with Wallace, who had also been briefly accosted by the mutineers in their relatively bloodless uprising.[7]

Canales tried to rule from Matamoros, but Foreign Minister Sebastián Lerdo de Tejada nullified all of his edicts, and President Juárez appointed Gen. Santiago Tapia as military governor. In turn, Canales had Tapia arrested in Matamoros, and Canales' ally, Gen. Pedro Hinojosa, took his place. Ford initially joined with Canales, understanding that he supported Juárez, but when Canales declared against Juárez and in favor of Gen. Jesús Gonzalez Ortega, the president of the Supreme Court of Mexico, Ford, and about one hundred Texans whom he had recruited, rebelled in early October 1866. The Texans were already unhappy because they had not been paid, and so they decided to join in a raid to free a Juárez representative held by Canales. Ford discussed the situation with his officers. He agreed to permit the attack, but he was not convinced it was a good idea, and he used illness as an excuse to be absent when the assault began at night in a thunderstorm. When it failed after lots of random firing but few casualties, Ford led his Texans aboard a gunboat for the short trip across the Rio Grande to Texas. There the commander of the gunboat, former Union Navy officer Bradley S. Osbon, surrendered his vessel to Federal authorities, and Ford's Texans disbanded.[8]

Ford's ignominious return to Texas did not go unnoticed. Ferdinand Flake, the outspoken editor of *Flake's Bulletin* in Galveston, condemned the Texans for their part in the fighting in Matamoros. Flake declared that "the doings of General Ford and Admiral Osborn [*sic*], the one commanding an army of 175 Americans and 13 Mexicans, and the other, a gunboat, manned by eight as gallant tars as ever drank rum, are notorious." He claimed that Ford's troops planned "to capture Matamoros, seize the Treasury, and pay themselves the wages due." Flake claimed that a storm drove Osbon's gunboat to the Texas side of the Rio Grande and his crew got drunk, forcing Ford to abandon his plans. Osbon's surrender of his gunboat to Federal officers, Flake added, made a bad situation worse and would take much time and money to resolve. Flake's solution was to call for the United States to assign more soldiers to the border to prevent such nonsense. Ford naturally was infuriated to learn that he had been characterized in such a manner, but he could do little about it. And years later he would admit, in his memoirs, that he was "rather ashamed" by the entire matter.[9]

Ford was not yet done with Canales. Escobedo again besieged Matamoros under the authority of Juárez, while Ortega, on his way to Mexico, was arrested by Sheridan's order at Brazos Santiago, thus ending that threat. Col. Thomas D. Sedgwick led troops from Brownsville to occupy Matamoros in late November 1866, insisting that he had to keep order and protect United States interests. Escobedo launched a bloody attack on November 27 that failed, and then withdrew and opened negotiations with Canales and Sedgwick. The latter, in order to secure a steady flow of supplies and facilitate transfers of any reinforcements, laid a pontoon bridge from Matamoros to Brownsville. During all this, rumors resurfaced that Cortina would attack Brownsville, perhaps in an attempt to advance his own claims to an office. Sedgwick, with his forces stretched thin, asked Mayor William Neale of Brownsville for assistance, and Neale called on Ford. Several hundred Union and Confederate veterans gathered at Fort Brown under Ford's command, and Sedgwick armed them. They listened nervously to Escobedo's attack and guarded the Texas end of Sedgwick's bridge, then were greatly relieved to learn that Cortina was not coming and that Canales had surrendered Matamoros to Escobedo on November 30. Sedgwick withdrew to Brownsville and dismantled his pontoon bridge, but Ford noted with amusement that he neglected to reclaim all the guns he had issued to the makeshift militia regiment.[10]

Ford's last role in the transfer of power at Matamoros was to serve as foreman of a grand jury empanelled at Brownsville in the spring of 1867 by Judge John C. Watrous of the United States District Court. Watrous had served as the attorney general for the Republic of Texas and as the first district judge after statehood, and had been forced to leave the state as a Unionist during the Civil War. His District Attorney, D. J. Baldwin, had been jailed as a Unionist in Texas during the Civil War and then banished to Mexico. Despite these credentials, they were denounced by some for allowing Ford to serve as a foreman in defiance of Maj. Gen. Charles Griffin's requirement that all who served on juries had to swear an oath that they had never supported the Confederacy. Ford presided as the grand jury, in response to instructions from Federal authorities, failed to indict any men brought before them for the raid on Bagdad in January 1866 despite the fact that, as Ford later admitted, the evidence against the accused was "mountain-high, and exhaustive."

At the same time Ford's jurors indicted others who had raided across the Rio Grande, and some were sent to the state prison. Perhaps the difference was that Weitzel had already held a court-martial for the soldiers involved in the attack on Bagdad. Apparently Judge Watrous was pleased with Ford; despite continued protests, he brought Ford to Galveston to serve as foreman of the grand jury there in May 1867, when Ford also enjoyed a final meeting with Maj. Gen. Samuel P. Heintzelman. In an epilogue to his sojourn in Mexico, Ford and Nestor Maxán served as defense counsels for Americans accused of robbing a saloon keeper while they were in Matamoros. Ford and Maxán lost the case, and the men were jailed, though Ford always believed they were innocent.[11]

Ford returned from Mexico in poor health only to face a series of personal losses. His father, William Ford, died on October 14, 1866, and was buried at Austin while his son remained entangled in events around Matamoros. A hurricane in early October 1867 destroyed Bagdad at the mouth of the Rio Grande and badly damaged Matamoros and Brownsville. Finally, Ford's father-in-law, Elihu D. Smith, died on October 16, 1868, at Brownsville after a long and painful illness. Ford and his wife Addie could take some comfort in three events. First, she bore them a son, named John William in honor of his father and grandfather, in April 1866. Second, Ford became a grandfather for the first time when his daughter Fannie and her husband William G. Thomas, who had settled in Austin to practice law, had a son, Gray. Last but certainly not least, Richard King during this period began depositing as much as $250 per month in a bank account for Ford, in appreciation for his efforts on behalf of King and his business associates during and after the Civil War.[12]

To help support his immediate family, which included Addie and three children by late 1866, Ford returned to the newspaper business. He became an assistant editor for the Brownsville *Ranchero,* owned by Somers Kinney and Henry A. Maltby, a fellow Mason who had served with William Walker in Nicaragua and as a delegate to the Texas Secession Convention. Among Ford's other colleagues in that enterprise was William M. O'Leary, an Irish-born Union veteran who married Ford's sister-in-law, Mary Louise Smith. Ford's poor health hindered his work for the *Ranchero,* so he quit and went to work for a rival, the *Courier,* owned and edited by Edmond P. Claudon. Exhausted from hard work and persistent illness, Ford had to leave that operation as well by 1868, but after a bedridden convalescence he rebounded and became the editor of a new paper, the Brownsville *Sentinel,* with the support of a partner, Jesse E. Dougherty. The editorial message of the *Ranchero* was bitterly anti-Republican and anti-Reconstruction, so much so that Maltby and Kinney were arrested by Col. Ranald S. Mackenzie in December 1867. Ford followed suit as the editor of the *Sentinel,* declaring that his purpose was to "reinstate the ballot box, and suspend the rule of the bayonet." As he explained in his memoirs, his newspaper remained staunchly Democratic, opposing "all the wild and oppressive measures of the Republican party in reference to the reconstruction of the Confederate states and other unconstitutional heresies they advocated and passed into laws." Ford did not focus only on politics—he continued to advocate temperance as he had always done—but his political writing seemed to draw the most attention.[13]

Ford's outspoken editorials led to at least one potentially deadly clash. He was playing billiards at Henry Miller's hotel in Brownsville on the evening of February 15, 1870, when Sheriff Rudolph Krause and Deputy Cruise Carson entered the room. The former, an immigrant from Germany, "directed insulting language at the Colonel." Ford finished his game and then approached Krause, who repeated his insults. Ford grabbed the sheriff "by the throat or ears," whereupon Krause drew his pistol and fired, wounding Ford in the hand when someone knocked the muzzle aside. Editor Maltby, in recounting the event, pointed out that Krause was a military appointee who had come to Brownsville after the Civil War, while Ford was a well-known leader of good character. Krause, he added, was a "good officer," but he "forgot himself" and disgraced his office. During the ensuing excitement a group of citizens called upon Brig. Gen. Henry B. Clitz to intervene with troops, but he declined, as he did for the next few days despite demands from acting mayor Jeremiah Galvan. The mayor issued an arrest warrant for Krause and Carson, but the sheriff fled, and Carson refused to allow coroner

Jacob Huth, the next legal officer in succession, to arrest him. Frustrated, Galvan met with the city council on February 18 and submitted his resignation, but the members persuaded him to stay. Soon afterward, Krause surrendered to Judge Henry Haupt of the state district court and was released on bail. Maltby took that opportunity to declare: "When the time has come that the sheriff of Cameron County can enter a hotel and insult an honorable citizen and attempt to take his life with impunity we are solemnly reminded of the propriety of keeping one's thoughts to himself, lest he himself may be the next subject for the licensed blade of an assassin." Strangely, when the court convened in late March 1870, Krause was still serving as sheriff, and there was no mention of indictments against him or Carson.[14]

Ford retired as the editor of the Brownsville *Sentinel* in the fall of 1871, in part because he was becoming involved in other business interests. King and Mifflin Kenedy had been given a charter in 1866 to operate a railroad from Brownsville to Point Isabel, using some of the equipment left behind by a military railroad operation, but the 1867 hurricane destroyed much of the equipment, and they did not rebuild. When Brownsville businessmen protested the lack of development and the partnership's continued high rates for conveyance on their steamboats, the Texas legislature pulled the charter and gave it to another group headed by Simon Celaya, a businessman and vice-consul for Spain at Brownsville. Ford and Maxán were among the directors of the new Rio Grande Railroad Company, for which Celaya served as president. They built a narrow-gauge railway from Brownsville to Point Isabel by 1872, despite two unsuccessful lawsuits from Kenedy, and the line operated under their original charter until early in the twentieth century.[15]

A rising tide of cattle theft and violence along the Rio Grande involved Ford in law enforcement, and indirectly drew him back into Texas politics. Brevet Maj. Gen. Alexander McD. McCook replaced Mackenzie as commander of the subdistrict of the Rio Grande in early 1868 after Mackenzie suppressed the Brownsville *Ranchero,* and McCook had Ford guide his single company of the Fourth United States Cavalry into the field on a three-day hunt for raiders. Nothing was accomplished, and the raids continued. When King and Kenedy

Alexander McD. McCook. Prints and Photographs Division, Library of Congress.

conducted an inventory in preparation for dissolving their ranching partnership, they were disturbed to discover how many cattle had been lost, and they hired private security forces that may have included Ford, whose continued presence on the border was often the subject of hateful articles in Mexican newspapers. The appointment of Cortina to a military command on the Rio Grande in 1870 alarmed many Anglos, who believed he orchestrated much of the theft. Ford's *Sentinel* estimated that 7,000 head of cattle were taken during one week in the summer of 1871 in Cameron and Hidalgo counties. Clitz, who as a Federal officer had given Ford a guided tour of Fort Brown in 1861, may have refused to intervene when Ford clashed with Sheriff Krause in 1870, but by the next year he was asking for his help in patrols "against cow-thieves and other disturbers of peace and quietude." Also in 1871, when McCook returned to investigate allegations of corruption against Maj. Gen. Joseph J. Reynolds, Ford, who had praised both McCook and Clitz in the *Sentinel,* rode with him during his inquiries along the Rio Grande and then accompanied him to Austin.[16]

A Cameron County grand jury convened during August 1871 to investigate cattle thefts called upon the federal government to intervene, and McCook added a warning that inaction might lead to war between the United States and Mexico. Ford served as foreman of a federal grand jury that met in Brownsville in March 1872 to consider the same problem. Three weeks of testimony ended with their impassioned condemnation of Cortina and other Mexican officials for a "reign of terror" from the Rio Grande to the Nueces River. Since the conclusion of the Civil War, they declared, "mercenary bands of marauders, Mexican officers and soldiers, and Mexican outlaws and bandits, have been . . . holding a saturnalia of crime, violence, and rapine upon the soil of Texas." About Cortina, "it may be truly said that he has written the history of his career on this side of the Rio Grande in letters of blood and fire." No fewer than 420,000 cattle had been stolen, worth a total of $6.3 million, and four hide inspectors appointed by the Army had been murdered. The jurors asked the federal government to send cavalry to guard the border.[17]

Congress passed a joint resolution calling for an investigation in May 1872, and Pres. Ulysses S. Grant in response appointed a three-man commission: Thomas P. Robb, Fabius J. Mead, and Richard H. Savage. Known as the Robb Commission, they came to Brownsville in July 1872 and departed in October 1872, then returned about March 1873, with Thomas O. Osborn in place of Mead, and toured the area south of the Nueces River. They returned once more to Washington, DC, in October 1873, and there they produced a report that included almost 1,100 pages of testimony documenting more than $48 million in claims for losses, more than 90 percent of which was attributed to Mexican raiders. In truth, only $11 million was claimed for actual losses, while much of the rest relied on laborious and sometimes comical calculations of potential losses. For instance, Ford represented the owner of a stage line who had lost 150 goats in 1867. This man wanted to be compensated for his goats and for the kids they might have had if they had not been stolen. Allegedly asked to calculate the actual and potential loss, Ford struggled valiantly and arrived at a preposterous figure of 2,521,018 goats. Ordered to declare his total, Ford commented, "If the figures don't lie, and the goat business ain't stopped, in ten years, sir, Texas won't hold her goats."[18]

Ford later wrote about the Robb Commission in a manner that reflected both amusement and regret. He did not recall the goats, but he did recount how the members of the commission feared snakes and scorpions. He remembered that Osborn one day during a march from Rio Grande City to Corpus Christi "began cutting peculiar capers," yelling and firing his rifle into the ground. When it was learned that the source of his terror was a lizard, the escorting black soldiers laughed heartily. On a more serious note, Ford admitted that considering any potential losses "was allowing consequential damages at a very large figure, in violation of a principle recognized by courts in all civilized countries." He personally presented claims for more than $3,000,000. Not surprisingly, the claims were ignored in Washington. Robb, as president of the commission, tried to meet with Grant and was not received at the White House. An attorney was retained to press the case, and Ford arranged for him to be paid 10 percent of each claim, but the man died before anything was resolved. When Robb hired himself as the representative for the claimants, Ford decided he was "a man of questionable integrity." He traveled to Washington to confer with Robb, "and was not favorably impressed by his demeanor." Feeling foolish, Ford dropped the matter entirely. He later heard that Robb had sold the claims to someone for $30,000, but Ford refused to believe "any sane man" would invest in such a "shadowy" transaction. To add insult to injury for Ford, the government did pay Robb for his expenses.[19]

In response to the Robb Commission, Pres. Sebastián Lerdo de Tejada of Mexico sent his own investigating committee to the Rio

Grande border. They compiled almost 18,000 pages of evidence from both sides of the border, and then produced a long report in Spanish and English that countered almost every assertion of the Robb Commission. Americans, not Mexicans, were committing the crimes. Recounting the revolt led by Carvajal in 1851, they condemned Ford for his participation, declaring that his "conduct during the whole course of his life has ever been absolutely hostile to Mexico." Much of the subsequent violence along the border originated with smuggling and efforts by the Texans to recover slaves. Concerning Ford's operations along the Rio Grande in 1860, they denied that Mexicans initiated any attacks, while Ford had engaged in looting and murder without provocation and without official permission to be in Mexico. The same scenario occurred in Zapata County in April 1861, when "several inoffensive inhabitants were assassinated" by vicious Confederates. If Mexicans did raid into Texas, the Lerdo de Tejada commission argued, they did so at the request of Americans, especially the Union government during the Civil War. Understandably, Ford did not discuss this Mexican rejoinder to the Robb Commission in his memoirs.[20]

Both the Robb Commission and its Mexican counterpart agreed on one point: the solution to border violence was to send more troops. Demands by cattlemen on the Texas side of the Rio Grande, along with the creation of organizations that looked suspiciously like vigilante groups, led the United States government to increase its military presence in the region. With the assistance of Mexican guides, and the effective cooperation of the Mexican military, much of the damage done by cattle thieves, many of whom did work for Cortina, lessened by 1873. At the same time, Mackenzie returned to the border with the Fourth United States Cavalry and led six of its companies in an attack on Kickapoo and Apache villages in Mexico, ending their involvement in the cattle thefts. The Mexican government filed only a mild protest at Mackenzie's brazen violation of its sovereignty.[21]

Amid the turmoil along the border, Ford reentered politics. Texas was readmitted to the Union in the spring of 1870, officially ending Reconstruction in the state. By the fall he was Chief of Police and Health Officer for Cameron County, struggling with the problem of drunkenness among the soldiers assigned to assist his officers in the hopeless task of monitoring border crossings. An amnesty act adopted by Congress in May 1872, which removed voting restrictions on ex-Confederates, broadened Ford's opportunities. He attended the Democratic state convention in June 1872 at Corsicana, where he placed third in the first balloting for Congress, then faded as Roger Q. Mills pushed to the front and won on a seventh ballot. Mills also outpolled James W. Throckmorton, who had been removed from the governor's office in 1867 as an "impediment" to Reconstruction. Noting that Mills resided in Corsicana, the Clarksville *Standard* declared, "The old war-horse of the Rio Grande, Col. John S. Ford, got a highly complimentary vote all over the state; but had too many rivals at home." Others attributed Ford's convention loss to his lack of preparation. He did impress many with a fiery speech denouncing Gov. Edmund J. Davis for not properly protecting the frontier, and so he was chosen by the delegates to attend the national convention in July. There he became infuriated when the Democrats endorsed liberal Republican Horace Greeley for the presidency, and he claimed he was leaving politics. Instead, he was appointed by Governor Davis as an Inspector of Hides and Animals for Cameron County, a practical choice that probably recognized Ford's continued involvement in law enforcement on the border and overlooked his politics.

Later, in 1873, Ford was discussed as a candidate for lieutenant governor on a ticket with Throckmorton as "The Impediment and Old Rip" (and got a few votes for governor at the state convention), and he was elected mayor of Brownsville in the fall, when Democrats swept the state elections.[22]

Ford traveled to Austin with the newly elected legislators from Cameron County in December 1873 as a conflict loomed between Governor Davis and the Conservatives, most of whom were Democrats. Davis argued that the 1873 elections were void because the polls opened for only a single day, not the four days required by the Constitution of 1869. Two weeks after the elections resulted in a Democratic landslide, Davis filed suit to challenge the results. The Republican-dominated Texas Supreme Court agreed that the election law was unconstitutional, and Davis announced his intention to block Democrats from taking office.

Richard Coke. Prints and Photographs Division, Library of Congress.

Angry Democrats, including Ford, converged on Austin, determined to install their candidate, Richard Coke, as governor. President Ulysses S. Grant advised Davis to accept majority rule, and Conservatives such as Throckmorton tried to negotiate, but Davis stood fast. Defiant, the Fourteenth Legislature, dominated by Democrats, met on January 13, 1874, elected officers, and notified Davis that they were ready to conduct business. Ford and others watched from the gallery or waited tensely in the Capitol halls. Two days later, the legislators declared Coke to be the governor of Texas. That night he was inaugurated in the Capitol, despite Davis sending state troops to block his entry.[23]

Anticipating an armed clash with Davis, Coke chose Henry E. McCulloch to act as his temporary adjutant general until his permanent appointee, William Steele, could arrive. McCulloch had no troops, but a militia company, the Travis Rifles, soon arrived at the Capitol led by Ford, allegedly singing "The Yellow Rose of Texas." Lt. Albert S. Roberts, their commander, had them sworn as a posse by Sheriff George B. Zimpleman, who had served in the Eighth Texas Cavalry with Roberts, and McCulloch posted them in the upstairs hall between the legislative chambers. Coke thus had troops on the second level, while Davis and his militia occupied the floor below them. The next morning, January 16, McCulloch suddenly announced that he was too ill to continue. Coke told Guy M. Bryan, a former Congressman who had been elected speaker, that he was responsible for defending the members of the House and its chambers in the Capitol. A worried Bryan encountered William N. Hardeman and asked him to find his cousin, William P. "Old Gotch" Hardeman, who had fought in all the wars of Texas since 1836, and "Old Rip" Ford, under whom William N. Hardeman had served as a conscription officer during the Civil War. When the three reported to Bryan at the speaker's rostrum, Bryan made a short speech calling upon them to serve Texas as they had previously, then appointed all three as "assistant sergeants-at-arms." He admonished them to protect the Capitol and the legislators, but to do so peacefully.[24]

Ford and the Hardemans remained involved with the showdown at the Capitol even after Steele arrived to assume the title of adjutant general. When Coke demanded that Davis surrender his office on January

William P. Hardeman. Brown, *Indian Wars and Pioneers of Texas.*

16, Davis responded the following day with a letter refusing to do so. The Travis Rifles in turn were ordered to occupy the nearby state arsenal, but when they arrived there they found the building defended by Davis' militia. To make matters worse, Mayor Thomas B. Wheeler, who had accompanied the Travis Rifles, was captured by another detachment of Davis' militia arriving from the Capitol under the command of Capt. Asa C.

Hill, who had served under Ford against Cortina in 1859 and 1860. After a heated argument, Wheeler simply walked away from his captors and made his way to Congress Avenue, where he found Ford at work. An angry mob had gathered with the intention of rescuing Wheeler, but Ford spoke to them, promising that if the "radicals and darkies" attacked first they would suffer "the worst whipping ever inflicted on any set of men since the world began." He also cagily explained that if the mob fired the first shot, military government would return. When Mart H. Royston, who had served under Ford in 1861 and had been removed as state treasurer in 1867, appeared and reported that "Old Gotch" Hardeman had asked for more militia, Ford called for all men who were interested in sustaining the laws to join Royston. Many rushed to do so, and Royston led them to the Capitol. The rest of the crowd dispersed, perhaps because Wheeler ordered all the saloons to close.[25]

Ford and the Hardemans were determined to avoid a fight if it was at all possible. When Hill later appeared at the Capitol to announce that he had stopped the Travis Rifles from occupying the arsenal, "Old Gotch" grabbed one of his men's rifles to prevent him from shooting Hill. Ford also blocked his militia from firing at Davis' troops twice, and he enforced strict discipline by threatening to pummel anyone who acted rashly. Coke later credited Ford with ensuring that the confrontation with Davis never became violent. Until Davis quit, Ford remained in the Capitol, "spending the nights on a straw couch in the executive office." Davis ordered his militia out of the Capitol on the night of January 17, 1874, and resigned two days later. Ford and the Hardemans were retained by Bryan until February 7 in response to rumors that Republicans would try to seize the Capitol at night. To ensure that did not happen, the three again slept in the building for days, and they spiked the two cannon on the Capitol lawn. On their last day of service, Speaker Bryan publicly thanked his three defenders, having them stand before his platform as he addressed the legislature, which responded with grateful applause.[26]

Ford remained in Austin through San Jacinto Day, April 21, 1874, then went home to Brownsville, where he continued as mayor. Thomas P. Robb arranged for him to write for the Chicago *Inter-ocean*

Showdown in Austin. *Frank Leslie's Illustrated Weekly,* February 21, 1874.

for a nickel per column, but Ford had more pressing issues to confront. The circuit court of the Eastern District of Texas employed him as an official translator in 1875, and Tejanos in Cameron County hired him to translate their petition to be compensated for losses in border raids, which once more resurged. Cortina, in control of Matamoros as well as commander of the troops in Tamaulipas, encouraged the raiders rather than try to control them. Both Ford and his former subordinate, Santos Benavides, testified to a legislative committee on border problems in March 1875. The following month, in response to remarks made by Ignacio Mariscal, Lerdo de Tejada's minister to the United States, as well as another raid in Nueces County, Ford and fifteen others produced a short tract insisting that Mexican policies and Cortina were to blame for continued violence on the Rio Grande, and that in fact only the United

States had ever effectively intervened on the border. They once more asked for federal or state military assistance to cope with the continuing threat of theft and murder.[27]

The turmoil on the Rio Grande prompted Governor Coke to appeal to Grant for help and to send a company of Rangers into the field led by Capt. Leander H. McNelly. McNelly and his Rangers arrived in Brownsville by May 1875 and began searching the region for cattle thieves. In June they encountered Mexican raiders, all of whom were alleged to be Cortina's men, and killed eleven in a fierce firefight. McNelly lost one of his Rangers, a young man named L. B. "Berry" Smith, and he returned with the body to Brownsville, where he asked Sheriff James Browne to retrieve the dead Mexicans. A detachment of cavalry accompanied Browne, who found eight bodies that had not been recovered by family members and displayed them in Brownsville. Ford agreed to serve as marshal for Smith's funeral together with Col. Henry C. Merriam of the Twenty-Fourth Infantry (USCT), and Texas Rangers marched with Merriam's black troops in the procession. Rumors flew that Cortina would cross from Matamoros, where he served as mayor, to exact revenge. Brig. Gen. Edward O. C. Ord as the commander of the Department of Texas ordered an ironclad gunboat, the USS *Rio Bravo,* and troops to Brownsville, if only to keep Texans from provoking a fight. Lerdo de Tejada wanted to avoid trouble, and so Cortina and others were arrested during July 1875 while the Mexican government assured the United States of its desire for a peaceful resolution. But once he arrived, Lt. Comm. Dewitt C. Kells of the *Rio Bravo* conspired with McNelly and others to initiate a confrontation with Mexican officials in Matamoros. Kelly's removal from command derailed the scheme, but McNelly attacked Las Cuevas in Mexico in November 1875, mistakenly expecting support from a detachment of cavalry. Outnumbered, he was forced to withdraw into Texas after initially attacking the wrong ranch, killing dozens of Mexicans in a bloody gunfight, and infuriating officials in both Washington and Mexico City.[28]

Ford, frustrated at the lack of resolution on the border, chaired yet another angry meeting in Brownsville in December 1875. McNelly attended the long discussion, which focused on the continuing trouble with Mexican raiders and how to keep McNelly and his Rangers on the Rio Grande. A committee of eleven, including Ford, was chosen to write a memorial to Governor Coke asking for McNelly's Ranger force to be increased. The chair of this committee was John L. Haynes, who had served under Ford with Carvajal in 1851 but commanded the Second Texas Cavalry (USA) during the Civil War. Yet another delegation, also chaired by Haynes and including both Ford and McNelly, was asked to present the same petition to Congress. McNelly carried the missive to Austin and then continued to Washington, where he testified during January 1876 before a House of Representatives committee on border unrest chaired by the Texans' nemesis during the Civil War, Nathaniel P. Banks. Not satisfied with the congressmen's response, which may well have been shaped by their disapproval of his invasion of Mexico, McNelly returned to Texas and continued to lobby for the return of his Rangers to the field.[29]

Ford was not a conspirator with McNelly and Kells because he was in Austin as a delegate to the constitutional convention that began on September 7, 1875, and continued for sixty-eight days. Congressional elections in the fall of 1874 created a Democratic majority in the United States House of Representatives, so Texas Democrats decided that it was safe to replace the state's 1869 Constitution, which contained many Republican reforms. The legislature passed a bill for a convention, Governor Coke signed it and issued a call for elections, and Ford won for the Twenty-Ninth Senate District. He was similar to most of his fellow delegates in that he was a Southern-born Democrat, but he was older than almost all of the others and unlike a majority of the delegates had attended a previous convention and had legislative experience. Some prominence attached to the fact that he was one of only eight who had attended the 1861 convention, and many remembered his campaigns before and during the war. With such credentials, he was in a good position to become a leader during the constitutional convention, and in fact he chaired the Committee on State Affairs and served on five others as well.[30]

Ford's Committee on State Affairs recommended provisions in the new Texas Constitution for maintaining public roads through citizen labor rather than a tax, building a new Capitol, and providing pensions for Texas Revolution veterans. The idea of reducing taxes appealed to other delegates, but the provisions for the Capitol and veterans led to angry debates. Ford in his memoirs hotly defended the idea of setting aside 3,000,000 acres for a new Capitol, asking, "Has it occurred to any brawling opposer of the measure that the land appropriated was far outside the settled parts of the state, and could not have been sold, in 1875, at five cents an acre?" The grant was included in the new Constitution, and Alexander W. Terrell introduced the enabling bill in the legislature that resulted in a new Capitol being built by 1888 after the old one burned. Ford was not as successful in his fight to raise pensions for Revolution veterans, who had been paid a base pension of $250 a year under the 1869 Constitution. The new Constitution reduced that amount to $150 per year, in keeping with recent legislation, despite the protests of Ford and a minority. He sarcastically recalled this as a "grand gift," adding, "After this display of generosity who dares say republics are ungrateful?"[31]

Ford had similarly strong opinions on his work with other committees and as an individual. He served on a select committee that focused on frontier defense, producing a petition that was sent to Congress on behalf of the convention to demand protection for the Rio Grande area and compensation for those who had suffered losses. Like previous Texas Constitutions, the new charter provided for the confiscation of abandoned lands, including Spanish or Mexican grants that had never been documented, and confiscation of lands held by those who had been supporters of Mexico in its conflicts with Texas. Ford successfully introduced a special section into Article XIV of the new Constitution that gave those who lived between the Nueces River and the Rio Grande an extension of time, until 1880, to prove all land claims due to the "unsettled condition of the country," which he claimed began with an 1839 evacuation order from General Valentín Canalizo of Mexico. Ford also argued in vain for the appointment of judges rather than electing them, but he joined the majority in favor of allowing local option on liquor sales, creating the office of Commissioner of Insurance, Statistics and History, and giving the governor the power to lease or sell public land to the national government for military posts.[32]

Ford and Fletcher S. Stockdale, who had been the last Confederate governor of Texas, signed separately from the other members of the committee created to present the new Constitution to the voters. The two endorsed the document, and recommended that people vote for it, but made it clear that they, unlike the rest of the committee, did not "concur in all the particulars of the address of the Committee." Ford in fact remembered that he signed the Constitution under protest. He objected to the overwhelming fiscal conservatism that had led, among other things, to a lowering of state salaries to a point where he thought it would be difficult to convince good men to serve. He blamed those that belonged to the Patrons of Husbandry, or "Grangers," for being petty with money. He recalled that the Grangers, which numbered forty and included such prominent men as John H. Reagan, joined with the fifteen Republicans to outvote the forty-six Democrats who wanted a more liberal Constitution. He always believed the Republicans did this to make the public vote against the new Constitution, but Democratic unity ultimately foiled this tactic. Both Ford and Stockdale served prominently on the committee on the platform and resolutions at the Democratic state convention in January 1876, and the next month the voters of Texas overwhelmingly endorsed the new charter.[33]

Attending the Democratic convention in January 1876 prevented Ford from going with McNelly to Washington, but he made time to honor an old friend and settle matters with an old enemy that month. John B. Magruder had died and was buried in Houston in February 1871; when his body was moved to Galveston in January 1876, Ford served as a pall bearer. Burying a living foe proved more complex. Carvajal had written to Ford as early as February 1872 to protest against Lerdo de Tejada's apparent support of Cortina. Cortina was removed as commander of troops along the Rio Grande after the conflicting commission reports were published, but he remained a general. His taking charge of Matamoros in 1874, in conjunction with an increase in border violence, forced Lerdo de Tejada to send troops to arrest him, but he still

Porfirio Díaz. Prints and Photographs Division, Library of Congress.

worried Ford and other Texans. Porfirio Díaz, planning his own challenge to Lerdo de Tejada, visited Brownsville in January 1876 seeking support. He met with Ford, who explained the situation in simple terms: promise to keep Cortina away from the Rio Grande, and Díaz would find it easy to get money from Americans. Díaz promised Ford, King, Kenedy, and others that he would remove Cortina and also support a railroad from the Rio Grande into central Mexico, and so thousands of dollars flowed into his hands, including some from Savas Cavazos, Cortina's half-brother. During Díaz's subsequent attack on Lerdo de Tejada, whom Ford regarded as "an astute lawyer, with more brains than principles and less patriotism than selfishness," Ford again worked as a translator and reporter, sending pro-Díaz material to the Galveston *News* and other Texas papers.[34]

Díaz kept his word about Cortina. Watching from Mexico City, where Lerdo de Tejada had detained him, Cortina pronounced in favor of Díaz, then fought for him along the Rio Grande. Ordered to report to Díaz in Mexico City after he took power, Cortina stalled. Díaz, unwilling to tolerate rivals, had Cortina arrested during late February 1877. Servando Canales, whom Ford had given sanctuary from Cortina in 1864 and then plotted to remove at Matamoros in 1866, became military governor of Tamaulipas as well as the commander of troops along the Rio Grande for his support of Díaz, and it fell to him to decide Cortina's fate. He held a military trial that condemned Cortina to be executed. Ford, who had tried but failed to warn Cortina that Canales had troops looking for him, crossed the Rio Grande to speak with Canales, declaring that killing Cortina might lead to unrest and violence. Ford later said that he did this in keeping with the understanding that began with his promise to Cortina's mother and continued with Cortina's courtesy to Ford's wife during the Civil War. Canales was unmoved, but two days before Cortina's execution Díaz sent a telegram ordering the prisoner transferred to Mexico City. There Cortina remained a prisoner until he was permitted to settle in Azcapotzalco under house arrest, where he stayed until his death in October 1894. After Cortina left, cattle thefts on the border gradually declined.[35]

Having reestablished himself in Texas politics with his work for the Democratic Party and his activism in the constitutional convention, Ford in 1876 won the first of two consecutive terms in the Texas Senate. There he continued many of the initiatives for which he had pressed hard in the convention. He had pushed unsuccessfully for a provision promoting immigration into Texas, and in the Senate he continued to lobby for this idea. He failed, for which he blamed "rutabagaism," a dismissive reference to the agrarian faction within the Democratic Party. Ford was also noted as an advocate of frontier defense and education, although his efforts in the latter focused on providing for the sale of public lands to create an endowment rather than supporting tax increases for the benefit of schools. He always argued "that efficiency in the public service was the only true measure of a wise economy." Ford had fought for the inclusion of the office of Commissioner of Insurance, Statistics, and History in the new state Constitution, and as a senator he introduced, at the suggestion of Comptroller Stephen H. Darden, an enabling act for that agency. The duties had previously been done by a "clerk in the Comptroller's office," who did not have the time or resources to tend properly to such matters. Of great concern to Ford was the distressing fact that "the men who assisted to make Texas a free and independent republic were passing away, and very few of them had left written statements of the affairs in which they were efficient actors." The office he helped to create would work to gather their papers, and thus assist in preserving their legacy.[36]

As a Texas senator, Ford found himself in a position to assist McNelly in his law enforcement effort on the Rio Grande. McNelly returned from Washington to the border and in June 1876 arrested John King Fisher and eight of his men. Fisher, an outlaw who had killed at least a half-dozen men, had forcefully taken control of parts of Dimmitt and Zavala counties. McNelly left him and his men with officials at Eagle Pass, who quickly released the prisoners on bond. A frustrated McNelly complained to Adj. Gen. William Steele that he did not have the time to bring witnesses against Fisher and his gang, seven of whom could be indicted for murder, before they were freed. The Ranger commander angrily added that he had recovered hundreds of stolen cattle from Fisher, but the hide inspector and sheriff refused to look at them, and so he turned them loose. McNelly also wrote to Ford, suggesting that a measure for an automatic change of venue in such cases would be helpful. He then made his way to Austin, where he testified before the Texas Senate Committee on Indian Affairs and Frontier Protection, chaired by Ford. After McNelly described his frustration, Ford prepared a bill for a new Ranger company to be led by McNelly. Rather than having to deliver prisoners to sheriffs or other officials, each Ranger was empowered to make his own arrests. The bill passed in an amended form, and McNelly by August 1876 was again on the border, where he campaigned for two more months before tuberculosis forced him to leave his command. Concerning the extraordinary power granted to McNelly's Rangers, Ford wrote, "If any one . . . misused the power vested in him by the law the writer has never heard of the fact."[37]

Impatient with the slow subsidence of violence along the border, Ford became involved in one last scheme to invade Mexico. Handbills circulated in Brownsville and Corpus Christi in the fall of 1877 claiming that Gov. Richard B. Hubbard had authorized Ford to recruit a regiment to march into that country. The Galveston *News* in October reported that Ford had gone to Corpus Christi "on some special and confidential mission, the nature of which has not fully transpired." Ford did travel to Corpus Christi with a cavalry escort, and he delivered a "spirited lecture" to a crowd at the city hall there on October 4. Emotions were high because Lt. John L. Bullis, who had repeatedly raided into Mexico with Army troops and Seminole scouts, was feared lost, but Bullis returned and Ford's plans fizzled. Only a few volunteers answered his call, and similar meetings chaired by him in San Antonio and Austin failed to gather many more recruits. He did not conduct a rally for his proposed filibuster in Brownsville, where apparently Cortina's arrest and the operations of law enforcement officials had greatly reduced the concern for Mexican unrest. Too, he may have had other matters weighing on him when he returned home to Brownsville: his mother-in-law, Mary S. Smith, died in November 1877.[38]

Texans may have lost interest in Ford's plans to invade Mexico, but Congress was not so complacent. An investigating committee in January 1878 interviewed a series of witnesses. Julius G. Tucker, a Brownsville businessman and Army contractor, testified about Ford's activities during the previous fall. Tucker had asked Ford if Hubbard had given him a commission; Ford denied it, then disappeared from Brownsville and surfaced to speak in Corpus Christi, San Antonio, and Austin. Tucker supported Díaz, but he was uncertain whether Ford intended to fight for or against him. Newly elected Congressman Edward S. Bragg asked if Ford was actually a "buccaneer," accusing him of having his own people steal cattle and report them as stolen by Mexicans. Bragg then added, "He avails himself of every opportunity to get up sensational items about wrongs perpetrated on Texans by Mexicans, does he not?" Tucker responded, "He may." Bragg also declared Ford talked "continually" about invading Mexico, to which Tucker said, "He is talking of war frequently." Questioned further, Tucker described Ford as one of the local leaders who wanted to invade Mexico, though he was not the most prominent. Bragg continued his hard queries with John L. Haynes, the former filibusterer and Union colonel who now served in Brownsville as collector of customs. Haynes proved more reluctant to speak ill of Ford, insisting that he did have a commission from Hubbard and supported Díaz. But he had to admit that Ford made it clear that he still thought the Sierra Madres made a better boundary between the United States and Mexico than the Rio Grande.[39]

Haynes revealed that Ford himself was in Washington in January 1878 and ready to answer any questions. The news that "Old Rip" had answered the committee's call led to a flurry of angry denunciations from anonymous enemies along the border. Telegrams were sent to the Chicago *Tribune* and New York *Herald* denouncing him as a bandit and worse. One angry dispatch from Brownsville was quoted in the Dallas *Herald,* accusing Ford of having led filibusters to burn Matamoros during Carvajal's 1851 revolt, of being in the pay of both Díaz and Cortina in 1876, and of trying to recruit volunteers to invade Mexico in 1877. As for what he would try to do in Washington, the writer declared that "Ford and his fillibusters [*sic*] will show that war is positively necessary and absolute inevitable." Ford's supporters in Brownsville organized and sent a protest in his favor to the Dallas *Herald,* but apparently all the

John L. and Angelica Haynes. Lawrence T. Jones III Collection, Southern Methodist University.

fuss was for nothing: he did not appear before the Congressional committee. Instead, he stayed in Washington until August 1878 to attend to a series of other issues. He met with Pres. Rutherford B. Hayes to discuss the frontier, and perhaps to lobby for his own application to be a United States marshal. He did testify to Congress, but it was about border unrest, its impact on sheep farmers, and how the construction of the Galveston and Camargo Railroad, with federal subsidies, would aid in defensive operations as well as economic development. He did not get his appointment, nor did the railroad ever get its subsidies. Instead, King and Kenedy got new partners and built a narrow gauge line from Corpus Christi to Laredo, bypassing Brownsville and Matamoros.[40]

Ford returned to the Texas Senate for his final term in 1879. There were many issues to confront, so all of the senators accepted multiple assignments. Ford served on at least a dozen committees and chaired the Committee on Frontier Protection. He spoke at length in March on the latter subject, beginning with long quotations from Swiss legalist Emerich de Vattel on the obligation of nations to defend their people, as well as several Supreme Court cases on the same issue. He also recalled seeing the white woman captive in a Comanche camp, declaring, "It may be reprehensible for me to say it; I have done some tolerably rough Indian fighting but I have never led a headlong charge without having the figure of that woman before my mind's eye just as she appeared on Brady's creek; and my conscience does not accuse me of a failure to avenge her sad fate." He dwelt on the memory for a moment, adding, "I wish to God she could stand before this Senate, and appeal to its members with the mute eloquence of grief to protect the exposed families which constitute the advance guard of progress and civilization, and not to allow human blood and human suffering to be placed in one scale and money in the other." His plea for additional Rangers "to protect the brave spirits who are bearing aloft the flag of civilization" fell largely on deaf ears. Despite the angry opposition of Ford, who even traveled to the state Democratic convention in San Antonio during the legislative session to denounce those who balked at paying Ranger expenses, the legislators in 1879 cut funding for the Rangers by a third, reasoning that the advancing frontier itself, with its growing population, made special protection unnecessary.[41]

Ford proved equally passionate about settling the remaining claims against the Republic of Texas. He was appalled when the Senate refused to pay the claims of the heirs of Thomas Toby, who had helped to finance the Texas Revolution. Despite the endorsement of Comptroller Darden and other prominent leaders, the vote was sixteen to ten against paying the claim, with the majority arguing that to pay such a claim would open the door to fiscal danger. Ford wrote a protest against the vote, which was signed by him and three other senators on Texas Independence Day, March 2, 1879. This said, in part, that paying the Toby heirs would be "shielding Texas from the charge of repudiating a claim she is morally bound to pay as an act of gratitude and justice to a noble man who was her friend and benefactor in the dark days of danger and peril." Toby's son, with the endorsement of the legislature, later sued in the Court of Claims at Washington and won a judgment that was paid by the United States Treasury from the funds set aside in the Compromise of 1850 to pay Texas debts. When this issue was presented before Congress to secure enabling legislation, Ford's protest was one of the documents presented in favor of payment, which was approved in March 1881. Ford applauded this result, writing that it "saved [Texas] from the charge of meanness and ingratitude."[42]

History became an increasing concern for Ford, foreshadowing the last stage of his life when he spent much of his time writing his memoir. He had served twice under the command of Thomas J. Rusk, in 1838 and 1839, and very much admired him. On March 2, 1879, Ford was the first speaker before a joint session of the legislature when a portrait of Rusk, by John S. Morton of Kentucky, was hung in the Senate chamber. This was fitting since Ford had successfully introduced a bill just a few months earlier to have portraits painted of all of the presidents and governors of Texas. His succinct but florid remarks were followed by a much longer speech from Ashbel Smith, and later by an address from Oran M. Roberts. Ford also pushed through a bill for funding the state library and setting aside space for it in the Capitol, but he could

Alexander W. Terrell. Daniell, *Personnel of the Texas State Government, 1892.*

become obstructive if he thought that one history was being favored over another. When a bill for a monument to the Eighth Texas Cavalry, popularly known as Terry's Texas Rangers, was put to a vote in the Senate on April 18, 1879, Ford was among the minority who voted in favor of an amendment from Alexander W. Terrell to sponsor monuments to all of the Texas veterans "who fought in any war of the United States prior to 1861 or in the late civil war." After Terrell's proposal failed, Ford joined a majority who voted against a substitute bill introduced by Walter P. Lane that endorsed monuments for all Texas veterans of Confederate units, apparently because Lane did not include state organizations or antebellum veterans. Terrell then announced he would "cheerfully vote for permission to erect a similar monument by the friends of any who fell in the defense of whom they believed to be right, and in obeying the call of the state or government which they believed was entitled to their allegiance." Lane then withdrew his substitute, and the original bill passed and became law.[43]

There were many other issues in which Ford became involved during his last term as a Texas senator. He and Terrell were friends; in fact, they were baptized together by Richmond K. Smoot, the energetic pastor of the First Southern Presbyterian Church in Austin. Not only did the two men as senators ally over monuments, but they were also appointed to serve along with two members of the Texas House of Representatives as a committee to inspect the governor's mansion. When they reported the sad condition of the building and its furnishings, funds were appropriated by the House to pay for repairs and new furniture. Ford was also one of the legislators appointed to a special committee to receive the body of United States Representative Gustave Schleicher, who had pushed hard for reparations for his Rio Grande constituents, from a congressional committee in late January 1879 and oversee his burial in the state cemetery. Interestingly, Schleicher was a German immigrant, and Ford had spent much energy that same month arguing that the governor's annual message should be published in German and Spanish as well as English. When the legislature met in a special session during June 1879, Ford expanded his horizons by amending a bill for Prairie View Normal Institute, increasing its funding by $1,600. The institute, which opened within a few months as the only public institution of higher education for blacks in Texas, later became Prairie View A&M University.[44]

By the time Prairie View opened, Ford had undertaken yet another new role for Texas. He was appointed as superintendent of the Deaf and

Dumb Asylum at Austin in place of Henry E. McCulloch in late August 1879. McCulloch had endured a turbulent term, and the legislature in April 1879 transferred the power to appoint a superintendent from the asylum's governing board to the governor, Oran M. Roberts, subject of course to legislative approval. Roberts chose Ford, his friend, who did his best to improve the asylum. He found that his new students "had been for many months previously in a state of dissatisfaction and occasional insubordination, which it seemed [McCulloch] was not able to allay and control, so as to produce harmony in the institution." McCulloch had gotten an appropriation of $2,500 in the spring of 1879, and that summer had asked for $26,200 more to remodel or complete existing buildings, build new structures such as a dining hall and chapel, replace cisterns with city water systems, install gas lines, hire new teachers, and buy groceries. All of these tasks fell to Ford, who did not get an increase in funding. One month after the legislators confirmed his appointment in January 1881, a Senate committee visited the asylum and found enrollment had increased from twenty-two in the fall of 1879 to eighty in the spring of 1881. Ford struggled with no increase in faculty, with facilities that had never been completed or updated, and with an annual budget that was already exhausted. He asked for $44,000, more than twice what he asked from the state one year earlier. He apparently never got what he requested, but when senators came again in early 1882 they found the asylum well managed and without a deficit, and in a few months water lines were finally laid.[45]

Ford's appointment upset many people, who argued that he had no experience in education, especially with deaf and dumb students. He proved them wrong by learning sign language and working hard to instill a real system of education. He expanded the curriculum, initiated an honor system, and provided new student positions in farming, shoe repair, printing, and book binding. He was especially proud of his work with the *Texas Mute Ranger,* a student newspaper which began publication in 1878 and continued until 1888. Under Ford, it presented poetry as well as articles on history, politics, current events, culture, hunting, and even science in an effort to promote both learning and good character. Ford himself wrote some contributions; for instance, the May 1880 edition had a long article on his Canadian River expedition and another on John C. Hays. He also, in the April 1882 edition, printed a transcript of his 1875 interview with Francisco Becerra, who claimed to have fought as a Mexican sergeant at the Alamo and served under Ford at Brownsville in 1861. In March 1883 the *Texas Mute Ranger* reported on a fire in a New York school, where fourteen children had been crushed in a panic. Ford had an excellent reason for including this article: an asylum barn had burned to the ground on March 1. He asked, "What would have been the terrible results had these children [in New York] been deaf mutes?" His buildings were mostly wooden, crowded close together, with wooden exterior stairways. Calling for state money to build fireproof facilities, he rephrased his plea for maximum impact: "How many innocent children would be burned alive, roasted like so many rats?" If nothing else, the involvement of students in writing and printing such articles demonstrated that they could be productive employees.[46]

Ford's tenure as superintendent of the Deaf and Dumb Asylum was a personally taxing one for him as a father as well as a teacher. He and his wife Addie adopted a baby girl, Lillian Alva Ford, born June 21, 1878, so Ford became responsible for an infant at the advanced age of sixty-three. Far more distressing was the death of his only son, John William Ford, on February 25, 1880, at the age of thirteen. The boy, who attended the Military Institute of Austin, was showing a pistol to some of his father's students when it discharged, hitting him in the left leg. The elder Ford immediately applied a tourniquet, but his son died of "nervous depression" weeks later. Ford had served on the vestry of the Episcopal Church of the Advent, where he apparently also taught Sunday school, in Brownsville after the Civil War, and the boy was buried in an Episcopal service. Ford may have wondered how much worse things could get when his oldest daughter, Mary Louise Ford, whom he called Lula, was kidnapped by an unidentified man and woman in November 1882. Her struggle forced them to abandon her on a bridge over the Colorado River a half mile from the asylum. A man discovered her, handcuffed to the railing and gagged, and with the assistance of the bridge tender and Samuel De Cordova he freed her and took her home. Ford tried to track the kidnappers, but to no avail.[47]

Somehow Ford managed to retain a sense of humor, macabre as it might be. He wrote a jovial letter to his old subordinate, John J. Dix Jr., in March 1883, reporting that his second daughter, Addie, married De Cordova, the man who rescued her older sister in November. As for "The Mustang," Lula, "She may marry, provided she does not flirt herself 'out of the ring.'" Her less-than-doting father added, "She is now patronising [*sic*] the drama, and is of [the] opinion she has a voice for the opera. I opine it is more suited to calling hogs, and eating bacon and eggs, than for trilling on the stage." Their mother, whom Ford called a "Red-headed Institution," apparently suffered from ill health, but she had not convinced her husband of the seriousness of her afflictions. Ford declared, "She has gone quite through the catalogue of ailments. She is showing premonitory symptoms of itch, and that is the last on the bill of fare promulgated by the pill peddlers. Won't I be glad when the old critter has trotted down the home-stretch, fooled the doctors, and swindled any body else!!" Recalling Dix's problems with his own family, Ford remarked that Richard M. Swearingen, who also served under Ford and now was the state health officer for Texas, had been "very successful in that line. He charges very high—fifteen dollars for getting up a female funeral in the most approved and artistic style. Should he come down to five dollars, within easy reach of hundreds of loving husbands, I shall think of employing him."[48]

Ford as superintendent of the Deaf and Dumb Asylum was a political appointee, and politics led to his removal from that post in December 1883. His fiery challenge to the legislature for construction money led to angry debates on the Senate floor, in which his ally Terrell declared he would not trust his horse's life in the wooden buildings of the asylum. An appropriation passed, as well as a land grant, and by the summer of 1883 an extensive rebuilding of the campus was underway that included the removal of all wood structures. Unfortunately, the legislature also ceded control of the superintendent's job back to the board of directors, chaired by Thomas W. Folts. By the fall of 1883 he and Ford were fighting, perhaps because construction delayed the opening of the asylum that year. The board met in a "private meeting" and sent a letter to Ford telling him he was removed based upon charges from

Richard M. Swearingen. Prints and Photographs Division, Library of Congress.

"Thommie," as he caustically referred to Folts. Ford recalled in his memoirs that he was not allowed to attend that meeting or to confront Folts or any other witnesses in "this kangaroo, hidden, and one-sided affair." When he told the board that he intended to resign, they withdrew their dismissal and allowed him to do so, effective December 31, 1883. In his departing report as superintendent, Ford added a final salvo against his political enemies: "I have not endeavored to please any one in particular, but to do my duty. I have not abandoned my purpose for smiles or frowns—the first have not induced undue complacency, and the latter caused no intimidation." His replacement was William Shepard, who came under fire from the Texas Senate and was removed, along with Folts, by Gov. Lawrence S. "Sul" Ross, to the delight of Ford.[49]

Despite the satisfaction of seeing his enemies removed, Ford had to realize that his time on the political stage in Texas had ended. Anticipating a Democratic triumph in Washington in 1877, he had tried to secure an appointment as the collector of customs at Brazos Santiago. The accession of Republican Rutherford B. Hayes to the presidency, and Ford's continued advocacy of an invasion of Mexico, ended any realistic hope for a significant federal appointment. On the state level, he remained active on the Democratic Executive Committee for Texas during his term in the Senate, and Brownsville delegates to the convention were told to support him for governor, but his friend Roberts won that office in 1878. Others such as Hamilton P. Bee still sought Ford's support for candidates and political appointments, acknowledging his influence, and he served as a delegate to the Democratic state convention in 1882, but he was no longer discussed as a candidate.

Months before stepping down at the asylum, Ford remarked that for him, "the political chess-board is almost idle." Mainline Democrats had to be quite cautious, while the independent faction of that party was "watching and waiting." As for any chance that he would join the Texans who opposed the Democrats, he characterized them as a "mongrel brood," adding, "The ground-work is radical, and the corpus is made up of Greenbackers, discontented democrats, and worn out office-seekers."[50] He saw no future there. Instead, he would find yet another role in the public arena. The story of the Texians, including himself, had not been properly told, and he would seize the opportunity to do just that. Unlike his beloved revolutionary grandfathers, Ford would take pen in hand to ensure that the contributions of his generation, and his legacy, were not forgotten.

CHAPTER 8 HISTORIAN

As Ford passed the age at which most people contemplate a quiet retirement, he found himself drawn into a new role: historian. He had always had an interest in the history of Texas, or at least the Anglo colonization and development of the state, and in the 1880s he began writing his magnum opus—a memoir. Unfortunately for those who would consider publishing it, it included every good story he had ever heard about Texas, because Ford was not just concerned that he would be forgotten. He tried to record the history of his entire generation. Spurred by the inaccurate tales of his exploits to be found in prominent works such as Hubert Howe Bancroft's multivolume history of north Mexico and Texas, Ford combed archives, interviewed former associates, and published a significant amount of history in newspapers and other people's books. In the process, he reinforced his own reputation as a historical legacy, to the point that when Texans finally did establish an enduring state historical association, Ford had to be invited to serve as one of its most prominent members. Historian proved to be the last role he played for Texas, and as usual, he embraced it with great passion. Ford was determined not to be forgotten as he perhaps realized that his revolutionary grandfathers had been, even while their generation as a whole continued to be revered.

Ford left Austin in 1885 for San Antonio, where until 1889 he served as a deputy collector of internal revenue taxes for the southern and western sub-districts of Texas. The two sub-districts had been merged after the former deputy collector at El Paso failed to support Republican president Chester A. Arthur for re-election, and then Arthur lost to Grover Cleveland, who took office in 1885. Ford, a staunch Texas Democrat, thus was appointed to office by the only Democrat to win the presidency during the Gilded Age. It was certainly no accident that

John S. "Rip" Ford. Institute of Texan Cultures, UTSA, #072-3518.

he worked for Isham G. Green, the Third District collector who was a former Confederate officer and Democratic secretary of state for Texas from 1877 to 1879, when Ford served in the state senate. At the same time, among Green's other deputy collectors was George B. Zimpleman, the sheriff who deputized the Travis Rifles after Ford led them to the Texas Capitol during the standoff between Democrats and Republicans in 1874. Ford appreciated the appointment, but his new assignment was somewhat overwhelming. His territory sprawled from Brownsville west to El Paso, and from the Rio Grande north to Corpus Christi and New Braunfels. From his home in San Antonio, as Ford quietly noted, "it was difficult to visit all the points." He recalled that "in the discharge of these duties the first object was execute the law, and if possible to cause injury to no man." But he was firm, and he secured indictments for those who did not obey.[1]

Ford also became involved in other federal tasks after he moved to San Antonio. He helped another federal employee find a suitable site for a federal courthouse and post office in the city. A lot owned by Samuel and Albert Maverick was selected, and Ford delivered the payment of $24,000 for the property. Ford also had James Riely Gordon appointed as architect for the project and was pleased when he lobbied successfully for alteration of the plans into something "more nearly . . . that of a southern building." Ford declared the "good looking edifice," completed in 1889, was "well worth the $176,000 it cost." Ford also testified before a federal commission on whether Greer County properly belonged in Texas or the Indian Territory, a question that was not definitively answered until many years later (and not in Texas' favor). The transformed ex-Ranger made an impression on his granddaughter, Lucille Thomas (née Cowen), who remembered that he always came to Austin wearing a "Prince Albert coat, striped pants and a black bow tie . . . a Stetson hat, and Congress gaiters." As usual, Ford always wanted to make a proper impression. But she also noted that one could still see the scar left on his forehead by a bullet in 1851, when he fought for José María de Jesús Carvajal in Mexico.[2]

Ford also received at least one last special assignment from the state of Texas. In 1889, Gov. Lawrence S. "Sul" Ross appointed him,

Thomas W. Dodd of Laredo, and Peter C. Wood of San Marcos as a committee to select a location for a new state insane asylum for southwest Texas. Ford served as chair, while Wood was the secretary. With state funds, and what Ford described as "very liberal" gifts from their many hosts, the trio visited sites in at least thirteen communities. Their work was facilitated by the assistance of many old colleagues. Like Ford, Dodd and Wood were Confederate veterans (both in fact were disabled), and the three of them were escorted to a possible site in Beeville by Alexander C. Jones, who served with Ford under James E. Slaughter. The committee decided to accept a San Antonio site offered by Nathaniel G. Mitchell and D. Morrill Poor, a San Jacinto veteran and a former captain in the Second Texas Cavalry, respectively, but there was a snag: the two did not intend to donate the property, but wanted to sell it. Governor Ross suggested that the committee wait a few days, and finally Mitchell agreed to cut his price while donors stepped forward to pay the remaining cost. Ford later noted that some of those who pledged money did not pay, and so Mitchell and Poor had to sue them. Other troubles emerged when the legislative appropriation for the building proved inadequate, and delays ensued in completing the edifice, but it opened in 1892.[3]

Ford's public retirement after 1889 allowed him to devote more energy to one of his principal interests—Texas history. His first venue for recounting the experiences of early Texans had been the *Texas State Times,* the newspaper he published at Austin in the 1850s. When Ford traveled to Goliad to muster William R. Henry's Ranger company in the fall of 1854, he visited the chapel of the Spanish presidio popularly known as La Bahia. He also met with an "old comrade of the Mexican war," Henry Scott, who as a six-year-old boy had witnessed some of the events connected with the massacre of the Texas revolutionaries near Goliad in 1836. Ford printed some of what Scott told him in his paper, and he later provided this material to Austin publisher Lewis E. Daniell, who produced many books on Texas history after the Civil War. Ford also published a series of historic lectures on Texas given by Edward Fontaine, Episcopal rector of the Church of the Epiphany in Austin and a great-grandson of Patrick Henry. The publication of Henderson

Yoakum's two-volume *History of Texas* in 1855 marked the appearance of what could be considered the first significant history of Texas. It was generally well-received, and it remained the standard by which all others were judged until well into the next century. Within a year of its appearance, Ford published a call for the organization of a statewide historical society for Texas in his newspaper, but other matters apparently proved to be of more importance.[4]

It would be more than forty years before another group founded a successful state historical association in Texas, but Ford was among those who made yet another abortive attempt in the waning days of Reconstruction. On San Jacinto Day, April 21, 1874, just months after the confrontation over political power at the Capitol, Oran M. Roberts, then the Chief Justice of the Texas Supreme Court, presided over a meeting in his office. Eighteen men joined him, including former Confederate Postmaster General John H. Reagan and Guy M. Bryan, who as Speaker of the House had enlisted Ford to help protect the Texas legislature just a few months earlier. Their purpose was to organize a history society—Bryan for instance was a nephew of Stephen F. Austin—and Ford again played a prominent role. He served on the committee established to write a constitution for the organization, and at their invitation he read that document aloud at a subsequent meeting. Certain they were on the verge of success, the prospective members of the society chose a board of directors, which included Ford. Unfortunately for their plans, not much money was available for the effort, and many of those present would soon be diverted to other activities. Within just a few years, for example, Reagan would be elected to Congress, Ford would be elected to the state constitutional convention and the Texas Senate, and Roberts would be elected governor.[5]

Leaving others to resurrect the idea of a state historical society, Ford became involved in veterans' organizations. In March and April 1874, during the same period when he met with Roberts and his allies, Ford chaired a series of meetings for Mexican War veterans in Austin. They met first in the offices of Swante Palm and E. W. Shands, but so many attended that they soon moved to the office of Mayor Thomas B. Wheeler. Formally organized as the "Association of the Soldiers of the

John G. Walker. Lawrence T. Jones III Collection, Southern Methodist University.

Mexican War of the State of Texas," the members elected Ford as their first president. Among those who chose him were many colleagues who had served the Confederacy as well, including William N. Hardeman, James M. Swisher, William Steele, and John G. Walker, who chaired the committee on organization. Ford then presided as they also voted to extend honorary memberships to Peter H. Bell and Ford's old commander, John C. Hays. The group met regularly at Austin until 1878, then not again until 1881, when they decided it was too difficult to meet so often. Ford remained as president for one year, then served on several committees, including recruitment, as membership increased from thirty-nine to more than a thousand. One of their major purposes was to get pensions for Mexican War veterans, which Congress approved in 1887. That year, Ford applied for a pension, but of course he did not get it because he still worked for the Internal Revenue Service and therefore was not wholly disabled or destitute.[6]

One month after attending the establishment of the organization for Mexican War veterans, Ford traveled to Houston for the second annual meeting of the Texas Veterans Association, founded in 1873 for all those who fought for Texas independence or in any military units of the Republic of Texas. Ford qualified as a first-class member because he served several times in the militia of the Republic. He apparently attended association meetings, which convened in many different towns around the state, until his death in 1897. He and Hamilton P. Bee together politely declined an invitation from Bryan, the group's president, to address the association in 1894, declaring that "circumstances beyond our control prevent us from accepting the proffered honor you pay us." That same year, Ford accepted an appointment to an association committee, chaired by Henry E. McCulloch, which was charged with acquiring battlefields for preservation. The remaining members of the committee were Bee, Stephen H. Darden, John C. Duval, William P. Hardeman, James M. Hill, and Francis R. Lubbock. Hardeman, Hill, and Lubbock visited San Jacinto in 1894 and recommended its purchase, and in 1897 Hill was one of three commissioners for the state charged with buying the property. Ford enjoyed this work. As he wrote to the ladies who invited him to the 1896 association meeting, he worked not only to memorialize the men who had fought for Texas independence, but also the "illustrious men who labored, fought, and bled for the Lone Star Republic and state."[7]

Ford of course became involved in Confederate veterans' organizations as well. He commanded the United Confederate Veterans camp at San Antonio, named in honor of Albert Sydney Johnston, in 1893 and 1894, and during May 1895 he presided over a reunion of the Second Texas Cavalry at the state convention in Houston. It must have been a bittersweet experience for Ford, who had lost his commission as their colonel in the fall of 1862. Mostly, though, he relished such events. His granddaughter, Lucille Cowen, remembered riding with him on a "black charger" in a Confederate veterans' parade, and that both of them were quite delighted with themselves. Perhaps the highlight of Ford's career as a former Confederate came in 1897, when other veterans paid his expenses to travel to Nashville and participate in the national convention. He knew almost no one among the thousands of ex-Confederates there, but he was repeatedly introduced as "the officer who won the last fight of the war." He and Reagan were supposed to ride in an open carriage decorated with flags during a five-mile march to the Tennessee state fairgrounds, but someone took it, and they had to settle for a covered conveyance. This proved fortunate because a torrential downpour drenched both marchers and onlookers, forcing them to abandon the march short of its goal. Nonetheless, Ford once more had a great time. While he never became a state officer for the United Confederate Veterans, he remained active to the end, and by 1896 the chapter in Del Rio, on the Rio Grande, had been named in his honor.[8]

Ford did not neglect the many Rangers he had commanded. He wrote a letter in 1892 that was published in the San Antonio *Express* and reprinted elsewhere, calling for a reunion in San Antonio. Ford made his purpose quite clear: "Let us meet once more, exchange salutations, fight over our battles in words and leave data for the historian to write a true history of our successes and failures." Ford's summons did not get immediate results, but in 1896 he received a proposal for a gathering of former Rangers from Will Lambert, a journalist and prominent

Confederate Veterans Parade, Houston, May 1895. Brown, *Indian Wars and Pioneers of Texas.*

Democrat who had served under Ford against Juan N. Cortina. Ford happily endorsed the idea, declaring that "God made the old Texians honest and honorable, and circumstances, the operations against their enemies, the defence [*sic*] of their homes and their families, converted them into heroes." Ford could not attend the meeting held at Austin on March 2, 1897, when it was decided to organize the Ex-Texas Rangers Association, because he was at the organizational meeting for the Texas State Historical Association that same day. Ford wrote to Lambert, the secretary of the Rangers' organization, in July 1897, "The rangers did all brave men could do. In God's name let them organize, and give to the world an idea of their services and their sacrifices." Ford had long been an "unceasing advocate" of a Ranger organization, and Lambert was making it happen. Tragically, the first Ranger reunion took place at Austin in early October 1897, by which time Ford had been cruelly incapacitated by a stroke and could not attend.[9]

While Ford expended much energy in veterans' organizations, he also began to write again for newspapers, usually in response to an inaccuracy in someone's account of an event in which he was involved. He was determined that his efforts would be recalled properly. For instance, when the story of the meeting at Point Isabel with Lew Wallace in March 1865 resurfaced in the San Antonio *Express* twenty years later, Ford responded with his own fairly accurate version, which was reprinted in the Dallas *Morning News* in late December 1885. Ford's former commander, Walker, supported him by writing his own response for the *Morning News* a little more than a year later, insisting there was nothing underhanded or treasonous planned by Ford and James E. Slaughter. While some may have considered Ford's purpose in taking up his pen again to be self-serving, he was quick to declare otherwise, sending a letter to the Galveston *News* that read, in part, "Write no more history, and you will strike a death-blow to many of the impulses which lead men to do good and eschew evil."[10]

Several factors combined to push Ford to think in terms of writing on a grander scale. A recurrence of his Mexican War malady felled him during 1885, leading him to consider his own mortality in light of his advancing years. This concern was attenuated by the celebration of the fiftieth anniversary of Texas independence in 1886, when Ford and many others realized that the generation who had founded the Republic of Texas might soon be gone. Ford certainly was not the only Texas veteran to attend the reunion at Dallas in April 1886 and draw inspiration from the enthusiastic event, but he would be among the few who actually put something on paper. Finally, Ford was outraged at the inaccuracies contained in Hubert Howe Bancroft's *History of the North Mexican States and Texas, 1531–1889,* the second volume of which appeared in 1889. Bancroft actually employed a host of assistants to produce his works, but Ford blamed him personally for the inaccurate accounts of many events in Texas history, and his rage perhaps kept Ford writing long after others would have quit.[11]

Ford arguably had good reason to be upset with Bancroft and his host of writers. Not only did they ignore many of the Texans whom Ford thought should be immortalized in print, they also overlooked or slandered Ford. He was not mentioned in their account of the fighting with Juan N. Cortina on December 27, 1859, when Ford and his Rangers broke the Mexican lines and retrieved two cannons, nor did he appear in the remainder of their brief narrative on the suppression of Cortina in early 1860. To add further insult, the Bancroft writers declared that Cortina not only defeated Ford and the French together on September 6, 1864, at Brownsville, but in fact Ford was driven from the town three days later by Cortina, who then offered it as a prize to the Federals at Brazos Santiago. Finally, Ford was incensed to discover that he did not appear in a narrative of the Palmito Ranch fight in May 1865 that ludicrously recounted how the Confederates, led by Slaughter, were driven from the battlefield and failed in repeated efforts to disrupt the Federals as they withdrew in good order to Brazos Island. This final claim pushed Ford to exclaim in a newspaper article, based upon his memoirs, that "Bancroft's assertion that Colonel Barrett caused the Confederates to abandon their position would do honor to the inventive genius of Baron Münchhausen." The combined effect of all of these unintended insults led Ford to condemn Bancroft's volumes as a "bungling and untruthful history of Texas."[12]

Ford scribbled furiously in longhand at night and on Sundays, producing "about one thousand pages of foolscap" in just a few years. For editing, he called on his friend Oran M. Roberts, who sparingly annotated the sheets Ford shipped to him. The greatest obstacle Ford encountered in his writing was the loss of his own papers. He had left his Mexican War records aboard the ship that brought him back to Texas at the end of that conflict, and his letters to fellow editor Michael Cronican had been discarded as being too lengthy. Most of the papers concerning his military operations from 1849 to 1862 had been put in a trunk and entrusted to the care of John M. Swisher in 1864, when Ford left for the Rio Grande. Swisher put the trunk in his mother's smokehouse, where water ruined many pages. Ford years later visited Swisher and discovered that his report on the Canadian River expedition was being used as a heat pad under a hot iron. Ford admitted, "I went for him in rather an extravagant manner." When Swisher stuttered that he had lost his papers in the same way, Ford became even more incensed, "but that did not bring my papers back." Some documents that survived Swisher's neglect "fell into the hands of a lady," who sent them to Isaac H. Julian, a newspaper editor in San Marcos, who in turn notified Ford that he had the papers. When Ford arrived to get them, Julian told him that since he did not answer immediately, he assumed Ford did not care about the documents and burned them. Ford in his memoirs remarked sarcastically, "Will the reader pardon the comparison of the fiddling of Nero on the burning of Rome to the conflagration at San Marcos? Let him imagine Mr. Julien [*sic*] playing an inspiriting tune on the hurdy gurdy as Mr. Rip's papers are being reduced to ashes."[13]

Determined to complete his task, and to be as accurate as possible, Ford asked old friends and associates to find materials for him. Hamilton P. Bee, in a letter asking Ford to help secure the endorsement of Texas Democrat Henry C. King for Lawrence S. Ross' bid for the governorship in 1886, mentioned that he knew of many historical documents in the state archives, including material on Cortina, that Ford could use. Bee well knew the files because they were in his charge as the Commissioner of Insurance, Statistics, and History for Texas, and he offered to make them available to Ford as he needed them. Ford must have been elated because many state records had been destroyed when a fire gutted the Capitol in Austin, which, in his "historical point of view," was the severest calamity Texas ever suffered. He apparently availed himself of Bee's offer as John E. Hollingsworth, one of Bee's successors, in 1892 had to ask Ford to return volumes of legislative records that he borrowed in the fall of 1886. Ford did not miss many chances to expand his work. In 1886 he was called to testify before the Joint Commission on the Boundary regarding the line between Texas and the Indian Territory in Greer County. One of the others who testified was Hugh F. Young, and Ford convinced him to sit down and write an account of the Snively Expedition. Young did so, and Ford, after checking it against a published account by Young and others in the Clarksville *Northern Standard* of 1843, included it in his growing memoir.[14]

Ford especially targeted his military colleagues, or their families, in his quest for information. He contacted James W. Truitt, son of

James W. Throckmorton. Prints and Photographs Division, Library of Congress.

Alfred M. Truitt, and asked if he had any material concerning his father, with whom Ford had served in Mexico. Ford heard that John A. Green, who had also been a delegate to the Secession Convention, had some of Ford's papers from that era, but Green confessed that the material had been "lost in a storm" and referred Ford to John Henry Brown, who served in the convention as well. Former governor James W. Throckmorton provided details on his own military career in the Civil War in response to Ford's inquiry. James A. Ware, a captain under Ford during 1864 and 1865, wrote to Judge Thomas A. Falvey in El Paso, asking him to assist Ford in "writing a history of his times." Santos Benavides received a letter written by Ford on Christmas Day, 1890, bluntly telling him that if an account of his defense of Laredo in March 1864 appeared in Ford's book, Benavides would have to write it. Disappointed at Benavides' failure to respond to several previous letters, Ford concluded, "If you are not hostile to me and unwilling to do me any harm I shall surely endeavor not to assail your official conduct in a manner to harm you."[15]

Ford's assurances to Benavides reveal an aspect of his work as a writer that he expanded upon in two letters to Throckmorton. He had no intention of using his memoir to retaliate against those who might have opposed him in the past. As he explained to Throckmorton, "I am anxious to say nothing extremely unpleasant of any one if I can help it." There were of course "sons-of-tinkers so cussedly mean" that Ford could not "say anything good of them and tell the truth," so he simply omitted them. After all, he had "almost quit lying, unless in a very tight place, and I see a good chance to get out." Ford's primary concern was that he had "put off what I intended writing too long," and Texas had many heroes whose deeds needed to be recorded before they were entirely forgotten. As for himself, and many like him, "we have had our day, and a rather nice one it was."[16]

Ford did not have any reservations about attacking Bancroft, and in January 1890 he got a windfall. He received a letter from DeWitt C. Foster, who had chased Cortina under Ford in 1859 and 1860 but was now living in Mexico City after having served in the Mexican Army. Foster mentioned that he had dinner with Cortina, which inspired Ford. He traveled to Mexico City in October 1891, when he was escorted to see Porfirio Díaz by Ignacio Sepúlveda, a California judge and diplomat who was an intermediary for Americans in Mexico. More important, Ford met Cortina and received an invitation to visit him at his home in Atzcapotzalco, a suburb about six miles northwest of the city center. Ford rode the streetcar there with Nathaniel M. Stukes, a fellow veteran from John C. Hays' regiment, and was received courteously by Cortina and his wife. After enjoying his old enemy's hospitality, Ford convinced him to sign a statement, which Sepúlveda translated, that declared Bancroft was wrong about events on the Rio Grande during September 1864. Interestingly, Ford later wrote in explanation of how he could spend time with Cortina that, "We condemn the acts he committed against our citizens, yet we can not wholly ignore the cause inducing their commission." Specifically, Ford referred to Cortina's complaints about the Treaty of Guadalupe Hidalgo, which ceded so much territory from Mexico to the United States and led to the displacement of many Mexicans, a trend Ford himself tried to combat as a state senator after the Civil War.[17]

Ford did not wait to publish his completed memoir before assailing Bancroft in print. One early newspaper article by Ford, entitled "Mr. Bancroft's Mistakes in the History of Texas," included a copy of a general order from Winfield Scott identifying Ford as the officer who led the advance that captured Cortina's artillery and baggage in December 1859. Another article focused on the battle at Palmito Ranch and quoted from Slaughter's congratulatory message to Ford on his victory, which read, in part, "It comes like a bright gleam of hope, to illuminate the dark cloud of disaster which has lowered upon us, and may be the harbinger of future successes and of prosperity and happiness." It was in this same article that Ford angrily declared that Bancroft's account "would do honor to the inventive genius of Baron Münchhausen." Supporting letters from Charles A. Ogsbury, a newspaper correspondent at Brownsville in May 1865, and L. G. Aldrich, a staff officer for John B. Magruder, were published in the same newspaper a few weeks later and confirmed that Ford commanded at Palmito Ranch, not Slaughter, and that the Confederates had won the day.[18]

Ford attacked Bancroft through other channels as well. Asked to preside over the reunion of the Second Texas Cavalry at Houston in May

1895, Ford waited patiently while his fellow veterans adopted a glowing memorial in honor of John R. Baylor, who had died the previous year, then launched his attack. After listening to their former commander, those present agreed to have his denunciation of Bancroft, complete with a copy of the statement signed by Cortina, read by Ford into the minutes of their meeting. Two years later, Ford spent a month confined to his bedroom by influenza and pleurisy, so he passed the time by penning another correction to Bancroft. He sent this to United States Senator Roger Q. Mills of Texas, with directions to show it to his fellow senator John B. Gordon, who was the national commander of the United Confederate Veterans. Ford believed his ex-Confederate colleagues could get his latest diatribe published "in some periodical or newspaper of extensive circulation," but there is no evidence that this was done.[19]

Ford's memoir was never published in its entirety, nor was the biography of Hays that he wrote in the 1890s. Following a well-established practice, he issued a prospectus in 1886 asking for subscribers to his forthcoming book. This call bore the endorsements of eleven prominent men, including the previously mentioned Bee, Isham Green, King, Roberts, and Hugh Young, as well as Judge Thomas J. Devine, former adjutant general Wilburn H. King, Republican lawyer Charles W. Ogden, Presbyterian minister Richmond K. Smoot (who baptized Ford), former state health officer Richard M. Swearingen (who served under Ford in 1861), and former Confederate general William H. Young. Despite this support, Ford raised only enough money to continue writing, not to print the resulting manuscript of more than a thousand pages, not including his material on Hays. Part of the problem of course lay in the size of Ford's manuscript and its lack of focus, but he also fell victim to bad timing. John Henry Brown in 1892 published *History of Texas from 1685 to 1892,* two volumes that were almost as idiosyncratic as Ford's memoir. Readers hungry for more about frontier conflict could read John W. Wilbarger's *Indian Depredations in Texas,* which was published in 1889 and contained an account of the Canadian River expedition that featured Ford, or Brown's *Indian Wars and Pioneers of Texas,* which appeared in 1896 with an account of the battle at Palmito Ranch approved by Ford. Two years later, Dudley G. Wooten produced

A Comprehensive History of Texas from 1685 to 1897. As the editor of this compilation, Wooten included all of Henderson Yoakum's 1855 history of the Lone Star State, then convinced many writers to contribute chapters. Among them was Wilburn H. King, who with Ford's assistance wrote the first published history of the Texas Rangers for Wooten.[20]

Ford did not live long enough to read Wooten's finished work, and he clearly disliked Brown's literary efforts. In an 1897 letter to John J. Dix Jr., his old friend and former subordinate, Ford angrily denounced "Brown's pretended history of [the] Indian wars of Texas." Somehow Brown identified Ford as a captain in the army and credited Lawrence S. "Sul" Ross with commanding the Canadian River expedition in 1858. Ford could not complain to Brown, who had died in 1895, so he apparently planned to contact Brown's publisher, Lewis E. Daniell, who he declared was "better qualified for a high position in Hell than a place in decent society." It probably made matters much worse that Brown had quoted from Ford's memoir in his book on Indian wars, and that Ford had canvassed the state to sell subscriptions for that work, traveling as far west as El Paso. Ford remained convinced, as he wrote to Roberts in March 1897, that "the proper history of Texas is yet unpublished." Interestingly, Wooten shared Ford's opinion, condemning the sorry state of Texas history in a tirade published in the *Baptist Standard* in December 1898, more than a year after Ford died.[21]

While he never published his memoir, Ford did have a stream of letters and articles appear in print, many of which were drawn from his memoir and related research. The editors of the Dallas *Morning News* proved especially eager to publish contributions. The December 26, 1892, edition, for example, contained Ford's account of his meeting in 1876 with Porfirio Díaz, a synopsis of Cortina's career on the border, and a recounting of Ford's visit to Mexico City in 1891. The next year, readers of the same paper enjoyed articles by Ford on James H. Callahan's expedition into Mexico in 1855, Indians in Texas during the Republic era, and Robert M. Williamson, popularly known as "Three-Legged Willie," with whom Ford had served in the Congress of the Republic of Texas. The piece on Williamson was laudatory, and Ford was polite in his comments about Cortina to a San Antonio *Express* reporter in 1894, but he could be publicly acerbic to those whom he thought were trying to harm his heroes. When W. G. Slaughter, a San Jacinto veteran, had an article published that presented an uncomplimentary account of Sam Houston prior to that battle, Ford attacked. In comments printed in the San Antonio *Express,* he admitted that "It is charitable to suppose that revered gentleman has outlived a correct memory of the scenes he portrays," but he concluded that in fact Slaughter's portrayal of Houston was "purely imaginary—fantastic images conjured up by a worn-out brain." Ford could also be poetic, writing in 1896 of "Texas in times gone by, when the plains, the hills, the woods of Texas were a sheen of loveliness which claimed the wanderer." His last published piece, a lengthy obituary for his friend, San Jacinto veteran Nathaniel G. Mitchell, appeared in the San Antonio *Express* in August 1897, just a little more than a month before Ford died.[22]

Ford expended much energy in writing about the Alamo. He published his first extract from his memoir on that topic in the San Antonio *Times* in April 1887. At about that time he joined the Alamo Monument Association and was appointed to a committee charged with producing a brief booklet on the Alamo to be sold as a fund-raiser. Mary A. Maverick recalled that Ford brought in his version first and the committee accepted it, although the manuscript was longer than expected. In fact, the booklet relied heavily on the eyewitness account of the Alamo written earlier by John Sutherland, and it suffered from Ford's usual literary sin: it included many interesting stories that had nothing to do with the Alamo. Another contribution by Ford on the Alamo was apparently sold by the association to L. F. Meyers, who combined it with other material on San Antonio and published a slim book under his own name. Ford denounced him as a "very common fellow" and, having failed to goad him into a fight, decided he was also a "coward."

Younger members of the association must have enjoyed having Ford as a resource because he was a contemporary of those who had fought in the Alamo. For example, Sutherland left the Alamo as a courier in the company of John W. Smith. Ford noticed one day that someone had published an article in the San Antonio *Express* declaring that Smith had died in the Alamo. He mailed a correction in which he

Nathaniel G. Mitchell. Daniell, *Personnel of the Texas State Government, 1892.*

pointed out that he had served with Smith in the Ninth Congress of the Republic, and that he attended Smith's funeral when he actually did die in January 1845 at Washington-on-the-Brazos, while serving as a Texas congressman.[23]

Ford pledged to become a regular contributor to the *Confederate Veteran,* the national magazine for the United Confederate Veterans, but he never did. He broke his silence in 1895 to sharply deny a claim that William B. Travis had offered to surrender the Alamo to Santa Anna and been refused, an allegation that had appeared in an earlier article for the magazine. The next year, he contributed some comments on the fight at Palmito Ranch to another piece on the last battle of the Civil War. Before his death in 1897, Ford shared his files with Oran M. Roberts, who was writing the Texas portion of the eleventh volume in Clement A. Evans' *Confederate Military History,* a landmark set of twelve volumes published in 1899. Roberts incorporated Ford's account of Palmito Ranch into his narrative almost verbatim, perhaps as yet another slap at the much more prominent, and published, Bancroft.[24]

Ford's literary output made him an accepted authority on Texas history, and many sought his help. In addition to the material he provided to Roberts during the last year of his life, Ford sent a correction for "the falsehood published in the spurious history by the Californian," regarding "Cortina's interference in our war," to the publisher of Yoakum's new history of Texas by Yoakum's son. At that time Ford had apparently just completed his work for James T. DeShields of Belton, who would become a prolific writer on Texas history. DeShields had been introduced to Ford in 1887 with letters from Belton attorney Wilson T. Davidson, Ford's former newspaper partner in Austin, and San Antonio newspaper editor Carrick W. Crozier, and Ford wrote at least forty-two articles for DeShields—on the major events of his own life, Texas history, and notable Texans—at the rate of fifty cents per page. Ford also discussed merging his work on Hays with additional material written by DeShields to create a more substantial book, but that did not happen. Unfortunately for Ford, he had many subscribers for the Hays volume but not enough money to publish it, and DeShields did not agree to Ford's offer to do most of the editing "and not charge the horns off a billy-goat." This was a lengthy unproductive period for DeShields, whose book on Texas frontier conflicts would not be published until 1912, fifteen years after Ford died. Ford apparently quit working for DeShields in the fall of 1896, but he continued to write for himself and others until he suffered a stroke in October 1897. Much of his last writing may well have been dictated to his youngest daughter, Lillian, who was the salutatorian of her graduating class from San Antonio High School that year.[25]

Ford's contributions to Texas history did not just include words. When William H. Huddle was creating his huge painting, *The Surrender of Santa Anna,* in 1886, Ford sent him two images, of Edward Miles and James A. Sylvester, who had captured Santa Anna. The Texas Legislature in 1891 purchased Huddle's monumental painting, and it became a permanent addition to the collection displayed in the Capitol at Austin. Perhaps having heard of Ford's offer of assistance to Huddle, another painter, Henry A. McArdle, wrote to Ford in 1890, asking for the image of Miles to be used in the production of his own massive painting, entitled *The Battle of San Jacinto.* Ford struggled for two years to fulfill this request, eventually also recovering Sylvester's image from Huddle and sending it to Miles' daughter, Esther Miles Crawford, so that she could forward both to McArdle.

It took Ford another year to secure an image of José Antonio Menchaca, who served as a lieutenant in Juan N. Seguín's company at San Jacinto. Ford explained that not only was Menchaca "during his whole life a faithful friend of Texas," but also that "it is just to the Mexicans who sided with the Americans to be represented in a painting of the battle of San Jacinto. I hope you will give Man chaca [*sic*] a place. It would cause you some more friends in San Antonio." Ford had seen McArdle's painting of Gen. Robert E. Lee and his Texas troops in the Battle of the Wilderness, which had been destroyed in the fire that gutted the Austin Capitol in 1881, and he took great pride in contributing to McArdle's new work on San Jacinto, which was purchased by the legislature in 1898 and placed in the House chamber along with McArdle's later work, *Dawn at the Alamo.*[26]

At some point during the last years of his life, Ford crossed the line between writing history and being history. William S. Speer and John Henry Brown as early as 1881, in their *Encyclopedia of the New West,* declared that "it is a delightful task to scan the life of one whose entire character will bear the closest scrutiny as a man, a citizen and a soldier." Going a step further, however, they added that Ford had become "inseparably connected with Texas history." These words were echoed in the *Biographical Souvenir of the State of Texas,* a rival publication that appeared in 1889. Ford's transition from historian to historical icon became national when Frederick Remington immortalized him in an article for *Harper's Magazine* in 1896. Remington was visiting a San Antonio club when a friend invited him to meet an old Ranger who "will tell you stories that will make your eyes hang out on your shirt front." He was introduced to Ford, whom he described as "a very old man, with a wealth of snow-white hair and beard—bent, but not withered." The men lit cigars, settled into chairs, and spoke for hours amid clouds of blue smoke.

Either Remington misunderstood, or Ford misled him, because Remington wrote that Ford was with Hays in his first big Indian fight, which was misdated as 1836. Ford may have also stumbled in recounting the battle with Father Celedonio Domeco de Jarauta in 1848, because Remington recorded that the priest was killed. However, Ford erred only slightly in telling Remington that he could hit a man with every shot from a Colt revolver at 125 yards; he had actually made one such shot and had seen others do it as well. Ford was also generous in giving credit to others, such as telling Remington that Ed Burleson Jr.'s fight in 1851 was the "most desperate" he could recall. The conversation ended late that night when Ford finally fell asleep. Remington, probably unaware of Ford's literary background, condescendingly noted that his rough stories "would fare better at the hands of one used to phrasing and capable also of more points of view than the colonel was used to taking." The article, embellished with Remington's drawings, confirmed Ford's image as a historical icon, albeit one with a pistol in each hand and stripped of literacy.[27]

Since Ford had become an icon of Texas history, it seemed proper to include him in establishing a lasting state historical organization. Unfortunately for those involved in this successful effort, this proved to be rather difficult. In response to invitations sent by Prof. George P. Garrison of the University of Texas, twenty to thirty people gathered on March 2, 1897, in the Capitol at Austin. Garrison served as secretary, while Zachary T. Fulmore chaired the meeting. When Garrison read the proposed constitution aloud, and reached the line about "members, life members and honorary members," Fulmore asked if anyone wanted any amendments. Ford loudly called for the insertion of the term "lady members" as a separate category. A silence fell over the room that was broken only by Ford's repeated demands that his motion be put to a vote. Garrison did not want such a distinction among the membership, and he mutely looked for support to three ladies who were present: Julia Lee Sinks, Dora Fowler Arthur, and Bride Neill Taylor. They did not speak at first while Ford glared at them, leaning on a gold-headed cane, but Taylor at last mustered her courage, rose to her feet, and quietly said the amendment was not needed. Ford, glowering, condemned Taylor's "brass" and thundered that women certainly could not be members unless the constitution was amended. Fulmore called for a vote, and the amendment lost. Garrison continued until he read aloud the word "fellows," when Ford erupted again, growling that he could not imagine a lady being called a fellow. Garrison explained that the term as an honorary title had a long lineage and resumed his reading, but Ford was finished. He "rose, grumbling his indignation audibly, and went stumping out of the room, the loud strokes of his big stick as it hit the tiled floor emphasizing his disapproval of us at every step down the long corridor outside."[28]

Ford's melodramatic exit might have been funny, but no one laughed. He was a revered historical icon, and his abandonment of the association might cause it to fail. The meeting halted while former governor Francis R. Lubbock and two others rushed to speak with Ford. They need not have bothered; Ford's daughter Lillian would become a women's rights activist, but her father came from an earlier age when men and women were not equal in voting matters, such as membership in the association. Other members of his generation might accept change as part of embracing the future, but Ford always looked to the past for his models. Perhaps even more important, he also was not used to having his authority questioned. Driven to match the legacy of his grandfathers, and to prove he was of the same "fighting stock" as they, Ford had little time for anyone who was disloyal or insubordinate, even in a gathering of ostensible equals. And women he did not consider to be his equal in all affairs. When Lubbock predictably failed to bring

Francis R. Lubbock. Daniell, *Personnel of the Texas State Government, 1892.*

Ford back, the crestfallen group finished the business of organizing the association.[29]

Garrison and Lubbock visited Ford in his Austin hotel room the next day, thinking that reconciliation might be achieved through a private conversation that did not have the appearance of a public challenge. They proved right; Ford penned a letter to Oran M. Roberts, who had been selected as the first president of the association, on March 20, 1897, telling his friend that "I anticipate remaining with the 'Texas Historical Society' as long as I can do anything to promote the interest of Texas history, however, I cannot promise that will be a long time. Indications of age have already developed, and there is no means of guessing when the end may come." In June 1897, Ford was elected as both an honorary life member and a fellow of the association, a dual distinction given to only four other people at that time: Guy M. Bryan (incumbent president of the Texas Veterans Association), John H. Reagan, Roberts, and Sinks, who was one of five women to share the title of fellow with Ford. Despite the honors extended to Ford, the association still almost lost him. When he sent them a copy of his manuscript on Hays, expecting it to be published, and asked for $145 in compensation, he received only a bill for five dollars in dues. Angry, he considered quitting, but the mistaken request for dues was withdrawn, and the organization included an (unpaid) article by Ford in the first volume of its new quarterly journal.[30]

Sadly, Ford was quite sincere in his demands to be paid for his work because by 1897 he had no money. He had moved from Austin to San Antonio to work as a deputy collector for the Internal Revenue Service, at an initial salary of $1,900 per year, but this appointment ended in 1889. The economic depression that beset the country during the 1890s, for which Ford blamed "Gold-men" and always voted for Democrats who favored minting more silver, made it difficult for the aging historian to support himself. Writing to DeShields, whose payments were often late, Ford mused that "poverty may not be a crime, yet it is quite inconvenient." He was deeply moved when a former Unionist whom he had protected in Brownsville in 1865 met with him in 1896 and offered to pay $180 for two months of work, "adding 'then we will talk further.'" A grateful Ford wrote to Dix, "Where is the rich Confederate who has done so much?" While this assistance kept Ford from starving, it did not allow him to enjoy many luxuries. As he explained to Dix in 1897, he and his wife Addie were "poorer than Job's turkey and verging towards meanness all the time." Ford had never accumulated much property, and

Guy M. Bryan. Daniell, *Personnel of the Texas State Government, 1892.*

he confessed in his memoirs that he regretted his "improvidence." He had received a second-class land grant of 1,280 acres for arriving in Texas in 1836, but he sold that to his former medical partner Oscar Fitzallen. He paid taxes only on a town lot and some personal property while living in Austin before the Civil War, and he apparently divested himself

John J. Dix Jr. Daniell, *Personnel of the Texas State Government, 1892.*

of that while serving in the Confederate army. Afterward, he bought another lot in Brownsville but sold that when he moved to San Antonio, where he rented a home at 325 North Cherry Street.[31]

Rapidly declining health during the last months of his life compounded Ford's money woes. In early 1894 he accidentally ingested carbolic acid, thinking it was his usual medication, but two years later he wrote to his friend Dix, "We are in good health. That is one thing the Gold-men can not control directly." To DeShields he declared that he had a "constitution few men possess," and that he could read without glasses and "walk over town without a cane." A few months later a horse and buggy ran over him, severely injuring his back. Early in 1897 he suffered from influenza and pleurisy. By July he blamed Dix for giving him a cold, via a letter, that made him cough until his teeth had all fallen out, his nose was "out of joint," and both of his big toes were "missing." Too, one of his ears was "busted," while his new pants had been "coughed into ribbons." Ford jovially admitted that in fact he and Dix were victims of time, declaring "for your particular benefit I will consider myself a venerable old lady of untold age, and yourself as you are, the remains of a once veritable Ranger, who fought for Texas because he loved the noble land, and hated whoever hated her people." On the first day of October 1897, Ford suffered a stroke that paralyzed him. He apparently was taken to the home of his oldest daughter, Mary Louise (or Lula), who had married Joseph W. Maddox, a Vanderbilt University graduate and San Antonio realtor. They lived at 322 King William Street, and there the old Texian died at the age of eighty-two on November 3, 1897, attended by his family.[32]

Ford's funeral reflected many aspects of his life. Jointly hosted by the Anchor Lodge of the Royal Arch Masons and the United Confederate Veterans, it featured six honorary pall bearers. Unionist and Republican George W. Brackenridge served along with at least two prominent Democrats: former Confederate officer and United States Representative Christopher C. Upson and former Texas Secretary of State John A. Green. Another Confederate veteran, William McMaster, had fought at San Jacinto. The other two were Horace W. "Wash" Tong, a Confederate veteran whose father fought in the American Revolution, and Bohne Stephenson, a local justice of the peace. In recognition that Ford's elderly contemporaries could not actually carry his remains, six actual pall bearers were selected as well. These included cattlemen M. K. Shiner and Jesse H. Presnall, Confederate veteran Augustus A. Ellison, Hamilton P. Bee's son Carlos (who later became a Congressman), Democratic politico

Henry C. King Jr., and B. B. Green. They laid Ford to rest in the section of Cemetery Number Four at San Antonio that was owned by the Albert Sydney Johnston camp of the United Confederate Veterans, close by the grave of Hamilton P. Bee, who had died one month earlier.[33]

Ford need not have worried that he might pass unnoticed. Several major papers in the state assigned reporters to produce lengthy memorials, several of which relied heavily on his unpublished memoir. Most of these articles focused on Ford's "brilliant military record," as a reporter for the Austin *Statesman* wrote in a front-page contribution, though attention was also paid to his work as a politician and historian. A second piece on Ford in the same newspaper declared that his name "was a household word in Texas," but this was greatly upstaged by the praise lavished upon Ford by Chicago *Times-Herald* writer H. S. Canfield, whose work was reprinted in the Dallas *Morning News.* According to him, Ford spoke six Indian languages and "was an expert with the rifle, the knife, the bow and the lance." Furthermore, he was a perfect representative of a bygone age of warriors who "believed it to be his duty when warring to smite and spare not, and his band left behind it a thirty-foot wide trail of blood." Refusing to be outdone, Charles L. Martin, who served under Ford in 1862 at Brownsville, opined that Ford was great at everything he ever did, but as a self-taught master of war he was best at fighting both Indians and Mexicans. Martin was certain that "among all this galaxy of immortals [early Texans] none will shine brighter, no name be blazoned higher than John S. Ford." The flow of memorials to Ford ended in March 1898 with Will Lambert's submission to the *Southern Tribute,* a United Daughters of the Confederacy publication printed in San Marcos. Lambert, like most of the others, made some grave errors of fact in recalling Ford's life, and then concluded that "in the death of Col. Ford Texas has lost one of its grandest landmarks."[34]

While Ford himself may have been a landmark, there remains no site named for him in Texas except for a building at the Texas School for the Deaf in Austin. This was done in 1995, almost a century after his death, through a concurrent resolution introduced by Texas Sen. Gonzalo Barrientos. There was some consideration of naming a county for

Ford in the early 1890s; Robert Potter, who had served under Ford in the Canadian River expedition of 1858, called for this in an article published in the Dallas *Morning News* in 1892. Unfortunately for him, and for those who wanted to honor Ford in this way, the previous year there had been a misunderstanding in the legislature. A Henderson County rancher had submitted a petition for the creation of a new county from part of Henderson. The request stalled until Texas Sen. Wells Townsend offered his support, in return for which the new county would be named in honor of his law partner, Robert Foard. Many legislators voted for the proposal thinking they were honoring the old Ranger who had won the last battle of the Civil War, not Townsend's friend Foard. Barrientos, perhaps unwittingly, thus provided at least a partial corrective to a legislative embarrassment of the previous century.[35]

Addie did not long survive the death of her husband. She remained in the house they had rented on North Cherry Street, where she received a pension from the state of Texas as an indigent Confederate widow beginning in September 1899. She had no real estate or other income, and asthma prevented her from working. She also noted that her late husband had never successfully applied for any other pension, nor had he received any land grants as a veteran. Certainly she received some support from her two married daughters, Mary Louise Maddox and Addie, who lived with her husband, Samuel De Cordova, in Austin. Lillian, Ford's youngest, apparently resided with her mother until she died in 1901, after which Lillian married Robert A. Votaw of Austin. Apart from her daughters, Ford's widow had few surviving immediate family members. Her son had died tragically in 1882, her parents and brother were both dead as well, and her younger sister, Mary Louise O'Leary, had died in 1890 at Dallas, where her husband William, Ford's former newspaper associate in Brownsville, served as postmaster. Even Fannie, Ford's daughter from his first marriage, was not listed among those who survived him in his obituaries, nor was her son Gray, although her daughter, Lucille Thomas, married Raphael Cowen of Brownsville in about 1902. When Addie died on February 19, 1901, and was interred beside her husband in the Confederate Cemetery, as that San Antonio burial ground had come to be known, there must have been very few people who attended the service.[36]

Ford's name may not have survived his passing, and there may be no monuments to him in Texas, but he certainly was not forgotten. And in that, he definitely surpassed his grandfathers, whose example of military and public service he tried hard to emulate. Not content to be just another face in the crowd of young men who immigrated to Texas during the era of the Republic, Ford had taken advantage of the opportunities that the growing republic and then state afforded him. Not satisfied to cultivate the land like his father, he forged an aggressive reputation for himself as a politician, soldier, Ranger, newspaperman, and historian. His grandfathers had been soldiers and politicians as well, but they did not follow the pathway to prominence provided by a well-written newspaper. Nor did they take the time to record the deeds of themselves and their generation, which could have afforded them an even greater measure of immortality. In one of Ford's last letters to his friend Oran M. Roberts, just after he had stormed out of the organizational meeting of the Texas State Historical Association, he lamented that many of the greatest leaders in the early history of Texas had died without writing memoirs, and they as yet had no biographers. Continuing in this vein, Ford ended with the directive, "You see I have allowed a subject to run away with me. I shall make no apology. If you get tired burn the sheets."[37] Fortunately Roberts ignored that order, as did the many people who cared for Ford's other papers through the years. Ford's last service to Texas, then, was to provide a compelling account of its early days, and in so doing to preserve his own story, and his legacy as a fighter in many roles.

NOTES

Introduction

[1] John S. Ford, Memoirs (Manuscript, n.d., in John S. Ford Papers, Dolph Briscoe Center for American History, University of Texas at Austin [hereinafter cited as CAH]), 269, 525; John S. Ford, *Rip Ford's Texas*, ed. Stephen B. Oates (Austin: University of Texas Press, 1963), 48–49, 157; Dallas *Morning News*, Dec. 28, 1892.

[2] Ford, *Rip Ford's Texas*, 15.

[3] Ford, *Rip Ford's Texas*, 7; Ford, Memoirs (Ford Papers, CAH), 4 [1st quote]; George B. Forgie, *Patricide in the House Divided* (New York: W. W. Norton & Company, 1979), 25 [2nd quote].

[4] R. H. Williams, *With the Border Ruffians: Memories of the Far West, 1852–1868* (New York: E. P. Dutton and Company, 1907), 364–365 [quotes]; William J. Hughes, *Rebellious Ranger: Rip Ford and the Old Southwest* (Norman: University of Oklahoma Press, 1964), 178.

[5] Walter P. Webb, *The Texas Rangers: A Century of Frontier Defense* (Boston: Houghton Mifflin, 1935), 454; Thomas W. Knowles, *They Rode for the Lone Star* (Dallas: Taylor Publishing Company, 1999), vi; Robert M. Utley, *Lone Star Justice: The First Century of the Texas Rangers* (New York: Oxford University Press, 2002), 90, 116; Mike Cox, *The Texas Rangers: Wearing the Cinco Peso, 1821–1900* (New York: Forge Books, 2008), 128; Michael L. Collins, *Texas Devils: Rangers and Regulars on the Lower Rio Grande, 1846–1861* (Norman: University of Oklahoma Press, 2008), 131.

[6] T. R. Fehrenbach, *Lone Star: A History of Texas and Texans* (New York: American Legacy Press, 1968), 374 [1st-4th quotes]; T. R. Fehrenbach, "Texas Mythology: Now and Forever," in *Texas Myths*, ed. Robert F. O'Connor (College Station: Texas A&M University Press, 1986), 218 [5th quote]; Jesus F. de la Teja, Paula Marks, and Ron Tyler, *Texas: Crossroads of North America* (New York: Houghton Mifflin, 2004), 265 [6th quote]; Gary C. Anderson, *The Conquest of Texas: Ethnic Cleansing in the Promised Land, 1820–1875* (Norman: University of Oklahoma Press, 2005), 304 [7th quote]; Mary M. M. Amberson, James A. McAllen, and Margaret H. McAllen, *I Would Rather Sleep in Texas: A History of the Lower Rio Grande Valley and the People of the Santa Anita Land Grant* (Austin: Texas State Historical Association, 2003), 4 [8th quote]. The best-selling textbook on Texas, Randolph B. Campbell's *Gone to Texas: A History of the Lone Star State* (New York: Oxford University Press, 2003), refers to Ford as a "famed Ranger" (p. 241) and adds only a passing reference on Ford's role in the secession crisis to the usual accounts of his work as a Ranger and soldier.

[7] Lucille T. Cowen, "Personal Reminiscences of My Grandfather, Col. John S. Ford" (Typescript, n.d., in possession of Linda Cain, Carthage, Texas), 3 [1st quote], 8;

Charles L. Martin, "The Last of the Ranger Chieftains," *The Texas Magazine* 4 (January 1898): 40 [2nd quote]; Dallas *Morning News,* December 19, 1897 [3rd and 4th quotes]; A. J. Sowell, *Early Settlers and Indian Fighters of Southwest Texas* (Austin: Ben C. Jones & Company, 1900), 827 [5th quote]; Tom Lea, *The King Ranch,* 2 vols. (Boston: Little, Brown and Company, 1957), 1: 164 [last quote]; Hughes, *Rebellious Ranger,* 79, 141–142; Webb, *Texas Rangers,* 124; Utley, *Lone Star Justice,* 335. The latest book that features Ford, Michael L. Collins' *Texas Devils: Rangers and Regulars on the Lower Rio Grande, 1846–1861* (Norman: University of Oklahoma Press, 2008), once more repeats the story that the nickname "Rip" originated with the notations he added to his letters reporting Texas Ranger deaths in the Mexican War (p. 40).

Chapter One: Texian

[1] Research notes (Typescript, n.d., Lucie Clift Price Papers, CAH); Ford, Memoirs (Ford Papers, CAH), 8; Ford, *Rip Ford's Texas,* 8; Hughes *Rebellious Ranger,* 3.

[2] Ford, *Rip Ford's Texas,* 6–8; Ford, Memoirs (Ford Papers, CAH), 2–4, 5, 7; Hughes, *Rebellious Ranger,* 3; Archie V. Huff Jr., *Greenville: The History of the City and County in the South Carolina Piedmont* (Columbia: University of South Carolina Press, 1995), 38, 40–42, 55. There is a significant discrepancy between what Ford wrote in his memoirs about George Salmon's escape from the British on King's Mountain and what Salmon wrote in his pension application, which can be found on the website entitled "The Salmon family," http://www.fortunecity.com/tinpan/nirvana/621/salmon.html (accessed March 5, 2009). Elizabeth Young Salmon moved west with family members and died in Missouri in 1849.

[3] Ford, *Rip Ford's Texas,* 5, 7, 8; Ford, Memoirs (Ford Papers, CAH), 2, 4, 5, 8; Hughes, *Rebellious Ranger,* 3; Huff, *Greenville,* 27–28, 41, 46, 49, 55, 64.

[4] Ford, *Rip Ford's Texas,* xviii [1st quote], 8–9; Ford, Memoirs (Ford Papers, CAH), 8 [2nd quote]; Hughes, *Rebellious Ranger,* 3–4. John Ford reported two slaves in the 1790 census for Greenville, while his son William Ford owned one slave in the 1820 census for Lincoln County, Tennessee. The latter had four slaves in the 1830 and 1840 censuses for the same location. United States Department of the Interior, Bureau of the Census, First Census, 1790, Fourth Census, 1820, Fifth Census, 1830, and Sixth Census, 1840 (Record Group 29, National Archives, Washington, DC). George Salmon's estate included 16 slaves ("The Salmon family").

[5] Ford, *Rip Ford's Texas,* xviii, 9; Ford, Memoirs (Ford Papers, CAH), 8; Hughes, *Rebellious Ranger,* 4–6. Wilkins Blanton died in August 1886, at the advanced age of eighty, according to his tombstone. See "Coffee County, TN Cemeteries—Old Grove Cemetery," http://files.usgwarchives.net/tn/coffee/cemeteries/oldgrove.txt (accessed March 5, 2009).

[6] Ford, *Rip Ford's Texas,* xvii-xviii, 9–10; Ford, Memoirs (Ford Papers, CAH), 9 [quote], 10; John S. Ford to Adina de Zavala, Sept. 13, 1892 (Vertical File: John S. Ford, CAH); Hughes, *Rebellious Ranger,* 5–6. John S. Ford's first daughter was named Frances, but she is most commonly referred to as "Fannie." Brownsville *Herald,* August 12, 1953.

[7] Ford, *Rip Ford's Texas,* xix, 14–15; Ford, Memoirs (Ford Papers, CAH), 10 [1st quote], 11, 12 [remainder of quotes]; Affidavit of G. W. Davis and [?] Wells, January 22, 1874 (Texas Veterans Association Papers, CAH); John M. Swisher, "Remembrances of Texas and Texas People" (Typescript, n.d. [1932], CAH), 74; Hughes, *Rebellious Ranger,* 6–7; Pat I. Nixon, *The Medical Story of Early Texas, 1528–1853* (San Antonio: Privately Printed, 1946), 375; Ron Tyler et al., eds., *The New Handbook of Texas,* 6 vols. (Austin: Texas State Historical Association, 1996), 1: 599–600, 825, 3: 485, 707, 6: 138 [hereinafter cited as *NHOT*].

[8] Ford, *Rip Ford's Texas,* 10, 13, 23–24; Ford, Memoirs (Ford Papers, CAH), 10–11, 143; Hughes, *Rebellious Ranger,* 6; *NHOT* 2: 1,036–1,037, 3: 41–42, 1,102; Register of Texas Veterans Reunion, Houston, May 18, 1874 (Texas Veterans Association Papers, CAH).

[9] Ford, *Rip Ford's Texas,* 25–26 [1st–4th quotes], 27; Ford, Memoirs (Ford Papers, CAH), 179 [also 1st–4th quotes], 181, 182 [5th quote]; Hughes, *Rebellious Ranger,* 7. Ford must have sold his grant of 1,280 acres (note that he got a household grant, not a single man's grant), because Oscar Fitzallen, his former partner, filed the patent for it in Kaufman County in February 1850, while Ford was patrolling in South Texas. See File 000246 (Nacogdoches 2nd class) in Texas General Land Office, Archives & Records, Land Grant Database [http://www.glo.state.tx.us/archives/landgrant.html (accessed March 5, 2009)].

[10] Ford, *Rip Ford's Texas,* xix, 26–27 [quotes]; Ford, Memoirs (Ford Papers, CAH), 180–181 [same quotes]; *NHOT,* 5: 299.

[11] Ford, *Rip Ford's Texas,* 35–37; Ford, Memoirs (Ford Papers, CAH), 183–186; Hughes, *Rebellious Ranger,* 7; *NHOT,* 1: 288, 2: 324–325; Stephen L. Moore, *Savage Frontier, Volume II: 1838–1839* (Denton: University of North Texas Press, 2006), 21–24, 26–27.

[12] Ford, *Rip Ford's Texas,* xix, 28–29; Ford, Memoirs (Ford Papers, CAH), 189–190, 191 [quotes]; Hughes, *Rebellious Ranger,* 8–9; *NHOT,* 1: 247–250, 837–838, 2: 63–64, 324–325, 1,036–1,037, 3: 1,055, 5: 721–722; Campbell, *Gone to Texas,* 169–170; Moore, *Savage Frontier, Volume II,* 237–239, 241, 244–267, 276, 281, 282; Stephen L. Moore, *Taming Texas: Captain William T. Sadler's Lone Star Service* (Austin: State House Press, 2000), 177, 179–185, 195, 301–303.

[13] Ford, *Rip Ford's Texas,* 15–17 [quotes]; Ford, Memoirs (Ford Papers, CAH), 176–178 [same quotes]; Cowen, "Reminiscences," 2; Hughes, *Rebellious Ranger,* 7–8; Frank Brown, Annals of Travis County and the City of Austin (Manuscript, n.d. [1875],

Frank Brown Papers, CAH), 13: 38; *NHOT,* 1: 648, 5: 822, 946, 982, 1,103. Red Land Lodge Number 3 opened in November 1838 and closed in 1845. Among Ford's fellow Masons in this lodge were Henry W. Augustine, Stephen W. Blount, Ed Burleson, Nicholas H. Darnell, William B. Ochiltree, and Richard A. Scurry. Masons would play prominent roles throughout Ford's life, including John C. Hays, Robert S. Neighbors, Oran M. Roberts, E. B. Nichols, and Hugh McLeod, among others. See James D. Carter, *Masonry in Texas: Background, History, and Influence to 1846* (Waco: Committee on Masonic Education and Service for the Grand Lodge of Texas, 1958), 314, 318, 426, 428, 430, 434, 437, 441, 451, 452, 456, 457; Austin *Texas State Gazette,* Feb. 19, 1850, Feb. 10, 1851.

[14] Ford, *Rip Ford's Texas,* xix, 19; Ford, Memoirs (Ford Papers, CAH), 142, 192 [quotes], 193; San Augustine [TX] *Red-Lander,* Sept. 8, 1841; Hughes, *Rebellious Ranger,* 9–10. Kenneth L. Anderson, the future vice-president of the Republic of Texas who had known Ford in Tennessee, and Nicholas H. Darnell, who like Anderson served as Speaker of the House of Representatives for the Congress of the Republic of Texas, won the 1841 election. See *NHOT,* 1: 1,666, 2: 512–513, San Augustine [TX] *Red-Lander,* Oct. 7, 1841.

[15] Ford, *Rip Ford's Texas,* xix; Receipt from estate of William B. Patterson of San Augustine County, Oct. 7, 1841 (John P. McGovern Historical Collections and Research Center, Houston Academy of Medicine—Texas Medical Center Library, http://mcgovern.library.tmc.edu/data/www/html/texascoll/thmd2/persons/ffolder/ford2.htm [accessed July 7, 2008]); Medical accounts book (Ford Papers, CAH); San Augustine [TX] *Red-Lander,* May 19 and 26, July 7 and 23, 1842, Oct. 17, 1843; John H. Reagan, *Memoirs: With Special Reference to Secession and the Civil War* (Austin and New York: Pemberton Press, 1968), 41–42; Hughes, *Rebellious Ranger,* 10–11; *NHOT,* 1: 166, 2: 554–555, 5: 945; Nixon, *Medical Story of Early Texas,* 375. Ford's bar examination was administered by Thomas Johnson, David S. Kaufman, and William C. Duffield. The first two men were quite prominent in Texas politics. See *NHOT,* 2: 962, 1,039; United States Department of the Interior, Bureau of the Census, Seventh Census, 1850, Schedule 1: Free Population [Nacogdoches County, TX] (Record Group 29, National Archives, Washington, DC). For more concerning Thomas H. Lister, see "Descendents of David Leister," http://www.geocities.com/~pamreid/leis_anc.html (accessed July 7, 2008).

[16] Ford, *Rip Ford's Texas,* xix, 42–49 [quotes on p. 45], Ford, Memoirs (Ford Papers, CAH), 142, 268–269; Dallas *Morning News,* Dec. 28. 1892, Hughes, *Rebellious Ranger,* 12–13, *NHOT,* 6: 803.

[17] Ford, *Rip Ford's Texas,* xx, 32; Ford, Memoirs (Ford Papers, CAH), 274–282; *Journals of the House of Representatives of the Ninth Congress of the Republic of Texas* (Washington, TX: Miller & Cushney, 1845), 18, 40–41, 85–86, 93–97, 181–183, 385–387; Washington [TX] *National Register,* Jan. 4, 11, 25, Mar. 22, 1845; Hughes, *Rebel-*

lious Ranger, 13–14; *NHOT,* 6: 820–821. More about the conflict surrounding Ward, as well as his life and contributions to Texas, can be found in David C. Humphrey, *Peg Leg: The Improbable Life of a Texas Hero, Thomas William Ward, 1807–1872* (Denton: Texas State Historical Association, 2009).

[18] Ford, *Rip Ford's Texas,* xx, 32–33; Ford, Memoirs (Ford Papers, CAH), 293–294 [quotes]; Moore, *Taming Texas,* 216.

[19] Ford, *Rip Ford's Texas,* 40–41, 49; Ford, Memoirs (Ford Papers, CAH), 310 [quote] 311–318, 338; John S. Ford, Annexation of Texas (Manuscript, n.d., John S. Ford Papers, Nita Stewart Haley Memorial Museum, Midland, TX); *NHOT,* 2: 676, 711–712, 828; Hughes, *Rebellious Ranger,* 14.

[20] Ford, *Rip Ford's Texas,* xx, 40–41; Ford, Memoirs (Ford Papers, CAH), 337 [quote], 339, 348; Washington [TX] *National Register,* June 19, 1845; *Journals of the House of Representatives of the Extra Session, Ninth Congress, of the Republic of Texas* (Washington, TX: Miller & Cushney, 1845), 5, 41, 48, 50, 51; Hughes, *Rebellious Ranger,* 14–15.

[21] Ford, *Rip Ford's Texas,* xx, 30–31; 53–54; Ford, Memoirs (Ford Papers, CAH), 364 [1st quote]-365 [other quotes]; *NHOT,* 6: 371; Hughes, *Rebellious Ranger,* 15.

[22] Ford, *Rip Ford's Texas,* xx-xxii, 54–55; Ford, Memoirs (Ford Papers, CAH), 367; Marriage License for John S. Ford and Louisa Lewis, Sept. 24, 1836 (Texas Ranger Archives, Texas Ranger Research Center, Texas Ranger Hall of Fame and Museum, Waco, TX); Washington [TX] *National Register,* Oct. 2, Nov. 15, 1845, Jan. 31, 1846; Marilyn M. Sibley, *Lone Stars and State Gazettes: Texas Newspapers Before the Civil War* (College Station: Texas A&M University Press, 1983), 172, 194–195; Hughes, *Rebellious Ranger,* 15, 16, 18, 19; *NHOT,* 1: 315.

[23] Ford, *Rip Ford's Texas,* 55–56 [quotes]; Ford, Memoirs (Ford Papers, CAH), 368–369 [same quotes]; Sibley, *Lone Stars and State Gazettes,* 195.

[24] Ford, *Rip Ford's Texas,* xxi; Austin *Texas Democrat,* Apr.15 and May 6, 1846; Ralph A. Wooster, "Early Texas Politics: The Henderson Administration," *Southwestern Historical Quarterly* 73 (October 1969): 184 [hereinafter cited as *SWHQ*]; Winkler, *Platforms of Political Parties in Texas,* 17, 18–20, 43–44; Hughes, *Rebellious Ranger,* 19–20; *NHOT,* 2: 27, 414, 586.

[25] Ford, *Rip Ford's Texas,* xxi-xxii, 55; Austin *Texas Democrat,* May 13, 20, 27, June 3, 10, and 17, July 15, Aug. 26, 1846; Research notes (Price Papers, CAH); Hughes, *Rebellious Ranger,* 20. The headstone for Louisa Ford, in the John S. Ford section of the Oakwood Cemetery in Austin, says she died on Aug. 5, 1846, but Ford's Austin *Texas Democrat* of Aug. 26, 1846, says she died on Aug. 21, 1846.

[26] Austin *Texas Democrat,* Sept. 9 [quotes], 16, 23, Oct. 28, Nov. 4, 18, 25, Dec. 16, 23, 30, 1846, Jan. 13, 20, 27, Mar. 4 and 20, 1847; Hughes, *Rebellious Ranger,* 20–21; *NHOT,* 3: 519.

[27] Ford, *Rip Ford's Texas,* 60–61; Ford, Memoirs (Ford Papers, CAH), 377, 379–380; Charles D. Spurlin, comp., *Texas Veterans in the Mexican War* (Nacogdoches, TX: Ericson Books, 1984), 88–90; United States Department of War, *Compiled Service Records of Volunteer Soldiers Who Served During the Mexican War in Organizations From the State of Texas* (Record Group 94, National Archives, Washington, DC [hereinafter cited as CSR, Mexican War]): John S. Ford; *NHOT,* 3: 519, 606; Hughes, *Rebellious Ranger,* 20–23. Ford probably left his daughter Fannie with his father, William Ford.

[28] Ford, *Rip Ford's Texas,* 61–62, 65–66; Ford, Memoirs (Ford Papers, CAH), 381, 384 [1st quote], 385 [2nd quote]; Austin *Texas Democrat,* Sept. 16, 1847; Hughes, *Rebellious Ranger,* 24–25. Ford later began referring to his horse as "Old Higgins."

[29] Ford, *Rip Ford's Texas,* 66–67, 70, 75; Ford, Memoirs (Ford Papers, CAH), 386–389 [quotes], 392; Hughes, *Rebellious Ranger,* 25–27, 30. For a detailed account of Texans' operations around Mexico City, see Chapter 11 of Frederick Wilkins, *The Highly Irregular Regulars: Texas Rangers in the Mexican* War (Austin: Eakin Press, 1990).

[30] Ford, *Rip Ford's Texas,* 68; Ford, Memoirs (Ford Papers, CAH), 389 [1st quote], 390 [2nd quote]; Hughes, *Rebellious Ranger,* 26.

[31] Ford, *Rip Ford's Texas,* 73–74; Ford, Memoirs (Ford Papers, CAH), 397–399; Hughes, *Rebellious Ranger,* 28–30.

[32] Ford, *Rip Ford's Texas,* xxiii, 72, 76, 78–79; Ford, Memoirs (Ford Papers, CAH), 395–396, 401 [quote], 402; Hughes, *Rebellious Ranger,* 28, 30–36.

[33] Ford, *Rip Ford's Texas,* xxiii, 76–79; Ford, Memoirs (Ford Papers, CAH), 403–404; Hughes, *Rebellious Ranger,* 30–38; Collins, *Texas Devils,* 31–32; James K. Greer, *Colonel Jack Hays: Texas Frontier Leader and California Builder* (Waco, TX: W. M. Morrison, 1973), 180–181.

[34] Ford, *Rip Ford's Texas,* 81–85; Ford, Memoirs (Ford Papers, CAH), 417–422; Greer, *Colonel Jack Hays,* 181–186; James K. Greer, *Texas Ranger: Jack Hays in the Frontier Southwest* (College Station: Texas A&M University Press, 1993), 184–186; Webb, *Texas Rangers,* 119–120; Hughes, *Rebellious Ranger,* 38–40; Collins, *Texas Devils,* 32–33.

[35] Ford, *Rip Ford's Texas,* 86–90; Ford, Memoirs (Ford Papers, CAH), 423–427, 429; John C. Hays to Joseph Lane, Mar. 1, 1848, Alfred M. Truitt to John S. Ford, Mar. 2, 1848 (Ford Papers, Haley Museum); Galveston *News,* Apr. 28, 1881 [quote]; Albert G. Brackett, *History of the United States Cavalry* (New York: Harper & Brothers, 1865), 120–121; Greer, *Colonel Jack Hays,* 187–189; Hughes, *Rebellious Ranger,* 40–45. Frederic Remington included Ford's account of the fight at San Juan Tenochtitlan with an illustration in his "How the Law Got into the Chaparral," *Harper's New Monthly Magazine* 94 (Dec. 1896): 60–69.

[36] Ford, *Rip Ford's Texas,* 91–92; Ford, Memoirs (Ford Papers, CAH), 435–437, 443, 449; Hughes, *Rebellious Ranger,* 45. Mariano Paredes had six brothers, and it is not clear which one John S. Ford and his comrades captured.

[37] Ford, *Rip Ford's Texas,* 71, 94–95, 97; Ford, Memoirs (Ford Papers, CAH), 393–394, 399, 402, 439–442, 453, 455, 456 [quote], 462; Hughes, *Rebellious Ranger,* 27, 47–49. Ford in *Rip Ford's Texas* (p. 95) says that fourteen Mexicans were killed and the same number were wounded, while about forty were taken prisoner.

[38] Ford, *Rip Ford's Texas,* 94–97; Ford, Memoirs (Ford Papers, CAH), 461; United States Congress, *Message from the President of the United States,* House Ex. Docs. No. 1, 30th Cong., 2nd Sess. [Serial Set 537], 97, 99, 100, 102, 103; Hughes, *Rebellious Ranger,* 49–50.

[39] Ford, *Rip Ford's Texas,* 100–104; Ford, Memoirs (Ford Papers, CAH), 467–468; Webb, *Texas Rangers,* 122–124; Hughes, *Rebellious Ranger,* 51–54; Greer, *Texas Ranger,* 209–210.

[40] Ford, *Rip Ford's Texas,* xxiii [quote], 68–69, 106–109; Ford, Memoirs (Ford Papers, CAH), 371 [quote]; Spurlin, *Texas Veterans in the Mexican War,* 89; CSR, Mexican War: John S. Ford; Greer, *Colonel Jack Hays,* 213–214; Sibley, *Lone Stars and State Gazettes,* 212; Greer, *Texas Ranger,* 213–214; Hughes, *Rebellious Ranger,* 54–55.

[41] Ford, *Rip Ford's Texas,* xxiii-xxiv, 141–142; Ford, Memoirs (Ford Papers, CAH), 503; Brown, Annals of Travis County (Brown Papers, CAH), 13: 42; Austin *Texas Democrat,* Aug. 16, Sept. 20, Nov. 4, 1848, Feb. 3, Mar. 10, June 23, 30, July 14, Aug. 4, 18, 1849; H. P. N. Gammel, comp., *The Laws of Texas, 1822–1897,* 10 vols. (Austin: Gammel Book Company, 1898–1902), 3: 195, 421–422; Harriet Smither, ed., *The Papers of Mirabeau Buonaparte Lamar,* 6 vols. (Austin: Vonn Boeckmann-Jones, 1921), 6: 168; Hughes, *Rebellious Ranger,* 58; *NHOT,* 2: 459, 6: 371. The Austin *Texas Democrat* became the Austin *Texas State Gazette* in late August 1849. See Austin *Texas Democrat,* Aug. 18, 1849.

[42] Ford, *Rip Ford's Texas,* xxiv, 108; Ford, Memoirs (Ford Papers, CAH), 476; Hughes, *Rebellious Ranger,* 57; Greer, *Colonel Jack Hays,* 217–226; Kenneth F. Neighbours, *Robert Simpson Neighbors And The Texas Frontier 1836–1859* (Waco: Texian Press, 1975), 68–69; A. B. Bender, "Opening Routes Across West Texas, 1848–1850," *SWHQ* 38 (Oct. 1934): 117–119; Kenneth F. Neighbours, "The Expedition of Major Robert S. Neighbors to El Paso in 1849," *SWHQ* 58 (July 1954): 36–37. John C. Hays, soon after getting lost on the expedition to El Paso, left Texas for California and never returned.

[43] Ford, *Rip Ford's Texas,* xxiv-xxv, 113–114; Ford, Memoirs (Ford Papers, CAH), 476; Hughes, *Rebellious Ranger,* 57–59; Neighbours, *Robert Simpson Neighbors,* 69–70; Bender, "Opening Routes," 119–125; Neighbours, "Neighbors Expedition," 36–37, 39; *NHOT,* 4: 971–972.

[44] Ford, *Rip Ford's Texas,* xxv, 108, 114–115, 439–440, 446–447; Ford, Memoirs (Ford Papers, CAH), 476, 478–480 [quotes]; Hughes, *Rebellious Ranger,* 60; Neighbours, *Robert Simpson Neighbors,* 69–70; Neighbours, "Neighbors Expedition," 39; *NHOT,* 1: 384–385, 813, 5: 690, 6: 533–534. Ford says David and John Torrey owned the trading post, but in fact George and Charles E. Barnard had bought it from the Torreys in 1848, and the Torreys then rode with Hays on an expedition.

[45] Ford, *Rip Ford's Texas,* xxv, 116–122; Ford, Memoirs (Ford Papers, CAH), 481, 486, 488; Hughes, *Rebellious Ranger,* 60–64; Neighbours, *Robert Simpson Neighbors,* 70, 72–74, Neighbours, "Neighbors Expedition," 45–46; *NHOT,* 4: 972.

[46] Ford, *Rip Ford's Texas,* 118–120; Ford, Memoirs (Ford Papers, CAH), 483 [3rd quote], 501 [1st quote], 502 [2nd quote]; Neighbours, *Robert Simpson Neighbors,* 73; Neighbours, "Neighbors Expedition," 46.

[47] Ford, *Rip Ford's Texas,* 121–124, 132; Ford, Memoirs (Ford Papers, CAH), 487–493, 495; Hughes, *Rebellious Ranger,* 63–67; Neighbours, *Robert Simpson Neighbors,* 75–77; Neighbours, "Neighbors Expedition," 45, 47–51.

[48] Ford, *Rip Ford's Texas,* xxv [2nd quote], 124–126; Ford, Memoirs (Ford Papers, CAH), 493–496 [1st quote]; Austin *Texas Democrat,* Sept. 9, 1846; Hughes, *Rebellious Ranger,* 68; Neighbours, *Robert Simpson Neighbors,* 78–79. The Great Western married another soldier, moved west, died in 1866 and was buried at Fort Yuma, where her name is recorded as Sarah Bowman-Phillips. See *NHOT,* 1: 677–678; Mercedes Graf, "Standing Tall with Sarah Bowman: The Amazon of the Border," *Minerva: Quarterly Report on Women and the Military* (Fall-Winter 2001) [http://findarticles.com/p/articles/mi_m0EXI/is_2001 Fall Winter/ai_92588782/pg_4?tag=artBody;col1, (accessed July 13, 2008)].

[49] Ford, *Rip Ford's Texas,* 126–128; Ford, Memoirs (Ford Papers, CAH), 496–498 [quote]; Neighbours, "Neighbors Expedition," 55–56; Hughes, *Rebellious Ranger,* 68–71; Neighbours, *Robert Simpson Neighbors,* 79–81.

[50] Ford, *Rip Ford's Texas,* xxv, 114; Ford, Memoirs (Ford Papers, CAH), 499; Austin *Texas Democrat,* June 23, 1849; Bender, "Opening Routes," 119–125; Hughes, *Rebellious Ranger,* 71; Neighbours, *Robert Simpson Neighbors,* 81–83; Neighbours, "Neighbors Expedition," 56–58; Kenneth F. Neighbours, ed., "The Report of the Expedition of Maj. Robert S. Neighbors to El Paso in 1849," *SWHQ* 60 (Apr. 1957): 527–532 [quote]; *NHOT,* 2: 404, 1,076, 3: 466, 6: 1,084.

[51] Ford, *Rip Ford's Texas,* xxv-xxvi, 129; Ford, Memoirs (Ford Papers, CAH), 499; John S. Ford, The Claim of Thomas Toby (Manucript, n.d., Ford Papers, Haley Museum); Austin *Texas Democrat,* June 15 and 23, 1849; Houston *Telegraph,* July 12, 1849; Campbell, *Gone to Texas,* 234–235; C. L. Greenwood, ed., "Opening Routes to El Paso, 1849," *SWHQ* 48 (Oct. 1944): 262–268; Neighbours, *Robert Simpson Neighbors,* 87–99; Hughes, *Rebellious Ranger,* 71–72; *NHOT,* 2: 253.

[52] Ford, *Rip Ford's Texas,* xxvi; Brown, Annals of Travis County (Brown Papers, CAH), 13: 38; Austin *Texas Democrat,* July 21, 1849 [quote]; Hughes, *Rebellious Ranger,* 72–73, 141.

Chapter Two: Rip

[1] Ford, *Rip Ford's Texas,* xxvii, 142, 143, 147; Ford, Memoirs (Ford Papers, CAH), 504, 507; Brown, Annals of Travis County (Brown Papers, CAH), 13:61; Austin *Texas Democrat,* Aug. 18, 1849; Hughes, *Rebellious Ranger,* 74–75; Collins, *Texas Devils,* 39; *NHOT,* 1: 478, 3: 357, 746, 4: 385–386, 5: 221; Lena Clara Koch, "The Federal Indian Policy in Texas, 1848–1860, Chapter III," *SWHQ* 29 (July 1925): 19–23, 25–26; Anderson, *Conquest of Texas,* 231, 234–236; Pekka Hämäläinen, *The Comanche Empire* (New Haven and London: Yale University Press, 2008), 292–303, 306–308. Ford remembered that he, Grumbles, and Henry E. McCulloch actually commanded the three companies. For a discussion of the violence along the Rio Grande, as well as comments on the ultimate abandonment of the treaty provisions for controlling it, see Brian DeLay, *War of a Thousand Deserts: Indian Raids and the U.S.-Mexican War* (New Haven and London: Yale University Press, 2008).

[2] Ford, *Rip Ford's Texas,* 142 [quote], 143–145, 147; Ford, Memoirs (Ford Papers, CAH), 505, 507–508; Hughes, *Rebellious Ranger,* 76–77; *NHOT,* 3: 1,111–1,112, 1,117, 6: 793.

[3] Ford, *Rip Ford's Texas,* 149, 154, 158, 172–173; Ford, Memoirs (Ford Papers, CAH), 514–515, 521 526, 575; John S. Ford, Gen. Edward Burleson the Younger (Manuscript, n.d., n.p., James T. DeShields Papers, Daughters of the Republic of Texas Library, San Antonio, TX [hereinafter cited as DRT]) Hughes, *Rebellious Ranger,* 77–78; J. W. Wilbarger, *Indian Depredations in Texas* (Austin: Hutchings Printing House, 1889), 7–14, 614; *NHOT,* 1: 838, 3: 329–330, 6: 793, 965.

[4] Ford, *Rip Ford's Texas,* xxiii, 146–147 [quote]; Ford, Memoirs (Ford Papers, CAH), 511 [same quote], 512, 521; Hughes, *Rebellious Ranger,* 78–79.

[5] Ford, *Rip Ford's Texas,* 145–146, 150 [quote], 151–153; Ford, Memoirs (Ford Papers, CAH), 512–513, 514 [same quote], 515–520; Hughes, *Rebellious Ranger,* 79–83; J. B. Wilkinson, *Laredo and the Rio Grande Frontier* (Austin: Jenkins Publishing Company, 1975), 249–250.

[6] Ford, *Rip Ford's Texas,* 150–154 ; Ford, Memoirs (Ford Papers, CAH), 515–520 ; Hughes, *Rebellious Ranger,* 80–83, 85 [quote]; Wilkinson, *Laredo,* 250.

[7] Ford, *Rip Ford's Texas,* 154–157; Ford, Memoirs (Ford Papers, CAH), 522–526; Hughes, *Rebellious Ranger,* 83–86.

[8] Ford, *Rip Ford's Texas,* 158–161; Ford, Memoirs (Ford Papers, CAH), 528–532; Hughes, *Rebellious Ranger,* 80; Collins, *Texas Devils,* 44–45. Ford believed the

arrow that killed William Gillespie was poisoned like the one that had earlier injured his hand. See Wilkinson, *Laredo,* 250–251.

[9] Ford, *Rip Ford's Texas,* 161–166; Ford, Memoirs (Ford Papers, CAH), 531–532, 534–542; Hughes, *Rebellious Ranger,* 87–91; Collins, *Texas Devils,* 45–49, 51–52; *NHOT,* 5: 880–881; Wilkinson, *Laredo,* 251–252, 255–256.

[10] Ford, *Rip Ford's Texas,* 170–172; Ford, Memoirs (Ford Papers, CAH), 546–549; Hughes, *Rebellious Ranger,* 78, 85, 92–93; Wilbarger, *Indian Depredations,* 614–616; Collins, *Texas Devils,* 49–50. Neill served under Ford in 1861 at Brownsville, and during that time an arrow point lodged in his lung since 1850 emerged. He showed it to Ford, who recalled that Neill survived the war "only to be killed by a Negro soldier after peace was brought about." A website for police killed in the line of duty reports that Neill responded to a domestic disturbance call in Waco on Feb. 6, 1877, and was shot by the husband. See Ford, *Rip Ford's Texas,* 173; Ford, Memoirs (Ford Papers, CAH), 549 [quote]; San Antonio *Express,* Aug. 17, 1896; "The Officer Down Memorial Page," http://www.odmp.org/officer/15617-police-officer-alpheus-d.-neill (accessed Mar. 7, 2009).

[11] Ford, *Rip Ford's Texas,* 169–170; Ford, Memoirs (Ford Papers, CAH), 537 [quotes], 543–544; John S. Ford, Maj. Andrew J. Walker (Manuscript, n.d., n.p., DeShields Papers, DRT); Collins, *Texas Devils,* 47–48; *NHOT,* 1: 483; Wilkinson, *Laredo,* 252, 257. Note that Ford was not present when the captive Comanche was executed.

[12] Ford, *Rip Ford's Texas,* 167–170, 181–183; Ford, Memoirs (Ford Papers, CAH), 542–543, 545, 563–565, 575; Hughes, *Rebellious Ranger,* 90, 93, 96–98; *NHOT,* 1: 838, 6: 793.

[13] Ford, *Rip Ford's Texas,* 173–179; Ford, Memoirs (Ford Papers, CAH), 552–554, 557–562; Hamilton P. Bee, Untitled Manuscript (n.d., n.p., DeShields Papers, DRT); Clarksville [TX] *Northern Standard,* Mar. 15, 1851; Victoria [TX] *Advocate,* Feb. 13, 1851; John H. Jenkins, *Recollections of Early Texas,* ed. John H. Jenkins III (Austin: University of Texas Press, 1958), 225–226; John Henry Brown, *Indian Wars and Pioneers of Texas* (Austin: L. E. Daniell, 1896), 720–721; Hughes, *Rebellious Ranger,* 95–96; *NHOT,* 6: 793; Wilkinson, *Laredo,* 258–259; Knowles, *They Rode for the Lone Star,* 162; Cox, *Wearing the Cinco Peso,* 129–130; Collins, *Texas Devils,* 52–53. Ford later remarked that he never knew exactly what happened to Carne Muerto after his transfer to San Antonio, but William J. Hardee reported that a Comanche captured by Ford was exchanged for a captive white girl. See United States Congress, *Message of the President,* Sen. Ex. Docs. No. 2, 31st Cong., 2nd Sess. [Serial Set 587], 122.

[14] Ford, *Rip Ford's Texas,* 177 [quote]; Ford, Memoirs (Ford Papers, CAH), 551, 555–556; Austin *Texas State Gazette,* Feb. 10, 1851; Wilkinson, *Laredo,* 259.

[15] Ford, *Rip Ford's Texas,* 185–188 [quotes]; Ford, Memoirs (Ford Papers, CAH), 571–572 [same quotes], 573–574, 576; Hughes, *Rebellious Ranger,* 98–99 [same quotes].

[16] Ford, *Rip Ford's Texas,* xxvii, 193–196, 205; Ford, Memoirs (Ford Papers, CAH), 591–596 [1st quote], 607 [last quotes], 612; Brown, Annals of Travis County (Brown Papers, CAH), 15: 19; Hughes, *Rebellious Ranger,* 100–101, 105; Amberson et al., *I Would Rather Sleep in Texas,* 134–136; Wilkinson, *Laredo,* 262; Collins, *Texas Devils,* 63–64; Joseph E. Chance, *José María de Jesús Carvajal: The Life and Times of a Mexican Revolutionary* (San Antonio: Trinity University Press, 2006), 88–90, 97–100, 102–105, 107–108, 161; Jerry D. Thompson, *Cortina: Defending the Mexican Name in Texas* (College Station: Texas A&M University Press, 2007), 22; Ernest C. Shearer, "The Carvajal Disturbances," *SWHQ* 55 (Oct. 1951): 208–209; Jeffrey A. Zemler, "The Texas Press and the Filibusters of the 1850s" (M.A. Thesis, University of North Texas, 1983), 108–110, 115–116; Michael G. Webster, "Texas Manifest Destiny and the Mexican Border Conflict, 1865–1880" (Ph.D. Diss., University of Indiana, 1972) 9; *NHOT,* 1: 971, 4: 631. For an interesting discussion of Texans' concerns about slaves running away to Mexico, see Sean Kelley, "'Mexico in his Head:' Slavery and the Texas-Mexican Border, 1810–1860," *Journal of Social History* 37 (Spring 2004): 709–723.

[17] Ford, *Rip Ford's Texas,* 196–198; Ford, Memoirs (Ford Papers, CAH), 596–597, 600, 609; Brown, Annals of Travis County (Brown Papers, CAH), 15: 19; Hughes, *Rebellious Ranger,* 101–102; Chance, *Carvajal,* 109, 111–112; Shearer, "Carvajal Disturbances," 209; Thompson, *Cortina,* 22; Robert E. May, *Manifest Destiny's Underworld: Filibustering in Antebellum America* (Chapel Hill: University of North Carolina Press, 2002), 174; *NHOT,* 3: 517, 696. Allegedly Ford and José María de Jesús Carvajal belonged to the same Masonic lodge, Rio Grande Lodge No. 81, but Ford must have joined later because he did not settle in Brownsville until about 1860. See Chance, *Carvajal,* 162.

[18] Ford, *Rip Ford's Texas,* 197–199, 200–201, 203; Ford, Memoirs (Ford Papers, CAH), 597–603; Hughes, *Rebellious Ranger,* 102–103; Chance, *Carvajal,* 112–117; Amberson et al., *I Would Rather Sleep in Texas,* 137–138; Thompson, *Cortina,* 22–23. At least one newspaper, the Brownsville *Rio Bravo,* claimed that losing Ford led to Carvajal's decision to withdraw. See Zemler, "Texas Press and Filibusters," 121.

[19] Ford, *Rip Ford's Texas,* 200–201, 203; Ford, Memoirs (Ford Papers, CAH), 602 [quote], 603–605; Hughes, *Rebellious Ranger,* 103–104; Chance, *Carvajal,* 110, 117–118, 120–123; Collins, *Texas Devils,* 64–65.

[20] J. Fred Rippy, "Border Troubles Along the Rio Grande, 1848–1860," *SWHQ* 23 (Oct. 1919): 98–100; Shearer, "Carvajal Disturbances," 210, 213, 223; Collins, *Texas Devils,* 67; Chance, *Carvajal,* 111, 133; May, *Manifest Destiny's Underworld,* 260.

[21] Ford, *Rip Ford's Texas,* 203, 207; Ford, Memoirs (Ford Papers, CAH), 606 [quote], 610–611; Austin *Texas State Gazette,* Jan. 17, 1852; Shearer, "Carvajal Disturbances," 216; Chance, *Carvajal,* 123; Hughes, *Rebellious Ranger,* 104–105. Ford recalled that the day of the special election was very cold and snow kept many voters at

home, but he stopped short of saying that this was why he won. See John S. Ford, Gen. Edward Burleson, Senior (Manuscript, n.d., n.p., DeShields Papers, DRT).

[22] Ford, *Rip Ford's Texas,* xxviii, 207; Ford, Memoirs (Ford Papers, CAH), 611; Hughes, *Rebellious Ranger,* 108; Neighbours, *Robert Simpson Neighbors,* 103, 104; Kenneth F. Neighbours, *Indian Exodus: Texas Indian Affairs, 1835–1859* (Privately printed, 1973), 90; Ralph A. Wooster, "Membership in Early Texas Legislatures, 1850–1860," *SWHQ* 69 (Oct. 1965): 164; *NHOT,* 5: 371–373.

[23] Ford, *Rip Ford's Texas,* 203–205, 207; Ford, Memoirs (Ford Papers, CAH), 607, 609–612 [quote]; Hughes, *Rebellious Ranger,* 105; Chance, *Carvajal,* 122, 140–148, 163; May, *Manifest Destiny's Underworld,* 38; Amberson et al., *I Would Rather Sleep in Texas,* 138–139; Shearer, "Carvajal Disturbances," 211, 220–224; Zemler, "Texas Press and Filibusters," 122–123; Hortense W. Ward, "The First State Fair of Texas," *SWHQ* 57 (Oct. 1953): 163–174.

[24] Ford, *Rip Ford's Texas,* xviii, xxix, xxxii, 207–208; Ford, Memoirs (Ford Papers, CAH), 613; Austin *Texas State Gazette,* Nov. 13, 1852 [quote]; Austin *Texas Democrat,* Aug. 18,1849; Hughes, *Rebellious Ranger,* 106, 110, 122–125, 127; Sibley, *Lone Stars and State Gazettes,* 253–257; *NHOT,* 1: 313–314, 2: 554, 3: 437, 992, 6: 796.

[25] Ford, *Rip Ford's Texas,* xviii, 208–211; Ford, Memoirs (Ford Papers, CAH), 613, 614 [last quote], 622–624 [1st quote]; 635–640; Brown, Annals of Travis County (Brown Papers, CAH), 17: 5; Austin *Texas State Times,* Jan. 6, 1855; Austin *Texas State Gazette,* Jan. 6, 13, 1855; Hughes, *Rebellious Ranger,* 113–115, 117–118, 121; *NHOT,* 4: 774–775.

[26] Ford, *Rip Ford's Texas,* xviii, 208, 313 [3rd quote], 314–315; Ford, Memoirs (Ford Papers, CAH), 613–614, 625, and "Miscellaneous: Secession," 1; Frederic Law Olmsted, *A Journey Through Texas* (New York: Dix, Edwards & Company, 1857), 323–325, 331–333; Ronnie C. Tyler, "The Callahan Expedition of 1855: Indians or Negroes?" *SWHQ* 70 (Apr. 1967): 574–575; Randolph B. Campbell, *An Empire for Slavery: The Peculiar Institution in Texas* (Baton Rouge: Louisiana State University Press, 1991), 62–64, 180; Hughes, *Rebellious Ranger,* 117, 125 [1st and 2nd quotes]; May, *Manifest Destiny's Underworld,* 260.

[27] Ford, *Rip Ford's Texas,* xviii; Ford, Memoirs (Ford Papers, CAH), 613 [1st quote]; Hughes, *Rebellious Ranger,* 106–107, 110, 114–116, 121, 125 [2nd quote]; Sibley, *Lone Stars and State Gazettes,* 254–256, 268–270; Zemler, "Texas Press and Filibusters," 119; *NHOT,* 1: 314 [3rd quote], 4: 519–520, 6: 796.

[28] Ford, *Rip Ford's Texas,* xviii [2nd quote], xxix; Hughes, *Rebellious Ranger,* 107–108 [1st quote]; Austin *Texas State Gazette,* June 25, 1853; Sibley, *Lone Stars and State Gazettes,* 256. Ford's trip to the Rio Grande did not prove entirely peaceful. He attended a party in his honor hosted by some of his former Rangers in San Patricio. A fight erupted about daybreak, just hours after Ford departed, and Henderson Miller, one of his former Rangers, was killed, sparking a blood feud. Saddened, Ford attended

Miller's funeral, returned to Austin, and apparently did not become involved in the violence. See John S. Ford, An Episode of Border Life, 1853–1854 (Manuscript, n.d., DeShields Papers, DRT).

[29] Ford, *Rip Ford's Texas,* xxix; Hughes, *Rebellious Ranger,* 108–109. William C. Walsh appears to be the principal source for the story about the troublesome gunman, which appears in the Austin *American Statesman,* Feb. 24, 1924. Ford does not tell this story in his memoirs.

[30] Ford, *Rip Ford's Texas,* xxx; Austin *Texas State Times,* Oct. 14 [1st and 2nd quotes] and 21 [3rd quote], 1854; Olmsted, *Journey Through Texas,* 163; Hughes, *Rebellious Ranger,* 112; Thompson, *Cortina,* 35; Paul D. Lack, "Slavery and Vigilantism in Austin, Texas, 1840–1860," *SWHQ* 85 (July 1981): 1–6, 7, 9, 10.

[31] Ford, *Rip Ford's Texas,* xviii, xxx, 211, 217; Ford, Memoirs (Ford Papers, CAH), 630 [quotes]; Austin *Texas State Times,* Oct. 21, 1854; Brown, Annals of Travis County (Brown Papers, CAH), 17: 44–45; Hughes, *Rebellious Ranger,* 119–122; Chance, *Carvajal,* 103–104; Robert E. May, *John A. Quitman: Old South Crusader* (Baton Rouge: Louisiana State University Press, 1985), 280, 288–291, 294–295; Earl W. Fornell, *The Galveston Era: The Texas Crescent on the Eve of Secession* (Austin: University of Texas Press, 1961), 195–196; Earl W. Fornell, "Texas and Filibusters in the 1850s," *SWHQ* 59 (Apr. 1956): 412–413. Many Austin residents regarded the Order of the Lone Star of the West as a practical joke, and they were told that the initiation ritual actually ended in a gag, but perhaps that is simply what Ford and others wanted them to think.

[32] United States Congress, *Claims of Texas Against the United States,* Sen. Ex. Docs. No. 74, 46th Cong., 2nd Session [Serial Set 1884], 29–31; Ernest C. Shearer, "The Callahan Expedition, 1855," *SWHQ* 54 (Apr. 1951): 431–442; Koch, "Federal Indian Policy, III," 29; Tyler, "Callahan Expedition," 579–580; Collins, *Texas Devils,* 79–86; Dallas *Morning News,* Jan. 13, 1893; *NHOT,* 1: 905, 3: 564.

[33] Ford, *Rip Ford's Texas,* 215; Ford, Memoirs (Ford Papers, CAH), 626–627; Austin *Texas State Times,* June 2, 1855 [quote], Oct. 27, 1855; Hughes, *Rebellious Ranger,* 120; May, *Quitman,* 295; Lack, "Vigilantism in Austin," 11; Tyler, "Callahan Expedition," 576–578; May, *Manifest Destiny's Underworld,* 260.

[34] William Kyle to Ed Burleson Jr., Oct. 7, 1855 (Ed Burleson Jr. Papers, CAH [1st quote]); Ford to James T. DeShields, Oct. 27, 1895 (DeShields Papers, DRT); Dallas *Morning News,* Jan. 13, 1893 [2nd quote]; Shearer, "Carvajal Disturbance," 443; Hughes, *Rebellious Ranger,* 120–121; Collins, *Texas Devils,* 83. Ford wrote a letter on Indian affairs from San Antonio on Oct. 5, 1855, which was published in the Austin *Texas State Times* on Oct. 13, 1855. That would have made it impossible for him to be with James H. Callahan in Piedras Negras.

[35] Ford to Ed Burleson Jr., Feb. 15, 1856 [quotes] (Ed Burleson Jr. Papers, CAH); Hughes, *Rebellious Ranger,* 122–123; Collins, *Texas Devils,* 92; May, *Manifest*

Destiny's Underworld, 261; Zemler, "Texas Press and Filibusters," 128. The reference in Ford's letter is to Ed Burleson Sr.

[36] Collins, *Texas Devils,* 93–98; Fornell, "Texas and Filibusters," 414–426; Fornell, *Galveston Era,* 200–214; San Augustine [TX] *Eastern Texian,* June 27, 1857 [quote]; Austin *Texas State Times,* Feb. 14, 21, 1857.

[37] Ford, *Rip Ford's Texas,* xxx; Austin *Texas State Times,* Oct. 13, 1855; Austin *Texas State Gazette,* Aug. 9, 1856; Brown, Annals of Travis County (Brown Papers, CAH), 17: 5; Jenkins, *Recollections of Early Texas,* 25; Hughes, *Rebellious Ranger,* 114, 119; Sibley, *Lone Stars and State Gazettes,* 257; Winkler, *Platforms of Political Parties,* 36–37, 39–40, 54–56, 58, 69–70; Ralph A. Wooster, "An Analysis of the Texas Know Nothings," *SWHQ* 70 (Jan. 1967): 414–417.

[38] Ford, *Rip Ford's Texas,* xxx, 211 [quote]; Ford, Memoirs (Ford Papers, CAH), 615 [same quote]; Austin *Texas State Times,* May 19, June 30, July 14, Aug. 18, Sept. 15, Oct. 13, Nov. 10, 1855, Jan. 26, Feb. 23, 1856; Adolf Douai, "Autobiography of Dr. Adolf Douai," trans. by Richard H. Douai Boerker (Typescript, n.d., Adolf Douai Papers, CAH), 120; Sibley, *Lone Stars and State Gazettes,* 230–236, 250, 257; Hughes, *Rebellious Ranger,* 118–119, 126.

[39] Ford, *Rip Ford's Texas,* xxx, 211–214, 314–315; Ford, Memoirs (Ford Papers, CAH), 615–616, 630; Austin *Texas State Gazette,* Aug. 18, 1855; Francis R. Lubbock, *Six Decades in Texas* (Austin: Ben C. Jones, 1900), 190–197, Winkler, *Platforms of Political Parties,* 39–40, 68–69; Hughes, *Rebellious Ranger,* 111–112, 116, 123.

[40] Ford, *Rip Ford's Texas,* xxx; Ford, Memoirs (Ford Papers, CAH), 631; Austin *Texas State Times,* June 14, Aug. 2, 9, 1856, May 23, 1857 [quotes]; Hughes, *Rebellious Ranger,* 123–127; Sibley, *Lone Stars and State Gazettes,* 258, 268–270; *NHOT,* 1: 313, 648, 5: 80.

[41] Ford, Memoirs (Ford Papers, CAH), 108; Ford to Peter H. Bell, Sept. 23, 1852, Elisha M. Pease to Ford, Oct. 12, 1854 (Texas Office of the Governor, Records, Texas State Library and Archives, Austin [hereinafter cited as GR and TSLA]); Austin *Texas State Gazette,* Sept. 4, 1852, Oct. 7, 1854, Nov. 29, 1856; Galveston *Weekly Journal,* Sept. 10, 1852; *Claims of Texas Against the United States,* 29; Hughes, *Rebellious Ranger,* 108, 112–113; Koch, "Federal Indian Policy, III," 28; Lack, "Vigilantism in Austin," 12–14; Anderson, *Conquest of Texas,* 265; *NHOT,* 6: 555.

[42] Ford, *Rip Ford's Texas,* 220; Clarksville [TX] *Northern Standard,* Nov. 26, 1859; Ford, Memoirs (Ford Papers, CAH), 650, 653; *Claims of Texas Against the United States,* 33–34; Hughes, *Rebellious Ranger,* 129–130; Anderson, *Conquest of Texas,* 299; Hämäläinen, *Comanche Empire,* 307–310.

[43] Ford, *Rip Ford's Texas,* xxxii [quote], 223–224; Ford, Memoirs (Ford Papers, CAH), 653–654; Hardin Runnels, order of Jan. 28, 1858 (GR); Runnels to Ford, Jan. 28, 1858 (Texas Office of the Adjutant General, Pre-War Ranger Records, TSLA) Austin *Texas State Gazette,* Jan. 30, 1858; *Claims of Texas Against the United States,* 33–34,

133; Gammel, *Laws of Texas,* 4: 949–950; Clarksville [TX] *Standard,* Nov. 26, 1859; Hughes, *Rebellious Ranger,* 130–131; Cox, *Wearing the Cinco Peso,* 144.

[44] Ford, *Rip Ford's Texas,* 224–225; Ford, Memoirs (Ford Papers, CAH), 654–656, 723–726; Robert S. Neighbors to David E. Twiggs, Jan. 17, 1858, Neighbors to Charles E. Mix, Feb. 3, 1858 (Robert S. Neighbors Papers, CAH); Runnels to Twiggs, Feb. 2, 1858, Twiggs to Runnels, Feb. 13, 1858 (GR); *Claims of Texas Against the United States,* 74, 133; Austin *Texas State Gazette,* May 22, 1858; Dallas *Morning News,* Aug. 7, 1892; Hughes, *Rebellious Ranger,* 132–133.

[45] Ford, *Rip Ford's Texas,* 225; Ford, Memoirs (Ford Papers, CAH), 656; Runnels to Ford, Jan. 28, 1858 (Ed Burleson Jr. Papers, CAH); Hughes, *Rebellious Ranger,* 141–142.

Chapter Three: Ranger

[1] Ford, *Rip Ford's Texas,* 226–227, 233; Ford, Memoirs (Ford Papers, CAH), 657–660; Hughes, *Rebellious Ranger,* 134–135; Ed Burleson Jr. to Ford, Mar. 30, 1858 (Texas Indian Papers, TSLA); Ford to Runnels, Feb. 27, 1858, Runnels to Ford, Mar. 7, 1858 (GR); *Claims of Texas Against the United States,* 36, 75; *NHOT,* 3: 836. Ford strictly forbade gambling among his Rangers in 1858; see Order No. __, June 20, 1858 (Ed Burleson Jr. Papers, CAH).

[2] Runnels to Ford, Mar. 10, 1858 (GR).

[3] Ford to Runnels, Apr. 7 [quotes], 26, 1858 (GR); Ford, *Rip Ford's Texas,* 220; Hughes, *Rebellious Ranger,* 135–136; Neighbours, *Robert Simpson Neighbors,* 197–198; Anderson, *Conquest of Texas,* 305; *NHOT,* 1; 423–424, 4: 971–972, 5: 690.

[4] Ford, *Rip Ford's Texas,* 228 [quote], 229; Ford, Memoirs (Ford Papers, CAH), 661–663 [same quote]; Hughes, *Rebellious Ranger,* 136–137 [same quote], 139.

[5] Ford, *Rip Ford's Texas,* xxxii, 229, 241; Ford, Memoirs (Ford Papers, CAH), 662–663, 734; Hughes, *Rebellious Ranger,* 137–139; Ford to Runnels, Apr. 26, May 22, 1858 (GR). The group included Caddos, Tonkawas, Wacos, Delawares, Shawnees, and even Tahuanacos—all united against the Comanches.

[6] Ford, *Rip Ford's Texas,* 229–232; Ford, Memoirs (Ford Papers, CAH), 664–666, 673; Ford to Runnels, May 22, 1858 (GR); Hughes, *Rebellious Ranger,* 139–141.

[7] Ford, *Rip Ford's Texas,* xxxii, 233–234; Ford, Memoirs (Ford Papers, CAH), 671–673; Allison Nelson to Ford, May 21, 1858, Ford to Runnels, May 22, 1858 (GR); *Claims of Texas Against the United States,* 34–35; Hughes, *Rebellious Ranger,* 142–145; Webb, *Texas Rangers,* 151–158; Cox, *Wearing the Cinco Peso,* 146–147; Anderson, *Conquest of Texas,* 273, 305–306; *NHOT,* 3:870–871. John S. Ford's battle with the Comanches on May 12, 1858, has come to be known as the Battle of Antelope Hills or

the Battle of Little Robe Creek. It is worth noting that a military map of Texas published in 1857 shows the site to be almost entirely in Texas, not in the Indian Territory.

[8] Ford, *Rip Ford's Texas,* 234–236; Ford, Memoirs (Ford Papers, CAH), 674; Ford to Runnels, May 22, 1858 (GR); Hughes, *Rebellious Ranger,* 145–148; Anderson, *Conquest of Texas,* 273, 306.

[9] Ford, *Rip Ford's Texas,* 231, 236, 238; Ford, Memoirs (Ford Papers, CAH), 674–675; Ford to Runnels, May 22 [1st and 2nd quotes], May 23, 1858 (GR); Cowen, "Reminiscences," 3 [last quotes]; Austin *Texas State Gazette,* June 5, 1858, Dallas *Morning News,* Aug. 7, 1892; Wilbarger, *Indian Depredations,* 323; Adam R. Johnson, *The Partisan Rangers of the Confederate States Army* (Louisville, KY; George G. Fetter Company, 1904), 23; Hughes, *Rebellious Ranger,* 132, 144, 148; Webb, *Texas Rangers,* 149, 158; William S. Speer and John H. Brown, *The Encyclopedia of the New West* (Marshall, TX: United States Biographical Publishing Company, 1881), 357. Hämäläinen in *Comanche Empire* agrees with Ford's report of Comanche casualties (310), as does Anderson in *Conquest of Texas* (306). Iron Jacket's coat of chain mail, or at least the large portion of it sent by Robert Potter to Gov. Hardin R. Runnels, was destroyed in the fire that devastated the Texas Capitol building in 1881. See Dallas *Morning News,* Jan. 30, 1892. Robert Cotter recalled about Little Owl that he never adjusted to life with a white family: "He was an Indian and died one." See Dallas *Morning News,* Aug. 7, 1892.

[10] Austin *Texas State Gazette,* May 29, 1858; Ford, *Rip Ford's Texas,* 234, 236, 238; Ford, Memoirs (Ford Papers, CAH), 671–672, 673 [2nd quote] 677 [1st quote]; Charles E. Barnard to George Barnard, May 25, 1858 (Neighbors Papers, CAH); Hughes, *Rebellious Ranger,* 146–149; *NHOT,* 1: 384; Robert G. Hartje, *Van Dorn: The Life and Times of a Confederate General* (Nashville: Vanderbilt University, 1967), 61–69. The Tonkawas were widely known for eating parts of dead enemies in an effort to absorb some of their bravery and skill; Ford later claimed they told him a creation myth in which they were told to live like wolves, which they did. See Remington, "How the Law Got into the Chaparral," 64; James T. DeShields, *Border Wars of Texas* (Tioga, TX: Herald Company, 1912), 287; William W. Newcomb, *The Indians of Texas* (Austin: University of Texas Press, 1961), 150–152, and David La Vere, *The Texas Indians* (College Station: Texas A&M University Press, 2004), 187.

[11] San Augustine [TX] *Eastern Texian,* May 29, 1858; Austin *Texas State Gazette,* May 22, 1858; Ford to Runnels, April 24, May 23, 1858, Runnels to Ford, May 28, 1858, Runnels to Texas Delegation in Congress, May 28, 1858 (GR); *Congressional Globe,* 35th Cong., 1st Sess. (1857–1858), 873–875; *Claims of Texas Against the United States,* 34; Hughes, *Rebellious Ranger,* 150; May, *Quitman,* 340–343; Clarksville [TX] *Standard,* Nov. 26, 1859.

[12] Ford, *Rip Ford's Texas,* 240; Ford, Memoirs (Ford Papers, CAH), 675; Ford to Runnels, June 2, 1858 [first quotes] (GR); Ford to Runnels, June 3, 1858 [last two quotes] (Texas Indian Papers, TSLA); Hughes, *Rebellious Ranger,* 150–151.

[13] Ford, *Rip Ford's Texas,* 221–223; Ford, Memoirs (Ford Papers, CAH), 562, 651–652; Austin *Texas Democrat,* Aug. 21, Sept. 25, Oct. 2, 1852; Dallas *Herald,* Aug. 21, 1858; Neighbours, *Indian Exodus,* 123; Robert J. Scarry, *Millard Fillmore* (Jefferson, NC: MacFarland & Company, 2001), 208; Cox, *Wearing the Cinco Peso,* 144–145, 147; Palestine [TX] *Trinity Advocate,* Apr. 20, 1859.

[14] Ford, *Rip Ford's Texas,* xxxii, 238; Ford, Memoirs (Ford Papers, CAH), 675; Runnels to Ford, May 28, 1858, Ford to Runnels, July 5, 1858, Runnels to Ford, July 6, 1858 (GR), Hughes, *Rebellious Ranger,* 150–151; Neighbours, *Indian Exodus,* 123.

[15] Ford, *Rip Ford's Texas,* xxxii, 239–240; Ford, Memoirs (Ford Papers, CAH), 670; Ford to Runnels, Apr. 14, 1858 (GR); Affidavit of John S. Ford, Nov. 22, 1858 (Neighbors Papers, CAH); Extract of letter from Ford to Josiah A. Wilcox, Apr. 12, 1859 (United States Office of Indian Affairs Letters, CAH [2nd-6th quotes]); Hughes, *Rebellious Ranger,* 149 [1st quote]; Neighbours, *Robert Simpson Neighbors,* 198–199; Anderson, *Conquest of Texas,* 304–305. Note that ironically Ford condemns vigilantes here, when he was one himself in Austin 1854.

[16] Affidavit of Ford, Nov. 22, 1858 (Neighbors Papers, CAH); Ford, *Rip Ford's Texas,* 239–240; Ford, Memoirs (Ford Papers, CAH), 670; Neighbours, *Robert Simpson Neighbors,* 199, 208–209, 221; Neighbours, *Indian Exodus,* 125; Webb, *Texas Rangers,* 168–169, *NHOT,* 1: 423–424, 4: 971–972, 976–977.

[17] Ford, *Rip Ford's Texas,* xxxii, 242–244; Ford, Memoirs (Ford Papers, CAH), 732–734; Dallas *Herald,* Oct. 10, Dec. 8, 1858; Austin *Texas State Gazette,* Nov. 27, 1858; Matagorda [TX] *Gazette,* Nov. 27, 1858 (Transcript in Vertical File: John S. Ford, CAH); *Claims of Texas Against the United States,* 38, 77, 78, 137, 138; Hughes, *Rebellious Ranger,* 152–153.

[18] Ford, *Rip Ford's Texas,* xxxii-xxxiii, 243–248; Ford, Memoirs (Ford Papers, CAH), 736–741, 762; Runnels to Ford, Dec. 12, 1858, Ford to Runnels, Feb. 24, 1859, S. G. Fidler to Runnels, Mar. 21, 1859; Ford to Runnels, Apr. 12, 1859 (GR); *Difficulties on Southwestern Frontier,* House Ex. Docs. 52, 36th Cong., 1st Sess. [Serial Set 1050], 10; Hughes, *Rebellious Ranger,* 155–157; Hartje, *Van Dorn,* 71–73.

[19] Ford, *Rip Ford's Texas,* xxxii-xxxiv, 247, 249–259; Ford, Memoirs (Ford Papers, CAH), 741–760; Dallas *Herald,* Feb. 23, 1859; Runnels, order of Jan. 28, 1858 [quote], Runnels to Ford, Feb. 13, 1858, Ford to Runnels, Dec. 28, 1858, Edward J. Gurley to Runnels, Feb. 3, 1859, Runnels to Ford, Feb. 11, 1859 (GR); Neighbours, *Robert Simpson Neighbors,* 223–228; Neighbours, *Indian Exodus,* 131–132; George Klos, "Our People Could Not Distinguish One Tribe from Another: The 1859 Expulsion of the Reserve Indians from Texas," *SWHQ* 97 (April 1994): 608–618; Hughes, *Rebellious Ranger,* 153–155; Webb, *Texas Rangers,* 169–170; Anderson, *Conquest of Texas,* 314–315; *NHOT,* 1: 418, 3: 390.

[20] Ford, *Rip Ford's Texas,* xxxiii-xxxiv; Ford, Memoirs (Ford Papers, CAH), 750–751, 760 [2nd quote], 761–762; Ford to Runnels, Feb. 16, 1859 [1st quote], Run-

nels to Ford, Mar. 3, 1859, Runnels to Ford, Apr. 3, 15, 1859 (GR); *Claims of Texas Against the United States,* 42; Austin *Texas State Gazette,* Mar.12, 1859; Dallas *Herald,* May 18, 1859; Koch, "Federal Indian Policy in Texas, 1848–1860, Chapter IV," *SWHQ* 29 (Oct. 1925): 115–117; Hughes, *Rebellious Ranger,* 158–159; Anderson, *Conquest of Texas,* 317–322.

[21] Ford, *Rip Ford's Texas,* 260, 264–265; Brown, Annals of Travis County (Brown Papers, CAH), 19: 20; Ford, Memoirs (Ford Papers, CAH), 763. 870; Ford to Ed Burleson Jr., Aug. 11, 1859 [quotes] (Ed Burleson Jr. Papers, CAH); *Claims of Texas Against the United States,* 43; Hughes, *Rebellious Ranger,* 160–161; Amberson et al., *I Would Rather Sleep in Texas,* 164–166; Collins, *Texas Devils,*111–118; Chance, *Carvajal,* 169–170; Thompson, *Cortina,* 7, 22, 36–37, 40–47, 50–51.

[22] Ford, *Rip Ford's Texas,* 265; Ford, Memoirs (Ford Papers, CAH), 662–663, 734; William G. Tobin to Runnels, Nov. 27, 1859 (GR); Jerry D. Thompson, ed., *Fifty Miles and a Fight: Major Samuel Peter Heintzelman's Journal of Texas and the Cortina War* (Austin: Texas State Historical Association, 1998), 131–132; Corpus Christi *Ranchero,* Dec. 3, 1859; *Claims of Texas Against the United States,* 44, 48; United States Congress, *Troubles on the Texas Frontier,* House Ex. Docs. 81, 36th Cong., 1st Sess. [Serial Set 1056], 5–7; Hughes, *Rebellious Ranger,* 161; Collins, *Texas Devils,* 118–122, 124–126, 128–130, 133; Amberson et al., *I Would Rather Sleep in Texas,* 167–169; Webb, *Texas Rangers,* 182; Thompson, *Cortina,* 52–65, 68–72, 74, 77, 78; Cox, *Wearing the Cinco Peso,* 154, 155; *NHOT,* 3: 543.

[23] Ford, *Rip Ford's Texas,* xxxiv, 265–266; Ford, Memoirs (Ford Papers, CAH), 769–771; Runnels to Ford, Nov. 17, 22, 1859, Ford to Runnels, Nov. 22, 1859 (GR); *Claims of Texas Against the United States,* 143–144; San Antonio *Express,* Jan. 19, 1890; Hughes, *Rebellious Ranger,* 161–162; Collins, *Texas Devils,* 123–124; Thompson, *Cortina,* 61–62. Ford tended to believe that Forbes Britton, in convincing Gov. Hardin R. Runnels to send Rangers to the Rio Grande in 1859, had shown himself to be a "first class actor." See John S. Ford, The Cortina War (DeShields Papers, DRT).

[24] Ford, *Rip Ford's Texas,* 266–267; Ford, Memoirs (Ford Papers, CAH), 771–773, 870; Ford to Runnels, Dec. 16, 1859 (GR); San Antonio *Ledger & Texan,* Dec. 10, 1859; Corpus Christi *Ranchero,* Dec. 3 [quote], 24, 1859; *Difficulties on Southwestern Frontier,* 87–88; *Troubles on the Texas Frontier,* 7–8; Collins, *Texas Devils,* 131–132, 136–137; Martin L. Crimmins, ed., "Colonel Robert E. Lee's Report on Indian Combats in Texas," *SWHQ* 39 (July 1935): 21–32; Thompson, *Fifty Miles and a Fight,* 138, 140–141; Hughes, *Rebellious Ranger,* 162–163; Thompson, *Cortina,* 73–74.

[25] Ford, *Rip Ford's Texas,* 268–269; Ford, Memoirs (Ford Papers, CAH), 774, 776, 777; Runnels to Ford, Nov. 17, 23 [1st quote], 1859 (GR); Ford to H. E. Woodhouse, Dec. 20, 1859 [receipt] (Texas Adjutant General, Pre-War Ranger Records, TSLA; Thompson, *Fifty Miles and a Fight,* 125, 140–142 [2nd quote], 143, 147–149;

Crimmins, "Lee's Report," 25; Hughes, *Rebellious Ranger,* 162, 164; Brackett, *United States Cavalry,* 202.

[26] Ford, *Rip Ford's Texas,* 269–272; Ford, Memoirs (Ford Papers, CAH), 777–780; *Claims of Texas Against the United States,* 45; Hughes, *Rebellious Ranger,* 164–165; Thompson, *Cortina,* 77–80; Corpus Christi *Ranchero,* Jan. 7, 1860; Austin *Texas State Gazette,* Jan. 14, 1860.

[27] Ford, *Rip Ford's Texas,* 274–275; Ford, Memoirs (Ford Papers, CAH), 782–785; Ford to Sam Houston, Dec. 29, 1859, Tobin to Houston, Jan. 30, 1860 (GR); Corpus Christi *Ranchero,* Jan. 7, 1860; Austin *Texas State Gazette,* Jan. 14, 1860; *Difficulties on Southwestern Frontier,* 96–98; *Troubles on the Texas Frontier,* 9, 72; Thompson, *Fifty Miles and a Fight,* 155; Hughes, *Rebellious Ranger,* 166–167; Collins, *Texas Devils,* 142–146; "Starr County Elected Officials," http://www.rootsweb.ancestry.com/~txstarr/elected.htm (accessed Dec. 28, 2008).

[28] Ford, *Rip Ford's Texas,* 274–276; Ford, Memoirs (Ford Papers, CAH), 772–773, 784–785, 791; Tobin to Samuel P. Heintzelman, Jan. 2, 1860 (Texas Adjutant General, Pre-War Ranger Records, TSLA); Tobin to Houston, Jan. 2, 1860 (GR); Thompson, ed., *Fifty Miles and a Fight,* 142, 164; Hughes, *Rebellious Ranger,* 168; Collins, *Texas Devils,* 125, 135, 139, 162–164; Amberson et al., *I Would Rather Sleep in Texas,* 169; Charles M. Robinson III, *The Men Who Wear the Star: The Story of the Texas Rangers* (New York: Random House, 2000), 130–132. A writer in the San Antonio *Ledger,* Jan. 14, 1860, opined that Ford's delay in holding the elections led to his defeat. Ford attributed his defeat to his strict discipline and the efforts of John D. Littleton, who understood that if William G. Tobin became a major, it would create a vacancy for a captain. Littleton was elected captain to succeed Tobin, but quickly switched sides and joined Ford, who later claimed that he always regarded both Tobin and Littleton as his friends. See Ford, The Cortina War (Manuscript, n.d., DeShields Papers, DRT).

[29] Ford, *Rip Ford's Texas,* 276–279; Ford, Memoirs (Ford Papers, CAH), 791–793; San Antonio *Ledger,* Feb. 18, 1860; Corpus Christi *Ranchero,* Feb. 25, 1860; Angel Navarro and Robert H. Taylor to Tobin, Jan. 12, 1860, Taylor to Houston, Jan. 16, 1860, Heintzelman to Navarro and Taylor, Feb. 2, 1860, Navarro and Taylor to Ford, Feb. 2, 1860, Navarro and Taylor to Houston, Feb. 4, 1860 (GR); *Claims of Texas Against the United States,* 45; Thompson, *Fifty Miles and a Fight,* 187; *Difficulties on Southwestern Frontier,* 118–119; Hughes, *Rebellious Ranger,* 168–170; Collins, *Texas Devils,* 164–167, 174–176; Thompson, *Cortina,* 87–90.

[30] Ford, *Rip Ford's Texas,* 154, 242, 279–280, 353; Ford, Memoirs (Ford Papers, CAH), 521, 736, 790–794; Corpus Christi *Ranchero,* Dec. 3, 1859; *Difficulties on Southwestern Frontier,* 122; Hughes, *Rebellious Ranger,* 153, 167, 169–170; *NHOT,* 2: 657; 4: 237–238.

[31] Ford, *Rip Ford's Texas,* xxxii, 229, 241; Ford, Memoirs (Ford Papers, CAH), 662–663, 734; Heintzelman to Tobin, Jan. 2, 1860 [quotes] (Texas Adjutant General,

Pre-War Ranger Records, TSL); Houston to Ford, Dec. 30, 1859 (GR); Corpus Christi *Ranchero,* Jan. 7, 1860); Amelia W. Williams and Eugene C. Barker, eds., *The Writings of Sam Houston, 1813–1863,* 8 vols. (Austin: University of Texas Press, 1938–1943), 7: 390, 409; Thompson, *Fifty Miles and a Fight,* 174, 179, 182, 195; Shearer, "Carvajal Disturbances," 443; Hughes, *Rebellious Ranger,* 167; Thompson, *Cortina,* 81–82, 87; Amberson et al., *I Would Rather Sleep in Texas,* 161–162.

[32] Ford, *Rip Ford's Texas,* 281–282, 245; Ford, Memoirs (Ford Papers, CAH), 739, 796, 807–808, 897–898; Hughes, *Rebellious Ranger,* 170–172; Corpus Christi *Ranchero,* Feb.11, 18, 1860; Austin *Texas State Gazette,* May 26, 1860.

[33] Ford, *Rip Ford's Texas,* 282–286; Ford, Memoirs (Ford Papers, CAH), 796–801, 813, 828, 830; Tobin to Houston, Feb. 6, 1860, Ford to Houston, Feb. 9, 1860 (GR) Ford to C. W. Thomas, Feb. 5, 1860 (Ford Papers, TSLA); Corpus Christi *Ranchero,* Feb. 11, 18, 1860; *Difficulties on Southwestern Frontier,* 110–111, 112–115, 119–120; *Claims of Texas Against the United States,* 45, 46; *Troubles on the Texas Frontier,* 10–11, 13, 63–70, 75, 96, 97; Thompson, *Cortina,* 83–84; Collins, *Texas Devils,* 168–173; Amberson et al., *I Would Rather Sleep in Texas,* 171–172.

[34] Ford, *Rip Ford's Texas,* 286–289; Ford, Memoirs (Ford Papers, CAH), 802, 806, 809–813; Thompson, *Fifty Miles and a Fight,* 188–189, 191; Runnels to Ford, Nov. 23, 1859 (GR); Ford to Heintzelman, Feb. 4, 1860 (Texas Adjutant General, Pre-War Ranger Records, TSLA); Heintzelman to Ford, Feb. 4, 1860 (Ford Papers, TSLA); Hughes, *Rebellious Ranger,* 172.

[35] Ford, *Rip Ford's Texas,* 291; Ford, Memoirs (Ford Papers, CAH), 807–808, 818–819; Ford to Houston, Feb. 9, Mar. 25 [quotes], 1860, John J. Dix to Ford, Mar. 4, 1860, Arthur Pue to Ford, Mar. 10, 1860, Ford to Thomas, Mar. 11, 1860, Heintzelman to Ford, Mar. 14, 1862 (GR); Thompson, *Fifty Miles and a Fight,* 195; Hughes, *Rebellious Ranger,* 172–173.

[36] Ford, *Rip Ford's Texas,* 290–293, 295; Ford, Memoirs (Ford Papers, CAH), 817–818, 819–822, 825; Heintzelman to Ford, Mar. 14, 1860, Ford to Houston, Mar. 17, 1860 (GR); Ford to Thomas, Mar. 15, 1860 (Ford Papers, TSLA); Corpus Christi *Ranchero,* Mar. 24, 1860; *Troubles on the Texas Frontier,* 80, 81; Hughes, *Rebellious Ranger,* 173–174; Collins, *Texas Devils,* 192–196; Chance, *Carvajal,* 172; Thompson, *Cortina,* 85.

[37] Ford, *Rip Ford's Texas,* 293–295; Ford, Memoirs (Ford Papers, CAH), 822–825; Hughes, *Rebellious Ranger,* 175; Thompson, *Cortina,* 83–85, 87.

[38] Ford, *Rip Ford's Texas,* 295–296; Ford, Memoirs (Ford Papers, CAH), 826–833, 834 [quote]; Will Lambert, "Col. John S. Ford," *The Southern Tribute* 1 (March 1898): 177–184 [quote on 181]; Ford to Heintzelman, Mar. 24, 1860 (Ford Papers, TSLA); *Troubles on the Texas Frontier,* 99; Hughes, *Rebellious Ranger,* 175–176; *NHOT,* 4:45–46; Lewis E. Daniell, *Personnel of the Texas State Government, with Sketches of Distinguished Texans* (Austin: City Printing Company, 1887), 196–197.

[39] Ford, *Rip Ford's Texas,* xxxii, 296–298; Ford, Memoirs (Ford Papers, CAH), 835–839; Ford to Heintzelman, Mar. 24, 1860 (Ford Papers, TSLA); Hughes, *Rebellious Ranger,* 176–177; Thompson, *Cortina,* 85; Webb, *Texas Rangers,* 184–193.

[40] Ford, *Rip Ford's Texas,* 299–303; Ford, Memoirs (Ford Papers, CAH), 825, 840–845; Hughes, *Rebellious Ranger,* 178–181; Collins, *Texas Devils,* 198–202; Thompson, *Cortina,* 85; Corpus Christi *Ranchero,* Apr. 14, 21, 1860; San Antonio *Ledger,* Apr. 28, 1860.

[41] Ford, *Rip Ford's Texas,* 303–304; Ford, Memoirs (Ford Papers, CAH), 846–848; Hughes, *Rebellious Ranger,* 181–183; Thompson, *Cortina,* 86; San Antonio *Ledger,* Apr. 28, 1860.

[42] Ford, *Rip Ford's Texas,* 305–308; Ford, Memoirs (Ford Papers, CAH), 848–851; Thompson, *Fifty Miles and a Fight,* 183–184, 214, 227–230; Williams and Barker, *Writings of Houston,* 7: 444, 490, 499–500, 523, 541–543; Navarro to Houston, Jan. 31, 1860, Ford to Houston, Mar. 2, 1860 (GR); *Troubles on the Texas Frontier,* 86–89, 100; *Claims of Texas Against the United States,* 47; Hughes, *Rebellious Ranger,* 179–180, 183–184; Thompson, *Cortina,* 92–93; James L. Haley, *Sam Houston* (Norman: University of Oklahoma Press, 2002), 366–367; Carl Coke Rister, *Robert E. Lee in Texas* (Norman: University of Oklahoma Press, 1946), 115, 121–123; Collins, *Texas Devils,* 176–178, 203–206; Webb, *Texas Rangers,* 203–207; *NHOT,* 4: 423; Brackett, *United States Cavalry,* 206–207. Albert G. Brackett, as the captain of a company of the 2nd United States Cavalry, was the officer sent by Robert E. Lee to speak with community leaders in Reynosa.

[43] Ford, *Rip Ford's Texas,* 298, 307–308; Ford, Memoirs (Ford Papers, CAH), 851, 853; Robert E. Lee to Houston, Apr. 20, 1860 (GR); Thompson, *Fifty Miles and a Fight,* 244–247; Rister, *Lee in Texas,* 123–127; Hughes, *Rebellious Ranger,* 177, 184; Thompson, *Cortina,* 86.

[44] Ford, *Rip Ford's Texas,* 307–308; Ford, Memoirs (Ford Papers, CAH), 852; Austin *Texas State Gazette,* June 30, 1860; Dallas *Herald,* Oct. 1, 1860; San Antonio *Ledger,* Oct. 13, 1860; *NHOT,* 3: 1,145–1,146; Jimmie Hicks, ed., "Some Letters Concerning the Knights of the Golden Circle in Texas, 1860–1861," *SWHQ* 65 (July 1961): 86; Hughes, *Rebellious Ranger,* 186–187; Collins, *Texas Devils,* 215–217, 225–227; C. A. Bridges, "The Knights of the Golden Circle: A Filibustering Fantasy," *SWHQ* 44 (Jan. 1941): 287, 288, 290, 291–295, 297, 300–301; Roy Sylvan Dunn, "The KGC in Texas, 1860–1861," *SWHQ* 70 (Apr. 1967): 551, 555–556, 561.

[45] Ford to Runnels, June 3, 1858 (Texas Indian Papers, TSLA); Ford, *Rip Ford's Texas,* xxxv; Ford, Memoirs (Ford Papers, CAH), 124 and Miscellaneous, 161; Dallas *Morning News,* Feb. 20, 1901; John S. Ford, Remarks [1st-3rd quotes] (Manuscript, n.d., n.p., Ford Papers, Haley Museum); Cowen, "Reminiscences," 3 [4th-6th quotes]; Hughes, *Rebellious Ranger,* 187.

[46] Ford to Ed Burleson Jr., June 20, 1860 (Ed Burleson Jr. Papers, CAH). Ford sometimes referred to his former attendant as "Don Monkey Shit." The denunciation of

Ford appears in the Palestine [TX] *Trinity Advocate,* June 20, 1860. Rep. Abram B. Olin also denounced Texans in general as "horse-thieves, cowards, and inhuman murderers of poor innocent Indian women and children." Rep. John H. Reagan, whom Ford had once rescued from freezing to death, of course took angry exception to Olin's words.

Chapter Four: Secessionist

[1] Campbell, *Gone to Texas,* 239–240; Walter L. Buenger, *Secession and the Union in Texas* (Austin: University of Texas Press, 1984), 120–122. For an excellent discussion of the panic surrounding the secession movement in Texas, see Donald E. Reynolds, *Texas Terror: The Slave Insurrection Panic and the Secession of the Lower South* (Baton Rouge: Louisiana State University Press, 2007).

[2] Ford, *Rip Ford's Texas,* xxxvi, 313–315, 317; Ford, Memoirs (Ford Papers, CAH), 855, Miscellaneous: Secession, 1, 26; Ford to Ed Burleson Jr., June 20, 1860 [1st quote] (Ed Burleson Jr. Papers, CAH); Austin *Texas State Gazette,* Aug. 11, 25, Sept. 1, 1860; Hughes, *Rebellious Ranger,* 187, 188 [2nd quote]. Ford in his letter to Ed Burleson Jr. refers to Wilkins Micawber, the perpetually optimistic but indecisive character in Charles Dickens' novel, *David Copperfield.*

[3] Ford, *Rip Ford's Texas,* 315–317; Ford, Memoirs (Ford Papers, CAH), 855, Miscellaneous: Secession, 2, 3, 5, 10; Buenger, *Secession in Texas,* 123–125; Hughes, *Rebellious Ranger,* 188–189; *NHOT,* 1: 314, 2: 1,039, 5: 611–612.

[4] Ford, *Rip Ford's Texas,* xxxv, xxxvi; Ford, Memoirs (Ford Papers, CAH), Miscellaneous: Secession, 5; Brown, Annals of Travis County, 21: 6–7 (Brown Papers, CAH); Austin *Texas State Gazette,* Jan. 5, 12, 1861; Aaron B. Burleson to Ed Burleson, June 28, 1854, Nov. 19, 1860 (Ed Burleson Jr. Papers, CAH); Ernest W. Winkler, ed., *Journal of the Secession Convention of Texas, 1861* (Austin: Austin Printing Company, 1912), 9–10; Hughes, *Rebellious Ranger,* 188–190; J. J. Bowden, *The Exodus of Federal Forces from Texas 1861* (Austin: Eakin Press, 1986), 32–33; Anna Irene Sandbo, "The First Session of the Secession Convention of Texas," *SWHQ* 18 (Oct. 1914): 179–180; *NHOT,* 5: 1,125.

[5] Ford, *Rip Ford's Texas,* 198, 200, 317; Ford, Memoirs (Ford Papers, CAH), Miscellaneous: Secession, 27, and Miscellaneous: Ford as a Confederate, 1; Winkler, *Secession Convention,* 16, 22, 406, 449; Buenger, *Secession in Texas,* 142–143; Hughes, *Rebellious Ranger,* 189–191; Sandbo, "First Session," 182; Ralph A. Wooster, "An Analysis of the Membership of the Texas Secession Convention," *SWHQ* 62 (Jan. 1959): 322–335(323, 326, 327; *NHOT,* 3: 696. Cameron County was officially represented by Ford and James Walworth, a business associate of Mifflin Kenedy and Richard King.

[6] Ford, *Rip Ford's Texas,* xxxvi, 318; Ford, Memoirs (Ford Papers, CAH), Miscellaneous: Secession, 33, and Miscellaneous: Ford as a Confederate, 1; John S. Ford,

"Memoirs," (Typescript, n.d., 7 volumes, Ford Papers, CAH), 5: 995 [quote; hereinafter cited as "Typed Memoirs"]; Winkler, *Secession Convention,* 321–324; *The War of the Rebellion: A Compilation of the Official Records of the Union and Confederate Armies,* 130 vols. (Washington, DC: Government Printing Office, 1880–1902), Series I, Vol. 53: 649–651, 654 [hereinafter cited as *OR*]; Hughes, *Rebellious Ranger,* 189, 192, 193; Buenger, *Secession in Texas,* 125–126, 143–144; Clement A. Evans, ed., *Confederate Military History,* Extended edition, 17 vols. (Atlanta, 1899; extended ed., Wilmington, NC: Broadfoot Publishing Company, 1989), 15: 21–22, *NHOT,* 4. 329–330, 384–385. The material on Texas that appears in Evans' volume was written by Oran Milo Roberts, a close friend of Ford and the president of the Texas Secession Convention.

[7] Ford, *Rip Ford's Texas,* 318–319; *OR,* I, 53: 647–649; Hughes, *Rebellious Ranger,* 193–194; Bowden, *Exodus,* 83; Evans, *Confederate Military History* (Extended ed.), 15: 23, 38–39, 41; Stephen B. Oates, "John S. 'Rip' Ford: Prudent Cavalryman, C.S.A.," in Ralph A. Wooster, ed., *Lone Star Blue and Gray: Essays on Texas in the Civil War* (Austin: Texas State Historical Association, 1995), 314–315 [this article by Oates first appeared under the same title in *Southwestern Historical Quarterly* 64 (Jan. 1961): 289–314]; *NHOT,* 4: 434, 1,010, 6: 265. McLeod and Ford served together with Thomas J. Rusk in 1838 and 1839, and in the Texas House of Representatives in 1844–1845, and both supported José M. J. Carvajal in 1851–1852.

[8] Ford, *Rip Ford's Texas,* 318; *OR,* I, 1: 537–538, 53: 646–649, 651–652, 658; Bowden, *Exodus,* 83–85; Paul N. Spellman, *Forgotten Texas Leader: Hugh McLeod and the Texas Santa Fe Expedition* (College Station: Texas A&M University Press 1999), 173–175; Evans, *Confederate Military History* (Extended ed.), 15: 38–39; Amberson et al., *I Would Rather Sleep in Texas,* 186.

[9] Hughes, *Rebellious Ranger,* 195; *OR,* I, 1: 538–540 [quotes on 539], 53: 620, 650, 655, 659–660; Buenger, *Secession in Texas,* 154, 174–175; Evans, *Confederate Military History* (Extended ed.), 15: 39–40; Austin *Texas State Gazette,* Mar. 2, 23, 1861; Bowden, *Exodus,* 85–86; Oates, "Ford," 316; *NHOT,* 5: 958–959, 6: 602–603. Having secured the overwhelming approval of the Texas voters for secession on February 23, 1861, the Secession Convention reconvened and, having already sent delegates to meet with the Confederate government at Montgomery, Alabama, quickly allied Texas with the new Confederacy. See Buenger, *Secession in Texas,* 153, 176.

[10] Ford, *Rip Ford's Texas,* 320–321 [quote]; Ford, "Typed Memoirs" (Ford Papers, CAH), 5: 937–938, 999–1000; *OR,* I, 53: 656; Hugh McLeod to Ford, Mar, 1, 2, 1861 (Ford Papers, Haley Museum); Austin *Texas State Gazette,* Mar. 23, 1861; Corpus Christi *Ranchero,* Mar. 16, 1861; Hughes, *Rebellious Ranger,* 196; Evans, *Confederate Military History* (Extended ed.), 15: 40–41; Bowden, *Exodus,* 86.

[11] Ford, *Rip Ford's Texas,* 320–321; Ford, "Typed Memoirs" (Ford Papers, CAH), 5: 1000; McLeod to Ford, Mar. 4, 1861, Ford Papers, Haley Museum and Ford Papers, TSLA); Winkler, *Secession Convention,* 324–365; *OR,* I, 53: 652–653 [quotes]; Austin *Texas State Gazette,* Mar. 23, 1861; Corpus Christi *Ranchero,* Mar. 16, 30, 1861;

Hughes, *Rebellious Ranger,* 196–197; Bowden, *Exodus,* 87–90; Evans, *Confederate Military History* (Extended ed.), 15: 41.

[12] Ford, *Rip Ford's Texas,* 318; Ford, "Typed Memoirs" (Ford Papers, CAH), 5: 997; *OR,* I, 53: 652, 654, 664; Benjamin F. Terry to Ford, Mar. 11, 1861, McLeod to Ford, Mar. 11, 1861 (Ford Papers, Haley Museum); Hughes, *Rebellious Ranger,* 197; Bowden, *Exodus,* 137; Edward T. Cotham Jr., *Battle on the Bay: The Civil War Struggle for Galveston* (Austin: University of Texas Press, 1998), 12; Edward T. Cotham Jr., *Sabine Pass: The Confederacy's Thermopylae* (Austin: University of Texas Press, 2004), 40–41.

[13] Ford to Joseph E. Love, Mar. 15, 1861, Ford to William Edwards, Apr. 28, 1861 (Ford Papers, Haley Museum). The literary quotation in Ford's first letter is from Alexander Pope, "Essay on Man," Epistle 1: Line 200.

[14] Ford, *Rip Ford's Texas,* 324, 326; Winkler, *Secession Convention,* 200–201; Gammel, *Laws of Texas,* 4: 1534; *OR,* I, 1: 574–575, 577–578, 617–623, 631; Leroy Pope Walker to John Hemphill, Apr. 11, 1862, Walker to Edward Clark, Apr. 23, 1861, Walker to Jefferson Davis, Apr. 26, 1861 (Confederate States of America Records, Manuscript Division, Library of Congress, Washington, DC), Walker to Clark, Apr. 23, 1861 (GR); Dallas *Herald,* May 22, 1861; CSR, 2nd Texas Cavalry: John S. Ford; Hughes, *Rebellious Ranger,* 197, 200; Bowden, *Exodus,* 90; Campbell, *Gone to Texas,* 251–252; Evans, *Confederate Military History* (Extended ed.), 15: 34, 38. Stephen B. Oates, in *Confederate Cavalry West of the River* (Austin: University of Texas Press, 1961), declares that Ford's commission dates from May 23, 1861 (p. 8), as does Ralph A. Wooster in *Lone Star Regiments in Gray* (Austin: Eakin Press, 2002), 205. But Bruce S. Allardice, in *Confederate Colonels: A Biographical Register* (Columbia: University of Missouri Press, 2008), says the date was May 18, 1861 (p. 151). This conflict indicates how unclear the official records are.

[15] Ford, *Rip Ford's Texas,* xxxvii, xxxix, 326; Ford, Remarks (Ford Papers, Haley Museum); Texas Secretary of State, Confederate Pension Files: 00356, Bexar County, Addie N. Ford (TSLA); Corpus Christi *Ranchero,* Apr. 6, 1861; Dallas *Morning News,* Feb. 20, 1901; Hughes, *Rebellious Ranger,* 200; Benjamin W. Dwight, *The History of the Descendants of Elder John Strong* (Albany, NY: Joel Munsell, 1871), 185. William Ford lived in Webberville, a town east of Austin in Travis County, with Jesse F. Burdett in 1860. For William G. Thomas, see United States Ninth Census, 1870 [Travis County, Texas]; Houston *Telegraph,* July 29, Aug. 10, 12, 17, 1863, Mar. 21, 28, 1864; *NHOT,* 2: 718.

[16] Ford, "Typed Memoirs" (Ford Papers, CAH), 5: 938–939; *OR,* I, 1: 601; Felix A. Blucher et al. to Ford, Mar. 10, 1861, Ebenezar B. Nichols to Ford, Mar. 19, 1861 [quote], John Littleton to Ford, Mar. 20, 1861 (Ford Papers, Haley Museum); Winkler, *Secession Convention,* 401–402; Hughes, *Rebellious Ranger,* 197;

[17] Ford, *Rip Ford's Texas,* 325, 326 ; Ford to Clark, Apr. 1 [1st quote], 21, May 12, 1861 (GR); Ford to George Dye, Apr. 19, 1861, Ford to John Donelson, Apr. 19, 1861,

Ford to Littleton, Apr. 19, 1861 (Ford Papers, Haley Museum); Ford to Matt Nolan, Apr. 18, 1861 [2nd quote], Ford to Santos Benavides, Apr. 19, 1861 (Ford Papers, Haley Museum, and Ford Papers, TSLA); Corpus Christi *Ranchero,* Apr. 27, 1861; Jerry D. Thompson and Lawrence T. Jones III, *Civil War and Revolution on the Rio Grande Frontier* (Austin: Texas State Historical Association, 2004), 40.

18 Ford, *Rip Ford's Texas,* 327–328; Ford, Memoirs (Ford Papers, CAH), Miscellaneous: Ford as a Confederate, 4; Ford, "Typed Memoirs" (Ford Papers, CAH), 5: 931; Ford to Nolan, Apr. 28, 1861 (Ford Papers, Haley Museum); Ford to Clark, May 12, 1861, (GR); Corpus Christi *Ranchero,* May 3, 10, 1861; Brownsville [TX] *Rio Grande Sentinel,* June 26, 1861; Hughes, *Rebellious Ranger,* 199; Gilman B. Howe, *Genealogy of the Bigelow Family of America* (Worcester, MA: C. Hamilton, 1890), 382–383; Amberson et al., *I Would Rather Sleep in Texas,* 108, 128.

19 Ford, *Rip Ford's Texas,* 323; Ford, "Typed Memoirs" (Ford Papers, CAH), 5: 914, 915; *OR,* I, 53: 654; Winkler, *Secession Convention,* 329–331 [1st quotes]; Ford to Edwards, Apr. 18, 1861 [last quote] (Ford Papers, Haley Museum); Corpus Christi *Ranchero,* Mar. 23, 1861; Hughes, *Rebellious Ranger,* 197.

20 Ford, *Rip Ford's Texas,* 186, 317–318, 324; Ford, Memoirs (Ford Papers, CAH), 569; Ford, "Typed Memoirs" (Ford Papers, CAH) 5: 1002; Henry Redmond to Ford, Apr. 12, 1861, Ford to Clark, Apr. 21, 1861 (GR); Ford to Redmond, Apr. 15, 1861 [last quote], Nolan to Ford, Apr. 16, 17 [1st quote], 1861, Ford to Santos Benavides, Apr. 17, 1861 (Ford Papers, Haley Museum); *NHOT,* 6: 718; Hughes, *Rebellious Ranger,* 199; Thompson, *Cortina,* 97–98, 109; Thompson and Jones, *Civil War & Revolution on the Rio Grande Frontier,* 47. Ford declares in his memoirs that Isidro Vela was hanged in Zapata County in April 1861, and William J. Hughes repeats this mistake. In fact, Vela was lynched by Mexican raiders in December 1862 at his Zapata County ranch.

21 Nolan to Ford, Apr. 16, 1861 [all quotes but last], Ford to Nolan, Apr. 28, 1861 [last quote] (Ford Papers, Haley Museum, also Ford Papers, TSLA); Ford to Clark, Apr. 21, 1861 (GR); Corpus Christi *Ranchero,* Apr. 27, 1861; Thompson and Jones, *Civil War & Revolution on the Rio Grande Frontier,* 34–37; Jerry D. Thompson, *Vaqueros in Blue and Gray,* (Austin: State House Press, 2000), 15–19; Thompson, *Cortina,* 97–99.

22 Ford, *Rip Ford's Texas,* 324; Ford, "Typed Memoirs" (Ford Papers, CAH) 5: 918–925, 1002–1003; Nolan to Ford, Apr. 16, 1861, Santos Benavides to Ford, May 23, 1861 (Ford Papers, Haley Museum, and Ford Papers, TSLA); Matt Nolan to Ford, May 5, 1861 (Ford Papers, Haley Museum, and Walter P. Webb Papers, CAH); Ford to Clark, May 8, 13, 1861 (GR); Corpus Christi *Ranchero,* June 1, 8, 1861; *New York Times,* Sept. 22, 1873; Hughes, *Rebellious Ranger,* 199; Thompson, *Cortina,* 99–101; Thompson and Jones, *Civil War & Revolution on the Rio Grande Frontier,* 37–40; Thompson, *Vaqueros in Blue and Gray,* 19–23; *NHOT,* 1: 483–485.

[23] Ford to Clark, May 12 [quotes], 29, 1861, June 9, 1861 (GR); Ford, "Typed Memoirs" (Ford Papers, CAH), 5: 918–925, 1002–1003; Ford to Santos Benavides, May 27, 1861 (Ford Papers, Haley Museum, and Ford Papers, TSLA); Thompson, *Cortina,* 101–102.

[24] Oates, "Prudent Cavalryman," 317–318; J. P. Austin to Ford, Apr. 17, 1861, Ford to Clark, Apr. 21, June 23, 1861 (GR); Ford to Santos Benavides, May 26, 1861 [1st quote], June 2, 1861 (Ford Papers, Haley Museum); Ford to Santos Benavides, May 29, 1861 [2nd and 3rd quotes] (Ford Papers, Haley Museum, and Ford Papers, TSLA); *OR,* I, 1: 577; Ford, *Rip Ford's Texas,* 325; Winkler, *Secession Convention,* 332; Hughes, *Rebellious Ranger,* 199; Thompson, *Cortina,* 101.

[25] Ford to Clark, July 14, 1861 (GR).

[26] *OR,* I, 4: 131–132, 136–137, II, 1, pt. 1: 93–94; Ford, "Typed Memoirs" (Ford Papers, CAH), 5: 934–936; Ford, *Rip Ford's Texas,* 319, 328–329; Evans, *Confederate Military History* (Extended ed.), 15: 226; Hamilton P. Bee to Clark, Sept. 22, 1861 (GR); Ford to Oran M. Roberts, Sept. 30, 1861 [quotes] (Oran M. Roberts Papers, CAH); Corpus Christi *Ranchero,* July 13, 1861.

[27] Ford, *Rip Ford's Texas,* 329–330; Ford to Littleton, June 14, 1861, Ford to Santos Benavides, July 19, 1861 (Ford Papers, Haley Museum); Charles G. T. Lovenskiold to Clark, Sept. 9, 1861 [1st and 2nd quotes], Oct. 6, 1861 [3rd quote], Bee to Clark, Sept. 22, 1861, Lovenskiold to Lubbock, Nov. 6, Dec. 5, 1861, Jan. 15, 1862 (GR); Hughes, *Rebellious Ranger,* 20; Thompson, *Vaqueros in Blue and Gray,* 43–47; *NHOT,* 4: 307.

[28] *OR,* I, 4: 107–108, 118–119. Ford's and Henry E. McCulloch's regiments mustered into Confederate service as the 2nd and 1st Texas Cavalry, respectively.

[29] *OR,* I, 4: 152–153, 164–166, 9: 706; Henry E. McCulloch to Francis R. Lubbock, Apr. 15, 1862 (GR); Ford, *Rip Ford's Texas,* 329; Hughes, *Rebellious Ranger,* 202; Oates, "Prudent Cavalryman," 318–319; *NHOT,* 1: 458.

[30] Ford, *Rip Ford's Texas,* 329, 460, 464; Ford, Memoirs (Ford Papers, CAH), 860–864, 866–867, 873–874; Ford, "Typed Memoirs" (Ford Papers, CAH), 5: 1105–1106; Hughes, *Rebellious Ranger,* 202–203; Stephen R. Wise, *Lifeline of the Confederacy: Blockade Running During the Civil War* (Columbia: University of South Carolina Press, 1991), 88; Rodman L. Underwood, *Waters of Discord: The Union Blockade of Texas During the Civil War* (Jefferson, NC: MacFarland and Company, 2003), 68–69; Thompson and Jones, *Civil War & Revolution on the Rio Grande Frontier,* 40–42; Don Graham, *Kings of Texas: The 150-Year Saga of an American Ranching Empire* (New York: John Wiley & Sons, 2003), 100–101; Amberson et al., *I Would Rather Sleep in Texas,* 156, 189, 195–196; Lea, *King Ranch,* 1: 185–186 [quote]; Oates, "Prudent Cavalryman," 319; Harbert Davenport, "Notes on Early Steamboating on the Rio Grande," *SWHQ* 49 (Oct. 1945): 286–289; Robert W. Delaney, "Matamoros, Port for Texas during the Civil War," *SWHQ* 58 (Apr. 1955): 473–474, 479–480; Ronnie C. Tyler,

"Cotton on the Border, 1861–1865," *SWHQ* 73 (Apr. 1970): 457; L. Tuffly Ellis, "Maritime Commerce on the Far Western Gulf, 1861–1865," *SWHQ* 77 (Oct. 1973): 204, 205, 213; Marilyn M. Sibley, "Charles Stillman: A Case Study of Entrepreneurship on the Rio Grande, 1861–1865," *SWHQ* 77 (Oct. 1973): 234; *NHOT,* 3: 1,064–1,065, 1,107–1,108, 6: 102. Charles Stillman of course was ridiculing the proud Aztec-inspired eagle that appears on the national flag of Mexico.

[31] Ford, *Rip Ford's Texas,* 329; *Official Records of the Union and Confederate Navies in the War of the Rebellion,* 30 vols. (Washington: Government Printing Office, 1894–1922), Ser. I, Vol. 18: 458 [quotes]; Hughes, *Rebellious Ranger,* 204.

[32] Santiago Vidaurri to Clark, July 1, 1861, José A. Quintero to Clark, June 3 [2nd quote], July 11, 1861, Ford to Clark, July 14, 1861 [1st quote] (GR); Corpus Christi *Ranchero,* June 22, 1861; James D. Richardson, ed., *A Compilation of the Messages and Papers of the Confederacy,* 2 vols. (Nashville: United States Publishing Company, 1905), 2: 77–81; Hughes, *Rebellious Ranger,* 202; Thompson, *Cortina,* 101; Amberson et al., *I Would Rather Sleep in Texas,* 189–190; Thompson and Jones, *Civil War & Revolution on the Rio Grande Frontier,* 45–46; Ronnie C. Tyler, *Santiago Vidaurri and the Southern Confederacy* (Austin: Texas State Historical Association, 1973), 50–52, 59, 70; Tyler, "Cotton on the Border," 459–460; J. Fred Rippy, "Mexican Projects of the Confederates," *SWHQ* 22 (Apr. 1919): 292–293, 298–299; *NHOT,* 5: 393–394.

[33] Redmond to Ford, Nov. 1, 1861 (Ford Papers, Haley Museum); Ford, Memoirs (Ford Papers, CAH), Miscellaneous, 125–126; Ford, "Typed Memoirs" (Ford Papers, CAH), 5: 928; Thompson and Jones, *Civil War & Revolution on the Rio Grande Frontier,* 40; Hughes, *Rebellious Ranger,* 202; Amberson et al., *I Would Rather Sleep in Texas,* 192–193; Tyler, "Cotton on the Border, 464; Darryl E. Brock, "José Agustín Quintero: Cuban Patriot in Confederate Diplomatic Service," in *Cubans in the Confederacy,* ed. Phillip T. Tucker (Jefferson, NC: MacFarland and Company, 2002), 10, 22–23, 28, 30–31, 35–36, 42–43, 47–53; Chance, *Carvajal,* 173–175.

[34] Jesús de la Serna to Philip N. Luckett, Feb. 27, 1862, Vidaurri to "Commanding Officer, Fort Brown, Texas," Mar. 3, 1862, José M. J. Carvajal to Ford, Mar. 15, 1862 [1st and 2nd quotes], Robert Williams to Ford, Mar. 19, 1862, L. S. Lawhon to Ford, Mar. 28, 1862, Littleton to Ford, Mar. 29, 1862 (Ford Papers, Haley Museum); Julian Quiroga to "Sr. Commandante del Fuerte Brown," Mar. 11, 1862, Quiroga to Ford, Mar. 23, 1862 [3rd quote] (Ford Papers, Haley Museum, and Ford Papers, TSLA); Quintero to Lubbock, Mar. 24, 1862 (GR); Tyler, *Vidaurri,* 61–64, 66; Chance, *Carvajal,* 174–175; Rippy, "Mexican Projects," 302. The Brownsville [TX] *Fort Brown Flag,* Apr. 17, 1862, reported that Ford delivered arms taken from Carvajal to officers commanding at Matamoros on April 12, but other sources say Ford never did so, and that seems to be corroborated by the firepower of Carvajal's troops in this period.

[35] Quintero to Lubbock, Mar. 28, Apr. 13, 1862, Vidaurri to Lubbock, Apr. 6, 1862, McCulloch to Lubbock, Apr. 16, 19, 1862 (GR); Tyler, *Vidaurri,* 67–75; Chance,

Carvajal, 176–177; Hughes, *Rebellious Ranger,* 203–204; Tyler, "Cotton on the Border," 465; Frank L. Owsley, *King Cotton Diplomacy: Foreign Relations of the Confederate States of America,* 2nd ed. (Chicago: University of Chicago Press, 1959), 121–123; *NHOT,* 1: 971.

[36] Quintero to Lubbock, Mar. 24, 28, 1862, McCulloch to Lubbock, Mar. 15, 1862, Bee to Lubbock, Mar. 24, 1862 (GR); CSR, 2nd Texas Cavalry; *OR,* I, 9: 708–709; Brock, "Quintero," 56–57; Tyler, "Cotton on the Border," 465; Owsley, *King Cotton Diplomacy,* 122–123; Hughes, *Rebellious Ranger,* 203–204.

[37] Judah P. Benjamin to Quintero, Apr. 30, 1862 [quotes] (Confederate States of America Records, Manuscript Division, Library of Congress, Washington, DC); San Antonio *Semi-Weekly News,* May 22, 1861; James A. Irby, *Backdoor at Bagdad: The Civil War on the Rio Grande* (El Paso: Texas Western Press, 1977), 21; Evans, *Confederate Military History* (extended edition), 15: 69; Hughes, *Rebellious Ranger,* 205. The removal of Ford mollified Vidaurri, and trade again increased across the Rio Grande. See Amberson et al., *I Would Rather Sleep in Texas,* 195.

[38] Hughes, *Rebellious Ranger,* 205; Gammel, *Laws of Texas,* 5: 578.

Chapter Five: Phoenix

[1] Ford, *Rip Ford's Texas,* 332–333; Brown, Annals of Travis County (Brown Papers, CAH), 21: 6–7; Research notes (Price Papers, CAH); *OR,* I, 9: 715–716; Houston *Telegraph,* June 27, Oct. 1, 1862; United States Department of the Interior, Bureau of the Census, Eighth Census, 1860, Schedule 1: Free Population [Travis County, Texas] (Record Group 29, National Archives, Washington, DC); Hughes, *Rebellious Ranger,* 206; Oates, "Prudent Cavalryman," 320; Evans, *Confederate Military History* (Extended ed.), 15: 69; *NHOT,* 1: 937, 6: 815–816; Albert B. Moore, *Conscription and Conflict in the Confederacy* (New York: MacMillan Company, 1924), 13–14, 34, 140, 185–186. It is ironic that while Ford tried to enforce the draft fairly, Camp Ford at Tyler became a hated prison that held both civilian Unionists and Federal soldiers. Concerning William Ford, he lived in Webberville, a town east of Austin in Travis County, with Jesse F. Burdett in 1860.

[2] John S. Ford, Conscript Duty, (Manuscript, n.d. [1892], n.p., Ford Papers, Haley Museum); John Sayles to Lubbock, June 26, 1862 (Texas Adjutant General, Civil War Records Concerning Conscription, TSLA); Houston *Telegraph,* July 4, 1862; James A. Marten, *Texas Divided: Loyalty and Dissent in the Lone Star State, 1856–1864* (Lexington: University Press of Kentucky, 1993), 95–105; Oates, "Prudent Cavalryman," 320; *NHOT,* 3: 539, 5: 907. Printed copies of Ford's 1862 orders concerning the draft in Texas can be found in *Confederate Imprints,* 144 reels (New Haven, CT: Primary Source Microfilm, 1974), on reel 12, items numbered 737–1, 737–2, 737–3, 737–4, 737–6.

[3] Ford, Memoirs, (Ford Papers, CAH), Miscellaneous: Untitled [Wartime Reminiscences], 2–4; Mifflin Kenedy, Francisco Yturria, Simon Celaya, and H. E. Woodhouse to Phillip N. Luckett, July 10, 1862 (Texas Adjutant General, Civil War Records Concerning Conscription, TSLA); Ford, *Rip Ford's Texas,* 332–333 [quote]; Moore, *Conscription and Conflict,* 16, 53, 67–68; Hughes, *Rebellious Ranger,* 206–207; Marten, *Texas Divided,* 71, 100; Oates, "Prudent Cavalryman," 320; *NHOT,* 3: 438–439, 492.

[4] Ford, *Rip Ford's Texas,* 337; Ford, Memoirs (Ford Papers, CAH), Miscellaneous: Untitled [Wartime Reminiscences], 6 [1st quote], 7 [2nd and 3rd quotes], 51 [4th quote]; Ford, "Typed Memoirs" (Ford Papers, CAH), 7: 1,205; *OR,* I, 9: 735–736; Ford to C. M. Mason, Sept. 12, 1862, in CSR, 11th Texas Cavalry: William C. Young; Marten, *Texas Divided,* 103–105; Alwyn Barr, ed., "Records of the Confederate Military Commission in San Antonio, July 2-October 10, 1862," *SWHQ* 73 (October 1969): 247; *NHOT,* 3: 309–310, 4: 1,054. For more on the Great Hanging, see Richard B. McCaslin, *Tainted Breeze: The Great Hanging at Gainesville, Texas, October 1862* (Baton Rouge: Louisiana State University Press, 1994).

[5] Ford, *Rip Ford's Texas,* 330; Ford, Memoirs (Ford Papers, CAH), Miscellaneous: Ford as a Confederate, 5 [1st quote]; Ford, "Typed Memoirs" (Ford Papers, CAH), 5: 1,007 [2nd quote]; George F. Moore to John H. Reagan, Nov. 6, 1862, in CSR, 2nd Texas Cavalry: John S. Ford; Hughes, *Rebellious Ranger,* 201, 205–207; Evans, *Confederate Military History* (Extended ed.), 15: 587; *NHOT,* 1. The Compiled Service Records for the 2nd Texas Cavalry note that Ford's commission as a colonel dates from May 23, 1861, but the mustering of his companies occurs from May 1861 to September 1862.

[6] Texas Congressional Delegation to Jefferson Davis, Sept. 20, 1862, Moore to Reagan, Nov. 6, 1862; Reagan to James Seddon, Dec. 1, 1862; Petition from Sixteen East Texas Leaders, n.d. [Feb. 1863], Petition from Texas Legislators to Texas Delegation in Congress, Feb. 2, 1863, CSR, 2nd Texas Cavalry: John S. Ford; Hughes, *Rebellious Ranger,* 207–208.

[7] Ford, *Rip Ford's Texas,* 332; CSR, 2nd Texas Cavalry: John S. Ford; Ford, Memoirs (Ford Papers, CAH), Miscellaneous, 51; Ford, Conscript Duty (Ford Papers, Haley Museum); Ford, "Typed Memoirs" (Ford Papers, CAH), 5: 1,008; CSR, General and Staff Officers: James P. Flewellen; *OR,* I, 26, pt. 2: 21–22 [quote], 42, 47, 65; Houston *Telegraph,* July 15, Dec. 30, 1863, Jan. 4, 6, 8, 13, 1864; Thomas M. Settles, *John Bankhead Magruder: A Military Reappraisal* (Baton Rouge: Louisiana State University Press, 2009); 244–251, 258–259; Campbell, *Gone to Texas,* 253–254; Hughes, *Rebellious Ranger,* 208–209; *NHOT,* 4: 464–465, 5: 1,093–1,094; Stephen B. Oates, "Texas Under the Secessionists," *SWHQ* 67 (Oct. 1963): 195; Cotham, *Battle on the Bay,* passim.

[8] Lubbock to Jefferson Davis, Nov. 13, 1862, Elkanah B. Greer to Lubbock, Sept. 17, 1863, Ford to Lubbock, Sept. 18, 1863 (GR); Dorman H. Winfrey and James M.

Day, eds., *The Indian Papers of Texas and the Southwest, 1825–1916,* 5 vols. (New York, 1966; reprint, Austin: Texas State Historical Association, 1995), 4: 77–78; Rena M. Green, ed., *Samuel Maverick, Texan: 1803–1870* (San Antonio: Privately Printed, 1952), 372; Houston *Telegraph,* Apr. 22, 1863; Moore, *Conscription and Conflict,* 202, 224, 247; Robert L. Kerby, *Kirby Smith's Confederacy: The Trans-Mississippi South, 1863–1865* (New York: Columbia University Press, 1972), 258; Settles, *Magruder,* 270–272; Oates, "Texas Under the Secessionists," 196–200; *NHOT,* 3: 325, 4: 895–896. Ford wrote an interesting letter in early 1863 to H. C. Cook, in which he declared that he was not a candidate for governor. He added that any officer, civilian or military, should abide by the constitution and the laws. At the same time, Texans should support the Confederate national government, which "has given us no just cause of complaint." Finally, frontier defense was paramount, and an "aggressive policy" would be the only effective one against Indians. Ford concluded that "Cost what it may the pioneer settlers must be protected. It is the imperative duty of the State to do so. It matters not what motive carried them to the frontier. They had a right to go, and they are entitled to the fostering care of the Government." See Austin *Texas Almanac Extra,* Mar. 17, 1863. For a personal account of a Texan being assigned to the frontier by Ford rather than serving with a Confederate unit, see William J. Maltby, *Captain Jeff: Frontier Life in Texas with the Texas Rangers* (Colorado, TX: Whipkey Printing Company, 1906), 19–20.

[9] John S. Ford, Memorandum [1st quote] (Manuscript, Nov. 9, 1863. n.p., Ford Papers, Haley Museum); Ford, *Rip Ford's Texas,* 337–338 [2nd quote]; Ford, Memoirs (Ford Papers, CAH), Miscellaneous: Untitled [Wartime Reminiscences], 9–10; Ford, "Typed Memoirs" (Ford Papers, CAH), 7: 1,208–1,209; *OR,* I, 9: 733–734, 22: 963–964, 26, pt. 2: 119–120; Hughes, *Rebellious Ranger,* 210; Marten, *Texas Divided,* 95; Oates, "Texas Under the Secessionists," 201; *NHOT,* 3: 390.

[10] Ford, *Rip Ford's Texas,* 335–337, 343; Ford, "Typed Memoirs" (Ford Papers, CAH), 7: 1,203–1,205 [1st quote]; *OR,* I, 26, pt. 2: 377–378, 393; Ford to William T. Townsend, Jan. 18, 1864, Ford to William Herbert, Jan. 18, 1864, William C. Walsh to Ford, Jan. 15, 1864 (Ford Papers, Haley Museum); Hughes, *Rebellious Ranger,* 209–210.

[11] Stephen A. Townsend, *The Yankee Invasion of Texas* (College Station: Texas A&M University Press, 2006), 3, 8–11, 14, 15, 17, 19–21, 26–32; Campbell, *Gone to Texas,* 254–257; Hughes, *Rebellious Ranger,* 211; Amberson et al., *I Would Rather Sleep in Texas,* 226; *NHOT,* 1: 369, 5: 745; Cotham, *Sabine Pass,* passim; Richard G. Lowe, *The Texas Overland Campaign* (Abilene, TX: McWhiney Foundation, 1996), passim.

[12] James A. Ware to Edmond P. Turner, Dec. 13, 1863 [quote], Turner to Ford, Dec. 19, 1863 (Ford Papers, Haley Museum); Pryor Lea et al. to Pendleton Murrah, Dec. 15, 1863, John B. Magruder to Murrah, Dec. 30, 1863 (GR); Ford, "Typed Memoirs" (Ford Papers, CAH), 6: 1,034; *OR,* I, 26, pt. 2: 524–526, 534–535 [quote], 540, 543–544, 34, pt. 2: 835, 979; Austin *Texas State Gazette,* Dec. 23, 1863; Evans, *Con-*

federate Military History (Extended ed.), 15: 122; Ford, *Rip Ford's Texas,* 343; Hughes, *Rebellious Ranger,* 212–213; Graham, *Kings of Texas,* 109–110.

[13] Ford, *Rip Ford's Texas,* 344; Ford, statement on Dec. 27, 1863 [1st and 2nd quotes], Ford to Ware, Jan. 11, 1864 [3rd and 4th quotes] (Ford Papers, Haley Museum); Townsend, *Yankee Invasion,* 94.

[14] Ford to Santos Benavides, Dec. 28, 1863, Ford to Turner, Dec. 29, 1863, Jan. 6, 1864, Ford to Andrew G. Dickinson, Jan. 17, 1864, and n.d. [Jan. 1864] (Ford Papers, Haley Museum); Ford to Turner, Dec. 27, 1863, Ford to James Duff, Dec. 28, 1863, in John S. Ford Letterbook, Dec. 4, 1863 to Feb. 17, 1864 (Manuscript, n.p., Ford Papers, Haley Museum); *OR,* I, 26, pt. 2: 543–544, 560–561 [quote], 53: 922.

[15] *OR,* I, 26, pt. 2: 516, 517 [1st quote], 524, 530 [2nd quote], 34, pt. 2: 835, 882, 1,011, 1,053–1,054 [quote], pt. 4: 695; Murrah to Ford, Dec. 28, 1863, Ford to Turner, Mar. 4, 1864 Ford Papers, Haley Museum); Magruder to Murrah, Dec. 30, 1863 (GR); Ford to Murrah, Dec. 30, 1863, in Ford Letterbook, Dec. 4, 1863 to Feb. 17, 1864 (Ford Papers, Haley Museum); General Orders No. ___, Apr. 27, 1864, in CSR, 2nd Texas Cavalry: John S. Ford [last quote]; Special Orders No. 178, Headquarters, District of Texas, June 26, 1864 (Ford Papers, Haley Museum, and Ford Papers, TSLA). Francis B. Heitman includes Ford on his list of Confederate generals in his *Historical Register and Dictionary of the United States Army,* 2 vols. (Washington: Government Printing Office, 1903), 2: 177. Bruce S. Allardice does the same in *More Generals in Gray* (Baton Rouge: Louisiana State University Press, 1995), 89–90. Ralph A. Wooster, in *Lone Star Generals in Gray* (Austin, TX: Eakin Press, 2000), correctly lists Ford in an appendix as a state brigadier general (p. 243).

[16] W. R. Boggs to Santos Benavides, Nov. 3, 1863, Special Order No. 108, Nov. 26, 1863, Turner to Ford, Dec. 22, 1863, Ford to Santos Benavides, Dec. 27, 28, 1863, Ford to Turner, Jan. 6, Feb. 5, 1864, Duff to Ford, Jan. 8, 1864, Santos Benavides to Ford, Jan. 10, 1864, Spruce M. Baird to Ford, Feb. 11, 1864 [quotes], Ford to Daniel Showalter, Feb. 18, 1864 (Ford Papers, Haley Museum); Ford to Santos Benavides, Jan. 9, 23, 1864, Ford to Turner, Jan. 12, 1864, Ford to Duff, Jan. 15, 1864, Ford to Baird, Feb. 5, 1864 in Ford Letterbook, Dec. 4, 1863 to Feb. 17, 1864 (Ford Papers, Haley Museum); *OR,* I, 34, pt. 2: 946–947; Hughes, *Rebellious Ranger,* 215; *NHOT,* 1: 341.

[17] Ford, *Rip Ford's Texas,* 346, 348, 350; Felix A. Blucher to Ford, Feb. 10, 1864, Ford to Turner, Feb. 5, 1864, Ford to Alexander P. Root, Sept. 30, 1864 (Ford Papers, Haley Museum); Ford to Turner, Jan. 27, 1864, in Ford Letterbook, Dec. 4, 1863 to Feb. 17, 1864 (Ford Papers, Haley Museum); *OR,* I, 34, pt. 2: 947; Hughes, *Rebellious Ranger,* 214 [2nd quote], 243; *NHOT,* 1: 601–602.

[18] *OR,* 1, 26, pt. 1: 529–531, pt. 2: 528–530, 534–535, 34, pt. 2: 906, 1,074, pt. 3: 749, 53: 922–923; Thomas H. O'Callaghan to Ford, Dec. 25, 1863, Ford to Turner, Jan. 6, 1864 (Ford Papers, Haley Museum); Dates of Muster of the Companies of Ex. Forces [a list of ten companies, with captains and dates of muster from May 14,

1862 (Thomas E. Cater) to March 14, 1864 (J. H. Fry)] in John S. Ford Special Order Book, Dec. 27, 1863 to Feb. 4, 1865 (Manuscript, n.p., Ford Papers, Haley Museum); Ford to Murrah, Jan. 6, 1864 (GR); Townsend, *Yankee Invasion,* 95; *NHOT,* 3: 153–154.

19 *OR,* I, 26, pt. 2: 543–544 [1st and 2nd quotes]; Ford to Dickinson, n.d. [Jan. 1864] [3rd quote], Ford to John B. Davis, Jan. 4, 1864, Special Order No. 35, Headquarters, Dist. of TX, NM, and AZ, Feb. 4, 1864, General Order No. 55, Headquarters, Dist. of TX, NM, and AZ, Mar. 3, 1864, Turner to Ford, Mar. 8, 1864 (Ford Papers, Haley Museum); Ford, *Rip Ford's Texas,* 347.

20 Ford to J. H. Fry, Jan. 15, 1864, Ford to L. M. Rogers or James A. Ware, Feb. 10, 1864, Ford to Turner, Feb. 10, 1864, in Ford Letterbook, Dec. 4, 1863 to Feb. 17, 1864 (Ford Papers, Haley Museum); Duff to Ford, Feb. 2, 1864, Ford to W. W. Martin, Feb. 15, 1864, Ford to _____ Adams, Thomas E. Cater, William Armstrong, _____ Barker, and Santos Benavides, Feb. 6, 1864, Ford to E. M. Fly, Feb. 17, 1864, Ford to A. C. Jones, Feb. 22, 1864, Cater to Ford, Feb. 24, 1864, _____ Malone to _____ Moncure, Apr. 30, 1864, John F. Tom to "Captain," July 5, 1864 [with endorsements of Duff, July 18, 1864, and McCulloch, n.d.] (Ford Papers, Haley Museum); Ford to James G. Slaughter, July 7, 1864, in John S. Ford Letterbook, June 9, 1864, to Sept. 10, 1864 (Manuscript, n.p., Ford Papers, Haley Museum); Ford, Memoirs (Ford Papers, CAH), 569, Miscellaneous, 71; Ford, *Rip Ford's Texas,* 186, 347 [quote]; Houston *Telegraph,* Feb. 15, 1864.

21 George H. Giddings to Ford, Feb. 4, 12, 1865 (Ford Papers, Haley Museum); Endorsement by Ford, Dec. 30, 1864, in Ford Special Order Book, Dec. 27, 1863 to Feb. 4, 1865 (Ford Papers, Haley Museum); *NHOT,* 5: [James W. Robinson].

22 Ford to Turner, Dec. 29, 1863, Jan. 15, Mar. 25, 1864, Ford to Dickinson, n.d. [Jan. 1864], Ford to Hugh Timon, June 6, 1864 (Ford Papers, Haley Museum); Ford to Turner, May 5, 1864, in Retained Copies of Communications From March 11, 1864, to June 6, 1864 (Manuscript, n.p., Ford Papers, Haley Museum); *OR,* I, 26, pt. 2: 560–561, 34, pt. 2: 1,083–1,084; Hughes, *Rebellious Ranger,* 217; Thompson and Jones, *Civil War & Revolution on the Rio Grande Frontier,* 62–65; Thompson, *Cortina,* 106, 110, 114–120, 122–128, 133–136.

23 *OR,* I, 26, pt. 2: 543–544, 41, pt. 2: 989; Ford to Turner, Dec. 29, 1863, Ford to Dickinson, n.d. [Jan. 1864], Walter W. Blow to Ford, Feb. 8, 10, 1864, Special Orders No. 20, Feb. 8, 1864 [1st quote], Special Orders No. 58, Headquarters, Dist. of TX, NM, and AZ, Feb. 27, 1864, Ford to Turner, Feb. 28, Mar. 6, 22, 1864 [2nd quote], H. H. Christmas to H. Wilkie, May 18, 1864 (Ford Papers, Haley Museum), Ford to Slaughter, July 2, 1864, in John S. Ford, Letterbook, Apr. 25 to Aug. 25, 1864 (Manuscript, n.p., Ford Papers, Haley Museum); Ford to Theodore Herman, Feb. 1, 1864 (Ford Papers, TSLA); Houston *Telegraph,* Apr. 4, 1864; Tyler, *Vidaurri,* 122–127.

[24] Ford to Dickinson, n.d. [Jan. 1864] [quote], Santos Benavides to Ford, Jan. 10, 1864, Ford to Santos Benavides, Jan. 22, Feb. 4, 1864, F. M. Campbell to Ford, Feb. 10, 1864, John M. Swisher to Ford, Feb. 23, 1864 (Ford Papers, Haley Museum); Francis J. Herron to Edward O. C. Ord, Feb. 11, 1864 (Military Operations in Texas Collection, 1862–1864, CAH); *OR,* I, 34, pt. 2: 295–296, 961, 968–969, 1,042–1,043; Austin *Southern Intelligencer,* Jan. 25, 1860; Thompson and Jones, *Civil War & Revolution on the Rio Grande Frontier,* 66; Brock, "Quintero," 70–72; Tyler, "Cotton on the Border," 463, 470–472; Hughes, *Rebellious Ranger,* 218–219. Swisher was a San Jacinto veteran who also served as the clerk for the 9th Congress of the Republic of Texas, in which Ford served. See *NHOT,* 6: 180–181.

[25] Nolan to Ford, Mar. 6, 1864, Lovenskiold to Ford, Mar. 9, 1864, Ford to Edward P. Alsbury, Apr. 8, 1864 [4th quote], Ford to Lovenskiold, Apr. 11, 1864 [2nd and 3rd quotes], Ford to Dix, Apr. 12, 1864, Ford to Charles H. Merritt, Apr. 8 [5th quote], 28, 1864 [6th quote] (Ford Papers, Haley Museum); Lovenskiold to Ford, Mar. 20, 1864 [1st quote] (Ford Papers, Haley Museum, and Ford Papers, TSLA); Ford to Herman, Feb. 1, 1864 (Ford Papers, TSLA); Ford to B. F. Fly, May 21, 1864, in Ford Letterbook, Mar. 11 to June 6, 1864 (Manuscript, n.p., Ford Papers, Haley Museum).

[26] Ford to Turner, Dec. 29, 1863, in Ford Letterbook, Dec. 4, 1863 to Feb. 17, 1864 (Ford Papers, Haley Museum); Lieuen M. Rogers to Ford, Feb. 3, 1864 [1st quote], Ford to Turner, Jan. 21, Feb. 7, 1864 [2nd quote] (Ford Papers, Haley Museum); Ford, *Rip Ford's Texas,* 347–348, 350; *OR,* I, 26, pt. 2: 560, 53: 952, 34, pt. 2: 402, 948–950; Ford, "Typed Memoirs" (Ford Papers, CAH), 6: 1,037–1,038, 1,041; Evans, *Confederate Military History* (Extended ed.) 15: 125; Hughes, *Rebellious Ranger,* 215–216; Graham, *Kings of Texas,* 112; Oates, "Prudent Cavalryman," 324.

[27] Ford to Dickinson, n.d. [Jan. 1864], Charles Human to Albert Walthersdorff, Jan. 17, 24, 1864, E. Kapp to Ford, Feb. 20, 1864 [2nd quote], James A. Lucas to Ford, Jan. 20, 1864, Palatino Robinson to Ford, Jan. 20, 1864, Ford to Turner, Jan. 21, 24, 28, Feb. 8, 12 [1st, and 3rd quotes], 15, 21, 22 [4th quote], 26, 27, 1864, Ford to Thomas Riordan, Jan. 24, Feb. 15, 1864, Ford to W. J. Alexander, Jan. 24, 1864, Walthersdorff to Ford, Jan. 28, Feb. 17, 24, 1864, Ford to Walthersdorff, Feb. 28, 1864, Riordan to Ford, Feb. 5, 1864 (Ford Papers, Haley Museum); Ford to Herman, Feb. 1, 1864 (Ford Papers, TSLA); *OR,* I, 34, pt. 2: 961–962; Ford, *Rip Ford's Texas,* 351.

[28] Ford to Turner, Feb. 26, Mar. 9, 1864, Ford to Santos Benavides, Feb. 27, 1864, Nolan to Ford, Mar. 6, 21, 1864 (Ford Papers, Haley Museum); Ford to Turner, Mar. 25, 1864 [quote], Ford to Nolan, Apr. 11, 1864 in Ford Letterbook, Mar. 11 to June 6, 1864 (Ford Papers, Haley Museum); San Antonio *Herald,* Mar. 19, 1864; *OR,* I, 34, pt. 1: 638–639, pt. 3: 129, 177–178; Ford, *Rip Ford's Texas,* 354–355; Evans, *Confederate Military History* (Extended ed.), 15: 123; Oates, "Prudent Cavalryman," 324–325; Townsend, *Yankee Invasion,* 70–79; *NHOT,* 1: 356.

[29] Napoleon J. T. Dana to Charles P. Stone, Jan. 7, 15, 1864, Herron to Ord, Feb. 11, 1864 (Military Operations in Texas Collection, CAH), *OR,* I, 34, pt. 2: 84–86, 232, 295–296, pt. 3: 176 [quote]; Santos Benavides to Ford, Jan. 10, 1864 (Ford Papers, Haley Museum, and Ford Papers, TSLA); Ford to Turner, Feb. 17, 1864, in Ford Letterbook, Dec. 4, 1863, to Feb. 17, 1864 (Ford Papers, Haley Museum).

[30] *OR,* I, 34, pt. 2: 979, 992, 1,004–1,005, 1,033, 1,068–1,069; Ford to Turner, Feb. 7, [2nd quote], Mar. 22, 1864, Ford to Showalter, Mar. 14, 1864 [1st quote] (Ford Papers, Haley Museum); Samuel A. Maverick to Murrah, Mar. 17, 1864 (GR); Hughes, *Rebellious Ranger,* 215–216; Campbell, *Gone to Texas,* 257; Townsend, *Yankee Invasion,* 69, 70; Kerby, *Kirby Smith's Confederacy,* 194.

[31] *OR,* I, 34, pt. 1: 647–649, pt. 2: 278, 402, 962, 968, 1,004–1,005, 1,081, 1,084, 1,106, pt. 3: 754, 775 [quote], 776; Ford to Santos Benavides, Mar. 31, 1864, Ford to Turner, March 22, 31, Apr. 17, 1864 (Ford Papers, Haley Museum); Ford to Dickinson, Mar. 29, 1864, in Ford Letterbook, Mar. 11 to June 6, 1864 (Ford Papers, Haley Museum); Ford, "Typed Memoirs" (Ford Papers, CAH), 6: 1,060–1,062; Ford, *Rip Ford's Texas,* 355–360; Evans, *Confederate Military History* (Extended ed.), 15: 123–124; Oates, "Prudent Cavalryman," 324; Wilkinson, *Laredo,* 295–296; Thompson, *Vaqueros in Blue and Gray,* 107–110, Hughes, *Rebellious Ranger,* 216; Townsend, *Yankee Invasion,* 98, 99.

[32] *OR,* I, 34, pt. 3: 775–776 [quotes]; Ford to Turner, Apr. 17, 1864 (Ford Papers, Haley Museum); Ford, *Rip Ford's Texas,* 359–360; Thompson, *Vaqueros in Blue and Gray,* 111; Thompson, *Cortina,* 132–133; Hughes, *Rebellious Ranger,* 217; Tyler, *Vidaurri,* 141–142.

[33] *OR,* I, 34, pt. 1: 1,053–1,054, pt. 3: 783–784, 797 [1st quote], 798–799, 807–808, 53: 1,001; Ford to Santos Benavides, May 2, 1864, Ford to Turner, May 2, 1864, J. Maria Garcia Villarreal to Ford, May 5, 1864, Ford to Villarreal, May 6, 1864 [4th and 5th quotes], Ford to Slaughter, May 25, 1864 [6th quote], in Ford Letterbook, Mar. 11 to June 6, 1864 (Ford Papers, Haley Museum); General Order No. 10, Apr. 24, 1864 [2nd and 3rd quotes] in Ford Special Order Book, Dec. 27, 1863 to Feb. 4, 1865 (Ford Papers, Haley Museum); Ford, *Rip Ford's Texas,* 360; Oates, "Prudent Cavalryman," 326.

[34] Ford, Memoirs (Ford Papers, CAH), Miscellaneous: Ford as a Confederate, 11 [1st quote]; Ford, Memoirs (Ford Papers, CAH), 5: 1,016; Ford to Turner, Apr. 17, May 2, 1864, Ford to Giddings, May 6, 1864, D. L. Angier et al. to Ford, May 29, 1864 (Ford Papers, Haley Museum); Ford to Santos Benavides, May 29, 1864 [2nd and 3rd quotes], in Ford Letterbook, Apr. 25 to Aug. 25, 1864 (Ford Papers, Haley Museum); Ford to Turner, May 5, 1864, in Retained Copies of Communications From March 11, 1864, to June 6, 1864 (Ford Papers, Haley Museum); Ford to Slaughter, May 25, 1864, in Ford Letterbook, Mar. 11 to June 6, 1864 (Ford Papers, Haley Museum); *OR,* I, 34, pt. 4: 684–685; Brock, "Quintero," 75–76; Ford, *Rip Ford's Texas,* 364; *Reports of the*

Committee of Investigation Sent in 1873 by the Mexican Government to the Frontier of Texas (New York: Baker & Godwin, 1875), 151; Wilkinson, *Laredo,* 283; Thompson, *Cortina,* 132, 135, 136; Hughes, *Rebellious Ranger,* 218–219.

[35] Ford, *Rip Ford's Texas,* 332, 351; Ford, Memoirs (Ford Papers, CAH), 898, Miscellaneous, 161, Miscellaneous: Untitled [Wartime Reminiscences], 2–3; *OR,* I, 53: 975; Ford, "Typed Memoirs" (Ford Papers, CAH), 5: 906–907; Ford to Merritt, Mar. 22, 29, 1864, F. M. Campbell to Ford, Feb. 10, Mar. 28, 1864 (Ford Papers, Haley Museum); Hughes, *Rebellious Ranger,* 184, 207, 217, 218; Brown, *Indian Wars and Pioneers of Texas,* 592; *NHOT,* 4: 843.

[36] Swisher to Ford, May 25, [1st and 2nd quotes], July 14, 1864, Charles B. Combe to Ford, June 25 [1864] [3rd, 4th, and 5th quotes], Robert West to Ford, July 14, 1864 (Ford Papers, Haley Museum); Brownsville *Herald,* Aug. 12, 1953; Ford, *Rip Ford's Texas,* 361; United States Eighth Census, 1860 [Cameron County, TX]; Thompson, *Cortina,* 69.

[37] Ford to Giddings, May 2, 1864 [1st and 2nd quotes], Ford to Slaughter, May 27, 1864, Ford to Santos Benavides, June 4, 1864 in Ford Letterbook, Mar. 11 to June 6, 1864 (Ford Papers, Haley Museum); Ford to Murrah, May 8, 1864 (GR); General Order No. 11, May 10, 1864 [3rd quote], in Ford Special Order Book, Dec. 27, 1863 to Feb. 4, 1865 (Ford Papers, Haley Museum); Ford, *Rip Ford's Texas,* 361, 362.

[38] General Order No. 11, May 10, 1864 [1st-3rd quotes], in Ford Special Order Book, Dec. 27, 1863 to Feb. 4, 1865 (Ford Papers, Haley Museum); Ford to Littleton, June 9, 1864 [4th quote], in Ford Letterbook, June 9 to Sept. 10, 1864 (Ford Papers, Haley Museum); Ford to Slaughter, June 15, 1864 (Ford Papers, Haley Museum).

[39] Ford to Slaughter, June 15, 1864 (Ford Papers, Haley Museum, and in CSR, 2nd Texas Cavalry: John S. Ford); General Orders No. 18, June 16, 1864 [1st quote], in Ford Special Order Book, Dec. 27, 1863 to Feb. 4, 1865 (Ford Papers, Haley Museum); Showalter to Ford, June 15, 1864, Ford to Showalter, June 16, 1864 (Ford Papers, Haley Museum); Ford to Slaughter, July 2, 1864, in Ford Letterbook, June 9 to Sept. 10, 1864 (Ford Papers, Haley Museum); Ford, *Rip Ford's Texas,* 362–363; *OR,* I, 34, pt. 1: 1,053–1,054, pt. 4: 676, 684–685; Hughes, *Rebellious Ranger,* 218–219; Townsend, *Yankee Invasion,* 81, 100, 101; *NHOT,* 6: 867.

[40] Ford to Slaughter, July 2, 1864, Ford to J. J. Richardson, July 2, 1864, in Ford Letterbook, June 9 to Sept. 10, 1864 (Ford Papers, Haley Museum); Ford, "Typed Memoirs" (Ford Papers, CAH), 5: 1,013–1,015 and 6: 1,082–1,084; Receipt for Prisoners of War, July 6, 1864 (Ford Papers, Haley Museum); Ford to John J. Fisher, May 18, 1864, in Ford Letterbook, Apr. 25 to Aug. 25, 1864 (Ford Papers, Haley Museum); Houston *Telegraph,* July 18, 1864; Ford, *Rip Ford's Texas,* 360, 362–363; Hughes, *Rebellious Ranger,* 220–221; Thompson, *Vaqueros in Blue and Gray,* 92–93, 114–115; Townsend, *Yankee Invasion,* 101, 102. John J. Fisher was serving as a lieutenant colonel

in Benito Juárez's army in May 1864, but he left that command and was given the same rank by Ford that month.

[41] Ford to Slaughter, July 2, 3, 7, 1864, in Ford Letterbook, June 9 to Sept. 10, 1864 (Ford Papers, Haley Museum); Herron to William Dwight, June 26, July 2, 1864 (Military Operations in Texas Collection, CAH); Swisher to Ford, July 7, 1864 (Ford Papers, Haley Museum); Houston *Telegraph,* July 18; 1864; *OR,* I, 34, pt. 1: 1,053–1,054, pt. 4: 559–560; Ford, *Rip Ford's Texas,* 362–363; Hughes, *Rebellious Ranger,* 221; Oates, "Prudent Cavalryman," 326–327. Concerning the number of Federals who returned to Brownsville after Las Rucias, a letter intercepted by Swisher declared that thirty men rejoined the garrison.

[42] Ware to Ford, June 24, 1864 (Ford Papers, Haley Museum); Ford, "Typed Memoirs" (Ford Papers, CAH), 6: 1,095–1,099; Ford, Memoirs (Ford Papers, CAH), Miscellaneous, 56–58; Herron to Dwight, July 2, 1864 (Military Operations in Texas Collection, CAH); *OR,* I, 34, pt. 1: 1,053–1,054; San Antonio *Express,* May 22, July 3, 1892; Tyler, *Vidaurri,* 122–127; Tyler, "Cotton on the Border," 470–472.

[43] *OR,* I, 41, pt. 2: 994–996, 1,001 [quote]; Ford to Turner, Mar. 6, 1864, W. A. Alston to Oliver Steele, Mar. 13, 1864, Ford to Steele, Mar. 29, 1864, Ford, endorsement of July 2, 1864, L. G. Aldrich to Ford, July 12, 1864, Robert J. Samuel to Ford, July 20, 1864 (Ford Papers, Haley Museum); Ford to Slaughter, July 9, 1864, in Ford Letterbook, June 9 to Sept. 10, 1864 (Ford Papers, Haley Museum); Settle, *Magruder,* 276; Ford, *Rip Ford's Texas,* 346–347, 349, 360–361; Ford, Memoirs (Ford Papers, CAH), Miscellaneous, 52.5; Hughes, *Rebellious Ranger,* 219.

[44] Swisher to Ford, July 14, 1864 [quotes] (Ford Papers, Haley Museum, and Ford Papers, TSLA); W. Kearny to Ford, July 21, 1864 (Ford Papers, TSLA); Ford to Tobin, July 15, 16, 1864, in Ford Letterbook, June 9 to Sept. 10, 1864 (Ford Papers, Haley Museum); Ford to Tobin, July 23, 1864 (Ford Papers, Haley Museum); Ford, Memoirs (Ford Papers, CAH), Miscellaneous, 59–62, Miscellaneous: Ford as a Confederate, 11; Ford, *Rip Ford's Texas,* 363–364; Hughes, *Rebellious Ranger,* 221–222; Townsend, *Yankee Invasion,* 103.

[45] Ford, "Typed Memoirs" (Ford Papers, CAH), 5: 1,016–1,017, and 6: 1,100–1,103; Ford, Memoirs (Ford Papers, CAH), Miscellaneous, 61, 62 [quote], 65; Ford to Tobin, July 27, 31, 1864, in Ford Letterbook, June 9 to Sept. 10, 1864 (Ford Papers, Haley Museum); Eber W. Cave to Ford, July 31, 1864 (Ford Papers, Haley Museum); General Orders No. 27, July 29, 1864, in Ford Special Order Book, Dec. 27, 1863 to Feb. 4, 1865 (Ford Papers, Haley Museum); *OR,* I, 41, pt. 1: 185–186, 211–212, pt. 2: 1,069–1,070, 1,088; Ford, *Rip Ford's Texas,* 364–365; Hughes, *Rebellious Ranger,* 222–224; Oates, "Prudent Cavalryman," 327; Townsend, *Yankee Invasion,* 104; *NHOT,* 1: 1,045.

[46] Houston *Telegraph,* Aug. 17, 19 [1st quote], 24 [2nd quote], Sept. 30, 1864 [3rd and 4th quotes]; *OR,* I, 41, pt. 2: 1,069–2,070 [5th quote].

Chapter Six: Legacy

[1] *OR,* I, 48, pt, 1: 1,279.

[2] Ford, Memoirs (Ford Papers, CAH), 65, 73, 105; John D. Caldwell to Ford, Sept. 17, 1864, Alexander P. Root to Ford, Sept. 25, 1864, Special Orders No. 160, October 28, 1864, L. G. Aldrich to Ford, Nov. 11, 1864 (Ford Papers, Haley Museum); Ford to William Kearny, Aug. 16, 26, 1864, James H. Fry to Henry De Wolf, Sept. 5, 1864, in Ford Letterbook, June 9 to Sept. 10, 1864 (Ford Papers, Haley Museum); Ford to Joseph E. Dwyer, Sept. 3, 1864, James H. Fry to De Wolf, Oct. 9, 1864, in John S. Ford, Letterbook, Aug. 24 to Dec. 18, 1864, (Manuscript, n.p., Ford Papers, Haley Museum); James H. Fry to William J. Stokes, Oct. 30, 1864, in John S. Ford, Letterbook, Sept. 11, 1864, to Feb. 22, 1865 (Manuscript, n.p., Ford Papers, Haley Museum); General Orders No. 28, Aug. 1, 1864, in Ford Special Order Book, Dec. 27, 1863 to Feb. 4, 1865 (Ford Papers, Haley Museum); *OR,* I, 41, pt. 1: 211–212, pt. 2: 1,069–1,070; United States Department of State, *Papers Relating to the Foreign Relations of the United States, 1865–1866,* 4 vols. (Washington: Government Printing Office, 1865–1866), 3: 369–370; Ford, *Rip Ford's Texas,* 368–369; Hughes, *Rebellious Ranger,* Thompson, *Cortina,* 137. Ford also held the crew of the *Florence B. Beavers* in Brownsville after Com. Leon Smith captured and burned the schooner on Sept. 28, 1864. See Ford to Root, Oct. 2, 1864, in Ford Letterbook, Aug. 24, 1864, to Dec. 18, 1864 (Ford Papers, Haley Museum); Ford, Memoirs (Ford Papers, CAH), Miscellaneous: 72, 92.

[3] Ford, Memoirs (Ford Papers, CAH), Miscellaneous, 75; Ford, "Typed Memoirs" (Ford Papers, CAH), 6: 1,121–1,123; (Ford Papers, Haley Museum); Ford to Francis W. Latham, Aug. 22, 1864, Ford to Kearny, Aug. 22, 23, 26, 1864, Ford to "The Officer in Command of the French Forces on the Rio Grande," Aug. 24, 1864; Ford to José M. Cortina, Aug. 10, 1864 [quote], in Ford Letterbook, June 9 to Sept. 10, 1864 (Ford Papers, Haley Museum); Ford to Slaughter, May 25, 1864 in Ford Letterbook, Apr. 25 to Aug. 25, 1864 (Ford Papers, Haley Museum); Special Orders No. 125, Headquarters Expeditionary Forces, Aug. 24, 1864, A. Veron to Ford, n.d. [Aug. 25, 1864] (Ford Papers, Haley Museum); John J. Fisher and Waldemar Hyllested to Ford, Aug. 27, 1864 (Ford Papers, Haley Museum, and Ford Papers, TSLA); Ford to Veron, Aug. 27, 1864, in Ford Letterbook, Aug. 24 to Dec. 18, 1864 (Ford Papers, Haley Museum); *OR,* I, 34, pt. 2: 1,068, 41, pt. 2: 1,088–1,089 [quotes], 1,090, pt. 3: 910–911; Austin *Texas State Gazette,* Sept. 21, 1864; Ford, *Rip Ford's Texas,* 369–370; Hughes, *Rebellious Ranger,* 225–226; Thompson, *Cortina,* 9, 137; Rippy, "Mexican Projects of the Confederates," 304–307; Oates, "Prudent Cavalryman," 328.

[4] Ford, Memoirs (Ford Papers, CAH), 898–899, Miscellaneous, 66, 78.5; Ford, "Typed Memoirs" (Ford Papers, CAH), 5: 907; James H. Fry to Showalter, Aug. 31, 1864, Ford to Juan N. Cortina, Aug. 31, 1864, Ford to Showalter, Sept. 1, 1864, in

John S. Ford, "Letter Book, August 24, 1864 to December 30, 1864" (Typescript, n.d., Ford Papers, TSLA), 20, 21, 23; Ford to Juan N. Cortina, Aug. 29, 1864; Ford to Dwyer, Aug 29, Sept. 3 [quotes], 1864, in Ford Letterbook, June 9 to Sept. 10, 1864 (Ford Papers, Haley Museum); Ford to Showalter, Aug. 31, 1864 (Ford Papers, Haley Museum); *Reports of the Committee of Investigation Sent in 1873 by the Mexican Government,* 152; Houston *Telegraph,* Sept. 30, 1864; *OR,* I, 41, pt. 2: 1,088–1,089, 3: 912; Ford, *Rip Ford's Texas,* 369; Hughes, *Rebellious Ranger,* 226; Thompson, *Cortina,* 139; Townsend, *Yankee Invasion,* 109; *NHOT,* 5: 195.

[5] Ford, Memoirs (Ford Papers, CAH), Miscellaneous: 78.25, 93.25–102; Ford, "Typed Memoirs" (Ford Papers, CAH), 6: 1,125; Showalter to Ford, Sept. 5, 1864 [two letters of same date], De Wolf to Ford, Sept. 6, 1864 (Ford Papers, Haley Museum); James H. Fry to Giddings, Sept. 6, 1864, in Ford Letterbook, June 9 to Sept. 10, 1864 (Ford Papers, Haley Museum); Ford to Dwyer, Sept. 8, 1864, in Ford, "Letter Book, Aug. 24 to Dec. 30, 1864" (Ford Papers, TSLA), 38–39; Ford, *Rip Ford's Texas,* 370, 377–382; Hughes, *Rebellious Ranger,* 227; Townsend, *Yankee Invasion,* 101–102, 110; Thompson, *Cortina,* 140–143.

[6] Ford, Memoirs (Ford Papers, CAH), Miscellaneous, 81, 93.25–102; Ford, "Typed Memoirs" (Ford Papers, CAH), 5: 1,023, 6: 1,127–1,129; Showalter to Ford, Sept. 7, 1864 [endorsements indicate correct date is Sept. 6, 1864] (Ford Papers, Haley Museum); Ford to Root, Oct. 2, 1864, in Ford Letterbook, Aug. 24 to Dec. 18, 1864 (Ford Papers, Haley Museum); Ford to Dwyer, Sept. 8, 1864, in Ford, "Letter Book, Aug. 24 to Dec. 30, 1864" (Ford Papers, TSLA), 38–39; Ford to Root, Sept. 22, 1864, in John S. Ford, "Letter Book, September 22, 1864, to November 29, 1864" (Typescript, n.d., Ford Papers, TSLA), 1–5; Ford to Showalter, Sept. 6, 1864, in Ford Letterbook, June 9 to Sept. 10, 1864 (Ford Papers, Haley Museum); Ford to Root, Sept. 30, 1864, in Ford, Letterbook, Sept. 11, 1864, to Feb. 22, 1865 (Ford Papers, Haley Museum); *OR,* I, 41, pt. 1: 742 [quote]; Ford, *Rip Ford's Texas,* 365–366, 371–372, 377–382; Hughes, *Rebellious Ranger,* 227–229; Townsend, *Yankee Invasion,* 110–111; Thompson, *Cortina,* 142–143; Oates, "Prudent Cavalryman," 329.

[7] Ford, Memoirs (Ford Papers, CAH), Miscellaneous, 82; Ford, "Typed Memoirs" (Ford Papers, CAH), 5: 1,026, 6: 1,131–1,132 [3rd quote]; Ford to Veron, Sept. 8, 1864, Veron to Ford, n.d. [Sept. 9, 1864] [2nd quote] (Ford Papers, Haley Museum); Ford to Root, Sept. 22, 1864, in Ford, "Letter Book, Sept. 22, 1864, to Nov. 29, 1864" (Ford Papers, TSLA), 1–5; Ford to Showalter, Sept. 6, 1864 [1st quote], Ford to Slaughter, Sept. 6, 1864, Ford to José M. Cortina, Sept. 9, 1864, Ford to [John N.] Rose, Sept. 9, 1864, James H. Fry to Giddings, Sept. 10, 1864, in Ford Letterbook, June 9 to Sept. 10, 1864 (Ford Papers, Haley Museum); Ford to Veron, Sept. 8, 1864, Ford to Dwyer, Sept. 8, 1864, Ford to José M. Cortina, Sept. 8, 1864, in Ford, "Letter Book, Aug. 24 to Dec. 30, 1864" (Ford Papers, TSLA), 38–41, 45–47; Ford to Root, Sept. 30, 1864, in Ford Letterbook, Sept. 11, 1864, to Feb. 22, 1865 (Ford Papers, Haley

Museum); Ford to Veron, Sept. 8, 1864, in Ford, Letterbook, August 24 to December 18, 1864 (Ford Papers, Haley Museum); *OR,* I, 41, pt. 1: 742, pt. 3: 911, 100; Ford, *Rip Ford's Texas,* 372–373; Thompson, *Cortina,* 144.

[8] Ford to Rose, Sept. 9, 1864, in Ford, "Letter Book, Aug. 24 to Dec. 30, 1864" (Ford Papers, TSLA), 49; Ford to Root, Sept. 22, 1864 [quote], in Ford, "Letter Book, Sept. 22 to Nov. 29, 1864," (Ford Papers, TSLA), 1–5; Ford, *Rip Ford's Texas,* 373–374.

[9] Ford, Memoirs (Ford Papers, CAH), Miscellaneous, 85–87; Ford, "Typed Memoirs" (Ford Papers, CAH), 5: 1,027–1,028, 6: 1,135–1,141; W. H. D. Carrington to Ford, n.d. [Sept. 9, 1864], Sept. 15, 1864, Carrington to Giddings, n.d., Giddings to Ford, Sept. 9, 11, 1864 (Ford Papers, Haley Museum); James H. Fry to Giddings, Sept. 9, 1864 [quote], in Ford Letterbook, June 9, 1864, to Sept. 10, 1864 (Ford Papers, Haley Museum); Ford to Root, Sept. 22, 1864, in Ford, "Letter Book, Sept. 22 to Nov. 29, 1864" (Ford Papers, TSLA); *OR,* I, 41, pt. 3: 946–947; Ford, *Rip Ford's Texas,* 372, 374–375; Hughes, *Rebellious Ranger,* Townsend, *Yankee Invasion,* 111; Thompson, *Cortina,* 143–144.

[10] Carrington to Ford, Sept. 15, 1864, Agapito Longoria to [unknown], Sept. 17, 1864, Root to Longoria, Sept. 17, 1864 (Ford Papers, Haley Museum); Ford to Dwyer, Sept. 8, 1864, in Ford, "Letter Book, Aug. 24 to Dec. 30, 1864" (Ford Papers, TSLA), 38–39; Ford to "Comdg. Officer, U. S. Forces on Brazos Island," Sept. 11, 1864, Ford to José M. Cortina, Sept. 17, 1864, in Ford Letterbook, Aug. 24 to Dec. 18, 1864 (Ford Papers, Haley Museum); Ford to Root, Sept. 22, 1864, in Ford, "Letter Book, Sept. 22 to Nov. 29, 1864" (Ford Papers, TSLA); Ford to Root, Sept. 30, 1864, in Ford Letterbook, Sept. 11, 1864, to Feb. 22, 1865 (Ford Papers, Haley Museum); Ford, Memoirs (Ford Papers, CAH), Miscellaneous, 85–87, 91, 105, Miscellaneous: Ford as a Confederate, 15; *OR,* I, 41, pt. 3: 947; Ford, *Rip Ford's Texas,*365–366 [2nd quote], 371, 375–376; Hughes, *Rebellious Ranger,* 226–229; Thompson, *Cortina,* 144; Oates, "Prudent Cavalryman," 329.

[11] Ford, Memoirs (Ford Papers, CAH), Miscellaneous, 105; Special Orders No. 178, Headquarters, Dist. of TX &c., June 26, 1864 (Ford Papers, Haley Museum, and Ford Papers, TSLA); Ford to Rose, Sept. 9, 1864, in Ford, "Letter Book, Aug. 24 to Dec. 30, 1864" (Ford Papers, TSLA), 49; Root to Ford, Sept. 9, 1864, Thomas F. Drayton to Ford, Sept. 12, 1864 (Ford Papers, Haley Museum); James H. Fry to Root, Sept. 9, 1864, in Ford Letterbook, June 9 to Sept. 10, 1864 (Ford Papers, Haley Museum); Ford to Bee, Sept. 21, 1864 [quote], in Ford Letterbook, Aug. 24 to Dec. 18, 1864 (Ford Papers, Haley Museum); Ford to Root, Sept. 30, 1864, in Ford Letterbook, Sept. 11, 1864, to Feb. 22, 1865 (Ford Papers, Haley Museum); *OR,* I, 34, pt. 4: 695, 41, pt. 3: 946–947; Hughes, *Rebellious Ranger,* 230; Oates, "Prudent Cavalryman," 330–331.

[12] Ford, Memoirs (Ford Papers, CAH), 899–900, Miscellaneous, 91–92; Ford to Dwyer, Sept. 3, 1864, Ford to Slaughter, July 31, Sept. 6, 1864, in Ford Letterbook,

June 9 to Sept. 10, 1864 (Ford Papers, Haley Museum); Ford to Kearny, Aug. 26, 1864, Ford to Root, Oct. 2, 1864, in Ford, "Letter Book, Aug. 24-Dec. 30, 1864," (Ford Papers, TSLA), 7, 88; *Foreign Relations of the United States, 1865–1866,* 3: 75; *OR,* I, 34, pt. 4: 684–685, pt. 2: 990, pt. 3: 721–722, 909–911, 973–974, 43, pt. 3: 957–959; Galveston *News,* Oct. 21, 1864; Ford, *Rip Ford's Texas,* 376; Townsend, *Yankee Invasion,* 112–113; Hughes, *Rebellious Ranger,* 225, 230; Thompson, *Cortina,* 145.

[13] Ford, Memoirs (Ford Papers, CAH), Miscellaneous, 92–93, 93.25–102; Ford, "Typed Memoirs" (Ford Papers, CAH),) 6: 1,144–1,156, 7: 1,195; Ford to Root, Oct. 2, 1864, in Ford, "Letter Book, Aug. 24-Dec. 30, 1864," (Ford Papers, TSLA), 88; Austin *Texas State Gazette,* Oct. 12, 1864; Galveston *News,* Oct. 21, 1864; Ford, *Rip Ford's Texas,* 376–383; Drayton to Ford, Oct. 4, 1864, Tomás Mejía to Ford, Oct. 29, 1864 (Ford Papers, Haley Museum, and Ford Papers, TSLA); Ford to Mejía, Nov. 14, 1864, in Ford Letterbook, Sept. 11, 1864, to Feb. 22, 1865 (Ford Papers, Haley Museum); Carvajal to Ford, Oct. 6, 1864 (Ford Papers, TSLA); George L. Robertson to "Ma," Nov. 8, 1864 (George L. Robertson Papers, CAH); Hughes, *Rebellious Ranger,* 230; Thompson, *Cortina,* 145, 147.

[14] Ford, "Typed Memoirs" (Ford Papers, CAH), 7: 1,194; Ford, Memoirs (Ford Papers, CAH), Miscellaneous, 93; Ford to Root, Oct. 2, 1864, in Ford, "Letter Book, Aug. 24–Dec. 30, 1864" (Ford Papers, TSLA), 88; Ford statement, Jan. 20, 1897 (Ford Papers, Haley Museum); Robertson to [?], n.d. (Robertson Papers, CAH); *OR,* I, 41, pt. 3: 721–722, 957–959, 972–974; Ford, *Rip Ford's Texas,* 383; Austin *Texas State Gazette,* Nov. 2, 1864 [quotes]; Houston *Telegraph,* Oct. 26, Nov. 11, 1864; Hughes, *Rebellious Ranger,* 232; Thompson, *Cortina,* 147.

[15] Robertson to "Ma," Nov. 8, 1864 [quote] (Robertson Papers, CAH); Ford, Memoirs (Ford Papers, CAH), Miscellaneous, 106–108; Ford to Nestor Maxán and Latham, Sept. 17, 1864 (Ford Papers, TSLA; Ford to Dwyer, Oct. 11, 1864, in Ford Letterbook, Sept. 11, 1864 to Feb. 22, 1865 (Ford Papers, Haley Museum); Mejía to Ford, Oct. 29, 1864 (Ford Papers, Haley Museum, and Ford Papers, TSLA); Ford to Mejía, Oct. 29, 1864, in John S. Ford, General Order Book (Manuscript, n.d., n.p., Ford Papers, Haley Museum); Galveston *News,* Oct. 21, 1864; *OR,* I, 48, pt. 1: 1,355; Wise, *Lifeline of the Confederacy,* 183–184, 187–190, 214–220; Amberson et al., *I Would Rather Sleep in Texas,* 124, 252–253; Underwood, *Waters of Discord,* 70–75; Tyler, *Vidaurri,* 149–152; Townsend, *Yankee Invasion,* 6; *NHOT,* 1: 463, 6: 102; John M. Hart, *Revolutionary Mexico: The Coming and Process of the Mexican Revolution* (Berkeley: University of California Press, 1987), 111–114. Leonard Pierce resigned as the United States consul at Matamoros in November 1864, but E. Dorsey Etchison and Amzi Wood served as American consuls in that port during the last months of the Civil War.

[16] General Orders No. 163, Headquarters, Dist. of TX, NM, and AZ, Aug. 16, 1864, General Orders No. 165, Headquarters, Dist. of TX, NM, and AZ, Aug. 22, 1864, General Orders No. 1, Headquarters, Dist. of TX, NM, and AZ, Sept. 10, 1864,

General Orders No. 6, Headquarters, Dist. Of TX, NM, and AZ, Sept. 24, 1864 (Ford Papers, Haley Museum); Ford to Turner, Apr. 22, 1864, in Ford Letterbook, Mar. 11 to June 6, 1864 (Ford Papers, Haley Museum); Ford, *Rip Ford's Texas,* 383–384; Hughes, *Rebellious Ranger,* 231; Ralph A. Wooster, *Lone Star Regiments in Gray* (Austin: Eakin Press, 2002), 205.

[17] Ford to W. L. Newsom, Sept. 3, 1864, in Ford Letterbook, June 9 to Sept. 10, 1864 (Ford Papers, Haley Museum); Ford to Dwyer, Oct. 1, 1864, in Ford Letterbook, Sept. 11, 1864 to Feb. 22, 1865 (Ford Papers, Haley Museum); Giddings to Murrah, Oct. 21, 1864 (GR); Giddings to Ford, Oct. 25, 1864 (Ford Papers, Haley Museum); John S. Ford, Influence of the Benavides Family (Manuscript, n.d., n.p., Ford Papers, Haley Museum); *OR,* I, 34, pt. 2: 949 [quote], 950; Ford, Memoirs (Ford Papers, CAH), Miscellaneous, 123; Ford, "Typed Memoirs" (Ford Papers, CAH), 6: 1,126, 1,164–1,167; Ford, *Rip Ford's Texas,* 357–358, 383–385; Thompson, *Vaqueros in Blue and Gray,* 119–121; Hughes, *Rebellious Ranger,* 226, 231.

[18] Ford, Memoirs (Ford Papers, CAH), Miscellaneous, 79; Rufus [A.] Byler to "My Dear Wife" [Martha F. Byler], Dec. 29, 1864 (Dobie-Byler Family Papers, CAH); Ford to Nolan, Oct. 30, 1864, in Ford Letterbook, Sept. 11, 1864, to Feb. 22, 1865 [1st and 2nd quotes] (Ford Papers, Haley Museum); Ford, *Rip Ford's Texas,* 384, 385–386 [3rd quote]; *OR,* I, 48, pt. 1: 1,311–1,312, 53: 1,020–1,021; Hughes, *Rebellious Ranger,* 232; Townsend, *Yankee Invasion,* 114.

[19] *OR,* I, 48, pt. 1: 1,311–1,312, 1,353 [1st quote]-1,355, 53: 1,020–1,021; Robertson to "Fanny," Dec. 13, 1864 [2nd-4th quotes] (Robertson Papers, CAH); John H. Jenkins Sr., "Personal Reminiscences of Texas History" (Typescript, Apr. 1930, CAH), 121 [last quote]; Jenkins, *Recollections of Early Texas,* 232–233; Oates, "Prudent Cavalryman," 331.

[20] James H. Fry to John J. Dix, Sept. 24, 1864, R. W. Carr to Ed Duggan, Nov. 28, 1864, Giddings to Ed Duggan, Jan. 15, 18, 1865, Cater to Ford, Feb. 1, 9, 1865, Aldrich to Ford, Feb. 8, 1865 (Ford Papers, Haley Museum); Ford to W. R. Jones, Jan. 17, 1865, in Ford Special Order Book, Dec. 27, 1863 to Feb. 4, 1865 (Ford Papers, Haley Museum); *OR,* I, 41, pt. 4: 1,109 [quote], 1,085, 1,138, 48, pt. 1: 1,358, 1,457; Jane C. Monday and Francis B. Vick, *Petra's Legacy: The South Texas Ranching Empire of Petra Vela and Mifflin Kenedy* (College Station: Texas A&M University Press, 2007), 128.

[21] Ford, Memoirs (Ford Papers, CAH), Miscellaneous, 74; Ford to Root, Oct. 2, 1864. Ford to C. D. Evans, Oct. 24, 1864, in Ford Letterbook, Aug. 24 to Dec. 18, 1864 (Ford Papers, Haley Museum); Ford to Evans, Oct. 24, 1864 (Ford Papers, Haley Museum); *OR,* I, 41, pt. 3: 955; Ford, *Rip Ford's Texas,* 386–387; Hughes, *Rebellious Ranger,* 232; Townsend, *Yankee Invasion,* 113, 115; Chance, *Carvajal,* 180–183.

[22] Edwin De Leon, *Secret History of Confederate Diplomacy Abroad,* ed. William C. Davis (Lawrence: University Press of Kansas, 2005), 163–164; Kerby, *Kirby*

Smith's Confederacy, 144; Charles M. Hubbard, *The Burden of Confederate Diplomacy* (Knoxville: University of Tennessee Press, 1998), 156; Joseph H. Parks, *General Edmund Kirby Smith C.S.A.* (Baton Rouge: Louisiana State University Press, 1954), 451–452; Carland E. Crook, "Benjamin Theron and French Designs in Texas During the Civil War," *SWHQ* 68 (Apr. 1965): 432–454; Cotham, *Battle on the Bay,* 55–56.

[23] John Y. Simon, ed., *The Papers of Ulysses S. Grant, Volume Thirteen* (Carbondale: Southern Illinois University Press, 1985), 283; *OR,* I, 46, pt. 2: 201, 48, pt. 1: 512 [quotes]-513; Hubbard, *Confederate Diplomacy,* 172, 174; William S. McFeely, *Grant: A Biography* (New York: W. W. Norton & Company, 1981), 206; Irving McKee, *"Ben-Hur" Wallace* (Berkeley: University of California Press, 1947), 91–92; Harry T. and Marjorie L. Mahoney, *Mexico and the Confederacy, 1860–1867* (San Francisco: Austin & Winfield, 1998), 67; Townsend, *Yankee Invasion,* 117, 118; Hughes, *Rebellious Ranger,* 232–233; Rippy, "Mexican Projects of the Confederates," 295–296; Webster, "Texas Manifest Destiny," 33–34.

[24] Duggan to Giddings, Mar. 8, 1865, Duggan to Cater, Mar. 8, 1865, in Letters and Papers of Adjt. General Ed Duggan, Feb. 2 to May 27, 1865 (Manuscript, n.p., Ford Papers, Haley Museum); Evans, *Confederate Military History* (Extended ed.), 15: 125–126; Simon, *Grant Papers,* 13: 284–285; *OR,* I, 48, pt. 1: 937–938, 1,276–1,281; Dallas *Morning News,* Dec. 26, 1885; Ford, *Rip Ford's Texas,* 388; Townsend, *Yankee Invasion,* 85, 118.

[25] *OR,* I, 48, pt. 1: 1,166 [3rd quote], 1,167 [rest of quotes], 1,276 -1,277 [1st quote], 1,278–1,282; Simon, *Grant Papers,* 13: 285–288; Dallas *Morning News,* Dec. 26, 1885; Hughes, *Rebellious Ranger,* 233–236.

[26] Ford, Memoirs (Ford Papers, CAH), Miscellaneous, 122; Ford, "Typed Memoirs" (Ford Papers, CAH), 5: 1,030–1,031, 7: 1,174–1,186; Slaughter to "Genl", n.d. (Ford Papers, Haley Museum); Dallas *Morning News,* Dec. 26, 1885; Houston *Telegraph,* Apr. 4, 1865; *OR,* I, 48, pt. 1: 1,275–1,276, pt. 2: 122, 457–459 [quotes], 461–462 [last quote], 463; Hughes, *Rebellious Ranger,* 236; McKee, *"Ben-Hur" Wallace,* 93–94; Amberson et al., *I Would Rather Sleep in Texas,* 260. Ford later wrote that Lew Wallace said the 13th Amendment would not be ratified for years, if ever, while the Emancipation Proclamation was a "mistake," did not have widespread support, and would not be a problem. Ford of course claimed that he always strongly doubted these assertions.

[27] *OR,* I, 48, pt. 1: 1,358–1,359, pt. 2: 122, 460–461, 462 [1st and 2nd quotes], 463 [3rd quote], 1,277, 1,292–1,293; Simon, *Grant Papers,* 13: 288–290; Mahoney and Mahoney, *Mexico and the Confederacy,* 69; Hughes, *Rebellious Ranger,* 236; Parks, *Edmund Kirby Smith,* 451–452; Rippy, "Mexican Projects of the Confederates," 297–8, 308–309; Webster, "Texas Manifest Destiny," 36–37. Wallace's own account can be found in Lew Wallace, *An Autobiography,* 2 vols. (New York: Harper and Brothers, 1906), 2: 623–843. For another perspective, see Chapter 3 of Jeffrey W. Hunt, *The Last*

Battle of the Civil War: Palmetto Ranch (Austin: University of Texas Press, 2002). It is interesting to note that Maj. Gen. John M. Schofield, with the strong support of Federal officials, was recruited by the Juáristas in 1865 to lead an army composed of Union and Confederate veterans into Mexico to expel the French. Schofield agreed to the scheme, but wisely chose to try diplomacy first, which ultimately proved successful. See Donald B. Connelly, *John M. Schofield and the Politics of Generalship* (Chapel Hill: University of North Carolina Press, 2006), 182–186.

[28] Ford, "Typed Memoirs" (Ford Papers, CAH), 5: 1,031, 7: 1,189–1,190; Ford to Cater, Apr. 2, 17, 1865, Ford to Slaughter, Sept. 3, 1865 [misdated copy: Apr. 3, 1865], Ford to Sixto E. Navarro, Apr. 6, 1865, in Letters and Papers of Duggan, Feb. 2 to May 27, 1865 (Ford Papers, Haley Museum); Aldrich to Refugio Benavides, Apr. 6, 1865 (Ford Papers, Haley Museum, and Ford Papers, TSLA); *OR,* I, 48, pt. 2: 17–18; Evans, *Confederate Military History* (Extended ed.), 15: 125–126; Wallace, *Autobiography,* 2: 844–846, 862–863; Chance, *Carvajal,* 183–184; McKee, *"Ben-Hur" Wallace,* 95; Settle, *Magruder,* 278; Hunt, *Last Battle,* 39; Hughes, *Rebellious Ranger,* 237; Thompson, *Cortina,* 148–149; Webster, "Texas Manifest Destiny," 45–46.

[29] Duggan to Robinson, Apr. 29, May 10, 1865, Duggan to Cater, May 1, 1865, in Letters and Papers of Duggan, Feb. 2 to May 27, 1865 (Ford Papers, Haley Museum); *OR,* I, 48, pt. 2: 1,288–1,291; Thompson, *Cortina,* 148–149; Webster, "Texas Manifest Destiny," 45–46.

[30] Murrah, statement on Apr. 27, 1865 (GR); Special Order No. 59, Mar. 10, 1865 (Ford Papers, Haley Museum); John H. Brown, *History of Texas from 1685 to 1892,* 2 vols. (St. Louis, MO: L. E. Daniell, 1892), 2: 431; Hunt, *Last Battle,* 4, 41, 42–44, 46–47; Monday and Vick, *Petra's Legacy,* 129; Townsend, *Yankee Invasion,* 126; Amberson et al., *I Would Rather Sleep in Texas,* 262–263. Jefferson Davis was captured in Georgia on May 10, 1865, but that was not known in Texas until later.

[31] Robertson to "Julia," Apr. 15, 1864 [1865], May 8, 1865 (Robertson Papers, CAH); Carrington to Ford, May 8, 1865, A. J. Murry to Ford, May 10, 1865 [last quote] (Ford Papers, Haley Museum); Hunt, *Last Battle,* 48–49.

[32] *New York Times,* June 18, 1865; Irby, *Backdoor at Bagdad,* 47; Hughes, *Rebellious Ranger,* 237; Townsend, *Yankee Invasion,* 125–127; Hunt, *Last Battle,* 55, 57–58, 63–64. For another interesting study of the Battle of Palmito Ranch, see Phillip T. Tucker, *The Final Fury: Palmito Ranch, the Last Battle of the Civil War* (Mechanicsburg, PA: Stackpole Books, 2001).

[33] Ford to Aldrich, May 16, 1865 (Ford Papers, TSLA); San Antonio *Express,* Nov. 2, 1890; Dallas *Morning News,* Dec. 20, 1896; Ford, *Rip Ford's Texas,* 389; Evans, *Confederate Military History* (Extended ed.), 15: 126–127; Hughes, *Rebellious Ranger,* 237–238; Townsend, *Yankee Invasion,* 126–128; Hunt, *Last Battle,* 57–64, 68–79.

[34] Ford, "Typed Memoirs" (Ford Papers, CAH), 7: 1,190; General Order No. 3, May 12, 1865 (Confederate States of America Records, CAH); Ford to Aldrich,

May 16, 1865 (Ford Papers, TSLA); *New York Times,* June 18, 1865; Dallas *Morning News,* Nov. 27, Dec. 24, 1890, Dec. 20, 1896; San Antonio *Express,* Nov. 2, 1890; Ford, *Rip Ford's Texas,* 389–390, 394; Hughes, *Rebellious Ranger,* 238;Townsend, *Yankee Invasion,* 127–128; Hunt, *Last Battle,* 63, 80–83.

[35] Ford, "Typed Memoirs" (Ford Papers, CAH), 5: 1,031–1,033, 7: 1,186–1,189; Ford to Aldrich, May 16, 1865 (Ford Papers, TSLA); Ford, *Rip Ford's Texas,* 389–392; San Antonio *Express,* Oct. 10, 1890, Nov. 2, 1890; Dallas Morning *News,* Dec. 20, 1896; Evans, *Confederate Military History* (Extended ed.), 15: 127–129; Townsend, *Yankee Invasion,* 128–130; Hunt, *Last Battle,* 82–83, 85–88, 91–119, 128–129; Oates, "Prudent Cavalryman," 334–335; Hughes, *Rebellious Ranger,* 237–240.

[36] Ford, "Typed Memoirs" (Ford Papers, CAH), 5: 1,032, 7: 1,197, 1,209; Ford, Memoirs (Ford Papers, CAH), Untitled [Wartime Reminiscences], 10; Ford to Aldrich, May 16, 1865 (Ford Papers, TSLA); Ford, *Rip Ford's Texas,* 392, 395–396; Evans, *Confederate Military History* (Extended ed.), 15: 128–129; *New York Times,* June 18, 1865; San Antonio *Express,* Oct. 10, Nov. 2, 1890; Irby, *Backdoor at Bagdad,* 49; Townsend, *Yankee Invasion,* 129–132; Hunt, *Last Battle,* 109–110, 125–128, 131–137; Hughes, *Rebellious Ranger,* 238–241. Slaughter's congratulatory order can be found in *Confederate Imprints* (reel 14, item number 812–2).

[37] Duggan to Robinson, May 16, 1865, Ford to J. F. Lee, May 20, 1865 [quote], in Letters and Papers of Duggan, Feb. 2 to May 27, 1865 (Ford Papers, Haley Museum); Aldrich to Ford, May 19, 1865 (Ford Papers, Haley Museum); Ford, "Typed Memoirs" (Ford Papers, CAH), 7: 1,197–1,199; *OR,* I, 48, pt. 2: 300, 381–382, 564–565; Ford, *Rip Ford's Texas,* 396–397; Townsend, *Yankee Invasion,* 132–133, 135; Hughes, *Rebellious Ranger,* 241–242; Monday and Vick, *Petra's Legacy,* 131; Hunt, *Last Battle,* 138, 141.

[38] Ford to Egbert B. Brown, May 26, 1865 [1st quotes], in Letters and Papers of Duggan, Feb. 2 to May 27, 1865 (Ford Papers, Haley Museum); Ford, Remarks (Ford Papers, Haley Museum); Ford, "Typed Memoirs" (Ford Papers, CAH), 7: 1,211; Robertson to "Ma," May [?], 1865 (Robertson Papers, CAH); Carrington to Ford, May 22, 1865 [last quote] (Ford Papers, Haley Museum); *OR,* I, 48, pt. 2: 564 [quotes], 565; Hughes, *Rebellious Ranger,* 242.

[39] Ford, "Typed Memoirs" (Ford Papers, CAH), 7: 1,211; Ford, Memoirs (Ford Papers, CAH), Miscellaneous, 142; Duggan to Robinson, May 27, 1865, in Letters and Papers of Duggan, Feb. 2 to May 27, 1865 (Ford Papers, Haley Museum); Special Order No. ___, May 27, 1865 (Ford Papers, Haley Museum, and Ford Papers, TSLA); *OR,* I, 48, pt. 2: 813–814, 827–828; *Foreign Relations of the United States, 1865–1866,* 3: 510; Thompson, *Vaqueros in Blue and Gray,* 124; Hughes, *Rebellious Ranger,* 242–243; Townsend, *Yankee Invasion,* 138.

Chapter Seven: Statesman

[1] Ford, Memoirs (Ford Papers, CAH), 877, Miscellaneous, 143, 145, 146; Ford, *Rip Ford's Texas,* xl, 401–403; San Antonio *Express,* Oct. 10, Nov. 2, 1890; Webster, "Texas Manifest Destiny," 39, 41; Lea, *King Ranch,* 1: 238; William R. Richter, *The Army in Texas During Reconstruction* (College Station: Texas A&M University Press, 1987), 13–17; Townsend, *Yankee Invasion,* 139. Ford eventually returned the United States flag to an "agent" of the 34th Indiana Infantry at Matamoros.

[2] Ford, *Rip Ford's Texas,* xl, 397–398, 401–403, 465; Ford, Memoirs (Ford Papers, CAH), 877, Miscellaneous, 143–145; *OR,* I, 48, pt. 2: 727–728; Ford and J. Charles Black to Santos Benavides, June 30, 1865 (Ford Papers, Haley Museum, and Ford Papers, TSLA); [Santos Benavides] to Ford and Black, Aug. 23, 1865 (Ford Papers, Haley Museum); Dallas *Herald,* June 15, 1865; Hughes, *Rebellious Ranger,* 243; Monday and Vick, *Petra's Legacy,* 131; Thompson, *Cortina,* 147; Davenport, "Notes on Early Steamboating,"288–289. According to Tom Lea, in *The King Ranch,* Ford also helped Richard King with his application to Pres. Andrew Johnson for an executive pardon in the fall of 1865 (1: 241).

[3] Ford, Remarks, (Ford Papers, Haley Museum); Ford, Memoirs (Ford Papers, CAH), Miscellaneous, 64, Miscellaneous: Ford as a Confederate, 4; Thompson, *Fifty Miles and a Fight,* 181; Hunt, *Last Battle,* 151–163; "Point Isabel Lighthouse," http://atlas.thc.state.tx.us/common/viewform.asp?atlas_num=2076002014&site_name=Point+Isabel+Lighthouse&class=2001 (accessed Mar. 16, 2009).

[4] *Ford, Rip Ford's Texas,* 401–405; Ford, Memoirs (Ford Papers, CAH), Miscellaneous, 143, 150 [1st quote]; Ford, Remarks [2nd and 3rd quotes] (Ford Papers, Haley Museum); CSR, 2nd Texas Cavalry: John S. Ford; Hughes, *Rebellious Ranger,* 244.

[5] Ford, Memoirs (Ford Papers, CAH), Miscellaneous, 144; Thompson, *Cortina,* 152–155, 162–166; Webster, "Texas Manifest Destiny," 44–46.

[6] Dallas *Herald,* Aug. 11, 1866; Ford, *Rip Ford's Texas,* 404–405; Ford, Memoirs (Ford Papers, CAH), Miscellaneous, 148–49; Webster, "Texas Manifest Destiny," 48–50; Hughes, *Rebellious Ranger,* 245–246; Townsend, *Yankee Invasion,* 141; Thompson, *Cortina,* 178–180; Chance, *Carvajal,* 191–192, 195.

[7] Ford, *Rip Ford's Texas,* 406; Ford, Memoirs (Ford Papers, CAH), Miscellaneous, 150; Galveston *Flake's Bulletin,* Jan. 17, Feb. 14, 1866; Hughes, *Rebellious Ranger,* 246; Webster, "Texas Manifest Destiny," 46–48, 50; Thompson, *Cortina,* 181–182; Townsend, *Yankee Invasion,* 141; Chance, *Carvajal,* 187–190; McKee, *"Ben-Hur" Wallace,* 96–106, 111.

[8] *Reports of the Committee of Investigation sent in 1873 by the Mexican Government,* 202; Austin *Southern Intelligencer,* Sept. 6, 1866; Ford, *Rip Ford's Texas,* 406–407; Ford, Memoirs (Ford Papers, CAH), Miscellaneous, 150–152; Hughes, *Rebellious*

Ranger, 246–248; Chance, *Carvajal,* 193–198; Thompson, *Cortina,* 182; Webster, "Texas Manifest Destiny," 51.

[9] Ford, *Rip Ford's Texas,* 406–407 [quote]; Ford, Memoirs (Ford Papers, CAH), Miscellaneous, 151–152; Galveston *Flake's Bulletin,* Oct. 23, 1866; Hughes, *Rebellious Ranger,* 247; *NHOT,* 2: 1,024.

[10] *Reports of the Committee of Investigation sent in 1873 by the Mexican Government,* 202–204; Ford, Memoirs (Ford Papers, CAH), Miscellaneous, 154–155; Galveston *Flake's Bulletin,* Dec. 8, 1866; Ford, *Rip Ford's Texas,* 409–410; United States Department of State, *Papers Relating to the Foreign Relations of the United States, 1867–1868,* 2 vols. (Washington: Government Printing Office, 1868), 2: 498; Webster, "Texas Manifest Destiny," 52; Amberson et al., *I Would Rather Sleep in Texas,* 285–286, 288.

[11] Ford, Memoirs (Ford Papers, CAH), Miscellaneous, 152–153 [quote]; Galveston *Flake's Bulletin,* Jan. 17, Feb. 14, 1866, Mar. 30, Apr. 3, May 16, 18, 19, 21, 22, 23, 29, and 31, 1867; Ford, *Rip Ford's Texas,* 465; Cowen, "Reminiscences," 3; *Appleton's Annual Cyclopaedia and Register of Important Events* (New York: D. Appleton and Company, 1870), 676; Marten, *Texas Divided,* 62; Amberson et al., *I Would Rather Sleep in Texas,* 282; Thompson, ed., *Fifty Miles and A Fight,* 125; *NHOT,* 6: 848. As a federal judge, John C. Watrous presided in 1853 as the indictments against José María de Jesús Carvajal and his associates were dismissed or failed to secure a conviction. See Chance, *Carvajal,* 163.

[12] Ford, *Rip Ford's Texas,* xl-xli, 9; Ford, Memoirs (Ford Papers, CAH), 8, 160; Cowen, "Reminiscences," 1; Austin *Southern Intelligencer,* Oct. 25, 1866; United States Ninth Census, 1870 [Cameron County, Texas]; Research notes (Price Papers, CAH); Lea, *King Ranch,*1: 241–242; Hughes, *Rebellious Ranger,* 18, 245, 268; Dwight, *Descendants of Elder John Strong,* 185; Amberson et al., *I Would Rather Sleep in Texas,* 286, 288, 289; Lea, *King Ranch,* 1: 241–242; Irby, *Backdoor at Bagdad,* 48.

[13] Ford, *Rip Ford's Texas,* xl-xli, 434–435 [quote]); Ford, Memoirs (Ford Papers, CAH), Miscellaneous, 158; United States Ninth Census, 1870 [Cameron County, Texas]; Austin *Republican,* Nov. 14, 1868; Galveston *Flake's Bulletin,* Dec. 17, 19, 21, 1867, Feb. 18, 1868; Hughes, *Rebellious Ranger,* 248; *NHOT,* 4: 477.

[14] Brownsville *Ranchero,* Feb. 19, 24 [quotes], Mar. 29, 1870; United States Ninth Census, 1870 [Cameron County, Texas]; Amberson et al., *I Would Rather Sleep in Texas,* 172, 174, 308; Hughes, *Rebellious Ranger,* 248–249. At least one novel recounts the clash between Ford and Rudolph Krause, which it says occurred because Ford was so nasty in his editorials against Reconstruction and the Republicans. See Jim Sanderson, *Nevin's History: A Novel of Texas* (Lubbock: Texas Tech University Press, 2004), 34–35.

[15] Galveston *News,* Oct. 11, 1871; Gammel, *Laws of Texas,* 6:707–710; Ford, *Rip Ford's Texas,* 468; Monday and Vick, *Petra's Legacy,* 185–186; Amberson et al.,

I Would Rather Sleep in Texas, 296–297; *NHOT,* 5: 588, 876; Lea, *King Ranch,* 1: 248–250.

[16] Ford, *Rip Ford's Texas,* xli; 408–411, 468; Ford, Memoirs (Ford Papers, CAH), 879, 891, Miscellaneous, 156–158, 162, 163 [quote], 164–165; John S. Ford, Captain Nathan Mitchell (Manuscript, n.d., n.p., DeShields Papers, DRT); John S. Ford, Gen. McCook Investigates Gen. Reynolds (Manuscript, n.d., n.p., Ford Papers, Haley Museum); *Reports of the Committee of Investigation Sent in 1873 by the Mexican Government,* 153–158; Dallas *Herald,* Jan. 11, 1868; San Antonio *Express,* Aug. 11, 1871, Aug. 31, 1897; *New York Times,* Jan. 8, 1872; Graham, *Kings of Texas,* 118; Lea, *King Ranch,*1: 253, 255, 263–267; Thompson, *Cortina,* 202; Webster, "Texas Manifest Destiny," 68; Michael G. Webster, "Intrigue on the Rio Grande: The *Rio Bravo* Affair, 1875," *SWHQ* 74 (Oct. 1970): 150–151; Hughes, *Rebellious Ranger,* 248

[17] United States Department of State, *Papers Relating to the Foreign Relations of the United States, 1872–1873* (Washington: Government Printing Office, 1872–1873), 415–416 [quotes]; Thompson, *Cortina,* 207–208; Webster, "Intrigue on the Rio Grande," 150–151.

[18] John S. Ford, The Frontier Commission (Manuscript, n.d., n.p., Ford Papers, Haley Museum); Ford, *Rip Ford's Texas,* xli-xlii; Alexander E. Sweet and John A. Knox, *On a Mexican Mustang Through Texas* (Hartford, CT: S. S. Scranton & Company, 1883), 550–551 [quote]; United States Congress, *Depredations on the Frontier of Texas,* House Ex. Docs. No. 39, 42nd Cong., 3rd Sess. [Serial Set 1565], passim; Webster, "Intrigue on the Rio Grande," 151; Thompson, *Cortina,* 211, 212, 214; Hughes, *Rebellious Ranger,* 249–250.

[19] Ford, Frontier Commission (Ford Papers, Haley Museum).

[20] *Reports of the Committee of Investigation sent in 1873 by the Mexican Government,* 65–67 [quote], 182–183, 188–189 [quotes], 191–198, 207–208; Thompson, *Cortina,* 215–217.

[21] Thompson, *Cortina,* 209, 217; Ernest Wallace, *Ranald S. Mackenzie on the Texas Frontier* (Lubbock: West Texas Museum Association, 1963), 97–107; Amberson et al., *I Would Rather Sleep in Texas,* 313–323; *NHOT,* 4: 416–417, 5: 530–531.

[22.] J. R. Cranston to Ford, Oct. 21, 1870 (Ford Papers, Haley Museum); Clarksville [TX] *Standard,* June 29, 1872 [1st quote]; Dallas *Herald,* Sept. 28, 1872 [2nd quote]; Galveston *News,* June 19, July 31, Aug. 16, 1872, Jan. 22, Dec. 31, 1873; Ford, *Rip Ford's Texas,* xlii; Winkler, *Platforms of Political Parties in Texas;* 143–147; Hughes, *Rebellious Ranger,* 249–250; *NHOT,* 3: 857. Carl H. Moneyhon, in *Edmund J. Davis: Civil War General, Republican Leader, Reconstruction Governor* (Fort Worth: TCU Press, 2010), discusses Davis' concern for frontier violence in chapters 9 and 10.

[23] Ford, *Rip Ford's Texas,* 417–420; Campbell, *Gone to Texas,* 284; Hughes, *Rebellious Ranger,* 251–252; Carl H. Moneyhon, *Texas After the Civil War: The Strug-*

gle for Reconstruction (College Station: Texas A&M University Press, 2004), 197–198; *NHOT,* 2: 193, 195.

[24] Ford, *Rip Ford's Texas,* xliii, 420, 422–424, 428–429, 431–433; John S. Ford, Reply to General McCulloch, (Manuscript, n.d., n.p., Ford Papers, Haley Museum); Valentine O. Weed, Recollections of V. O. Weed, (Manuscript, Nov. 20, 1930, n.p., CAH); Hughes, *Rebellious Ranger,* 253; *NHOT,* 1: 790–791, 3: 450–451, 5: 607, 6: 555.

[25] Ford, *Rip Ford's Texas,* 282, 288, 420–421, 425 [quotes], 429–430; T. B. Wheeler, "Reminiscences of Reconstruction in Texas," *Quarterly of the Texas State Historical Association* 11 (July 1907): 56–62; Hughes, *Rebellious Ranger,* 254–255; *NHOT,* 3: 610–611, 5: 704–705.

[26] Ford, *Rip Ford's Texas,* xliii, 424–427, 432, 434; Hughes, *Rebellious Ranger,* 254–256. An undated, untitled manuscript in Ford's papers at the Haley Museum, probably written by Ford, says the three men served for eighteen days, for $8 a day.

[27] Ford, *Rip Ford's Texas,* xliii; John S. Ford, Hon. Gustave Schleicher (Manuscript, n.d., n.p., DeShields Papers, DRT); Thomas P. Robb to Ford, Apr. 24, 1875 (Ford Papers, Haley Museum); *Report of the Permanent Committee, Appointed at a Meeting of the Citizens of Brownsville, Tex., April 17, 1875* (Brownsville, TX: John S. Mansur, 1875), 2, 3, 7, 8–15, 22–23; Hughes, *Rebellious Ranger,* 256–257.

[28] United States Congress, *Testimony Taken by the Committee on Military Affairs in Relation to the Texas Border Troubles,* House Misc. Docs. No. 64, 45th Cong., 2nd Sess. [Serial Set 1820], 126–128, 147–148; Webb, *Texas Rangers,* 260–281; Utley, *Lone Star Justice,* 164–167; Cox, *Wearing the Cinco Peso,* 251–255; Graham, *Kings of Texas,* 145–147; Chuck Parsons and Marianne E. Hall Little, *Captain L. H. McNelly, Texas Ranger* (Austin: State House Press, 2001), 194–199, 201, 202; Webster, "Intrigue on the Rio Grande," 152–162; Thompson, *Cortina,* 228–230.

[29] United States Congress, *Texas Frontier Troubles,* House Reports No. 343, 44th Cong., 1st Sess. [Serial Set 1709], 1; Parsons and Little, *McNelly,* 253–254; Monday and Vick, *Petra's Legacy,* 136; Hughes, *Rebellious Ranger,* 102

[30] Dallas *Herald,* Aug. 28, 1875; Hughes, *Rebellious Ranger,* 257; J. E. Ericson, "The Delegates to the Convention of 1875: A Reappraisal," *SWHQ* 67 (July 1963): 22–25; *NHOT,* 2: 284–285.

[31] John S. Ford, Appropriation for the New Capitol [1st quote] (Manuscript, n.d., n.p., Ford Papers, Haley Museum); John S. Ford, Pensions to Texas Soldiers [2nd quote] (Manuscript, n.d., n.p., Ford Papers, Haley Museum); Hughes, *Rebellious Ranger,* 258; *NHOT,* 2: 284–285.

[32] John S. Ford, Lands Between the Nueces and the Rio Grande (Manuscript, n.d., n.p., Ford Papers, Haley Museum); Ford, *Rip Ford's Texas,* 143–145, 440; Ford, Memoirs (Ford Papers, CAH), 506, 690; Thompson, *Cortina,* 20; Hughes, *Rebellious Ranger,* 257–258; *NHOT,* 2: 285–285, 289–291, 5: 355. See Article XIV, Section 8, in 1876 Texas Constitution for quote.

[33] Ford, Appropriation for the New Capitol (Ford Papers, Haley Museum); John S. Ford, Pay of State Officers (Manuscript, n.d., n.p., Ford Papers, Haley Museum); John S. Ford, The Constitutional Convention (Manuscript, n.d., n.p., Ford Papers, Haley Museum); Campbell, *Gone to Texas,*285–286; Moneyhon, *Texas After the Civil War,* 200–201; Winkler, *Platforms of Political Parties in Texas,* 173–174; *NHOT,* 2: 289–291.

[34] Carvajal to Ford, Feb. 14, 1872 (Ford Papers, Haley Museum); Ford, Memoirs (Ford Papers, CAH), Miscellaneous, 167–168; Dallas *Morning News,* Dec. 26, 1892; Ford, *Rip Ford's Texas,* 412; Settle, *Magruder,* 299, 303; Chance, *Carvajal,* 199; Hart, *Revolutionary Mexico,* 105–109, 120, 121–124; Thompson, *Cortina,* 217–220, 228–229, 231; Hughes, *Rebellious Ranger,* 258–259; Monday and Vick, *Petra's Legacy,* 236–237.

[35] Ford, *Rip Ford's Texas,* 412–413; Ford, Memoirs (Ford Papers, CAH), Miscellaneous, 168–169; Dallas *Morning News,* Dec. 26, 1892; San Antonio *Express,* Nov. 2, 1890; Thompson, *Cortina,* 229–239.

[36] Martin, "Last of the Ranger Chieftains," 40 [1st quote]; Speer and Brown, *Encyclopedia of the New West,* 359 [2nd quote]; Ford, *Rip Ford's Texas,* xliii–xliv; Ford, Lands Between the Nueces and the Rio Grande [rest of quotes] (Ford Papers, Haley Museum); Lambert, "Col. John S. Ford," 177–184. Many thanks to my editor, Gregg Cantrell, for explaining the term "rutabagaism."

[37] Leander H. McNelly to Ford, June 8, 1876 (Ford Papers, Haley Museum); John S. Ford, Death of Capt. McNelly [quote] (Manuscript, n.d., n.p., Ford Papers, Haley Museum); Parsons and Little, *McNelly,* 263–274; *NHOT,* 3: 414, 4: 445–446.

[38] Galveston *News,* Oct. 8, 15, 1877; United States Congress, *Testimony Taken by the Committee on Military Affairs,* 250; Ford, Memoirs (Ford Papers, CAH), Miscellaneous, 161; *NHOT,* 1: 823–824.

[39] United States Congress, *Testimony Taken by the Committee on Military Affairs,* 236–240, 250 [quotes], 251–253, 260, 261; Webster, "Texas Manifest Destiny," 11; *NHOT,* 3: 517.

[40] Dallas *Herald,* Jan. 5 [quote], Feb. 2, 1878; Galveston *News,* Aug. 5, 1878; United States Congress, *Testimony Taken by the Committee on Military Affairs,* 261; United States Congress, *The Galveston & Camargo Railway,* House Misc. Docs. No. 46, 45th Cong., 2nd Sess. [Serial Set 1817], 12–17; United States Congress, *Sheep Husbandry,* Senate Ex. Docs. No. 25, 45th Cong., 3rd Sess. [Serial Set 1825], 105–106; Hart, *Revolutionary Mexico,* 117, 121, 124.

[41] John S. Ford, *Speech on Frontier Protection, Delivered in the Senate of Texas, March 1879* (Austin: n.p., 1879), 6 [1st and 2nd quotes], 8 [3rd quote]; Texas Legislature, *Journal of the Senate of the Sixteenth Legislature of the State of Texas, Regular Session, Convened in Austin, January 19, 1879* (Galveston: News Book and Job Establishment, 1879), 9–10; Galveston *News,* Mar. 24, 1879; Cox, *Wearing the Cinco Peso,* 300.

[42] John S. Ford, The Claim of Thomas Toby [quotes] (Manuscript, n.d., n.p., Ford Papers, Haley Museum); United States Congress, *Thomas Toby,* House Reports No. 249, 47th Cong., 1st Sess. [Serial Set 2065], 1, 3, 4, 6; Texas Legislature, *Journal of the Senate of the Sixteenth Legislature, Regular Session,* 432–433; *NHOT,* 6: 513.

[43] *Remarks of Senator Ford and Hon. Ashbel Smith on the Occasion of the Presentation of Gen. Rusk's Portrait in the House of Representatives, April 1, 1879* (Galveston: News Steam Book and Job Printing Establishment, 1879), passim; Ford, *Rip Ford's Texas,* 17–18; Ford, Memoirs (Ford Papers, CAH), 196; Texas Legislature, *Journal of the Senate of the Sixteenth Legislature, Regular Session,* 158, 449–450, 469–470, 792, 957–958, 1,065; *NHOT,* 4: 62–63, 6: 258–259.

[44] Cowen, "Reminiscences," 2; Ford, Hon. Gustave Schleicher (DeShields Papers, DRT); Texas Legislature, *Journal of the Senate of the Sixteenth Legislature, Regular Session,* 9, 65, 255–257; Texas Legislature, *Journal of the Senate of the Sixteenth Legislature of the State of Texas, Extra Session, Convened in Austin, June 10, 1879* (Galveston: News Book and Job Establishment, 1879), 167; *NHOT,* 5: 314–315, 918–919.

[45] Galveston *News,* Sept. 4, 1879, Mar. 25, 1880; Brown, Annals of Travis County (Brown Papers, CAH) 35: 20; Texas Legislature, *Journal of the Senate of the Sixteenth Legislature of the State of Texas, Extra Session,* 35–38; Texas Legislature, *Journal of the Senate of the Seventeenth Legislature of the State of Texas, Regular Session, Convened in Austin, January 11, 1881* (Galveston: A. H. Belo & Company, 1881), 28 [quote], 31, 35, 99; Texas Legislature, *Journal of the Senate of Texas, Being a Special Session of the Seventeenth Legislature, Begun and Held at the City of Austin, April 6, 1882* (Galveston: A. H. Belo & Company, 1882), 59, 84, 90. The Deaf and Dumb Asylum became the Texas State School for the Deaf in 1949. See *NHOT,* 6: 404–405.

[46] Cowen, "Reminiscences," 1; Swisher, "Remembrances of Texas and Texas People," 86; Rena M. Green, ed., *The Swisher Memoirs, by Col. John M. Swisher* (San Antonio: Sigmund Press, 1932), p. 59; Ford, *Rip Ford's Texas,* xliv; Galveston *News,* Mar. 25, 1880; Austin *Texas Mute Ranger,* May 1880, October 1881, March 1883, June 1888; Dan Kilgore, ed., *A Mexican Sergeant's Recollections of the Alamo & San Jacinto* (Austin: Jenkins Publishing Company, 1980), 9–10, 13–14.

[47] John W. Leonard, *Woman's Who's Who of America* (New York: American Commonwealth Company, 1914), 842; Brownsville *Herald,* Aug. 12, 1953; Galveston *News,* Mar. 4, 1880, Nov. 11, 1882; Austin *Democratic Statesman,* Jan. 10, Feb. 26, Mar. 2 [quote], 1880; Research notes (Price Papers, CAH); Amberson et al., *I Would Rather Sleep in Texas,* 110; John S. Ford, Sunday School (Manuscript, n.d., n.p. Ford Papers, Haley Museum); Hughes, *Rebellious Ranger,* 268.

[48] Ford to Dix, Mar. 12, 1883 (Ford Papers, TSLA); Dallas *Herald,* Jan. 18, 1863; Hughes, *Rebellious Ranger,* 268; Brown, *Indian Wars and Pioneers of Texas,* 747, 749; Lewis E. Daniell, *Personnel of the Texas State Government, with Sketches of Representative Men of Texas* (San Antonio: Maverick Printing House, 1892), 115.

[49] Brown, Annals of Travis County (Brown Papers, CAH), 35: 20; Texas Legislature, *Journal of the Senate of Texas, Being the Regular Session of the Eighteenth Legislature, Begun and Held at the City of Austin, January 9, 1883* (Austin, TX: E. W. Swindells, 1883), 36, 39, 223; Texas Legislature, *Journal of the Senate of Texas, Being the Called Session of the Eighteenth Legislature, Begun and Held at the City of Austin, January 8, 1884* (Austin, TX: E W. Swindells, 1884), 106; John S. Ford, Untitled Manuscript [Final Report (#1164)] [quotes] (n.d., n.p., Ford Papers, Haley Museum); Galveston *News,* Mar. 29, May 24, Aug. 9, 30, 1883, Dallas *Herald,* Mar. 29, Apr. 19, Nov. 29, 1883; *NHOT,* 6: 404–405.

[50] Ford to Roberts, Feb. 6, 1877, Ford et al. to Roberts, July 18, 1882 (Roberts Papers, CAH); Bee to Ashbel Smith, Jan. 28, 1879 (Bee Papers, CAH); Bee to Ford, June 9, 1886 [quote] (Ford Papers, Haley Museum); Ford to Dix, Mar. 12, 1883 (Ford Papers, TSLA); Galveston *News,* Jan. 28, 1878, Mar. 17, 1879; Winkler, *Platforms of Political Parties in Texas,* 175–176.

Chapter Eight: Historian

[1] John S. Ford, Moves to San Antonio [quotes] (Manuscript, n.d., n.p., Ford Papers, Haley Museum); Confederate Pension File 00356, Bexar County: Addie N. Ford (TSLA); *Official Register of the United States, 1885, Volume I: Legislative, Executive, Judicial* (Washington: Government Printing Office, 1886), 127; *Official Register of the United States, 1887, Volume I: Legislative, Executive, Judicial* (Washington: Government Printing Office, 1888), 130; *Official Register of the United States, 1889, Volume I: Legislative, Executive, Judicial* (Washington: Government Printing Office, 1890), 137; *NHOT,* 5: 955.

[2] Ford, Moves to San Antonio [1st-3rd quotes] (Ford Papers, Haley Museum); Cowen, "Reminiscences," 2 [4th quote], 9; Stephen B. Oates, "Hugh F. Young's Account of the Snively Expedition as Told to John S. Ford," *SWHQ* 70 (July 1966): 71, 72, 91; *NHOT,* 3: 248.

[3] John S. Ford, Lunatic Asylum (Manuscript, n.d. [1892], n.p., Ford Papers, Haley Museum); Dallas *Morning News,* Oct. 11, 15, 17, 21, 24, 1889; Alpine *Avalanche,* Dec. 23, 1915; *Memorial and Genealogical Record of Southwest Texas* (Chicago: Goodspeed Brothers, 1894), 297; *NHOT,* 5: 812–813. Ford may have met Nathaniel G. Mitchell for the first time along the Rio Grande in the 1860s, when they both operated along the border. See Daniell, *Personnel of the Texas State Government* (1892), 367.

[4] Ford, Memoirs (Ford Papers, CAH), 108, 115, 166, 175; Clarksville [TX] *Northern Standard,* Feb. 3, 1855 (extract from Austin *Texas State Times*); Ford, *Rip Ford's Texas,* xlvi; Hughes, *Rebellious Ranger,* 113; Daniell, *Personnel of the Texas State Government* (1892), 483–486; J. Marvin Hunter, ed., *The Trail Drivers of Texas,* rev.

ed. (Austin: University of Texas Press, 2003), 938–939; Laura McLemore, *Inventing Texas: Early Historians of the Lone Star State* (College Station: Texas A&M University Press, 2004), 6–7, 64, 68–69; Richard B. McCaslin, *At the Heart of Texas: One Hundred Years of the Texas State Historical Association, 1897–1997* (Austin: Texas State Historical Association, 2007), 5; *NHOT,* 2: 1,068, 6: 1,121–1,122. Interestingly, Henry Scott later commanded a company under Ford in 1864, and Ford revisited some of the same historic sites in Goliad in 1889 when he was serving on the committee to locate a site for a new state lunatic asylum. See Ford, Lunatic Asylum (Ford Papers, Haley Museum).

[5] Dallas *Morning News,* Apr. 21, 1940; McCaslin, *At the Heart of Texas,* 6–7; NHOT, 1: 790–791, 5: 466, 612.

[6] Brown, Annals of Travis County (Brown Papers, CAH), 33: 58; Veterans of the Mexican War Association, Records, CAH; Dallas *Morning News,* Apr. 7, 1929; United States Department of War, Adjutant General's Office, Mexican War Pension Applications (Record Group 94, National Archives, Washington, DC), C3967: Ford, John S. and Annie, Apr. 18, 1887; C. Luther Coyner, "Peter Hansborough Bell," *SWHQ* 3 (July 1899): 52; William H. Glasson, *Federal Military Pensions in the United States,* ed. David Kinley (New York: Oxford University Press, 1918), 116–118. The National Association of Veterans of the Mexican War organized in Washington, DC, in 1873, but there is no clear connection between it and the Texas organization to which Ford belonged. See Wallace E. Davies, "The Mexican War Veterans as an Organized Group," *Mississippi Valley Historical Review* 35 (Sept. 1948): 221–238.

[7] Affidavit of G. W. Davis and [?] Wells, Jan. 22, 1874, Register of Texas Veterans Reunion, Houston, May 18, 1874 Texas Veterans Association Roll Book, April 20, 1892, to 1901(Texas Veterans Association Papers, CAH); Rolls of Texas Veterans Association (Adina De Zavala Papers, CAH); Dallas *Morning News,* Apr. 21, 1886, Apr. 21, June 24, 1894; Ford and Bee to Guy M. Bryan, Mar. 21, 1894 [1st quote] (Guy M. Bryan Papers, CAH [also transcribed in Hamilton P. Bee Papers, CAH]); Ford to "Ladies," Apr. 3. 1896 [2nd quote] (Ford Papers, Haley Museum); NHOT, 2: 510–511, 741, 3: 450–451, 612–613, 4: 319, 6: 440.

[8] "United Confederate Veterans Camps," *Confederate Veteran* 1 (Dec. 1893): 359; "United Confederate Veterans Camps," *Confederate Veteran* 2 (Mar. 1894): 90; "List of Camps, Commanders, and Adjutants," *Confederate Veteran* 9 (Aug. 1901): 365; Dallas *Morning News,* Oct. 24, 25, 1892, July 25, 1893, May 25, 1895, June 25, 1896; *New York Times,* June 25, 1897; Cowen, "Reminiscences," 3; Ford to Dix, July 17, 1897 (Ford Papers, TSLA). In his July 17, 1897, letter to Dix, Ford, who had not returned to Lincoln County, Tennessee, since he left in 1836, explained that he tried to contact his Tennessee relatives while he was in Nashville, but ironically they were in the city as well for the festivities and so they missed each other.

[9] Dallas *Morning News,* Apr. 10, 1892 [1st quote], Oct. 5, 1897, Oct. 7, 1898; Houston *Daily Post,* Oct. 10, 1897; Ford to Will Lambert, Apr. 2, 1896 [2nd quote] (Ford Papers, Haley Museum); Ford to Lambert, July 8, 1897 [3rd and 4th quotes] (Texas Rangers Archives, Texas Ranger Museum, Waco); Cox, *Wearing the Cinco Peso,* 372; *NHOT,* 4:45–46; Daniell, *Personnel of the Texas State Government* (1887), 196. The organization that Ford helped to found became the Former Texas Ranger Association in 1965.

[10] Dallas *Morning News,* Dec. 26, 1885, Jan. 4, 1887; Jenkins, "Reminiscences of Texas History," 51 [quote].

[11] Alwyn Barr, "The Semicentennial of Texas Independence in 1886," *SWHQ* 91 (Jan. 1988): 351–354; McLemore, *Inventing Texas,* 8–9, 72–79, 83–85.

[12] Hubert Howe Bancroft, *History of the North Mexican States and Texas, 1531–1889, Volume 2* (San Francisco: A. L. Bancroft & Company, 1889), 443–448, 468, 475. Ford, *Rip Ford's Texas,* 377, 393 [1st quote]; Ford, Memoirs (Ford Papers, CAH), Miscellaneous, 103 [2nd quote]; Ford "Typed Memoirs" (Ford Papers, CAH), 7: 1,186–1,189; San Antonio *Express,* Oct. 10 [1st quote again], Nov. 2, 1890. What Bancroft published concerning the events in September 1864 is what appeared in the Houston *Telegraph* on Oct. 5, 1864, which in turn was a reprint of what had appeared in the *New York and Evening World Express* on Sept. 19, 1864.

[13] Ford to James W. Throckmorton, Mar. 13, 1888 (DeShields Papers, DRT) [1st quote]; Ford, Remarks (Ford Papers, Haley Museum) [remainder of quotes]; Ford to John Henry Brown, Feb. 25, 1888 (Ford Papers, TSLA); *NHOT,* 3: 1,016. Oran M. Roberts' annotations can be found on the manuscript edition of Ford's memoirs at CAH.

[14] Bee to Ford, June 9, 1886, John E. Hollingsworth to Ford, Jan. 15, 1892 (Ford Papers, Haley Museum); Ford to Brown, Feb. 25, 1888 [quote] (Ford Papers, TSLA); Oates, "Young's Account of the Snively Expedition," 71, 72, 91; *NHOT,* 3: 1,100, 5: 688–689.

[15] James A. Ware to Thomas A. Falvey, May 17, 1887 [1st quote], Throckmorton to Ford, Mar. 23, 1888, Ford to Santos Benavides, Dec. 25, 1890 [2nd quote] (Ford Papers, Haley Museum); Ford to James W. Truitt, Mar. 15, 1893 (James W. Truitt Papers, CAH); Ford to Brown, Feb. 25, 1888 (Ford Papers, TSLA).

[16] Ford to Throckmorton, Mar. 13, Apr. 4, 1888 (DeShields Papers, DRT).

[17] San Antonio *Express,* Jan. 19, 1890; *New York Times,* Nov. 13, 1881; Dallas *Morning News,* Dec. 26, 1892; John S. Ford, statement on Jan. 20, 1897, Ford to "My dear Sir," n.d. [quote] (Ford Papers, Haley Museum); Juan N. Cortina to Ford, Oct. 17, 1891, Giddings to Ford, Oct. 5, 1892 (DeShields Papers, DRT); Ford, Cortina Manuscript (n.d., n.p., DeShields Papers, DRT); Thompson, *Cortina,* 243. There is no record that Ford attended the banquet held in Matamoros in the spring of 1891, when Porfirio Díaz allowed Juan N. Cortina to visit one last time.

[18] Undated newspaper clipping entitled "Mr. Bancroft's Mistakes in the History of Texas, by John S. Ford" (Ford Papers, Haley Museum); Ford, *Rip Ford's Texas,* 393; San Antonio *Express,* Oct. 10 [quotes], Nov. 2, 1890.

[19] Dallas *Morning News,* May 25, 1895; Ford to Dix, Feb. 5, 1897 [quote] (Ford Papers, TSLA); *NHOT,* 4: 751.

[20] John S. Ford, untitled manuscript (n.d. [1886], n.p., Ford Papers, Haley Museum); Ford, *Rip Ford's Texas,* xlvii, xlix, 107; Ford to Dix, May 5, 1897 (Ford Papers, TSLA); Brown, *Indian Wars and Pioneers of Texas,* 747; Wilbarger, *Indian Depredations in Texas,* 320–326; Brown, *History of Texas from 1685 to 1892,* 2: 431–436; McLemore, *Inventing Texas,* 9, 86–88; Cox, *Wearing the Cinco Peso,* 371–372; Mary B. Fleischer, ed. "Dudley G. Wooten's Comment on Texas Histories and Historians of the Nineteenth Century," *SWHQ* 73 (Oct. 1969): 236; *NHOT:* 2: 613, 3: 1,108–1,109, 6: 167, 1,130. Wilburn H. King praised Ford in his contribution to Dudley G. Wooten's compilation. See Dudley G. Wooten, ed., *A Comprehensive History of Texas and Texans, 1865 to 1897,* 2 vols. (Dallas: William G. Scarff, 1898), 2: 338.

[21] Ford to Dix, May 5, 1897 [quotes] (Ford Papers, TSLA); Ford to Roberts, Mar. 20, 1897 (Roberts Papers, CAH); Brownsville *Daily Herald,* Aug. 7, 1893; Brown, *Indian Wars and Pioneers,* 101–102; Fleischer, "Wooten's Comment," 237. The same mistakes concerning Ford in the Canadian River campaign appear in a biographical article on Shapley P. Ross found in *Biographical Encyclopedia of Texas* (New York: Southern Publishing Company, 1880), 143–144.

[22] Dallas *Morning News,* Dec. 26, 1892, Jan. 13, 1893, Apr. 29, July 13, 1893; San Antonio *Express,* July 14, [1st and 2nd quotes], Nov. 3, 1894, Aug. 17, 1896, Aug. 31, 1897; *NHOT,* 6: 992; Ford, *Rip Ford's Texas,,* xliv; Thompson, *Cortina,* 246–247.

[23] San Antonio *Daily Times,* Apr. 12, 1887, San Antonio *Express,* Mar. 10, 1891; Ford, *Rip Ford's Texas,* xliv; Ford to DeShields, June 26, 1896 [quotes] (DeShields Papers, DRT); John S. Ford, *Origin and Fall of the Alamo* (San Antonio: Johnson Brothers Printing Company, 1896), passim; John Sutherland, *The Fall of the Alamo,* ed. Annie B. Sutherland (San Antonio: Naylor Press, 1936), vii-viii; Green, *Samuel Maverick,* 421; *NHOT,* 5: 1,104–1,105, 6: 156–157. The title of L. F. Meyer's publication was *History, Battles and Fall of the Alamo with Points of Interest, Etc., of San Antonio, Texas* (San Antonio: Privately printed, 1896).

[24] "Sketch of the Alamo," *Confederate Veteran* 3 (Jan. 1895): 10–11; "Col. Travis' Band at the Alamo," *Confederate Veteran* 3 (Mar. 1895): 88; "A Later 'Last Battle of the War,'" *Confederate Veteran* 4 (Dec. 1896): 416; Ford, *Rip Ford's Texas,* xlv.

[25] Ford to Dix, May 5, 1897 [quotes] (Ford Papers, TSLA); W. T. Davidson to Ford, Mar. 2, 1887, Carrick W. Crozier to Ford, Mar. 4, 1887 (Ford Papers, CAH); Ford to James T. DeShields, Jan. 8 and 18, Feb. 17, Oct. 16 and 27, Nov. 10, 11, 18, and 25, 1895, Jan. 14 [quote], May 30, June 26, July 18, Sept. 20, 1896 (DeShields Papers, DRT); Ford, *Rip Ford's Texas,* xliv-xlv, xlvii; Leonard, *Woman's Who's Who of America,*

842; *NHOT,* 2: 606. Henderson K. Yoakum had three sons who were alive in 1897: Robert, Houston, and Henderson. For examples of material contributed by Ford to James T. DeShields, see the latter's *Border Wars of Texas,* 74–81, 118–122, 140–142. The two men may have parted company because DeShields did not double Ford's pay to one dollar per page, as Ford asked, and he was not always timely in his payments. Ford also requested that his name appear under all of his contributions to DeShield's book, which was not done. See Ford to DeShields, Dec. 2 and 9, 1895 (DeShields Papers, DRT).

[26] Ford to Henry A. McArdle, Mar. 2, 1890, June 1, 1893 [quotes], Esther M. Crawford to McArdle, June 1, Aug. 25, 1892 (Henry A. McArdle, Battle of San Jacinto Notebook, TSLA); Sam D. Ratcliffe, *Painting Texas History to 1900* (Austin: University of Texas Press, 1992), 43–4, 46–48, 113; *NHOT:* 3: 760, 4: 365–366, 617, 723, 6: 185. Note that Manchaca, Texas, is named for José Antonio Menchaca, using the same mistake in spelling as Ford. See *NHOT,* 4: 482.

[27] Dallas *Morning News,* Dec. 6, 1896; Speer and Brown, *Encyclopedia of the New West,* 356 [1st and 2nd quotes]; *Biographical Souvenir of the State of Texas* (Chicago: F. A. Battey & Company, 1889), 299–303; Ratcliffe, *Painting Texas History,* 62–63; Remington, "How the Law Got Into the Chaparral," 60–69 [rest of quotes]; Ford, *Rip Ford's Texas,* 101; Ford, Memoirs (Ford Papers, CAH), 466. Frederic Remington's interview with Ford was reprinted in Frederic Remington, *Crooked Trails* (New York: Harper & Brothers, 1899), 1–20.

[28] Dallas *Morning News,* Sept. 10, 1897; Ford to Dix, May 5, 1897 (Ford Papers, TSLA); Bride Neill Taylor, "The Beginnings of the State Historical Association," 33 (July 1929): 1–6; McCaslin, *At the Heart of Texas,* 25–30.

[29] Taylor, "The Beginnings of the State Historical Association," 6–8; Ford, *Rip Ford's Texas,* xlvi; McCaslin, *At the Heart of Texas,* 27, 30; Leonard, *Woman's Who's Who of America,* 842.

[30] Taylor, "The Beginnings of the State Historical Association," 6–8; "The Organization and Objects of the Texas State Historical Association," *Quarterly of the Texas State Historical Association* 1 (July 1897): 74; "Affairs of the Association," *Quarterly of the Texas State Historical Association* 1 (Oct. 1897): 135–136; John S. Ford, "Fight on the Frio," *Quarterly of the Texas State Historical Association* 1 (Oct. 1897), 118–120; Thomas F. Harwood, "Review of the Work of the Texas State Historical Association," *SWHQ* 31 (July 1927): 4; Ford, *Rip Ford's Texas,* xlvi; Dallas *Morning News,* Sept. 10, 1897; Ford to Dix, May 5, 1897 (Ford Papers, TSLA); McCaslin, *At the Heart of Texas,* 30, 34, 50; *NHOT,* 1: 790–791, 5: 464–466, 1,061–1,062.

[31] Ford to DeShields, Nov. 10, 1895 [1st quote], June 14, July 18, Sept. 20, 1896 (DeShields Papers, DRT); Ford to Dix, July 15 [2nd quote], Sept. 20, 1896 [3rd and 4th quotes], May 5, 1897 [5th quote] (Ford Papers, TSLA); Ford, Memoir (Ford Papers, CAH), 182 [6th quote]; File 000246 (Nacogdoches 2nd class) in Texas General Land Office, Archives & Records, Land Grant Database; Confederate Pension File

00356, Bexar County: Addie N. Ford (TSLA); *Official Register, 1885,* p. 127; *Official Register, 1887,* p. 130; *Official Register, 1889,* p. 137. Ford did not name his Unionist benefactor. While he lived in Austin prior to the Mexican War, Ford paid his poll tax and the tax on his printing press. In 1848, when he returned, he paid a tax on Old Higgins, then disappeared from the tax rolls while serving on the frontier 1849–1851. As a bachelor in Austin in 1852–1854, he had horses and an expensive gold watch, and he paid his poll tax, but he paid no taxes at all from 1855 to 1857. In 1858 he paid a poll tax, then disappeared again to the frontier in 1859, and in 1860 and 1861 paid taxes on a lot in Austin and his poll tax. By 1862 he was gone. He appeared in the Cameron County tax rolls in 1866 with seven horses, and in 1867 and 1868 paid taxes on four horses, a lot in Brownsville ("As agent for Mary L. Ford" [daughter]), and $1,000 in miscellaneous property. By 1869 he had only a single horse, listed like the lot as his daughter's property, but he still had miscellaneous property worth $1,000. In 1870 he paid his first poll tax since the war ended, had one horse and his daughter's lot, and still had $500 in miscellaneous property. In 1871 he listed $34 as the value of his property and $1,375 as the value of his daughter's property, and again he paid a poll tax. For the next four years his daughter had her lot, while he paid the poll tax only in even numbered years. In 1876 he was finally listed as the owner of the lot, not Mary, and he also had $100 in miscellaneous property and paid a poll tax. In 1877 he paid taxes on the lot, but again Mary was listed as the owner. In 1878 I. L. Rudolph paid the taxes for Mary's lot; the next year Mary still had her town lot, and "Adel" Ford had a town lot for the first and only time. The taxes remained unpaid on Mary's lot from 1880 to 1883, then the taxes were paid in 1884, and finally the property disappeared from the rolls. See Travis County Tax Rolls (TSLA) and Cameron County Tax Rolls (TSLA).

[32] Ford to Dix, July 15, [1st quote], Sept. 20, 1896, Feb. 5, July 15, 1897 [last quotes] (Ford Papers, TSLA); Ford to DeShields, Dec. 9, 1895 (DeShields Papers, DRT) [2nd and 3rd quotes]; Ford, Memoirs (Ford Papers, CAH), Miscellaneous: Wartime Reminiscences, 2–3; Ford, *Rip Ford's Texas,* xlvii; Brownsville *Daily Herald,* Jan. 22, 1894, Nov. 7, 1896; Austin *Statesman,* Nov. 4, 1897; San Antonio *Express,* Nov. 4, 1897; Dallas *Morning News,* Jan. 26, 1949; Hughes, *Rebellious Ranger,* 268.

[33] San Antonio *Express,* Nov. 4, 1897, Jan. 31, Mar. 29, 1904, Mar. 7, 1905; Austin *Statesman,* Nov. 4, 1897; Houston *Daily Post,* Nov. 4, 1897; United States Department of the Interior, Bureau of the Census, Twelfth Census, 1900 [Bexar County, Texas] (Record Group 29, National Archives, Washington, DC); Brown, Annals of Travis County (Brown Papers, CAH), 16: 37; *NHOT:* 1: 458, 689–690, 3: 314, 6: 666. Nothing more about B. B. Green has been found.

[34] San Antonio *Express,* Nov. 4, 14, 1897; Austin *Statesman,* Nov. 4 [1st quote], Nov. 7, 1897 [2nd quote]; Dallas *Morning News,* Nov. 4, 7, Dec. 19, 1897 [3rd and 4th quotes]; Houston *Daily Post,* Nov. 7, 1897; Martin, "Last of the Ranger Chieftains," 41 [5th quote]; Lambert, "Col. John S. Ford," 184 [6th quote].

[35] Dallas *Morning News,* Aug. 7, 1892; John M. Morris, ed., *A Private in the Texas Rangers: A. T. Miller of Company B, Frontier Battalion* (College Station: Texas A&M University, 2001), 33–34. Texas Sen. Gonzalo Barrientos wrote and introduced Senate Concurrent Resolution 148, which was approved by the 74th Legislature and signed into law on June 16, 1995. It renamed the Vocational School at the Texas School for the Deaf as the John Salmon Ford Building.

[36] San Antonio *Express,* Nov. 4, 1897, Feb. 20, 1901; Dallas *Morning News,* Feb. 26, 1898, Feb. 20, 1901, May 9, 1903; Houston *Daily Post,* Feb. 20, 1901; Brownsville *Herald,* Aug. 12, 1953; Confederate Pension File 00356, Bexar County: Addie N. Ford (TSLA). Lillian Alva Ford, born June 21, 1878, in Austin, married Robert A. Votaw at Austin in 1901; she became a noted women's activist and author as well as the treasurer of the Bernard E. Bee Chapter of the United Daughters of the Confederacy (See Ford, Memoirs (Ford Papers, CAH), 161; Leonard, *Woman's Who's Who of America,* 842.) Mary Louise Smith O'Leary was born in 1843 and died in 1890; her husband William M. O'Leary was born in 1845 in Ireland and died in 1903. Both are buried in Calvary Cemetery, Dallas. Apparently Ford applied at least once for a pension; he wrote to John J. Dix on Feb. 5, 1897, that he went downtown to "send off my pension papers" (Ford Papers, TSLA). On Fannie's son Gray, see United States Department of the Interior, Bureau of the Census, Ninth Census, 1870 [Travis County, Texas] (Record Group 29, National Archives, Washington, DC). For Lucille and Raphael C. Cowen, see United States Department of the Interior, Bureau of the Census, Thirteenth Census, 1910 [Cameron County, Texas] and Fourteenth Census, 1920 [Cameron County, Texas] (Record Group 29, National Archives, Washington, DC).

[37] Ford to Roberts, Mar. 20, 1897 (Roberts Papers, CAH). Nearly a decade after Ford's death, James T. DeShields tried to convince Ford's daughters to let him publish their father's memoirs, promising them ten cents per copy in royalties and predicting he would sell 10,000 copies in the first year. He also inquired about Ford's biography of John C. Hays. Ever their father's daughters, and mindful that Ford had planned to charge ten dollars apiece for published copies of his memoirs, they refused the royalty offer and insisted on $250 for the Hays biography, which DeShields apparently would not pay. A poignant factor in their refusal to deal was a lien that Samuel De Cordova, the husband of Ford's second daughter Addie, had against the memoir for a loan he had provided to his father-in-law. See Louise Ford Maddox to DeShields, May 13, 17, 31, June 6, 1907 (DeShields Papers, DRT).

BIBLIOGRAPHY

Primary Sources

Unpublished

Bee, Hamilton P. Papers. Dolph Briscoe Center for American History, The University of Texas at Austin.

Brown, Frank. Papers. Dolph Briscoe Center for American History, The University of Texas at Austin.

Bryan, Guy M. Papers. Dolph Briscoe Center for American History, The University of Texas at Austin.

Burleson, Ed Jr. Papers. Dolph Briscoe Center for American History, The University of Texas at Austin.

Confederate States of America. Records. Dolph Briscoe Center for American History, The University of Texas at Austin.

———. ———. Manuscript Division, Library of Congress, Washington, DC.

Cowen, Lucille T. "Personal Reminiscences of My Grandfather, Col. John S. Ford." Typescript, n.d. In Possession of Linda Cain, Carthage, Texas.

DeShields, James T. Papers, Daughters of the Republic of Texas Library, San Antonio, Texas.

De Zavala, Adina. Papers. Dolph Briscoe Center for American History, The University of Texas at Austin.

Dobie-Byler Family. Papers. Dolph Briscoe Center for American History, The University of Texas at Austin.

Douai, Adolf. Papers. Dolph Briscoe Center for American History, The University of Texas at Austin.

Ford, John S. Papers. Dolph Briscoe Center for American History, The University of Texas at Austin.

———. ———. Nita Stewart Haley Memorial Museum, Midland, TX.

———. ———. Texas State Library and Archives, Austin.

Jenkins, John H. Sr. "Personal Reminiscences of Texas History." Typescript, April 1930. Dolph Briscoe Center for American History, The University of Texas at Austin.

McArdle, Henry A. Battle of San Jacinto Notebook. Texas State Library and Archives, Austin.

McGovern, John P. Historical Collections and Research Center, Houston Academy of Medicine - Texas Medical Center Library. [http://mcgovern.library.tmc.edu/data/ www/html/texascoll/thmd2/persons/ffolder/ford2.htm (accessed July 7, 2008)]

Military Operations in Texas Collection, 1862–1864. Dolph Briscoe Center for American History, The University of Texas at Austin.

Neighbors, Robert S. Papers. Dolph Briscoe Center for American History, The University of Texas at Austin.

Price, Lucie Clift. Papers. Dolph Briscoe Center for American History, The University of Texas at Austin.

Roberts, Oran M. Papers. Dolph Briscoe Center for American History, The University of Texas at Austin.

Robertson, George L. Papers. Dolph Briscoe Center for American History, The University of Texas at Austin.

Swisher, John M. "Remembrances of Texas and Texas People." Typescript, n.d. [1932]. Dolph Briscoe Center for American History, The University of Texas at Austin.

Texas. Bexar County. Tax Rolls. Texas State Library and Archives, Austin.

———. Cameron County. Tax Rolls. Texas State Library and Archives, Austin.

———. General Land Office. Archives & Records, Land Grant Database. [http://www.glo.state.tx.us/archives/landgrant.html (accessed March 5, 2009)]

———. Indian Papers. Texas State Library and Archives, Austin.

———. Office of the Adjutant General. Records. Texas State Library and Archives, Austin.

———. Office of the Governor. Records. Texas State Library and Archives, Austin.

———. Office of the Secretary of State. Confederate Pension Files. Texas State Library and Archives, Austin.

———. Rangers. Archives. Texas Ranger Research Center, Texas Ranger Hall of Fame and Museum, Waco, TX.

———. Travis County. Tax Rolls. Texas State Library and Archives, Austin.

Texas Veterans Association. Papers. Dolph Briscoe Center for American History, The University of Texas at Austin.

Truitt, James W. Papers. Dolph Briscoe Center for American History, The University of Texas at Austin.

United States. Department of the Interior. Bureau of the Census. First Census, 1790. Record Group 29. National Archives, Washington, DC.

———. ———. ———. Fourth Census, 1820. Record Group 29. National Archives, Washington, DC.

———. ———. ———. Fifth Census, 1830. Record Group 29. National Archives, Washington, DC.

———. ———. ———. Sixth Census, 1840. Record Group 29. National Archives, Washington, DC.

———. ———. ———.Seventh Census, 1850. Schedule 1: Free Population. Record Group 29. National Archives, Washington, DC.

———. ———. ———. Ninth Census, 1870. Record Group 29. National Archives, Washington, DC.

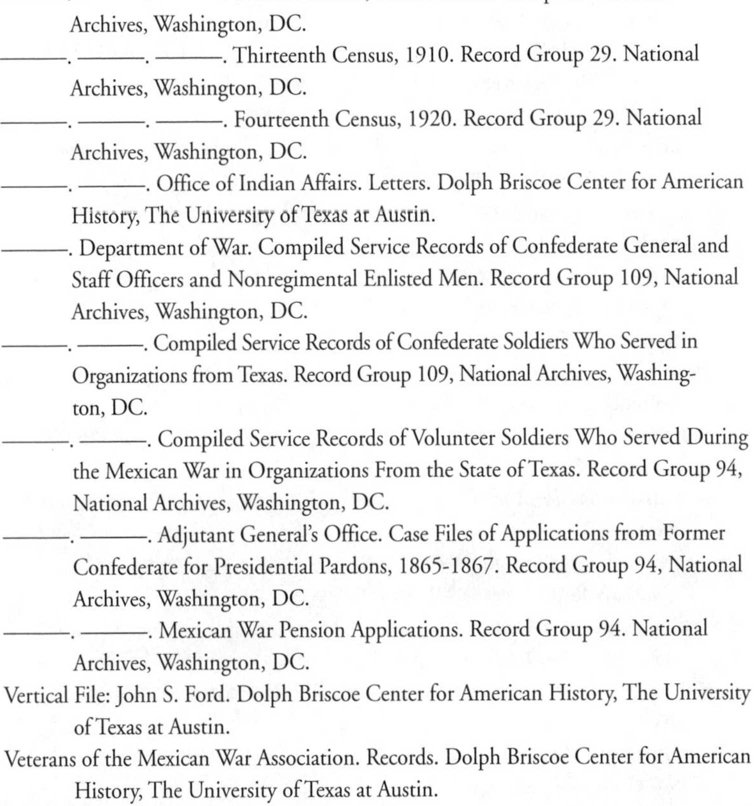

———. ———. ———. Twelfth Census, 1900. Record Group 29. National Archives, Washington, DC.

———. ———. ———. Thirteenth Census, 1910. Record Group 29. National Archives, Washington, DC.

———. ———. ———. Fourteenth Census, 1920. Record Group 29. National Archives, Washington, DC.

———. ———. Office of Indian Affairs. Letters. Dolph Briscoe Center for American History, The University of Texas at Austin.

———. Department of War. Compiled Service Records of Confederate General and Staff Officers and Nonregimental Enlisted Men. Record Group 109, National Archives, Washington, DC.

———. ———. Compiled Service Records of Confederate Soldiers Who Served in Organizations from Texas. Record Group 109, National Archives, Washington, DC.

———. ———. Compiled Service Records of Volunteer Soldiers Who Served During the Mexican War in Organizations From the State of Texas. Record Group 94, National Archives, Washington, DC.

———. ———. Adjutant General's Office. Case Files of Applications from Former Confederate for Presidential Pardons, 1865-1867. Record Group 94, National Archives, Washington, DC.

———. ———. Mexican War Pension Applications. Record Group 94. National Archives, Washington, DC.

Vertical File: John S. Ford. Dolph Briscoe Center for American History, The University of Texas at Austin.

Veterans of the Mexican War Association. Records. Dolph Briscoe Center for American History, The University of Texas at Austin.

Webb, Walter P. Papers. Dolph Briscoe Center for American History, The University of Texas at Austin.

Published

"The Affairs of the Association." *Quarterly of the Texas State Historical Association* 1 (October 1897): 129–144.

Barr, Alwyn, ed. "Records of the Confederate Military Commission in San Antonio, July 2-October 10, 1862." *Southwestern Historical Quarterly* 73 (October 1969): 243–274.

Confederate Imprints. 144 reels. New Haven, CT: Primary Source Microfilm, 1974.

Crimmins, Martin L., ed. "Colonel Robert E. Lee's Report on Indian Combats in Texas." *Southwestern Historical Quarterly* 39 (July 1935): 21–32.

De Leon, Edwin. *Secret History of Confederate Diplomacy Abroad,* ed. William C. Davis. Lawrence: University Press of Kansas, 2005.

Fleischer, Mary B., ed. "Dudley G. Wooten's Comment on Texas Histories and Historians of the Nineteenth Century." *Southwestern Historical Quarterly* 73 (October 1969): 235–242.

Ford, John S. "Fight on the Frio." *Quarterly of the Texas State Historical Association* 1 (October 1897), 118–120.

———. *Origin and Fall of the Alamo.* San Antonio: Johnson Brothers Printing Company, 1896.

———. *Rip Ford's Texas,* ed. Stephen B. Oates. Austin: University of Texas Press, 1963.

———. *Speech on Frontier Protection, Delivered in the Senate of Texas, March 1879.* Austin: n.p., 1879.

Gammel, H. P. N., comp. *The Laws of Texas, 1822–1897.* 10 volumes. Austin: Gammel Book Company, 1898–1902.

Green, Rena M., ed. *Samuel Maverick, Texan: 1803–1870.* San Antonio: Privately Printed, 1952.

———, ed. *The Swisher Memoirs, by Col. John M. Swisher.* San Antonio: Sigmund Press, 1932.

Greenwood, C. L., ed. "Opening Routes to El Paso, 1849." *Southwestern Historical Quarterly* 48 (October 1944): 262–272.

Hicks, Jimmie, ed. "Some Letters Concerning the Knights of the Golden Circle in Texas, 1860–1861." *Southwestern Historical Quarterly* 65 (July 1961): 80–86.

Jenkins, John H. *Recollections of Early Texas,* ed. John H. Jenkins III. Austin: University of Texas Press, 1958.

Johnson, Adam R. *The Partisan Rangers of the Confederate States Army.* Louisville, KY: George G. Fetter Company, 1904.

Kilgore, Dan, ed., *A Mexican Sergeant's Recollections of the Alamo & San Jacinto.* Austin: Jenkins Publishing Company, 1980.

Lambert, Will. "Col. John S. Ford." *The Southern Tribute* 1 (March 1898): 177–184.

"List of Camps, Commanders, and Adjutants." *Confederate Veteran* 9 (August 1901): 358–366.

Lubbock, Francis R. *Six Decades in Texas.* Austin: Ben C. Jones, 1900.

Maltby, William J. *Captain Jeff: Frontier Life in Texas with the Texas Rangers.* Colorado, TX: Whipkey Printing Company, 1906.

Martin, Charles L. "The Last of the Ranger Chieftains." *The Texas Magazine* 4 (January 1898): 33–41.

Morris, John M., ed. *A Private in the Texas Rangers: A. T. Miller of Company B, Frontier Battalion.* College Station: Texas A&M University, 2001.

Neighbours, Kenneth F., ed. "The Report of the Expedition of Maj. Robert S. Neighbors to El Paso in 1849." *Southwestern Historical Quarterly* 61 (April 1957): 527–532.

Oates, Stephen B. "Hugh F. Young's Account of the Snively Expedition as Told to John S. Ford." *Southwestern Historical Quarterly* 70 (July 1966): 71–92.

Official Records of the Union and Confederate Navies in the War of the Rebellion. 30 volumes. Washington: Government Printing Office, 1894–1922.

Official Register of the United States, 1885, Volume I: Legislative, Executive, Judicial.. Washington: Government Printing Office, 1886.

Official Register of the United States, 1887, Volume I: Legislative, Executive, Judicial.. Washington: Government Printing Office, 1888.

Official Register of the United States, 1889, Volume I: Legislative, Executive, Judicial.. Washington: Government Printing Office, 1890.

Olmsted, Frederic Law. *A Journey Through Texas.* New York: Dix, Edwards & Company, 1857.

"The Organization and Objects of the Texas State Historical Association." *Quarterly of the Texas State Historical Association* 1 (July 1897): 71–74.

Reagan, John H. *Memoirs: With Special Reference to Secession and the Civil War.* Austin and New York: Pemberton Press, 1968.

Remarks of Senator Ford and Hon Ashbel Smith on the Occasion of the Presentation of Gen. Rusk's Portrait in the House of Representatives, April 1, 1879. Galveston: News Steam Book and Job Printing Establishment, 1879.

Remington, Frederic. *Crooked Trails.* New York: Harper & Brothers, 1899.

———. "How the Law Got into the Chaparral." *Harper's New Monthly Magazine* 94 (December 1896): 60–69.

Report of the Permanent Committee, Appointed at a Meeting of the Citizens of Brownsville, Tex., April 17, 1875. Brownsville, TX: John S. Mansur, 1875.

Reports of the Committee of Investigation Sent in 1873 by the Mexican Government to the Frontier of Texas. New York: Baker & Godwin, 1875.

Richardson, James D., ed. *A Compilation of the Messages and Papers of the Confederacy.* 2 volumes. Nashville: United States Publishing Company. 1905.

Simon, John Y., ed. *The Papers of Ulysses S. Grant, Volume Thirteen.* Carbondale: Southern Illinois University Press, 1985.

Smither, Harriet, ed. *The Papers of Mirabeau Buonaparte Lamar.* 6 volumes. Austin: Vonn Boeckmann-Jones, 1921.

Spurlin, Charles D., comp. *Texas Veterans in the Mexican War.* Nacogdoches, TX: Ericson Books, 1984.

Sutherland, John. *The Fall of the Alamo,* ed. Annie B. Sutherland. San Antonio: Naylor Press, 1936.

Sweet, Alexander E., and John A. Knox. *On a Mexican Mustang Through Texas.* Hartford, CT: S. S. Scranton & Company, 1883.

Taylor, Bride Neill. "The Beginnings of the State Historical Association." *Southwestern Historical Quarterly* 33 (July 1929): 1–17.

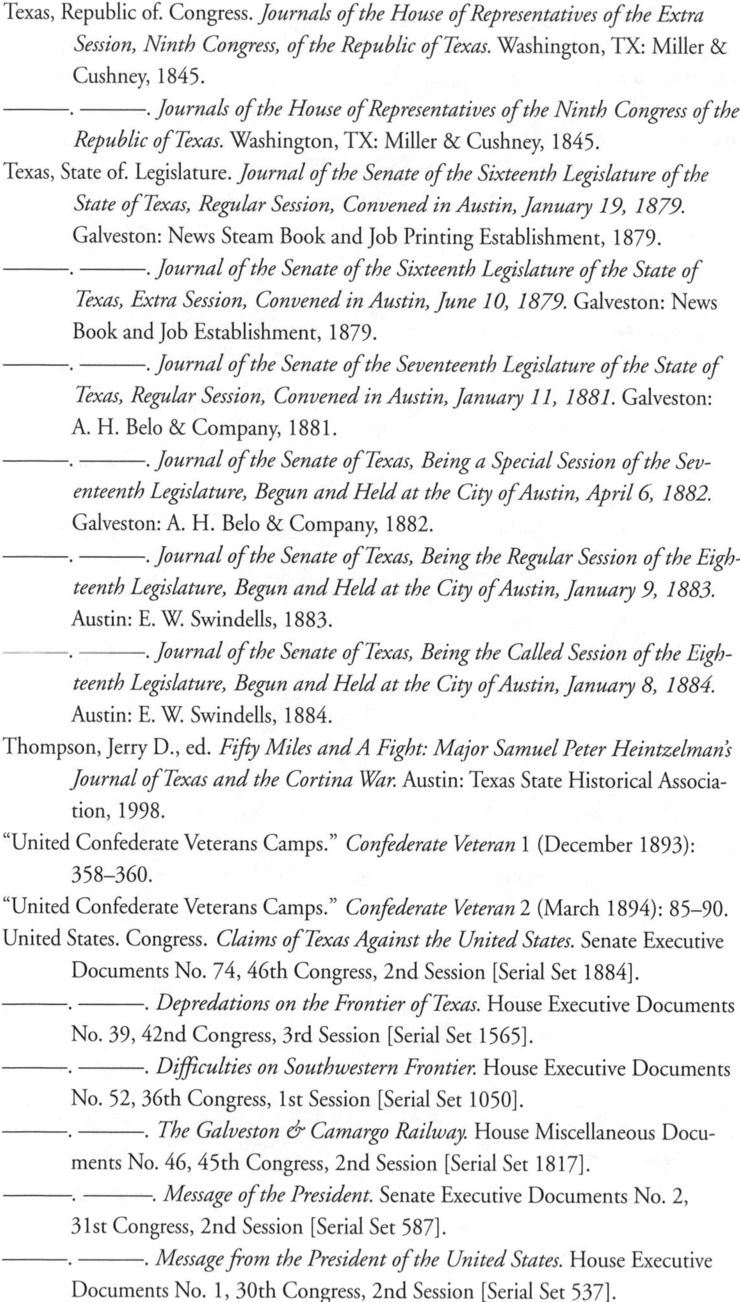

Texas, Republic of. Congress. *Journals of the House of Representatives of the Extra Session, Ninth Congress, of the Republic of Texas.* Washington, TX: Miller & Cushney, 1845.

———. ———. *Journals of the House of Representatives of the Ninth Congress of the Republic of Texas.* Washington, TX: Miller & Cushney, 1845.

Texas, State of. Legislature. *Journal of the Senate of the Sixteenth Legislature of the State of Texas, Regular Session, Convened in Austin, January 19, 1879.* Galveston: News Steam Book and Job Printing Establishment, 1879.

———. ———. *Journal of the Senate of the Sixteenth Legislature of the State of Texas, Extra Session, Convened in Austin, June 10, 1879.* Galveston: News Book and Job Establishment, 1879.

———. ———. *Journal of the Senate of the Seventeenth Legislature of the State of Texas, Regular Session, Convened in Austin, January 11, 1881.* Galveston: A. H. Belo & Company, 1881.

———. ———. *Journal of the Senate of Texas, Being a Special Session of the Seventeenth Legislature, Begun and Held at the City of Austin, April 6, 1882.* Galveston: A. H. Belo & Company, 1882.

———. ———. *Journal of the Senate of Texas, Being the Regular Session of the Eighteenth Legislature, Begun and Held at the City of Austin, January 9, 1883.* Austin: E. W. Swindells, 1883.

———. ———. *Journal of the Senate of Texas, Being the Called Session of the Eighteenth Legislature, Begun and Held at the City of Austin, January 8, 1884.* Austin: E. W. Swindells, 1884.

Thompson, Jerry D., ed. *Fifty Miles and A Fight: Major Samuel Peter Heintzelman's Journal of Texas and the Cortina War.* Austin: Texas State Historical Association, 1998.

"United Confederate Veterans Camps." *Confederate Veteran* 1 (December 1893): 358–360.

"United Confederate Veterans Camps." *Confederate Veteran* 2 (March 1894): 85–90.

United States. Congress. *Claims of Texas Against the United States.* Senate Executive Documents No. 74, 46th Congress, 2nd Session [Serial Set 1884].

———. ———. *Depredations on the Frontier of Texas.* House Executive Documents No. 39, 42nd Congress, 3rd Session [Serial Set 1565].

———. ———. *Difficulties on Southwestern Frontier.* House Executive Documents No. 52, 36th Congress, 1st Session [Serial Set 1050].

———. ———. *The Galveston & Camargo Railway.* House Miscellaneous Documents No. 46, 45th Congress, 2nd Session [Serial Set 1817].

———. ———. *Message of the President.* Senate Executive Documents No. 2, 31st Congress, 2nd Session [Serial Set 587].

———. ———. *Message from the President of the United States.* House Executive Documents No. 1, 30th Congress, 2nd Session [Serial Set 537].

———. ———. *Sheep Husbandry.* Senate Executive Documents No. 25, 45th Congress, 3rd Session [Serial Set 1825].

———. ———. *Testimony Taken by the Committee on Military Affairs in Relation to the Texas Border Troubles.* House Miscellaneous Documents No. 64, 45th Congress, 2nd Session [Serial Set 1820].

———. ———. *Texas Frontier Troubles.* House Reports No. 343, 44th Congress, 1st Session [Serial Set 1709].

———. ———. *Thomas Toby.* House Reports No. 249, 47th Congress, 1st Session [Serial Set 2065].

———. ———. *Troubles on the Texas Frontier.* House Executive Documents No. 81, 36th Congress, 1st Session [Serial Set 1056].

———. Department of State. *Papers Relating to the Foreign Relations of the United States, 1865–1866.* 4 volumes. Washington: Government Printing Office, 1865–1866.

———. ———. *Papers Relating to the Foreign Relations of the United States, 1867–1868.* 2 volumes. Washington: Government Printing Office, 1868.

———. ———. *Papers Relating to the Foreign Relations of the United States, 1872–1873.* Washington: Government Printing Office, 1872–1873.

Wallace, Lew. *An Autobiography.* 2 volumes. New York: Harper and Brothers, 1906.

The War of the Rebellion: A Compilation of the Official Records of the Union and Confederate Armies. 130 volumes. Washington, DC: Government Printing Office, 1880–1902.

Wheeler, T. B. "Reminiscences of Reconstruction in Texas." *Quarterly of the Texas State Historical Association,* 11 (July 1907): 56–65.

Williams, Amelia W., and Eugene C. Barker, eds. *The Writings of Sam Houston, 1813–1863.* 8 volumes. Austin: University of Texas Press, 1938–1943.

Williams, R. H. *With the Border Ruffians: Memories of the Far West, 1852–1868.* New York: E. P. Dutton and Company, 1907.

Winfrey, Dorman H., and James M. Day, eds. *The Indian Papers of Texas and the Southwest, 1825–1916.* 5 volumes. New York, 1966; reprint, Austin: Texas State Historical Association 1995.

Winkler, Ernest W., ed. *Journal of the Secession Convention of Texas, 1861.* Austin: Austin Printing Company, 1912.

Newspapers

Alpine *Avalanche*
Austin *American Statesman*
Austin *Democratic Statesman*
Austin *Republican*

Austin *Southern Intelligencer*
Austin *Statesman*
Austin *Texas Almanac Extra*
Austin *Texas Democrat*
Austin *Texas Mute Ranger*
Austin *Texas Sentinel*
Austin *Texas State Gazette*
Austin *Texas State Times*
Brownsville [TX] *Daily Herald*
Brownsville [TX] *Fort Brown Flag*
Brownsville [TX] *Ranchero*
Brownsville [TX] *Rio Grande Sentinel*
Clarksville [TX] *Northern Standard*
Clarksville [TX] *Standard*
Congressional Globe
Corpus Christi *Ranchero*
Dallas *Herald*
Dallas *Morning News*
Galveston *Flake's Bulletin*
Galveston *News*
Houston *Daily Post*
Houston *Telegraph*
New York Times
Palestine [TX] *Trinity Advocate*
San Antonio *Daily Times*
San Antonio *Express*
San Antonio *Herald*
San Antonio *Ledger*
San Antonio *Ledger & Texan*
San Antonio *Semi-Weekly News*
San Augustine [TX] *Eastern Texian*
San Augustine [TX] *Red-Lander*
Victoria [TX] *Advocate*
Washington-on-the-Brazos [TX] *Texas National Register*

Articles

Barr, Alwyn. "The Semicentennial of Texas Independence in 1886." *Southwestern Historical Quarterly* 91 (January 1988): 349–359.

Bender, A. B. "Opening Routes Across West Texas, 1848–1850." *Southwestern Historical Quarterly* 38 (October 1934): 116–135.

Bridges, C. A. "The Knights of the Golden Circle: A Filibustering Fantasy." *Southwestern Historical Quarterly* 44 (January 1941): 287–302.

"Col. Travis' Band at the Alamo." *Confederate Veteran* 3 (March 1895): 88.

Coyner, C. Luther. "Peter Hansborough Bell." *Southwestern Historical Quarterly* 3 (July 1899): 49–53.

Crook, Carland E. "Benjamin Theron and French Designs in Texas During the Civil War." *Southwestern Historical Quarterly* 68 (April 1965): 432–454.

Davenport, Harbert. "Notes on Early Steamboating on the Rio Grande." *Southwestern Historical Quarterly* 49 (October 1945): 286–289.

Davies, Wallace E. "The Mexican War Veterans as an Organized Group." *Mississippi Valley Historical Review* 35 (September 1948): 221–238.

Delaney, Robert W. "Matamoros, Port for Texas During the Civil War." *Southwestern Historical Quarterly* 58 (April 1955): 473–487.

Dunn, Roy Sylvan. "The KGC in Texas, 1860–1861." *Southwestern Historical Quarterly* 70 (April 1967): 543–573.

Ellis, L. Tuffly. "Maritime Commerce on the Far Western Gulf, 1861–1865." *Southwestern Historical Quarterly* 77 (October 1973): 167–226.

Ericson, J. E. "The Delegates to the Convention of 1875: A Reappraisal." *Southwestern Historical Quarterly* 67 (July 1963): 22–27

Fornell, Earl W. "Texas and Filibusters in the 1850s." *Southwestern Historical Quarterly* 59 (April 1956): 411–428.

Graf, Mercedes. "Standing Tall with Sarah Bowman: The Amazon of the Border." *Minerva: Quarterly Report on Women and the Military* (Fall-Winter 2001) [http://findarticles.com/p/articles/mi_m0EXI/is_2001 Fall-Winter/ai _92588782/pg_4?tag=artBody;col1, (accessed 7-13-2008)].

Harwood, Thomas F. "Review of the Work of the Texas State Historical Association." *Southwestern Historical Quarterly* 31 (July 1927): 3–32.

Klos, George. "Our People Could Not Distinguish One Tribe from Another: The 1859 Expulsion of the Reserve Indians from Texas." *Southwestern Historical Quarterly* 97 (April 1994): 598–619.

Kelley, Sean. "'Mexico in his Head:' Slavery and the Texas-Mexican Border, 1810–1860," *Journal of Social History* 37 (Spring 2004): 709–723.

Koch, Lena Clara. "The Federal Indian Policy in Texas, 1848–1860, Chapter III." *Southwestern Historical Quarterly* 29 (July 1925): 19–35.

———. "Federal Indian Policy in Texas, 1848–1860, Chapter IV." *Southwestern Historical Quarterly* 29 (October 1925): 98–127.

Lack, Paul D. "Slavery and Vigilantism in Austin, Texas, 1840–1860." *Southwestern Historical Quarterly* 85 (July 1981): 1–20.

"A Later 'Last Battle of the War.'" *Confederate Veteran* 4 (December 1896): 416.

Neighbours, Kenneth F. "The Expedition of Major Robert S. Neighbors to El Paso in 1849." *Southwestern Historical Quarterly* 58 (July 1954): 36–59.

Oates, Stephen B. "John S. 'Rip' Ford: Prudent Cavalryman, C.S.A." Ralph A. Wooster, ed., *Lone Star Blue and Gray: Essays on Texas in the Civil War.* Austin: Texas State Historical Association, 1995.

———. "Texas Under the Secessionists." *Southwestern Historical Quarterly* 67 (October 1963): 167–212.

Rippy, J. Fred. "Border Troubles Along the Rio Grande, 1848–1860." *Southwestern Historical Quarterly* 23 (October 1919): 91–111.

———. "Mexican Projects of the Confederates." *Southwestern Historical Quarterly* 22 (April 1919): 291–317.

Sandbo, Anna Irene. "The First Session of the Secession Convention of Texas." *Southwestern Historical Quarterly* 18 (October 1914): 162–194.

Shearer, Ernest C. "The Callahan Expedition, 1855." *Southwestern Historical Quarterly* 54 (April 1951): 430–451.

———. "The Carvajal Disturbances." *Southwestern Historical Quarterly* 55 (October 1951): 201–230

Sibley, Marilyn M. "Charles Stillman: A Case Study of Entrepreneurship on the Rio Grande, 1861–1865." *Southwestern Historical Quarterly* 77 (Oct. 1973): 228–240.

"Sketch of the Alamo." *Confederate Veteran* 3 (January 1895): 10–11.

Tyler, Ronnie C. "The Callahan Expedition of 1855: Indians or Negroes?" *Southwestern Historical Quarterly* 70 (April 1967): 574–585.

———. "Cotton on the Border, 1861–1865." *Southwestern Historical Quarterly* 73 (April 1970): 456–477.

Ward, Hortense W. "The First State Fair of Texas." *Southwestern Historical Quarterly* 57 (October 1953): 163–174.

Webster, Michael G. "Intrigue on the Rio Grande: The *Rio Bravo* Affair, 1875." *Southwestern Historical Quarterly* 74 (October 1970): 149–164.

Wooster, Ralph A. "An Analysis of the Texas Know Nothings." *Southwestern Historical Quarterly* 70 (January 1967): 414–423.

———. "An Analysis of the Membership of the Texas Secession Convention." *Southwestern Historical Quarterly* 62 (January 1959): 322–335.

———. "Early Texas Politics: The Henderson Administration." *Southwestern Historical Quarterly* 73 (October 1969): 176–192.

———. "Membership in Early Texas Legislatures, 1850–1860." *Southwestern Historical Quarterly* 69 (October 1965): 163–178 .

Books

Allardice, Bruce S. *Confederate Colonels: A Biographical Register.* Columbia: University of Missouri Press, 2008.

———. *More Generals in Gray.* Baton Rouge: Louisiana State University Press, 1995.

Amberson, Mary M. M., James A. McAllen, and Margaret H. McAllen. *I Would Rather Sleep in Texas: A History of the Lower Rio Grande Valley and the People of the Santa Anita Land Grant.* Austin: Texas State Historical Association, 2003.

Anderson, Gary C. *The Conquest of Texas: Ethnic Cleansing in the Promised Land, 1820–1875.* Norman: University of Oklahoma Press, 2005.

Appleton's Annual Cyclopaedia and Register of Important Events. New York: D. Appleton and Company, 1870.

Bancroft, Hubert Howe. *History of the North Mexican States and Texas, 1531–1889.* 2 volumes. San Francisco: A. L. Bancroft & Company, 1883, 1889.

Biographical Encyclopedia of Texas. New York: Southern Publishing Company, 1880.

Biographical Souvenir of the State of Texas. Chicago: F. A. Battey & Company, 1889.

Bowden, J. J. *The Exodus of Federal Forces from Texas 1861.* Austin: Eakin Press, 1986.

Brackett, Albert G. *History of the United States Cavalry.* New York: Harper & Brothers, 1865.

Brown, John H. *History of Texas from 1685 to 1892.* 2 volumes. St. Louis, MO: L. E. Daniell, 1892.

———. *Indian Wars and Pioneers of Texas.* Austin: L. E. Daniell, 1896.

Buenger, Walter L. *Secession and the Union in Texas.* Austin: University of Texas Press, 1984.

Campbell, Randolph B. *An Empire for Slavery: The Peculiar Institution in Texas.* Baton Rouge: Louisiana State University Press, 1991.

———. *Gone to Texas: A History of the Lone Star State.* New York: Oxford University Press, 2003.

Carter, James D. *Masonry in Texas: Background, History, and Influence to 1846.* Waco: Committee on Masonic Education and Service for the Grand Lodge of Texas, 1958.

Chance, Joseph E. *José María de Jesús Carvajal: The Life and Times of a Mexican Revolutionary.* San Antonio: Trinity University Press, 2006.

Collins, Michael L. *Texas Devils: Rangers and Regulars on the Lower Rio Grande, 1846–1861.* Norman: University of Oklahoma Press, 2008.

Connelly, Donald B. *John M. Schofield and the Politics of Generalship.* Chapel Hill: University of North Carolina Press, 2006.

Cotham, Edward T., Jr. *Battle on the Bay: The Civil War Struggle for Galveston.* Austin: University of Texas Press, 1998.

———. *Sabine Pass: The Confederacy's Thermopylae.* Austin: University of Texas Press, 2004.

Cox, Mike. *The Texas Rangers: Wearing the Cinco Peso, 1821–1900.* New York: Forge Books, 2008.

Daniell, Lewis E. *Personnel of the Texas State Government, with Sketches of Distinguished Texans.* Austin: City Printing Company, 1887.

———. *Personnel of the Texas State Government, with Sketches of Representative Men of Texas.* San Antonio: Maverick Printing House, 1892.

De la Teja, Jesus F., Paula Marks, and Ron Tyler. *Texas: Crossroads of North America.* New York: Houghton Mifflin, 2004.

DeLay, Brian. *War of a Thousand Deserts: Indian Raids and the U.S.-Mexican War.* New Haven and London: Yale University Press, 2008.

DeShields, James T. *Border Wars of Texas.* Tioga, TX: Herald Company, 1912.

Dwight, Benjamin W. *The History of the Descendants of Elder John Strong.* Albany, NY: Joel Munsell, 1871.

Dupree, Stephen A. *Planting the Union Flag in Texas.* College Station: Texas A&M University Press, 2008.

Fehrenbach, T. R. *Lone Star: A History of Texas and Texans.* New York: American Legacy Press, 1968.

Evans, Clement A. ed. *Confederate Military History,* Extended edition. 17 volumes. Atlanta, 1899; extended ed., Wilmington, NC: Broadfoot Publishing Company, 1989.

Forgie, George B. *Patricide in the House Divided.* New York: W. W. Norton & Company, 1979.

Fornell, Earl W. *The Galveston Era: The Texas Crescent on the Eve of Secession.* Austin: University of Texas Press, 1961.

Glasson, William H. *Federal Military Pensions in the United States,* ed. David Kinley. New York: Oxford University Press, 1918.

Graham, Don. *Kings of Texas: The 150-Year Saga of an American Ranching Empire.* New York: John Wiley & Sons, 2003.

Greer, James K. *Colonel Jack Hays: Texas Frontier Leader and California Builder.* Waco: W. M. Morrison, 1973.

———. *Texas Ranger: Jack Hays in the Frontier Southwest.* College Station: Texas A&M University Press, 1993.

Haley, James L. *Sam Houston.* Norman: University of Oklahoma Press, 2002.

Hämäläinen, Pekka. *The Comanche Empire.* New Haven and London: Yale University Press, 2008.

Hart, John M. *Revolutionary Mexico: The Coming and Process of the Mexican Revolution.* Berkeley: University of California Press, 1987.

Hartje, Robert G. *Van Dorn: The Life and Times of a Confederate General.* Nashville: Vanderbilt University Press, 1967.

Heitman, Francis B. *Historical Register and Dictionary of the United States Army.* 2 volumes. Washington: Government Printing Office, 1903.

Howe, Gilman B. *Genealogy of the Bigelow Family of America.* Worcester, MA: C. Hamilton, 1890.

Hubbard, Charles M. *The Burden of Confederate Diplomacy.* Knoxville: University of Tennessee Press, 1998.

Huff, Archie V. Jr. *Greenville: The History of the City and County in the South Carolina Piedmont.* Columbia: University of South Carolina Press, 1995.

Hughes, William J. *Rebellious Ranger: Rip Ford and the Old Southwest.* Norman: University of Oklahoma Press, 1964.

Humphrey, David C. *Peg Leg: The Improbable Life of a Texas Hero, Thomas William Ward, 1807–1872.* Denton: Texas State Historical Association, 2009.

Hunt, Jeffrey W. *The Last Battle of the Civil War: Palmetto Ranch.* Austin: University of Texas Press, 2002.

Hunter, J. Marvin, ed. *The Trail Drivers of Texas.* Revised edition. Austin: University of Texas Press, 2003.

Irby, James A. *Backdoor at Bagdad: The Civil War on the Rio Grande.* El Paso: Texas Western Press, 1977.

Kerby, Robert L. *Kirby Smith's Confederacy: The Trans-Mississippi South, 1863–1865* New York: Columbia University Press, 1972.

Knowles, Thomas W. *They Rode for the Lone Star.* Dallas: Taylor Publishing Company, 1999.

La Vere, David. *The Texas Indians.* College Station: Texas A&M University Press, 2004.

Lea, Tom. *The King Ranch.* 2 volumes. Boston: Little, Brown and Company, 1957.

Leonard, John W. *Woman's Who's Who of America.* New York: American Commonwealth Company, 1914.

Lowe, Richard G. *The Texas Overland Campaign.* Abilene, TX: McWhiney Foundation, 1996.

Mahoney, Harry T. and Marjorie L. *Mexico and the Confederacy, 1860–1867.* San Francisco: Austin & Winfield, 1998.

Marten, James A. *Texas Divided: Loyalty and Dissent in the Lone Star State, 1856–1864.* Lexington: University Press of Kentucky, 1993.

May, Robert E. *John A. Quitman: Old South Crusader.* Baton Rouge: Louisiana State University Press, 1985.

———. *Manifest Destiny's Underworld: Filibustering in Antebellum America.* Chapel Hill: University of North Carolina Press, 2002.

McCaslin, Richard B. *At the Heart of Texas: One Hundred Years of the Texas State Historical Association, 1897–1997.* Austin: Texas State Historical Association, 2007.

———. *Tainted Breeze: The Great Hanging at Gainesville, Texas, October 1862.* Baton Rouge: Louisiana State University Press, 1994.

McLemore, Laura. *Inventing Texas: Early Historians of the Lone Star State.* College Station: Texas A&M University Press, 2004.

McFeely, William S. *Grant: A Biography.* New York: W. W. Norton & Company, 1981.

McKee, Irving. *"Ben-Hur" Wallace.* Berkeley: University of California Press, 1947.

Memorial and Genealogical Record of Southwest Texas. Chicago: Goodspeed Brothers, 1894.

Monday, Jane C., and Francis B. Vick. *Petra's Legacy: The South Texas Ranching Empire of Petra Vela and Mifflin Kenedy.* College Station: Texas A&M University Press, 2007.

Moneyhon, Carl H. *Texas After the Civil War: The Struggle for Reconstruction.* College Station: Texas A&M University Press, 2004.

———. *Edmund J. Davis: Civil War General, Republican Leader, Reconstruction Governor.* Fort Worth: TCU Press, 2010.

Moore, Albert B. *Conscription and Conflict in the Confederacy.* New York: Macmillan Company, 1924.

Moore, Stephen L. *Savage Frontier, Volume II: 1838–1839.* Denton: University of North Texas Press, 2006.

———. *Taming Texas: Captain William T. Sadler's Lone Star Service.* Austin: State House Press, 2000.

Neighbours, Kenneth F. *Indian Exodus: Texas Indian Affairs, 1835–1859.* Privately printed, 1973.

———. *Robert Simpson Neighbors and the Texas Frontier 1836–1859.* Waco: Texian Press, 1975.

Newcomb, William W. *The Indians of Texas.* Austin: University of Texas Press, 1961.

Nixon, Pat I. *The Medical Story of Early Texas, 1528–1853.* San Antonio: Privately Printed, 1946.

Oates, Stephen B. *Confederate Cavalry West of the River.* Austin: University of Texas Press, 1961.

Owsley, Frank L. *King Cotton Diplomacy: Foreign Relations of the Confederate States of America.* 2nd edition. Chicago: University of Chicago Press, 1959.

O'Connor, Robert F., ed. *Texas Myths.* College Station: Texas A&M University Press, 1986.

Parks, Joseph H. *General Edmund Kirby Smith C.S.A.* Baton Rouge: Louisiana State University Press, 1954.

Parsons, Chuck, and Marianne E. Hall Little. *Captain L. H. McNelly, Texas Ranger.* Austin: State House Press, 2001.

Ratcliffe, Sam D. *Painting Texas History to 1900.* Austin: University of Texas Press, 1992.

Reynolds, Donald E. *Texas Terror: The Slave Insurrection Panic and the Secession of the Lower South.* Baton Rouge: Louisiana State University Press, 2007.

Richter, William R. *The Army in Texas During Reconstruction.* College Station: Texas A&M University Press, 1987.

Rister, Carl Coke. *Robert E. Lee in Texas.* Norman: University of Oklahoma Press, 1946.

Robinson, Charles M., III. *The Men Who Wear the Star: The Story of the Texas Rangers.* New York: Random House, 2000.

Sanderson, Jim. *Nevin's History: A Novel of Texas.* Lubbock: Texas Tech University Press, 2004.

Scarry, Robert J. *Millard Fillmore.* Jefferson, NC: MacFarland & Company, 2001.

Settles, Thomas M. *John Bankhead Magruder: A Military Reappraisal.* Baton Rouge: Louisiana State University Press, 2009.

Sibley, Marilyn M. *Lone Stars and State Gazettes: Texas Newspapers Before the Civil War.* College Station: Texas A&M University Press, 1983.

Sowell, A. J. *Early Settlers and Indian Fighters of Southwest Texas.* Austin: Ben C. Jones & Company, 1900.

Speer, William S., and John H. Brown. *The Encyclopedia of the New West.* Marshall, TX: United States Biographical Publishing Company, 1881.

Spellman, Paul N. *Forgotten Texas Leader: Hugh McLeod and the Texas Santa Fe Expedition.* College Station: Texas A&M University Press, 1999.

Thompson, Jerry D. *Cortina: Defending the Mexican Name in Texas.* College Station: Texas A&M University Press, 2007.

———. *Vaqueros in Blue and Gray.* Austin: State House Press, 2000.

———, and Lawrence T. Jones III. *Civil War and Revolution on the Rio Grande Frontier.* Austin: Texas State Historical Association, 2004.

Townsend, Stephen A. *The Yankee Invasion of Texas.* College Station: Texas A&M University Press, 2006.

Tucker, Phillip T., ed. *Cubans in the Confederacy.* Jefferson, NC: MacFarland & Company, 2002.

———. *The Final Fury: Palmito Ranch, the Last Battle of the Civil War.* Mechanicsburg, PA: Stackpole Books, 2001.

Tyler, Ron, et al., eds. *The New Handbook of Texas.* 6 volumes. Austin: Texas State Historical Association, 1996.

Tyler, Ronnie C. *Santiago Vidaurri and the Southern Confederacy.* Austin: Texas State Historical Association, 1973.

Underwood, Rodman L. *Waters of Discord: The Union Blockade of Texas During the Civil War.* Jefferson, NC: MacFarland and Company, 2003.

Utley, Robert M. *Lone Star Justice: The First Century of the Texas Rangers.* New York: Oxford University Press, 2002.

Wallace, Ernest. *Ranald S. Mackenzie on the Texas Frontier.* Lubbock: West Texas Museum Association, 1963.

Webb, Walter P. *The Texas Rangers: A Century of Frontier Defense.* Boston: Houghton Mifflin, 1935.

Wilbarger, J. W. *Indian Depredations in Texas.* Austin: Hutchings Printing House, 1889.

Wilkins, Frederick. *The Highly Irregular Regulars: Texas Rangers in the Mexican War.* Austin: Eakin Press, 1990.

Wilkinson, J. B. *Laredo and the Rio Grande Frontier.* Austin: Jenkins Publishing Company, 1975.

Winkler, Ernest W. Winkler, ed., *Platforms of Political Parties in Texas.* Bulletin of the University of Texas, No. 53: Sept. 20, 1916.

Wise, Stephen R. *Lifeline of the Confederacy: Blockade Running During the Civil War.* Columbia: University of South Carolina Press, 1991.

Wooster, Ralph A, ed., *Lone Star Blue and Gray: Essays on Texas in the Civil War* Austin: Texas State Historical Association, 1995.

———. *Lone Star Generals in Gray.* Austin: Eakin Press, 2000.

———. *Lone Star Regiments in Gray.* Austin: Eakin Press, 2002.

Wooten, Dudley G., ed. *A Comprehensive History of Texas and Texans, 1865 to 1897.* 2 volumes. Dallas: William G. Scarff, 1898.

Dissertations and Theses

Webster, Michael G. "Texas Manifest Destiny and the Mexican Border Conflict, 1865–1880." Ph.D. Dissertation, University of Indiana, 1972.

Zemler, Jeffrey A. "The Texas Press and the Filibusters of the 1850s." M.A. Thesis, University of North Texas, 1983.

Websites

"Descendents of David Leister" [http://www.geocities.com/~pamreid/leis_anc.html (accessed 7–7-2008)].

"The Officer Down Memorial Page" [http://www.odmp.org/officer/15617-police-officer-alpheus-d.-neill (accessed March 7, 2009)].

"Point Isabel Lighthouse" [http://atlas.thc.state.tx.us/common/viewform.asp?atlas_num=2076002014&site_name=Point+Isabel+Lighthouse&class=2001 (accessed Mar. 16, 2009)].

"The Salmon family" [http://www.fortunecity.com/tinpan/nirvana/621/salmon.html (accessed March 5, 2009)].

"Starr County Elected Officials," [http://www.rootsweb.ancestry.com/~txstarr/elected.htm (accessed 12-28-2008)].

INDEX

Page numbers in *italics* indicate illustrations. RF indicates John S. "Rip" Ford.

Fighting Stock: John S. "Rip" Ford of Texas
ISBN 978-0-87565-421-8
Case. $29.95.